MEDIA FRENCH

MEDIA FRENCH

A GUIDE TO CONTEMPORARY
FRENCH IDIOM

With English translations

Adrian C. Ritchie

UNIVERSITY OF WALES PRESS
CARDIFF
1997

British Library Cataloguing in Publication Data.
A catalogue record for this book is available from the British
Library.

ISBN 0-7083-1399-X

Cover design by Olwen Fowler
Typeset at the University of Wales Press
Printed in Great Britain by Dinefwr Press, Llandybïe

INTRODUCTION

Purpose and scope

In drawing up this handbook of French idiom, based in part on my *Newspaper French* (1990, 1993), I have tried to group together in a handy format the most useful terms and some of the more common idioms which the reader of contemporary French will regularly encounter.

For the translator and the advanced user of French in today's world, familiarity with specialized lexis in fields such as administration, economics, politics and social affairs is crucially important. In order to read, understand and use actively the French language of today, one needs a knowledge of these registers of contemporary French.

Words are always best understood in context, and so in this guide each headword is illustrated by one or more examples of its use, drawn from a wide range of situations and registers.

How to use this vocabulary

A strict alphabetical order has been adopted for all entries: thus **conseil**, **conseil général**, and **conseiller** occur as separate entries and in that sequence.

Headwords are printed in **bold type**, as also are those words and phrases within the illustrations which correspond precisely to the headword [e.g. **rejet** (*nm*): l'électorat manifeste son **rejet** de la classe politique (*rejection*)]. In more extended collocations, the whole sense-group is emboldened in order to highlight the use of the headword in a more complete context, as under **réintégrer** (*vt*), where the key element of the sentence: la femme refusa de **réintégrer le domicile conjugal** (*return to the marital home*) is highlighted, as also the expression **aboutir à une paix durable** (*achieve a lasting peace*) in the **aboutir** entry.

Translations, in round brackets and italicized, are given for headwords, e.g. **échelon** (*grade*, *rung*) when they appear in the illustrative examples. In the case of phrases incorporating the headword, e.g. **à l'échelon des villes**, the whole sense group (*at the urban/city level*) is translated. *Commas* are used to separate equivalents and near equivalents in the target language; a semicolon indicates a clear shift in meaning.

Illustrative examples are provided in order to clarify the use of the headword: consequently, in cases where more specialized terms are used – as in **code pénal**, **nue-propriété** or **usufruit** – explanatory glosses are preferred, not only to make clear the use of the word but also to clarify its meaning. Other culture-specific concepts such as **ceinture rouge**, **droit du sol** or **harki** are similarly glossed in order to convey their resonance for the French reader. For certain peculiarly French concepts [often legal or political terms such as **bâtonnier**, **cohabitation**, or **îlotier**; or acronyms such as **SMIC**, **ZUP** or **ZAC**], the nearest cultural equivalent in English is given.

Cross-referencing is used extensively throughout in order to widen the scope for comparing and contrasting uses of a given word. Under **eau**, for example, in addition to examples of **eaux territoriales**, **eaux ménagères** and **eaux usées**, a cross-reference alerts the user to the existence of other collocations under **adduction**, **dégât**, **évacuation** and **voie**. Similarly under the noun **base**, which has many and varied meanings according to context, I have grouped examples as different as **consulter leur base** (*consult rank and file opinion*), **jeter les bases** (*lay the foundations*) and **base de données** (*data base*).

Certain words in French appear very frequently *as an element in a set phrase or other common collocation*, such as **direction**, **état**,

exploitation, gestion, identité, impôt, jour, mouvement or **société,** and so cross-references are unavoidably numerous: under **gestion,** for example, the user is referred to **frauduleux, paritaire, quotidien** and **trésorerie** for further examples of its use. The noun **exploitation,** likewise, is cross-referenced to **chef, déficit, équilibre, perte** and **résultat.**

As a general principle, compound words which consist of attributive uses of French nouns, for example **article de fond, congé sans solde** and **garde à vue,** and other such collocations are put under the first word in the expression; hence **conseil des ministres** will be found under **conseil** and **évolution de carrière** under **évolution,** with cross-references under **ministre** and **carrière** respectively.

However, in the case of *compounds built on very common words* such as the adjective **mauvais,** the reader is cross-referred to the entries under **créance, payeur** and **traitement,** and under the headword **grand** to **bourgeois, commis, ensemble, muet, public, puissance, surface** and **travail.** *Phrases built on common verbs* such as **donner, faire, mettre** or **prendre** are treated in the same way: hence **donner lecture** appears under **lecture,** as the more 'significant' word in the expression. A collocation such as **prendre un bail** is given under the headword **bail** (*lease*); **renouvellement de bail** (*renewing of lease*), however, is found under **renouvellement.** The same principle is followed in the case of words, such as **mise** and **prise,** on which a large number of compounds are built: hence **mise au point** and **prise en compte** are ranged under **point** and **compte** respectively.

Adjectives in French commonly – though not always – are placed after the noun, and so decisions about how to deal with *noun + adjective groups* must be taken. In the majority of cases, such pairs of words are given under the noun: so **flambée terroriste** (*sharp rise in terrorist activity*) goes with **flambée des loyers** (*steep rent increases*) under the headword **flambée,** and the expression **flux migratoire** appears under **flux.** Similarly, an adjective such as **fiscal** (*pertaining to taxation, tax*), occurs as a qualifier in so many compounds and collocations that it seems wise to place it under the associated noun – in this case under **abattement, allégement, déduction, évasion, foyer, fraude, incitation, paradis, pression, redressement** and elsewhere. Adjectives such as **diplomatique, électoral, familial, général, judiciaire, municipal, patronal, pénal** or **social** are treated in the same way.

In some cases, however, e.g. **sujet conflictuel** or **commerce dominical**, where the adjective or other qualifier could be perceived as *the most significant element in the word group*, the reader will find the expression under the adjective, for example **conflictuel** and **dominical**, and suitable cross-referencing will be given under **sujet** and **commerce**. There is of course an element of editorial choice in these matters, and decisions may in some cases appear arbitrary.

Many *past participles which commonly have adjectival force*, such as **accru, avarié, éclaté, expérimenté** or **étudié**, are treated in this glossary as headwords.

Headwords which can be both noun and adjective, e.g. **clandestin, concurrent, horaire** or **policier**, are marked (*adj/nm,f*) or variants of same. *Verb/noun homographs*, e.g. **conseiller**, are, on the other hand, kept separate.

Where it seems necessary, some *syntactical information* may be included in the illustrative examples. In the case of verbs such as **s'échelonner** or **contrevenir**, both verb and associated preposition [**s'échelonner sur, contrevenir à**] or prepositional phrase [**tomber sous le coup de**] are emboldened to help the non-native speaker to use the word or expression correctly.

Symbols and abbreviations

In the interest of clarity and ease of reference, much lexicographical data normally provided in dictionaries [phonetic transcription of headwords, semantic categories, field and style labels, etc.] has been omitted. I have, however, incorporated a minimum of information, indicating the main parts of speech, the number [where necessary] and the gender of French nouns.

The following are the most commonly used symbols:

(*nm*)	masculine noun
(*nf*)	feminine noun
(*nmf*)	masculine and feminine nouns with invariable form
(*nm, f*)	masculine or feminine noun
(*nmpl*)	masculine plural noun
(*nfpl*)	feminine plural noun
(*nprm*)	proper name
(*pl*)	plural
(*adj*)	adjective
(*adj/nm*)	adjective or masculine noun
(*adj/nf*)	adjective or feminine noun
(*adj/nm, f*)	adjective or masculine or feminine noun
(*adj/nmf*)	adjective or invariable masculine and feminine noun
(*adv*)	adverb
(*inv*)	invariable
(*pref*)	prefix
(*prep*)	preposition
(*v impers*)	impersonal verb
(*vpr*)	reflexive verb
(*vi*)	intransitive verb
(*vt*)	transitive verb
(*excl*)	exclamation
[*fam*]	familiar/informal
[*fig*]	figurative use
[ ]	extra information, illustrations, etc., are given inside square brackets

Adrian C. Ritchie   Bangor, February 1997

A

A (*nm*): SEE **livret**

abaissement (*nm*): depuis l'**abaissement** de l'âge légal des relations homosexuelles; partisan de l'**abaissement** à 60 ans de l'âge de la retraite (*lowering, bringing down*)

abaisser (*vt*): **abaisser** à 16 ans le droit de vote; un accord visant à **abaisser** les barrières commerciales (*lower, bring down*); le nouveau gouvernement a promis d'**abaisser les taux d'intérêt** (*bring down/ reduce interest rates*)

abandon (*nm*): syndicats et manifestants exigent l'**abandon de la réforme** (*dropping of the [proposed] reform*); un projet européen qui exigera des **abandons de souveraineté** (*giving up of [national] sovereignty*)

abandonner (*vt*): il va **abandonner** son mandat de sénateur (*give up*)

abattement (*nm*): les **abattements fiscaux** en matière de succession (*tax allowance*); un **abattement forfaitaire** de 10% sur le revenu imposable (*standard [tax] relief*); réclamer un **abattement de zone** pour compenser la cherté de la vie en Corse (*reduction/allowance granted on a regional basis*)

abattre (*vt*): la négociation des prix permet d'**abattre** de 20% le tarif théorique (*lower, reduce*)

aberrant, -e (*adj*): des horaires **aberrants**; sans le SMIC, les salaires descendraient à des niveaux **aberrants** (*absurd, ridiculous*)

abonder (*vi*): le parquet semble **abonder dans leur sens** (*agree wholeheartedly; be in full agreement with them*)

abonné, -e (*nm,f*): 100 000 **abonnés** ont été privés d'eau courante (*customer*); le cable a gagné 245 000 **abonnés** en 1993 (*subscriber*); les **abonnés** ont priorité pour la location des places (*season-ticket holder*)

aborder (*vt*): il faut **aborder** la question sociale (*tackle, consider, deal with*)

aboutir (*vt*): le seul moyen d'**aboutir à une paix durable** (*achieve a lasting peace*); (*vi*): ces manœuvres pour isoler le Maroc pourraient **aboutir** (*succeed, come to fruition*)

aboutissement (*nm*): la France souhaite l'**aboutissement** des négociations (*[successful] outcome*)

abrogation (*nf*): l'**abrogation** des mesures édictées par les Conservateurs (*repeal, rescinding*); un projet de loi visant l'**abrogation de la loi de 1986** (*repeal of the 1986 act*)

abroger (*vt*): ils ont **abrogé** les récentes mesures de bannissement (*rescind, repeal [measure/law]*)

absorption (*nf*): rachat de trois firmes suisses, **absorption** de deux autres (*takeover*)

abstenir [s'] (*vpr*): le porte-parole du gouvernement **s'est abstenu de tout commentaire** (*decline to comment*)

abstention (*nf*): l'**abstention** communiste au deuxième tour (*abstention*); un **taux d'abstention** très élevé (*abstention rate*)

abus (*nm*): une loi qui peut donner lieu à des **abus** (*abuse; injustice*); huit employés ont été inculpés d'**abus de confiance** (*breach of trust*); on lui reproche des **abus de pouvoir** flagrants (*abuse of power*); l'**abus de biens sociaux**, ou l'utilisation de l'argent de l'entreprise pour des fins autres que son activité (*fraudulent use of company assets*); la question des **abus sexuels sur les enfants** (*child molesting*)

abuser (*vt*): le Premier ministre **abuse** des droits que lui accorde la Constitution (*misuse; abuse*); il est soupçonné d'avoir **abusé** de 17 élèves, garçons et filles (*[sexually] abuse*)

abusif, -ive (*adj*): des indemnités de rupture **abusive** du contrat de travail (*wrongful*); une utilisation **abusive** de la procédure; des plaintes pour dumping et subventions **abusives** (*unauthorized; improper*); SEE ALSO **clause, licenciement**

abusivement (*adv*): les journalistes **abusivement** assimilés à des fauteurs de troubles (*wrongfully*)

académie (*nf*): l'**Académie**, ou région administrative pour l'enseignement; un enseignant qui s'estime lésé peut s'adresser à l'**Académie** (*French regional education authority*); SEE ALSO **inspecteur, recteur**

accablant, -e (*adj*): le témoignage était **accablant** (*damning*); SEE ALSO **élément**

accabler (*vt*): décharger l'un du crime, c'est **accabler** l'autre (*condemn, damn*)

accalmie (*nf*): l'**accalmie** sur la Bourse de Paris n'a été que de courte durée (*period of quiet trading, lull*)

accaparer (*vt*): les militaires qui ont **accaparé le pouvoir** depuis l'indépendance (*seize power*)

accédant, -e (*nm,f*): un effort a été fait en faveur des **accédants à la propriété** (*house buyer; new homeowner*)

accéder (*vt*): il faut que la femme puisse **accéder aux** postes de responsabilité (*rise to, accede to*); une personne mise en examen ne peut **accéder directement** à son dossier (*have direct access*); l'an dernier, 50 000 ménages ont **accédé à la propriété** (*become a homeowner*)

acceptation (*nf*): l'**acceptation** par l'Irak du plan de paix soviétique (*accepting; agreeing to*)

accès (*nm*): le **libre accès** des femmes au planning familial (*free access*); des conditions d'**accès à la nationalité allemande** particulièrement strictes (*acquisition of German nationality*); SEE ALSO **bretelle**

accession (*nf*): après l'**accession à l'indépendance** de la Namibie (*achieving independence*); depuis son **accession au pouvoir** en 1985 (*coming to power*); un prêt à taux zéro destiné à relancer l'**accession à la propriété** (*home-ownership; owning one's own home*)

accommodement (*nm*): il faut **trouver un accommodement avec** l'Afrique du Sud (*come to terms with*)

accompagnement (*nm*): l'importance de l'**accompagnement** social et psychologique des sidéens (*support*); les crédits de l'État au titre de l'**accompagnement social** des demandeurs d'emploi (*social aid measures/programmes*)

accomplir (*vt*): il avait **accompli des missions confidentielles** à l'étranger (*carry out confidential missions*)

accord (*nm*): conclure un **accord** entre les deux pays (*agreement*); Renault: échec de l'**accord-cadre** (*outline agreement*); **accord salarial** dans la Fonction publique (*pay/wage settlement*); par convention ou **accord collectif** de branche (*collective agreement*); aux termes des **accords de paix** (*peace agreements*); SEE ALSO **amiable, conclure, parapher, protocole, valider**

accorder [s'] (*vpr*): les négociateurs ont pu **s'accorder sur un calendrier** de retrait des troupes (*agree on a timetable*)

accroc (*nm*): un nouvel **accroc** dans la cohabitation (*hitch, difficulty*); **sans accrocs** ni retards excessifs (*without a hitch, smoothly*)

accrochage (*nm*): des **accrochages** ont opposé manifestants et forces de l'ordre (*clash, incident*)

accroissement (*nm*): un **accroissement** de la corruption en France (*increase, growth*)

accroître (*vt*): l'État a progressivement **accru** son rôle (*increase, develop*); [s'] (*vpr*): le nombre des emplois **s'est accru** en douze ans de plus de 20 millions (*increase, grow*); SEE ALSO **tension**

accru, -e (*adj*): l'ouverture à l'extérieur implique une spécialisation **accrue** (*increased*); SEE ALSO **compétition, productivité**

accueil (*nm*): logé dans des conditions normales d'**accueil** (*accommodation*); SEE ALSO **famille, foyer, structure, terre**

accueillir (*vt*): l'OTAN **accueille** favorablement le projet français (*greet, welcome*); **accueilli** dans un centre d'hébergement (*accommodated*); on **accueillait** de plus en plus d'immigrés clandestins (*admit, let in*); **mal accueillis** au début, les Maghrébins ont réussi à s'intégrer (*[made] unwelcome*)

acculer (*vt*): une concurrence féroce **accula** la firme à la faillite (*force into; drive to the brink of*)

accusation (*nf*): il conteste en bloc les **accusations** dont il fait l'objet (*charge, accusation*); **répondre de l'accusation** de recel et d'abus de biens sociaux (*answer a charge*); l'**accusation** a fait valoir que l'inculpé avait été pris en flagrant délit (*prosecution*); instruire, **mettre en accusation** et juger les personnes coupables (*charge, indict*); la **mise en accusation** du Président des États-Unis (*impeachment; indictment*); SEE ALSO **chambre**

accusé, -e (*nm,f*): l'**accusé** nie avoir été mêlé à un trafic de devises; un **accusé** comparaît devant la cour d'assises (*accused, defendant*); envoyer un **accusé de réception** (*acknowledgement of receipt*); SEE ALSO **banc, box**

accuser (*vt*): le juge les **accusa** de meurtre (*indict, accuse, charge*); son parti **accuse** un retard de 21 points sur les travaillistes (*show, register*); [s'] (*vpr*): le décalage entre les deux partis **s'accuse** (*grow, increase; widen*)

acheminement (*nm*): des retards dans l'**acheminement du courrier** (*mail delivery*); les combats gênent l'**acheminement de l'aide humanitaire** (*transport/distribution of aid*)

acheminer (*vt*): afin d'**acheminer** l'aide humanitaire (*forward, transport*); [s'] (*vpr*): les négociations **s'acheminent vers** leur conclusion prévisible (*head/move towards*)

achèvement (*nm*): les sommes nécessaires à l'**achèvement** des travaux (*completion, conclusion*); d'importants travaux **en cours d'achèvement** (*nearing completion*)

achever (*vt*): l'économie **achève** sa convalescence (*complete*); [s'] (*vpr*): l'année 1982 vit **s'achever** le programme de nationalisations (*come to an end, terminate*); le congrès **s'est achevé** sur une démonstration d'unité (*conclude, end, close*)

achoppement (*nm*): le principal **point d'achoppement** concerne l'agriculture (*stumbling block; difficulty*); SEE ALSO **pierre**

achopper (*vi*): les discussions risquent d'**achopper** sur ce dossier difficile (*stumble; hit a snag*); la contestation risque de **faire achopper** les pourparlers de paix (*cause to falter; bring to a halt*)

acompte (*nm*): verser un **acompte** de 30% du prix d'achat (*payment on account, down payment*)

acquéreur (*nm*): chercher un **acquéreur** pour son unité de Kentucky (*buyer, purchaser*); **se porter acquéreur** d'un terrain construisible (*buy; offer to buy*)

acquérir (*vt*): des sociétés ont été cédées et d'autres **acquises** (*acquire; take over*); le leader du Labour sait que **leur soutien lui est acquis** (*he can be certain of their support*); il est d'ores et déjà **acquis au projet** (*in favour of the plan*); [s'] (*vpr*): les titres peuvent **s'acquérir** aux guichets de la Poste (*be obtained*)

acquêts (*nmpl*): les **acquêts,** les biens acquis pendant la durée du mariage (*estate comprising only property acquired after marriage*); SEE ALSO **communauté**

acquis (*nm*): les diplômes obtenus sont **un acquis incontestable** (*an undoubted asset*); il faut maintenir et renforcer les **acquis communautaires** (*what has been achieved by the [European] community*); les **acquis sociaux** auxquels tous ont droit (*social benefits, entitlements*)

acquisition (*nf*): une véritable fièvre d'**acquisitions** a gagné les pays membres de la CE (*takeover, esp. of company*)

acquittement (*nm*): la cour d'assises prononce un **acquittement** (*verdict of not guilty*); un contrôle de l'**acquittement** des droits d'entrée sera instauré (*payment*); SEE ALSO **plaider**

acquitter (*vt*): le tribunal correctionnel relaxe, la cour d'assises **acquitte** (*acquit, discharge*); les entreprises doivent **acquitter** la taxe professionnelle (*pay*); [s'] (*vpr*): **s'acquitter des** factures impayées (*pay, pay off, settle*)

acte (*nm*): l'usage de la langue arabe dans les **actes** officiels de l'administration (*deed; document*); un **acte authentique** passé devant notaire (*deed*); rédiger un **acte de l'état-civil** (*birth/marriage/death certificate*); la revalorisation de l'**acte médical** (*medical treatment/ consultation*); **passer à l'acte,** en arrêtant toute vente de pétrole aux pays occidentaux (*carry out a threat*); ces dispositions **prennent acte** de la nouvelle configuration des frontières (*take into account*); SEE ALSO **candidature**

actif, -ive (*adj/nm,f*): les **actifs** – qu'ils soient chômeurs ou salariés (*active/ working population*); le nombre d'**actifs occupés** a augmenté en France de 103 000 (*person in employment*); **à l'actif de** ce gouvernement, on cite sa législation sociale (*to the credit of*); SEE ALSO **population, vie**

action (*nf*): acquérir des **actions** en Bourse (*share*); travailler dans le cadre d'une **action** d'insertion (*initiative, programme*); l'**action sociale,** ou les mesures prises en faveur des plus démunis (*social programme*); une **action** de 24 heures paralyse les transports parisiens (*industrial action; strike*); sa décision d'**engager une action en justice** (*take legal action*); SEE ALSO **émission, journée, redresser**

actionnaire (*nmf*): le conseil d'administration conseille aux **actionnaires** d'accepter la proposition (*shareholder*); créer des milliers de **petits actionnaires** (*small shareholder*)

actionnariat (*nm*): un système d'**actionnariat** où les salariés détiennent 15% du capital (*shareholding; share ownership*); partisan de l'**actionnariat du personnel** (*employee share ownership*)

activité (*nf*): la croissance de l'**activité** féminine (*employment; work*); le ralentissement de l'**activité allemande** (*business activity in Germany*); la société de Lille a vendu ses **activités** de peignage et de tissus (*interests; operations*); SEE ALSO **appoint, artisanal, cessation, manufacturier, parc, salarié, séparer, service, zone**

actualisation (*nf*): l'**actualisation** d'une loi vieille de cent ans (*updating*); un programme d'**actualisation des connaissances** pour les personnels d'éducation (*updating of skills*)

actualiser (*vt*): cet accord a été **actualisé** au mois de juin 1987 (*renew*); pour **actualiser** ces chiffres, il faut les multiplier par deux (*update, bring up to date*)

actualité (*nf*): la question retrouve tout à coup toute son **actualité** (*topicality, relevance*); l'**actualité politique** est peu fournie en ces mois d'été (*political news; the political scene*)

actuel, -elle (*adj*): l'**actuel** chef de l'exécutif; l'**actuelle** majorité au parlement (*present, current*)

adaptation (*nf*): après un long processus d'**adaptation** (*adjustment*); l'**adaptation** de l'emploi aux aspirations des femmes (*adaptation, adapting*)

adapté, -e (*adj*): rechercher des **solutions adaptées** à chaque situation (*appropriate solutions*); la justice pénale est **mal adaptée** au monde des affaires (*ill-suited; inappropriate*)

additif (*nm*): un **additif** au règlement intérieur de l'école (*additional clause*)

adduction (*nf*): emporter un important marché d'**adduction d'eau** (*water supply*)

adepte (*adj/nmf*): une secte qui compte 3 millions d'**adeptes** au Brésil (*follower, disciple; member*); le service national conserve ses **adeptes** (*advocate; supporter*); l'argument des **adeptes de la chasse à courre** (*people in favour of hunting*); l'idée **fait des adeptes** dans les rangs socialistes (*gain support*)

adéquat, -e (*adj*): disposer de moyens **adéquats** pour se protéger (*adequate, sufficient*); la demande sera examinée par la commission **adéquate** (*appropriate; relevant*)

adéquation (*nf*): une meilleure **adéquation** entre l'offre et la demande (*matching*); le succès repose sur l'**adéquation** du produit au marché (*suitability*)

adhérent, -e (*adj/nm,f*): les **adhérents** du Parti conservateur sont favorables; financé par les cotisations des 5 000 **adhérents** (*member [trade union, political party]*); SEE ALSO **carte, revendiquer**

adhérer (*vt*): la volonté d'**adhérer** à la nation française (*be/become a member*); **adhérer** au traité de fraternité entre pays maghrébins (*join*); pourquoi tant d'ouvriers hésitent-ils à **adhérer**? (*join [esp. trade union/political party]*)

adhésion (*nf*): l'**adhésion** de la Grande-Bretagne à la CE risquait de faire éclater la Communauté (*membership; joining*); l'idée a **recueilli une très large adhésion** (*gain widespread support/approval*)

adjoint, -e (*adj/nm,f*): employé en tant qu'**adjoint** au directeur (*assistant; deputy*); les **adjoints au maire** font le gros du travail (*deputy mayor*); l'**adjoint à l'urbanisme** du maire de Paris (*deputy mayor in charge of town planning*)

adjudication (*nf*): des annonces signalant les plus importantes **ventes par adjudication** (*[sale by] auction*)

adjuger (*vt*): des logements **adjugés aux enchères publiques** sur décision de justice (*[sell by] auction*)

admettre (*vt*): seulement 34% des candidats **ont été admis** (*pass [examination]*)

administrateur (*nm*): l'Assemblée générale désigne les **administrateurs** (*director; trustee*); l'**administrateur gérant** du consortium Airbus Industrie (*chief executive*); les affaires en dépôt de bilan sont confiées à l'**administrateur judiciaire** (*receiver*); le groupe a **été placé sous administrateur judiciaire** (*be put under court administration; go into receivership*)

administration (*nf*): l'**administration directe** de la province par Londres (*direct rule/administration*); un désaccord avec un particulier ou une **administration** (*government service*); mars 1982 donna à l'**administration locale** un regain de vie (*local government*); la société nantaise a **été placée sous administration judiciaire** (*be put under court administration*); SEE ALSO **conseil, pénitentiaire**

administré, -e (*nm,f*): le maire est soutenu par ses **administrés** (*citizen; constituent*)

administrer (*vt*): une collectivité **s'administrant librement** dans le cadre de la République (*running its own affairs; self-governing*)

admissible (*adj*): il y avait 76% de candidats **admissibles [à l'oral]** (*eligible to sit the oral part of an exam*)

admission (*nf*): l'**admission** de l'Autriche dans la CE (*admission, admitting*); SEE ALSO **note**

adopter (*vt*): l'Espagne **adopte** un plan de réduction de ses dépenses publiques (*adopt*); le projet de loi a **été adopté** en première lecture à l'Assemblée nationale (*was passed/carried*)

adoptif, -ive (*adj*): sa famille **adoptive**, dont il ne voulait plus porter le nom (*adoptive*); SEE ALSO **parent**

adoption (*nf*): l'**adoption** d'enfants étrangers facilitée malgré les réticences du garde des Sceaux (*adoption*); l'**adoption** du projet de loi sur l'avortement (*adoption/passage [of a bill]*)

affaiblir (*vt*): la montée des taux d'intérêt **affaiblit** le franc; contribuer à **affaiblir** les partis d'opposition (*weaken*)

affaiblissement (*nm*): l'**affaiblissement** de la monnaie nationale (*weakening*); avoir pour effet un **affaiblissement** du rôle du gouvernement (*diminishing*)

affaire (*nf*): une **affaire** de vol (*case*); Paris n'a pas l'intention de se mêler des **affaires intérieures** du Canada (*internal affairs*); le Parti national, **depuis son arrivée aux affaires** fin 1990 (*since it came to power*); SEE ALSO **chiffre, expédier, expédition, retour, tribunal**

affairisme (*nm*): l'inquiétude de la gauche face aux accusations d'**affairisme** (*shady dealing; [political] racketeering*)

affaissement (*nm*): l'**affaissement** politique des communistes; l'**affaissement** du chiffre d'affaires des journaux (*fall, collapse*); on craignait un nouvel **affaissement des cours** à Wall Street (*fall in share prices*)

affaisser [s'] (*vpr*): le terrain **s'était affaissé** par endroits (*subside, give way*)

affectation (*nf*): 20% des recrues auront une **affectation** civile (*posting*); l'opposition s'inquiète de l'**affectation** du produit de ces privatisations (*allotment/allocation [of funds]*)

affecter (*vt*): les objecteurs de conscience, **affectés** dans une formation militaire non-armée (*attach; assign*); **affecter** les sommes économisées à l'aide au tiers monde (*allocate; earmark*)

afférent, -e (*adj*): les dépenses **afférentes à** l'habitation principale ouvrent droit à déduction d'impôt (*relating to*)

affichage (*nm*): une campagne d'**affichage** à l'échelon national (*billsticking; placarding*); les députés autorisent l'**affichage publicitaire** pour les boissons alcoolisées (*poster advertising*)

affiche (*nf*): dans la presse écrite et **par voie d'affiche** (*using posters/by poster*)

affiché, -e (*adj*): son approbation **affichée** de la politique du gouvernement (*open, declared*)

afficher (*vt*): côté français, on **affiche** une complète satisfaction (*display, express*); les statistiques récentes **affichent** une diminution de 5% du chômage (*reveal*)

affiliation (*nf*): la loi de 1972 rend obligatoire l'**affiliation** à un régime de retraite complémentaire (*registering with; subscribing to*); le Premier ministre **n'a pas d'affiliation partisane** (*belongs to no particular party*)

affilié, -e (*adj/nm,f*): les **affiliés** du régime général de la Sécurité sociale (*[affiliated] member*); les **Socialistes et affiliés** sont donnés gagnants (*Socialists and their allies*)

affilier [s'] (*vpr*): 20 000 membres supplémentaires **se sont affiliés** cette année (*join, become a member*)

affluer (*vi*): les réfugiés continuent d'**affluer** aux frontières (*flock/arrive in great numbers*); Libanais et Ghanéens **affluent en Allemagne** (*flock/flood into Germany*)

afflux (*nm*): l'**afflux** des demandeurs d'asile; un **afflux** massif de dollars risquait de provoquer une crise du système monétaire international (*influx, inflow*)

affranchir [s'] (*vpr*): les républiques veulent **s'affranchir** de la tutelle de Moscou (*break free*)

affranchissement (*nm*): son **affranchissement** de la tutelle russe (*freeing, emancipation*); l'**affranchissement** est à la charge de l'expéditeur (*postage*)

affrètement (*nm*): un contrat portant sur l'**affrètement** de trois supertankers (*chartering; hiring*); transport aérien: nouveaux **affrètements** pour Air Littoral (*charter flights*)

affréter (*vt*): un avion gros porteur **affrété** par la Croix-Rouge (*charter*)

affrontement (*nm*): les **affrontements** ont fait 16 morts et plusieurs blessés (*clash*)

affronter (*vt*): le pays **affronte** une sérieuse crise politique (*face, be faced by*); pour mieux **affronter** les difficultés de la presse (*face, face up to*); 2 000 jeunes émeutiers ont **affronté** les forces de l'ordre (*confront; clash with*)

âge (*nm*): SEE **classe, discrimination, limite, pyramide, tranche, troisième âge**

agenda (*nm*): cette visite, inscrite sur l'**agenda** du Premier ministre, a été annulée (*timetable, diary*)

agent (*nm*): deux **agents communaux** honorés (*municipal employee*); le salaire d'un **agent public** des DOM est majoré de 40%; le quart des **agents de l'État** travaillent en Île-de-France (*state employee; civil servant*); l'arrestation de 19 courtiers et **agents de change** (*exchange broker*); SEE ALSO **fonction, maîtrise**

agglomération (*nf*): une **agglomération**: un ensemble de communes sur lequel s'étend une zone bâtie (*town; built-up area*); une commune de l'**agglomération caennaise** (*Caen and its suburbs*); en zone rurale et dans les **petites agglomérations** (*small urban area*)

aggravant, -e (*adj*): SEE **circonstance**

aggravation (*nf*): Fidji: **aggravation** de la crise; face à l'**aggravation** du déficit extérieur (*worsening*); le chômage **dont l'aggravation est continue** (*ever worsening*)

aggravé, -e (*adj*): une peine maximale de deux ans pour les délits, même **aggravés** (*with aggravating circumstances*); SEE ALSO **peine, viol**

aggraver (*vt*): **aggravant** ainsi les inégalités et les tensions (*aggravate, make worse*); [s'] (*vpr*): le taux d'inflation pourrait même **s'aggraver** (*increase, rise*); la crise **s'aggrave** au fil des semaines (*worsen, deteriorate*)

agissement (*nm*): les **agissements** suspects du député socialiste (*schemes, intrigues*); l'ampleur des **agissements frauduleux** de l'ancien directeur (*malpractice, fraud*)

agitation (*nf*): l'**agitation** dans les territoires occupés; depuis le début de l'**agitation** islamiste (*unrest*); une recrudescence de l'**agitation sociale** (*social unrest*)

agréé, -e (*adj*): faire effectuer des travaux par un professionnel **agréé** (*authorized; accredited*); l'assistante maternelle doit être **agréée** (*approved; registered*)

agréer (*vt*): l'Allemagne ne saurait **agréer à** une baisse artificielle de ses taux d'intérêt (*agree to, accept*); une réduction **dont le principe a été agréé** lors du sommet d'octobre (*which has been agreed in principle*)

agrément (*nm*): l'**agrément** des pouvoirs publics est nécessaire pour procéder (*consent, approval*); lors de la demande d'**agrément** (*accreditation*)

agression (*nf*): des enfants victimes d'**agressions sexuelles** de la part de parents ou de proches (*sexual assault*)

aide (*nf*): l'octroi d'une **aide** occidentale à Moscou (*help, assistance*); des sommes allouées au titre de l'**aide extérieure** (*foreign aid*); environ 100 milliards de francs d'**aides publiques** (*government aid; public money*); recevoir 2 840 francs par mois d'**aide sociale** (*social security benefits; welfare [payment]*); se procurer une **aide à domicile** (*home help*); une réduction d'impôt pour **aide alimentaire** (*alimony*); SEE ALSO **acheminement, bénéficiaire, dépendance, exportation, pierre, venir**

aile (*nf*): avec l'accord de l'**aile modérée** du parti (*moderate wing*), l'**aile radicale** du terrorisme islamique algérien (*extreme/radical wing*)

aléa (*nm*): comme tous les placements, il est soumis aux **aléas** de la Bourse (*hazard; vagary*); **sauf aléa**, il sera au rendez-vous de Paris (*barring unforeseen circumstances*)

aléatoire (*adj*): malgré le caractère **aléatoire** des contrats avec l'étranger; le marché boursier peut être **aléatoire** (*uncertain, risky*); distribution **aléatoire** d'eau et d'électricité (*unreliable*)

alerte (*nf*): **alerte à la bombe** sur un avion d'Air France (*bomb alert/scare*); décréter l'**état d'alerte** (*state of emergency*); SEE ALSO **cote**

aliéner [s'] (*vpr*): au risque de s'**aliéner** les organisations syndicales (*alienate; antagonize*)

alignement (*nm*): un **alignement** des salaires sur ceux de la métallurgie parisienne; un **alignement** sur les normes occidentales demandera du temps (*bringing into alignment*)

aligner (*vt*): on essaie d'**aligner** la pratique française sur les dispositions en vigueur à l'étranger (*align; bring into alignment*); [s'] (*vpr*): la loi belge s'**aligne** sur la directive européenne (*fall into line with*)

alimentaire (*adj*): SEE **aide, autosuffisance, carence, pension, pénurie**

alimentation (*nf*): les sociétés ont la responsabilité de l'**alimentation en eau potable** de la ville (*supply of drinking water*)

alimenter (*vt*): attirer les investissements et **alimenter** la croissance (*feed, sustain*); payer des impôts et **alimenter les caisses de l'État** (*be a source of revenue for the state*)

alinéa (*nm*): le gouvernement fait grand usage de l'article 49, **alinéa** 3 de la Constitution (*paragraph*)

alléchant, -e (*adj*): des perspectives **alléchantes** pour les entreprises; des taux d'intérêt **alléchants** (*very attractive*)

allégation (*nf*): il dément formellement les **allégations** portées contre lui (*allegation, accusation*)

allégement (*nm*): un **allégement** des contrôles aux frontières (*lightening; relaxing; alleviating*); la répartition des 15 milliards d'**allégements fiscaux** (*tax relief/cuts*)

alléger (*vt*): **alléger** des programmes trop lourds (*lighten*); la volonté du gouvernement d'**alléger les impôts** (*reduce taxation*); [s'] (*vpr*): la procédure de nos jours **s'est allégée** (*become less complex; be simplified*)

alliance (*nf*): pas d'**alliance** RPR-FN pour le second tour des élections (*electoral alliance*); le chef d'État **fait alliance** avec l'armée (*form an alliance*); SEE ALSO **retournement**

allier [s'] (*vpr*): le français Thomson **s'allie** à British Aerospace (*link up with*)

allocataire (*nmf*): les **allocataires** du Fonds de solidarité; une incitation à la paresse pour les **allocataires** (*recipient [of allowance]; beneficiary*)

allocation (*nf*): on vient d'annuler l'**allocation** de famille unique (*allowance; benefit*); toucher l'allocation de solidarité à la suite de l'**allocation de fin de droits** (*final unemployment benefit entitlement*); SEE ALSO **caisse, veuvage**

allocution (*nf*): au cours de son **allocution** radiophonique (*speech, address*)

allongement (*nm*): l'**allongement** de la durée des études; il préconise un **allongement** de l'année scolaire (*lengthening; extension*); SEE ALSO **espérance**

allonger (*vt*): **allonger** la période de cotisation (*lengthen, extend*); [s'] (*vpr*): la durée de vie qui **s'allonge** (*get longer, increase*)

allouer (*vt*): l'État a **alloué** 1 500 MF au musée de la Villette; le gouvernement va **allouer** une nouvelle aide aux paysans (*allocate*); une grande partie du budget **est allouée aux dépenses sociales** (*is devoted to social expenditure*)

alourdir (*vt*): le gouvernement a choisi d'**alourdir l'impôt** (*increase taxes*); [s'] (*vpr*): le chômage de longue durée ne cesse de **s'alourdir** (*increase*); SEE ALSO **fiscalité**

alourdissement (*nm*): malgré l'**alourdissement** des impôts locaux (*increase, rise*); un **alourdissement des pertes** parmi les "casques bleus" (*heavier/increased losses*)

altérer (*vt*): une crise de confiance **altère** les relations entre Londres et Dublin (*impair, affect*)́

alternance (*nf*): la première **alternance** droite-gauche (*change of political power between two main parties*)

amalgame (*nm*): le FN profite de l'**amalgame** immigration-délinquance (*lumping [different] things together*)

ambiance (*nf*): l'**ambiance** à Alger est plutôt à l'apaisement (*mood, atmosphere*)

ambiant, -e (*adj*): ses propositions reflètent le discours libéral **ambiant** (*fashionable, current*); SEE ALSO **morosité**

aménagement (*nm*): depuis les traités de Rome, des **aménagements** ont été faits (*change, modification*); le projet de loi sur l'**aménagement du temps de travail** (*flexible management of time; flexible working hours*); un projet d'**aménagement du centre ville** (*redevelopment of the city centre*); des problèmes d'**aménagement urbain** (*urban development*); l'**aménagement du territoire** vise à remédier aux déséquilibres régionaux (*town and country/regional planning*); SEE ALSO **ZAC, ZAD**

aménager (*vt*): **aménager le temps de travail** pour créer des emplois (*adopt flexible working hours*)

amende (*nf*): une condamnation à une **amende** de 2 millions de francs (*fine*); SEE ALSO **passible**

amendement (*nm*): l'**amendement** de la loi sur la presse (*amending, amendment*)

amender (*vt*): un décret **amendant** la loi de 1988 (*amend*)

amener (*vt*): SEE **mandat**

amenuiser [s'] (*vpr*): l'écart **s'amenuisa** encore l'année dernière (*reduce, become less*)

amiable (*adj*): Panama: **accord à l'amiable** avec Washington (*amicable settlement*); le **règlement à l'amiable** d'un dossier (*out-of-court settlement*)

amicale (*nf*): une **amicale** de locataires (*association, group; club*)

amont (*nm*): petite ville **en amont de** Bordeaux (*upstream of*); [*fig*] les entreprises situées **en amont dans la chaîne de production** (*at an earlier stage of production*)

amorce (*nf*): l'**amorce** d'une décrue du chômage (*beginnings, first signs*); on a trouvé une **amorce de solution** (*initial elements of a solution*)

amorcer (*vt*): l'Éthiopie a **amorcé** un rapprochement avec les États-Unis (*begin, initiate*); le déclin **amorcé** en 1993 se poursuit (*starting/dating from*); [s'] (*vpr*): on ne voit pas encore **s'amorcer** la reprise tant attendue (*begin; get under way*)

amortir (*vt*): pour **amortir** les effets de la crise (*cushion*); le prêt sera **amorti** en cinq ans (*pay off, repay*); les petites entreprises n'arrivent pas à **amortir les investissements** (*recoup investment costs*)

amortissement (*nm*): l'**amortissement de la dette** exigera de longues années d'efforts (*paying off the debt*); compte tenu de l'**amortissement**, elle ne vaut plus que 5 000F (*depreciation*)

ampleur (*nf*): révélant l'**ampleur** du malaise qui traverse la société française (*scale*); devant l'**ampleur des combats** (*the scale of the fighting*)

amplifier [s'] (*vpr*): le terrorisme continuait à s'**amplifier** (*increase, spread*); SEE ALSO **appeler**

amputer (*vt*): le gouvernement a décidé d'**amputer de moitié** les salaires des fonctionnaires (*cut by half*)

ancien, -ienne (*adj/nm,f*): le rôle de l'**ancien** ministre de l'Intérieur; la France, **ancienne** puissance coloniale (*former*); les **anciens** des Grandes écoles prestigieuses (*former student*); SEE ALSO **bâti, habitat**

ancienneté (*nf*): l'**ancienneté** qu'a l'employé dans une société (*length of service, seniority*); la progression automatique, à l'**ancienneté** (*by virtue of length of service/seniority*); l'**ancienneté** moyenne de chômage est aujourd'hui de treize mois (*average duration*); SEE ALSO **bonification, prime**

ancrage (*nm*): l'**ancrage** du parti en Picardie reste fort (*solid [political] base*); préserver l'**ancrage à gauche** du Parti socialiste (*solid left-wing base*); l'**ancrage européen** de l'Allemagne unifiée (*anchorage/attachment to Europe*)

ancrer (*vt*): son souhait d'**ancrer** le PS à gauche (*anchor; establish firmly*)

animateur, -trice (*nm,f*): avoir des talents d'**animateur** exceptionnels (*organizer; leader*); les élus locaux sont de plus en plus les **animateurs** de leur communauté locale (*driving force*)

animation (*nf*): les fonctions de gestion et d'**animation** (*organization*); contribuer à l'**animation touristique** de la ville (*promotion of tourism*); **faire de l'animation sociale** dans les Maisons de jeunes (*take a lead in community activities*)

annexe (*adj/nf*): renvoyer une déclaration de revenus et les [pièces] **annexes** (*enclosure*)

annonce (*nf*): l'**annonce** de nouvelles mesures de compression du personnel (*announcement*); passer une **annonce** dans la presse locale (*[newspaper] advertisement*)

annoncer [s'] (*vpr*): la rentrée s'**annonce** "chaude" dans les lycées (*seems likely to be turbulent*); la tâche du gouvernement s'**annonce difficile** (*is likely to be difficult*); SEE ALSO **rude**

annonceur (*nm*): les **annonceurs** reçoivent un exemplaire gratuit (*advertiser*)

annuaire (*nm*): tout abonné reçoit l'**annuaire** [téléphonique] du département (*telephone directory*)

annuité (*nf*): une économie de 62 000F sur les **annuités des prêts** (*annual loan repayment*)

annulation (*nf*): les **annulations** de commandes (*cancellation*); la CGT exige l'**annulation** de 55 licenciements (*quashing*); des rumeurs d'**annulation des élections** avaient couru avant le premier tour (*calling off/ cancelling elections*)

annuler (*vt*): le sommet devra être **annulé** (*cancel, call off*); Paris décide d'**annuler les dettes restantes** de ces pays (*cancel outstanding debts*); on **annula** le verdict sur un vice de procédure (*quash*)

anonymat (*nm*): l'**anonymat** est garanti pour tous (*[complete] confidentiality*); préférant **garder l'anonymat** par peur de représailles (*remain anonymous*)

antécédent, -e (*adj/nm*): choisir un candidat en fonction de ses **antécédents scolaires** (*academic record*); compte tenu des **antécédents judiciaires** du prévenu (*criminal record*)

antenne (*nf*): avec des **antennes** en province; les locaux abritent l'**antenne** parisienne du mouvement (*agency; branch*); le **temps d'antenne** accordé aux petits partis est dérisoire (*broadcasting time*)

anticasseur (*adj*): les dispositions de la **loi anticasseurs** (*law banning violent behaviour during demonstrations*)

anticipé, -e (*adj*): SEE **élection, libération, retraite**

apaisement (*nm*): il faut aussi qu'Israël contribue à l'**apaisement** (*bringing of peace, reconciliation; reduction of tension*); lancer un appel à l'**apaisement du conflit** (*bringing the dispute to an end*); SEE ALSO **sens**

apaiser (*vt*): afin d'**apaiser** l'opinion publique (*appease*); [s'] (*vpr*): la tension en Cisjordanie **s'apaise** (*die down, subside*)

apatride (*adj/nmf*): l'Office français de protection des réfugiés et **apatrides** (*stateless person*)

apolitique (*adj*): les Français, de plus en plus **apolitiques** (*apolitical; indifferent to politics*); une grève **apolitique**, uniquement revendicative (*non political*)

appareil (*nm*): l'ensemble de l'**appareil** économique français (*system; organization*); l'**appareil du parti** est tout absorbé à la préparation du prochain congrès (*[political] party apparatus*)

appareiller (*vi*): le porte-avions Clemenceau **appareillera** lundi matin (*cast off, get under way*)

apparenté, -e (*adj/nm,f*): les Socialistes et leurs quinze **apparentés** ont voté l'amnistie (*political ally*); le député **apparenté** socialiste des Alpes-Maritimes (*closely allied to the Socialists*)

apparentement (*nm*): un système d'alliances pré-électorales, ou **apparentements** (*alliance of electoral lists*)

appartenance (*nf*): l'**appartenance** à une ethnie, une nation ou une race (*belonging to; membership of*); on ne connaît pas leur **appartenance** précise (*affiliation [esp. political]*)

appauvrir (*vt*): enrichir les très riches et **appauvrir** les très pauvres (*impoverish; make poorer*); [s'] (*vpr*): un sol qui **s'appauvrit** au fil des ans (*become poorer*)

appauvrissement (*nm*): l'**appauvrissement** des sols menace leur prospérité (*impoverishment*)

appel (*nm*): le volontariat implique l'abolition de l'**appel sous les drapeaux** (*conscription*); être relaxé **en appel** (*pending appeal*); **faire appel de** la décision du tribunal de Rennes (*appeal/lodge an appeal against*); la direction a **lancé un appel à la reprise du travail** (*appeal for a return to work*); **lancer un appel d'offres** pour la construction de l'autoroute (*invite tenders*); SEE ALSO **condamner, cour, devancer, interjeter, procès**

appelant, -e (*nm,f*): l'appel étant injustifié, l'**appelant** est condamné aux dépens (*appellant against a judgment*)

appelé (*nm*): le nombre d'**appelés** volontaires pour le service long; 400 postes de militaires de carrière et 2 183 postes d'**appelés du contingent** (*conscript; national serviceman*)

appeler (*vt*): un jeune Français est **appelé** à l'âge de 19 ans (*conscript/call up for service*); **appeler** à un changement de régime; **en appeler au** respect des droits de la personne (*appeal/call for*); l'immigration **est appelée à s'amplifier** au cours des prochaines années (*is likely to increase*); SEE ALSO **grève, vœu**

appellation (*nf*): des personnes répondant à cette **appellation** (*label, name, title*); les fromages **d'appellation d'origine** représentent 11% de la production fromagère totale (*bearing mark of the area of manufacture*)

application (*nf*): l'**application** d'un accord salarial signé en 1994; la **mise en application** du plan social (*implementation*); les diverses réformes qui vont **entrer en application** le mois prochain (*come into force*)

appliquer (*vt*): le règlement a été **appliqué** dès le premier jour (*implement*); la loi **sera appliquée** sans faille (*will be enforced*)

appoint (*nm*): les petits partis servent souvent d'**appoint** au gouvernement minoritaire (*[extra] help/support*); une **activité d'appoint** à domicile (*[extra] job/employment*)

appointements (*nmpl*): recevoir des **appointements** (*emoluments, salary attached to a post*)

appointer (*vt*): les maires, élus mais fonctionnaires **appointés par l'État** (*paid by the state*)

apport (*nm*): l'**apport** du tourisme étranger (*contribution; input*); faute d'**apport personnel** suffisant, les plus pauvres dépendent de l'aide publique pour l'achat d'un logement (*contribution; down payment*)

appréciation (*nf*): à Paris et à Bonn on a des **appréciations** assez différentes sur cette affaire (*view, assessment*); l'**appréciation** de la monnaie favorise les achats à l'étranger (*appreciation; increase in value*)

apprécier (*vt*): la justice aura pour tâche de désigner les responsables et d'**apprécier les conséquences** (*decide what action to take*); [s'] (*vpr*): une monnaie qui **s'apprécie**; l'indice CAC 40 **s'est apprécié** de près de 25% (*rise [in value], appreciate*)

apprenti, -e (*nm,f*): faire bénéficier les **apprentis** d'aides de l'état (*apprentice*); le **recrutement des apprentis** par les entreprises (*taking on apprentices*)

apprentissage (*nm*): Emploi: mesures pour développer l'**apprentissage** (*apprentice training, apprenticeship*); l'**apprentissage précoce** de l'anglais (*early learning of a skill [esp. at school]*)

approbation (*nf*): la politique des États-Unis **rencontre une large approbation** (*meet with general approval*)

approfondi, -e (*adj*): une étude **approfondie** de la question (*in depth*)

approfondir [s'] (*vpr*): la récession économique **s'approfondit** (*get worse*); les disparités entre riches et pauvres ne cessent de **s'approfondir** (*become more pronounced*)

approfondissement (*nm*): un **approfondissement du fossé** entre gauche et droite (*a widening gap/gulf*); il faudrait pour cela un **approfondissement du dialogue** (*further/more thorough discussions*)

approvisionnement (*nm*): les pays qui dépendent de la Russie pour leur **approvisionnement pétrolier** (*oil supplies*)

approvisionner (*vt*): les stocks permettent d'**approvisionner la demande** sans problème (*satisfy demand*); aubaine qui lui permit d'**approvisionner son compte en banque** (*pay money into a bank account*); un compte bancaire **non-approvisionné** (*overdrawn; in the red*)

appui (*nm*): Bagdad compte sur l'**appui** de la France (*support, backing*); le président cherche des **appuis diplomatiques** (*diplomatic backing*)

appuyer (*vt*): pour **appuyer** leurs revendications, ils menacent de faire grève (*support, back*)

apurement (*nm*): assurer l'**apurement** des dettes de l'entreprise (*settlement [of a debt]*)

apurer (*vt*): le déficit ne sera pas **apuré** avant l'année 2006 (*pay off, discharge [debt]*); augmenter les impôts de 11% pour **apurer le passif** (*pay off the debt*); la France et l'Iran **apurent leur contentieux** (*settle their dispute*); les dettes **s'apurent** au fil des mois (*be paid off/settled*)

arbitrage (*nm*): soumettre un litige à l'**arbitrage de l'ONU** (*United Nations arbitration*); **faire appel à l'arbitrage** pour éviter la publicité des tribunaux (*go to/have recourse to arbitration*)

arbitraire (*adj/nm*): arrestations **arbitraires** et exécutions sommaires (*arbitrary*); une accentuation de l'**arbitraire du pouvoir** (*high-handed action by government*); dans aucun pays le citoyen n'est à l'abri de l'**arbitraire de l'internement** (*arbitrary internment*)

arbitrer (*vt*): le FN pourrait **arbitrer les élections** dans les circonscriptions urbaines (*decide the election result*)

ardoise (*nf*): effacer une **ardoise** énorme (*debt, deficit*)

argent (*nm*): limiter les sorties d'**argent frais** (*new money*); sans avoir recours à l'**argent public** (*public funds*); SEE ALSO **loyer**

argentier (*nm*): l'ancien **grand argentier** de la RDA (*Finance Minister*)

arguer (*vi*): il veut faire annuler les élections, **arguant de fraudes** (*on the grounds of electoral fraud*); le parti peut **arguer à sa décharge** l'énorme travail accompli (*argue/point out in its defence*)

argumentaire (*nm*): les juges ont refusé l'**argumentaire** de la défense (*plea, argument*)

argumenter (*vi*): le ministre de l'Intérieur avait **argumenté dans le même sens** (*put forward the same argument*)

armateur (*nm*): les **armateurs** veulent briser la grève des marins; il faut apprendre aux **armateurs** à gérer et à prévoir les crises (*shipowner*)

arme (*nf*): SEE **commerce, livraison, pourvoyeur**

armé, -e (*adj*): SEE **bras**

armée (*nf*): le Président est aussi chef des **armées** (*armed forces*); cette réforme devrait toucher d'abord l'**armée de terre** (*the Army*); d'ici à 2015, l'**armée de l'air** perdra quelque 26 000 hommes (*the Air Force*); les partisans d'une **armée de métier** (*professional army*); les États-Unis et le Royaume-Uni **ont choisi l'armée professionnelle** (*have opted for a professional army*); SEE ALSO **heurter**

armement (*nm*): un important **armement** allemand suspend ses escales au port du Havre (*shipping company*); les armées et les **industries de l'armement** (*arms industry*); **ventes d'armement** en hausse de 13% (*arms sales*); SEE ALSO **course**

armer (*vt*): **armer** des volontaires (*arm*); avec 90 thoniers **armés** par 2 000 marins (*man, crew*)

arnaque (*nf*): une belle histoire d'**arnaque** et de magouilles politiciennes (*swindling; dishonesty*); une tortueuse affaire d'**arnaque immobilière** (*property fraud*)

arnaquer (*vt*): **se faire arnaquer** par un démarcheur peu scrupuleux (*be swindled*)

arraisonnement (*nm*): premier **arraisonnement** d'un pétrolier irakien par la marine américaine (*boarding and inspection*)

arraisonner (*vt*): le juge fit **arraisonner** le bateau (*stop and inspect*)

arranger (*vt*): le report du sommet **arrangerait** tout le monde (*suit, be convenient*); [s'] (*vpr*): les choses vont **s'arranger** d'ici à la date de la réunion (*improve; be settled*)

arrérages (*nmpl*): s'acquitter des **arrérages de loyer** et des factures impayées (*arrears of rent*)

arrestation (*nf*): procéder à l'**arrestation** des accusés (*arrest*)

arrêt (*nm*): une journée d'action, avec **arrêts de travail** et manifestations (*stoppage; stopping work*); son médecin **la met en arrêt de travail** pour longue maladie (*issue a medical certificate*); le tribunal a enfin rendu son **arrêt** (*judgment, decision*); prononcer un **arrêt de mort** (*death sentence*); un appelé du contingent a été **mis aux arrêts** par sa hiérarchie (*put under arrest*); SEE ALSO **maison**

arrêté (*nm*): encore sous le coup d'un **arrêté d'expulsion** (*expulsion order*); le SMIC sera augmenté **par arrêté du ministre** si l'indice des prix augmente de 2% (*by ministerial decree*); des **arrêtés municipaux** interdisant la mendicité publique (*local by-law*); SEE ALSO **préfectoral**

arrêter (*vt*): le gouvernement **arrête** un plan d'aide aux agriculteurs; **arrêter** un calendrier de réformes (*decide on; fix*); le conseil municipal vote et **arrête** le budget (*decide, draw up*)

arrhes (*nfpl*): le paiement des **arrhes** engage l'acheteur et le vendeur (*deposit*); **verser des arrhes** pour l'achat d'un terrain (*pay a deposit [esp. for purchase of property]*)

arriéré (*nm*): aucun nouveau contrat, tant qu'ils n'auront pas réglé les **arriérés** (*arrears of payment*); le fisc lui réclame 10 000F d'**arriérés d'impôts** (*unpaid tax*)

arrière (*adj/nm*): un port maritime doit disposer de liaisons avec un **arrière-pays** le plus large possible; Bayonne, qui tourne le dos à son **arrière-pays** (*hinterland*); cette initiative n'est certes pas sans **arrière-pensées** politiques (*ulterior motive*)

arrondissement (*nm*): huit **arrondissements** de Paris ont élu un nouveau maire (*administrative district [Paris, Marseille, Lyon]*); l'**arrondissement**, circonscription administrative intermédiaire entre le département et le canton (*administrative subdivision of department; district*)

article (*nm*): dans son **article de fond**, l'éditorialiste traite longuement de cette question (*leading article*); SEE ALSO **réprimer**

artisan (*nm*): les petits commerçants et les **artisans** sont les plus nombreux (*craftsman; self-employed person*); partout les **artisans pêcheurs** sont victimes des flottes industrielles (*self-employed fishermen*); [*fig*] il se proclame volontiers l'**artisan de l'Europe** (*the architect of the European idea*)

artisanal, -e, *pl* **-aux** (*adj*): des fromages français fabriqués **de façon artisanale** (*by small-scale production methods*); des **activités artisanales** lucratives (*small-scale craft industry*); SEE ALSO **fabrication**

artisanat (*nm*): un **artisanat** qui est en voie de disparition; le ministre des PME, du commerce et de l'**artisanat** (*artisan class; self-employed craftsmen*); un actif sur dix vit de l'**artisanat** (*craft industries*)

ascendance (*nf*): l'association des Français **d'ascendance polonaise** (*of Polish descent*)

ascension (*nf*): le chômage **poursuit son ascension** (*continues to rise*)

asile (*nm*): déposer une demande d'**asile** (*asylum*); 2 000 demandes d'**asile politique** enregistrées en novembre (*political asylum*); les réfugiés ayant **cherché asile** en France (*seek exile*); SEE ALSO **demandeur, requérant, terre**

asphyxie (*nf*): face à l'**asphyxie des transports** en Ile-de-France (*paralysis of the transport system*); l'**asphyxie politique et économique** du Zaïre (*political and economic paralysis*)

asphyxier (*vt*): la région parisienne reste engorgée, presque **asphyxiée** (*paralyzed*); la ville, **asphyxiée par la récession** (*paralyzed by the recession*)

assainir (*vt*): **assainir** les eaux du lac (*purify, treat*); il faut **assainir** une fois pour toutes le système bancaire argentin (*reform; put on a sounder financial basis*); [s'] (*vpr*): la situation des entreprises **s'est assainie** depuis lors (*improve; become more healthy*)

assainissement (*nm*): l'**assainissement** de la route forestière (*cleaning up*); une directive rendant obligatoire l'**assainissement des eaux usées** (*waste water treatment; sewerage*); dans le cadre de l'**assainissement** de l'appareil et des procédures judiciaires (*reform, reorganization*)

assassin (*nm*): les **assassins** et violeurs de mineurs (*murderer, killer*); SEE ALSO **présumé**

assassinat (*nm*): en cas d'**assassinat** de mineur; après la trêve électorale, violences et **assassinats** ont repris en Algérie (*murder, killing*)

assemblée (*nf*): les salariés de France 2 réunis en **assemblée générale** (*[annual] general meeting*); lors du débat à l'**Assemblée nationale** (*National Assembly*); occuper un fauteuil à la **haute Assemblée** (*Senate; Upper House*); SEE ALSO **rose**

assentiment (*nm*): obtenir par voie de référendum l'**assentiment** de la population (*assent, approval*)

asseoir (*vt*): utiliser sa fortune pour **asseoir** son influence (*consolidate, strengthen*); le Premier ministre eut à cœur de **mieux asseoir** son pouvoir (*consolidate; reinforce*)

assermenté, -e (*adj*): étant donné sa qualité de fonctionnaire **assermenté** (*on oath*); **être assermenté** et tenu au secret (*be on oath/sworn in*)

assesseur (*nm*): le Président de la cour d'assises, flanqué de deux **assesseurs** (*assessor; assistant judge*)

19

assiette (*nf*): l'impôt sur la fortune est calculé sur une **assiette** beaucoup plus large en France; l'**assiette de l'impôt** sur le revenu est devenue trop étroite et injuste (*tax base; tax bands*)

assignation (*nf*): le divorce prend effet dès la date de l'**assignation [à comparaître]** devant le tribunal (*summons, issuing of a writ*); quatre **assignations à résidence** après le coup manqué d'hier (*house arrest*)

assigner (*vt*): la société a été **assignée en justice** pour rupture de contrat (*serve writ on; summons*); **être assigné à résidence** depuis trois ans (*be under house arrest*)

assimilé, -e (*adj/nm,f*): sans compter les modérés et **assimilés** (*ally; person in the same category*)

assis, -e (*adj*): SEE **magistrature**

assise (*nf*): soucieux de ménager son **assise électorale** (*electoral base*); (*pl*) la **juridiction d'assises**, avec son jury populaire (*assize court*); en 1974, lors des **assises nationales** du mouvement (*national conference*); SEE ALSO **juré**

assistanat (*nm*): comment sortir d'une condition d'**assistanat** (*living on state aid/handouts*)

assistance (*nf*): un accroissement de l'**assistance** technique militaire (*aid, help*); les mécanismes de l'**assistance** tels que l'aide sociale ou l'assurance-chômage (*state aid*); du chômage massif et une **économie d'assistance** (*widespread dependence on state aid*); ses quatre enfants **placés à l'Assistance publique** (*[placed] in care*); SEE ALSO **non-assistance**

assistant, -e (*nm,f*): **assistant social** dans un quartier ouvrier de Mulhouse (*welfare/social worker*); faire garder son enfant à domicile par une **assistante maternelle** (*childminder*)

assisté, -e (*adj/nm,f*): une population d'**assistés**, où tous les risques sont pris en charge par l'État (*person living on state benefits/handouts*); encourageant ainsi une **mentalité d'assisté** (*dependency culture; a belief that one can live on state handouts*)

assister (*vt*): nous **assistons à** une recrudescence de la violence (*witness*)

associatif, -ive (*adj*): des mesures en faveur du **mouvement associatif** (*clubs and associations*); mettre tout en œuvre pour favoriser la **vie associative** dans les villes neuves (*community life*); SEE ALSO **local**

association (*nf*): la loi de 1901 régit toutes les **associations** (*association; organization*); la ville ne subventionne plus les **associations caritatives** (*charity agency, charitable body*); accusés de meurtre et d'**association de malfaiteurs** en relation avec une entreprise terroriste (*criminal conspiracy*)

associé, -e (*adj/nm,f*): être admis au rang d'**associé**; il a remercié son ancien **associé** (*partner*)

associer [s'] (*vpr*): les deux groupes **s'associent** pour la reprise de la firme allemande (*join together, link up*); il **s'est associé** avec son fils (*go into partnership*)

assortir (*vt*): rendre un rapport, **assorti de** quelques propositions (*together with*); des peines de 15 mois avec sursis, **assorties d'**amendes de 50 000F (*in addition to, plus*); [s'] (*vpr*): une condamnation **qui s'assortit d'une période de mise à l'épreuve** (*with/plus a period of probation*)

assouplir (*vt*): le chancelier n'envisage-t-il pas d'**assouplir sa position?** (*become less rigid*); [s'] (*vpr*): de nos jours, la procédure **s'est assouplie** et allégée (*become more flexible/easier*)

assouplissement (*nm*): un **assouplissement** des conditions de détention (*relaxing, easing*); Hongkong: l'**assouplissement de la censure** irrite Pékin (*relaxing of censorship*)

assujetti, -e (*adj/nm,f*): les **assujettis au régime ordinaire de la Sécurité sociale** y ont droit (*persons registered with the French health and pensions scheme*); taxe à laquelle **sont assujetties** les entreprises (*be liable*); les **assujettis à l'impôt nouveau** vont sans doute se plaindre (*person liable to the new tax*)

assujettissement (*nm*): l'**assujettissement** des avocats à la TVA (*[tax] liability*)

assurance (*nf*): un préjudice qui n'est pas couvert par les **assurances** (*insurance policy*); le fret et les **assurances** (*insurance*); bénéficier de l'**assurance-maladie** (*sickness insurance scheme*); SEE ALSO **caisse, escroquer, police, souscripteur**

assuré, -e (*adj/nm,f*): le courtier, défenseur de l'**assuré** (*insurance policy holder*)

assurer (*vt*): **assurer** des emplois aux diplômés (*provide; guarantee*); il se disait prêt à **s'assurer la direction du pays** (*take over the government of the country*); [s'] (*vpr*): **s'assurer** contre le vol (*take out insurance*); SEE ALSO **intérim, pérennité**

astreinte (*nf*): un métier qui implique jusqu'à 120 heures d'**astreinte** par semaine (*being on stand-by/on call*); verser une **astreinte** de 300 000 francs par infraction constatée (*financial penalty for failure to honour agreement/obey court order*)

atelier (*nm*): à l'**atelier** comme à l'usine (*in the workshop/workplace*); une partie du colloque sera consacrée à des **ateliers de travail** (*workshop; working-group*)

atermoiement (*nm*): après dix ans d'**atermoiements**, ils ont paraphé les accords; profitant des **atermoiements** de la communauté internationale (*procrastination, delaying tactics*)

atonie (*nf*): Suisse: **atonie** persistante de l'économie helvétique (*sluggishness [of market/economy]*)

atout (*nm*): sa présence est-ce un handicap ou un **atout**? (*asset, advantage*); cette région **a de sérieux atouts** pour l'industriel (*has considerable advantages*)

attaquer (*vt*): il menace de les **attaquer en justice** (*take to court*); le maire a annoncé son intention de **l'attaquer en diffamation** (*bring a libel action against him*); SEE ALSO **front**

atteinte (*nf*): une **atteinte** au principe de l'égalité entre les sexes (*infringement of; attack on*); les **atteintes aux personnes** [coups et blessures, viols] ont continué à progresser (*attacks on the person*); SEE ALSO **crédibilité, environnement**

attendu (*nm*): le juge donne, dans son **attendu [de jugement]**, une justification raisonnée de sa sentence (*explanation, reason adduced [for a verdict]*)

attentat (*nm*): un **attentat** à l'explosif a été commis dans la soirée (*[terrorist] attack*); auteur de plusieurs viols et d'**attentats à la pudeur** (*indecent assault*); SEE ALSO **lier, outrage**

attente (*nf*): l'école est loin de répondre aux **attentes** des entreprises (*expectations, requirements*); **dans l'attente de** l'arrêt de la cour d'appel (*pending*); son dossier **demeure en attente** (*remains pending*); SEE ALSO **prévenu**

attentisme (*nm*): **attentisme** et prudence à Amman (*caution*); du côté de la France, l'**attentisme** semble la règle (*wait-and-see attitude*)

attentiste (*adj/nmf*): observer une attitude **attentiste** (*cautious; wait-and-see*)

atténuant, -e (*adj*): SEE **circonstance**

attestation (*nf*): il faut joindre au dossier l'**attestation de prise en charge Sécurité sociale** (*proof of social security entitlement*)

attester (*vt*): **attester** la vérité d'une affirmation; **attester du** caractère libre et équitable des élections (*certify, attest; vouch for*); une réponse qui **attestait** sa mauvaise foi (*demonstrate, bear witness to*)

attitré, -e (*adj*): le négociateur **attitré** de la CFTC (*officially recognized; accredited*)

attractif, -ive (*adj*): les salaires de la fonction publique ne sont pas très **attractifs** (*attractive*); octroyer des prêts **à des taux très attractifs** (*at attractive rates [of interest]*)

attribuer (*vt*): le meurtre d'un Israélien **attribué** à l'OLP (*impute, attribute*); détenir le pouvoir d'**attribuer des marchés** (*award contracts*); [s'] (*vpr*): l'IRA **s'attribuait** le nouvel attentat (*claim responsibility for*)

attributaire (*nmf*): c'est la préfecture qui établit la liste des **attributaires** des tickets de rationnement (*recipient [of a state benefit]*)

attribution (*nf*): l'**attribution** d'actions gratuites dans le cadre de l'action-nariat des salariés (*allotting, allocation*); l'**attribution** du prix Nobel de la paix (*award*); les conditions d'**attribution des marchés** ne respectent pas la législation (*awarding of contracts*); quatre ministres **conservent leurs attributions** dans le nouveau cabinet (*retain their post*); ils ont jugé que leur collègue **sortait de ses attributions** (*went beyond his remit*)

atypique (*adj*): la même protection sociale pour les **emplois atypiques** (*temporary/seasonal/part-time employment*)

aubaine (*nf*): ce faux pas commis par le ministre fut une **aubaine** pour l'opposition (*godsend; stroke of luck*)

audience (*nf*): lors de la dernière **audience** du procès; l'**audience** fut consacrée à l'audition des témoins (*session; hearing*); la **salle d'audience** était pleine à craquer (*court room*)

audiovisuel, -elle (*adj/nm*): SEE **paysage, redevance**

audit (*nm*): lors de l'**audit** des comptes d'Adidas; un **audit** a mis en lumière de graves irrégularités de gestion (*audit; financial analysis*); SEE ALSO **cabinet**

audition (*nf*): une série de huit **auditions publiques** (*public hearing*); après une ultime **audition de témoins** (*examining of witnesses*); être conduit à la gendarmerie **pour audition** (*for questioning*)

auditionner (*vt*): 97 personnes ont été **auditionnées** par la commission (*hear, interview; question*); la nouvelle procédure permet d'**auditionner un témoin** en présence de ses conseils (*question/examine a witness*)

auditoire (*nm*): exposer les faits devant un **auditoire** très attentif (*audience*)

augmentation (*nf*): le projet anticipe une forte **augmentation** de la population (*increase*); une nette **augmentation des coûts** (*increase in costs*); réclamer de fortes **augmentations salariales** (*wage rise/increase; pay award*); procéder à une **augmentation de capital** (*share issue; issue of share capital*)

augmenter (*vt*): les employés **augmentés** le mois dernier (*given/awarded a pay rise*); Phénix **augmente son capital** (*raise fresh capital*); (*vi*): les droits d'inscription vont **augmenter** de 5% (*rise*)

austérité (*nf*): en 1983, **en pleine austérité** (*in a period of austerity measures*); SEE ALSO **budget, cure, drastique**

austral, -e, *mpl*, **-s** (*adj*): le Mozambique mise sur le développement de l'**Afrique australe** (*Southern Africa*)

autarcie (*nf*): la région a trop longtemps vécu en **autarcie** (*self-sufficiency; autarky*)

auteur (*nm*): l'**auteur** du coup de feu mortel a été arrêté (*person responsible [for offence/crime]*); les **auteurs de crimes** ou de délits graves (*person who has committed a crime*)

23

authentifier (*vt*): la signature permet d'**authentifier** la carte lors de son utilisation (*authenticate, validate; prove the validity of*); **authentifier** un document (*witness; legalize*)

authentique (*adj*): SEE **acte**

autochtone (*adj/nmf*): les **habitants autochtones** de la région (*indigenous population*); les **autochtones** insistent sur leur identité (*native inhabitant*)

autodétermination (*nf*): il était hostile à l'idée du référendum d'**autodétermination** (*self-determination*)

autofinancement (*nm*): une partie des bénéfices est consacrée à l'**autofinancement**; l'**autofinancement** désigne le financement des investissements à partir des ressources propres de l'entreprise (*self-financing; ploughing back of profits*)

autogestion (*nf*): l'**autogestion**, un vieux rêve du socialisme français; dans l'**autogestion** l'entreprise est gérée et contrôlée par les travailleurs (*worker management, worker's control*)

autonome (*adj*): une liste centriste **autonome** aux élections européennes (*separate; independent*); une grève des conducteurs CFDT, CGT et **autonomes** (*independent; unaffiliated*)

autonomie (*nf*): son **autonomie** par rapport aux organismes qui le soutiennent (*freedom of manœuvre*); l'aspiration à l'**autonomie** sinon à l'indépendance (*autonomy; home rule; self-government*)

autonomiste (*adj/nmf*): les **mouvements autonomistes** ne sont pas les seuls à utiliser la violence (*separatist movement*); les **autonomistes** basques revendiquent l'attentat (*separatist*)

autoproclamer [s'] (*vpr*): il s'**est autoproclamé** hier président par intérim (*proclaim oneself*); la république **autoproclamée** du Somaliland (*self-proclaimed*)

autorisation (*nf*): 175 **autorisations** de permis de construire enregistrées cette année (*authorization; permit*); obtenir une **autorisation de séjour** (*residence permit*)

autorisé, -e (*adj*): SEE **milieu**

autoriser (*vt*): les trois situations dans lesquelles le code civil **autorise** l'avortement (*permit, allow*); autant d'éléments qui l'**autorisent à être confiant** dans l'avenir (*entitle one to be confident*)

autorité (*nf*): l'**autorité parentale** est en général conjointe (*parental authority*); (*pl*) les **autorités** empêchent les journalistes de faire correctement leur travail (*the authorities*)

autoroute (*nf*): SEE **information**

autosatisfaction (*nf*): il leur reste deux motifs d'**autosatisfaction** (*satisfaction, self-congratulation*)

autosuffisance (*nf*): ce pays mène une politique d'**autosuffisance** (*self-sufficiency*); compromettant l'**autosuffisance alimentaire** de ces pays (*self-sufficiency in food*)

autosuffisant, -e (*adj*): le continent africain pourrait être **autosuffisant** en matière alimentaire (*self-sufficient*)

autruche (*nf*): SEE **politique**

auxiliaire (*adj/nmf*): des emplois d'**auxiliaire**, de vacataire, ou de contractuel (*temporary worker*)

aval (*nm*): le président a besoin de l'**aval** de ses ministres et du Sénat (*agreement, endorsement; approval*); l'usine est située à 15 kilomètres **en aval** de Rouen (*downstream*); [*fig*] fournisseur, la société de Rennes peut encore récupérer des bénéfices **en aval**; **en aval**, dans la valorisation industrielle du poisson (*later, at a later stage*)

avaliser (*vt*): le Conseil constitutionnel doit **avaliser** le découpage électoral; il reste à faire **avaliser** le budget par les parlementaires (*endorse, ratify*)

avance (*nf*): la droite **prend une sérieuse avance** dans les sondages (*build up a considerable lead*); une **avance** sur la prime d'intéressement sera distribuée aux salariés de Peugeot (*advance on salary/payment*)

avancée (*nf*): **avancée** du 20e congrès au mois d'octobre 1990 (*bringing forward*); une nouvelle **avancée** dans le traitement du sida (*advance; progress*); la principale **avancée sociale** de cette législature (*social victory*)

avancement (*nm*): le conseil municipal sera informé de l'**avancement** des négociations (*progress*); l'**avancement** est à l'ancienneté (*promotion*)

avancer (*vt*): personne ne souhaite **avancer** les élections (*bring forward*); **avancer** des propositions concrètes et crédibles (*put forward*); (*vi*): lutter pour **faire avancer** la justice sociale (*promote*)

avanie (*nf*): une nouvelle **avanie** infligée à la France par ses partenaires (*snub*)

avant (*prep/adv*): il faut **mettre en avant** les avantages de l'ouverture (*point out, emphasize*); il a aussi **mis en avant** sa proposition de réduire le temps de travail (*put forward [plan, proposal]*); la **mise en avant** des produits régionaux (*promotion*); SEE ALSO **fuite**

avantage (*nm*): le cumul des **avantages en nature** représente le quart du salaire d'un cadre (*perk, payment in kind*); SEE ALSO **bénéficier, donner**

avantageux, -euse (*adj*): proposer des marques **à prix avantageux** (*at attractive prices*)

avant-projet (*nm*): l'**avant-projet** de rapport, publié à la mi-juin 1994 (*first draft; pilot study*)

avarie (*nf*): subir des **avaries** (*damage*); **constater une avarie** dès réception des marchandises (*report damage*)

avarié, -e (*adj*): des produits **avariés** (*spoiled, damaged*)

avenant (*nm*): une lettre valant **avenant** au contrat initial; les syndicats ont obtenu un **avenant** à l'accord (*additional clause, endorsement; codicil*)

avènement (*nm*): l'**avènement** d'une société plus juste; l'**avènement** d'une nouvelle ère en Italie (*advent, arrival*)

avéré, -e (*adj*): la seule action **avérée** du terrorisme sur le sol allemand; des bailleurs de fonds **avérés** du Parti républicain (*confirmed, proven*)

avérer (*vt*): même si l'authenticité du document **est avérée** (*be proved/ confirmed*); [s'] (*vpr*): la rentrée sociale **s'avère** "chaude" cette année (*prove/turn out to be*); SEE ALSO **déterminant**

avertissement (*nm*): un **avertissement** au gouvernement à deux ans des élections; être l'objet d'un **avertissement en règle** de ses partenaires européens (*formal warning*); SEE ALSO **multiplier**

aveu, pl -x (*nm*): les *mafiosi* qui sont **passés aux aveux** (*confess, make a confession*); SEE ALSO **extorquer, revenir**

avis (*nm*): un texte voté par les députés contre l'**avis** du gouvernement (*advice*); le Conseil d'État **rendra son avis** avant la fin du mois (*give a ruling*); le gouvernement vient de **donner un avis favorable** (*give the go-ahead; give a positive response*); **émettre un avis défavorable** à un projet de construction d'un supermarché (*turn down, reject*); un **avis de concours** pour la réalisation de quinze logements neufs (*invitation to tender*)

aviser (*vt*): **aviser** le client de la date de livraison (*notify, advise*)

avocat (*nm*): un échange d'arguments entre le ministère public et les **avocats** (*defence lawyer*); on choisit les juges parmi les **avocats en exercice** (*practising barrister*); l'**avocat général** a demandé une peine de dix ans (*public prosecutor [in Assize/Crown court]*); [*fig*] l'Algérie **se fait l'avocat** de Tunis auprès du colonel Kadhafi (*represent, act on behalf of*); SEE ALSO **honoraires, ordre**

avoir (*nm*): l'**avoir** du livret épargne-logement est plafonné à 100 000F (*credit [balance]*); après le gel des **avoirs panaméens** aux États-Unis (*Panamanian assets/holdings*)

avoisiner (*vt*): la population **avoisine** les 300 000; la charge de la Sécurité sociale **avoisine** 30% du budget de l'État (*be in the region of/close to*)

avorté, -e (*adj*): [*fig*] des tentatives de vols **avortés** (*failed*); **coup d'état avorté** en Guinée (*failed coup*)

avorter (*vi*): [*fig*] une tentative de coup d'état qui avait **avorté** (*fail*)

avoué, -e (*adj/nm*): les partisans **avoués** de l'Europe dominent (*avowed, declared*); les fonctions du *solicitor* s'apparentent à celles de l'**avoué** et du notaire; c'est l'**avoué** qui représente les plaideurs (*solicitor [UK]; attorney*)

avouer (*vt*): les trois adolescents ont **avoué les faits** (*confess*); (*vi*): les auteurs des attentats ont **avoué** (*confess, make a confession*)

axe (*nm*): [*fig*] Aérospatiale: l'**axe** germano-nippon (*axis*); préciser **les grands axes** de sa politique (*the main thrust, the main directions*)

axer (*vt*): une campagne électorale **axée sur** l'emploi local (*focused on*)

ayant droit (*nm*): l'abaissement de l'âge de la retraite a pour effet d'augmenter le nombre d'**ayants droit** (*beneficiary; person entitled to receive a benefit*); l'assuré mais aussi ses **ayants droit** (*dependant [relative]*)

azimut (*nm*): la force de frappe **tous azimuts** (*multi-directional*); [*fig*] **mener une offensive tous azimuts** contre la corruption (*launch an all-out attack*)

B

baccalauréat (*nm*): titulaire d'un **bac[calauréat]** option Sciences économiques (*baccalaureate, secondary school examination allowing entry into higher education*); les titulaires d'un diplôme **bac +2** trouvent facilement du travail (*[in France] qualification gained after two years of post-baccalaureate study*)

bachelier, -ière (*nm,f*): 30% des **bacheliers**, tous types de bacs confondus (*holder of [French] baccalauréat*)

bafouer (*vt*): **bafouant** une loi inscrite dans la constitution (*flout, defy*); les Albanais de Macédoine **se sentent bafoués** par la majorité slave (*feel slighted; feel their rights are flouted*)

bagage (*nm*): ce **bagage** minimum que doit posséder un jeune à sa sortie d'école (*[educational] qualifications; skills*)

bail, *pl* **baux** (*nm*): les **baux locatifs** sont en général de 25 ans (*tenant's lease*); **prendre un bail** de dix ans sur une propriété (*take out a lease*); SEE ALSO **renouvellement**

bailleur, -euse (*nm,f*): une réforme des relations entre **bailleurs** et locataires (*lessor; landlord*); ses **bailleurs de fonds** étrangers qui lui ont apporté leur aide (*[financial] backer, sponsor*)

baisse (*nf*): nette **baisse** de la production: mises en chômage en perspective (*downturn, fall*); préférer des **baisses de salaire** à des licenciements (*wage/pay cut*); les vins de Bordeaux **à la baisse**: les prix chutent de 15% (*falling in price*); SEE ALSO **diffusion, pression, réviser**

baisser (*vt*): il ne faudrait pas **baisser** l'impôt sur le revenu (*lower, reduce*); (*vi*): ceci a permis de **faire baisser** le chômage (*bring down, reduce*); **les commandes baissent** pour les usines d'armement (*there is a fall in orders*)

baissier, -ière (*adj*): sur le marché des changes, le dollar était **baissier** hier; la tendance reste donc globalement **baissière** (*tending to fall, falling*)

balance (*nf*): un excédent record de la **balance commerciale** allemande (*trade balance*); la **balance des paiements courants** [commerce extérieur, transferts et services] est déficitaire pour le mois de mai (*balance of payments*)

balbutiant, -e (*adj*): l'instauration **encore balbutiante** de la démocratie (*in its infancy; very recent*)

balbutiement (*nm*): [*fig*] cette activité en France **n'est qu'aux balbutiements** (*is only in its infancy/in the early stages of development*)

ballet (*nm*): le **ballet diplomatique** pour sa succession s'intensifie (*flurry of diplomatic activity*)

ballon (*nm*): [*fig*] un simple **ballon d'essai** pour tester les réactions de l'opinion (*test of public opinion; trial run*)

ballottage (*nm*): le premier tour s'est soldé par un **ballottage** (*second ballot at parliamentary election*); le député sortant se trouve **en ballottage** avec le candidat socialiste (*without overall majority; required to stand in a run-off ballot*)

banalisation (*nf*): la **banalisation** des rapports sexuels avant le mariage (*spread, generalization*); la **banalisation du crime** et des menus larcins est inquiétante (*spread of crime*)

banalisé, -e (*adj*): deux policiers à bord d'un **véhicule banalisé** (*unmarked [police] car*); disposer d'un **local banalisé** en banlieue (*general-purpose premises*)

banaliser [se] (*vpr*): une pratique qui **se banalise** (*spread; become commonplace*)

banc (*nm*): la présence du Premier ministre **au banc du gouvernement** (*on the government front bench*); **sur le banc des accusés** aux assises de Rouen (*in the dock*); [*fig*] le gouvernement de Téhéran, **placé au banc des prévenus** (*put in the dock*)

bancaire (*adj*): SEE **découvert, référence, virement**

banditisme (*nm*): la répression du **grand banditisme** (*organized crime*)

banlieue (*nf*): la gauche est majoritaire dans les **banlieues ouvrières** (*working class/industrial suburbs*); dans les quartiers défavorisés ou dans les **banlieues résidentielles** (*residential suburbs*); SEE ALSO **mal**

banque (*nf*): une des principales **banques de dépôt** (*clearing bank*); une **banque de données**, accessibles en ligne (*data bank*); SEE ALSO **créancier**

banqueroute (*nf*): mener son pays au bord de la **banqueroute** (*bankruptcy*); inculpé d'escroquerie et de **banqueroute** (*[fraudulent] bankruptcy*)

barème (*nm*): un **barème des prix** doit obligatoirement être affiché devant l'établissement (*price list*); les tranches du **barème des impôts** ont été relevées de 3,3% (*tax scale*); un réajustement des **barèmes salariaux** (*salary scales*)

baron (*nm*): un authentique **baron** du gaullisme (*leading personality*); les **grands barons** du régime (*political heavyweight*)

baroud d'honneur (*nm*): la population va opposer bien plus qu'un simple **baroud d'honneur** à la construction de l'autoroute (*last-ditch stand; gesture of defiance*)

barrage (*nm*): désister en faveur du socialiste afin de **faire barrage** au Front national (*block, obstruct*)

barre (*nf*): les témoins se sont succédés à **la barre [des témoins]** (*in the witness box*); dans l'une des **barres** HLM de cette cité difficile (*high-rise apartment block*)

barreau, *pl* **-x** (*nm*): reçu au **barreau** en 1976 (*called to the Bar*); la cour d'assises l'a **renvoyé derrière les barreaux** (*send to prison*)

barrière (*nf*): l'élimination des **barrières aux échanges** (*trade barriers*); une industrie protégée par des **barrières douanières** (*customs/tariff barriers*); SEE ALSO **élever**

bas, basse (*adj*): la concurrence des **pays à bas salaires** (*low-wage country*); (*adv*): le chômage **est au plus bas** depuis cinq ans (*is at its lowest point*); tenter de **mettre à bas** le régime de Khartoum (*overthrow, topple*); SEE ALSO **chambre**

bas (*nm*): [*fig*] inciter les Français à **puiser dans leur bas de laine** (*dip into their savings*)

basculement (*nm*): le **basculement** de l'opinion en faveur des républicains (*swing*); le **basculement à droite** de la région Poitou-Charentes (*swing to the right*)

basculer (*vi*): depuis trois ans, l'opinion publique américaine a **basculé** (*shift; undergo a radical change*); le conseil général va-t-il **basculer à droite** en 1996? (*swing to the right*); les États-Unis pourraient **basculer dans la récession** (*go into recession*)

base (*nf*): un accord devant encore être ratifié par la **base** (*rank-and-file members; shop floor*); les organisations syndicales vont **consulter leur base** (*consult rank-and-file opinion*); on a **jeté les bases** d'un consensus (*lay the foundations*); constituer une **base de données** informatiques (*database*); SEE ALSO **durcissement, surenchère**

bassin (*nm*): des aides à la formation dans les **bassins d'emploi** du Nord (*regional employment area*); dans le **bassin minier** lorrain (*coalfield*)

bastion (*nm*): dans ce **bastion socialiste** qu'est le Nord (*Socialist stronghold*)

bâti (*nm*): la préservation du **bâti ancien** (*old/historic buildings*)

29

bâtiment (*nm*): dix **bâtiments de guerre** circulant dans le détroit de Formose (*warship*); la bonne activité du **bâtiment** et des travaux publics (*building trade*)

bâtir (*vt*): SEE **terrain**

bâtonnier (*nm*): une plainte a été déposée par le **bâtonnier** du barreau de Nancy; le **bâtonnier** de l'ordre des avocats de Paris (*president of the bar/barristers in the French legal system*)

battage (*nm*): le gouvernement **fait un énorme battage** autour de cette affaire (*make a great fuss*); faire l'objet d'un énorme **battage médiatique** (*media hype*)

battre (*vt*): SEE **pavillon, rappel**

bavure (*nf*): des **bavures** et des maladresses ont été commises; la triple **bavure** policière, politique et judiciaire de Marseille (*unfortunate mistake, blunder*)

belligérant, -e (*adj/nm*): des discussions entre les représentants des **belligérants** (*warring party/faction*); SEE ALSO **partie**

bémol (*nm*): [*fig*] le seul **bémol** de ce débat a été donné par les Socialistes (*discordant note*); un autre sondage est venu pourtant **apporter un bémol** (*add a discordant note*)

bénéfice (*nm*): les **bénéfices réalisés** sur les ventes d'armes (*profits [earned]*); hausse de 20% du **bénéfice semestriel** (*half-year profits*); l'impôt sur les **bénéfices des sociétés** (*company profits*); cette nouvelle a donné un prétexte à quelques **prises de bénéfice** (*profit taking*); SEE ALSO **dégager, optimiser**

bénéficiaire (*adj/nmf*): la sidérurgie française serait **bénéficiaire** en 1998 (*profitable, in profit*); ce pays est le deuxième **bénéficiaire de l'aide publique** française (*recipient of state aid*); SEE ALSO **marge**

bénéficier (*vt*): ce type de placements **bénéficient d'une déduction fiscale** (*be deductible for tax purposes*); les Français **bénéficient d'avantages sociaux** largement supérieurs (*enjoy welfare benefits*)

bénévolat (*nm*): le **bénévolat**: service assuré par une personne bénévole, sans obligation et gratuitement (*system of voluntary work*)

bénévole (*adj/nmf*): collaborateur **bénévole** de l'association (*unpaid*); travailler d'abord **à titre bénévole** avant d'être rémunéré (*on a voluntary unpaid basis*); une équipe d'amateurs dirigés par des **bénévoles** (*unpaid voluntary worker*)

benjamin, -e (*adj/nm,f*): **benjamin** d'une famille de six enfants (*youngest [child]*)

bétonner (*vt*): [*fig*] Perrier **bétonne** sa première place mondiale en eaux minérales (*consolidate*); il ne reste plus qu'à **bétonner** la nouvelle formation et à lui donner un programme (*consolidate, give a solid base*)

beur (*adj/nmf*): les **beurs**, ou les Français issus de l'immigration maghrébine; appeler aux jeunes **beurs** à s'inscrire sur les listes électorales (*person born in France of North African parents*)

biais (*nm*): s'implanter en Corée **par le biais de** partenaires locaux (*via, through*); s'insérer dans la société **par le biais du travail** (*via work, by finding employment*)

bien (*nm*): les importations de **biens de consommation courante** (*consumer goods*); ils continuent à exporter, notamment des **biens d'équipement** (*capital goods*); maisons, terrains ou autres **biens immeubles**, ou biens fonciers (*real estate, landed property*); inventorier tous ses **biens meubles**; tous ses **biens mobiliers** ont été saisis par la justice (*personal estate; moveables*); SEE ALSO **mener, séparation**

bienfait (*nm*): profitant des **bienfaits** de la politique agricole commune (*benefit, beneficial effect*)

bien-fondé (*nm*): vérifier le **bien-fondé** d'une plainte (*legitimacy; grounds*); mettre en cause le **bien-fondé** des assurances soviétiques (*reliability*); convaincre les compagnies du **bien-fondé** de sa stratégie (*rightness; validity*)

biens et services (*nmpl*): les importations de **biens et services** ont progressé de près de 5% (*goods and services*)

bilan (*nm*): le **bilan** d'une entreprise (*balance sheet, statement of accounts*); le **bilan** de quatre jours d'affrontements s'élève à 44 morts (*final toll/tally*); [*fig*] **faire le bilan** de l'aide française aux territoires occupés (*assess, make an assessment of*); SEE ALSO **déposer, dépôt**

billet (*nm*): un vendredi noir pour le **billet vert** (*US dollar, greenback*); SEE ALSO **planche**

bisbille (*nf*): [*fam*] nouvelle **bisbille** entre l'Élysée et Matignon; les **bisbilles** entre les formations de droite (*squabble, tiff*)

blanc, blanche (*adj/nm,f*): Thomson licencie dans les **produits blancs** (*white goods*); un certain nombre d'électeurs ont préféré **voter blanc** (*return a blank vote*); SEE ALSO **bulletin, livre, mariage, seing**

blanchiment (*nm*): le **blanchiment** de fonds d'origine criminelle (*'laundering' [money]*)

blanchir (*vt*): une loi d'amnistie est venue **blanchir** les coupables (*clear, exonerate*); [*fig*] soupçonné de **blanchir** de l'argent en provenance des pays de l'Est (*'launder' [money]*)

bleu, -e (*adj*): la réforme de l'**Europe bleue** (*EC fisheries policy*); trois hommes, en **bleu de travail** (*[worker's] overalls*); SEE ALSO **casque**

bloc (*nm*): les pays du **bloc soviétique** (*Soviet bloc*); la majorité municipale **fait bloc** autour du maire (*stand together, unite*)

blocage (*nm*): un **blocage total** des négociations (*impasse; stalemate*); sur les deux **points de blocage** subsistants (*sticking point*); le gouvernement opte pour un **blocage des prix** pour résoudre le problème (*price freeze/controls*); la direction décide le **blocage des salaires** (*wage restraint/freeze*); SEE ALSO **minorité**

blocus (*nm*): le **blocus** imposé par l'Iran aux exportations irakiennes (*blockade*); les États-Unis **décrètent un blocus** naval d'Haïti (*decide a blockade*)

bloqué, -e (*adj*): la situation reste **bloquée** (*in stalemate; insoluble*)

bloquer (*vt*): il faudrait **bloquer les pensions** pendant trois années consécutives (*freeze pensions*)

bombardement (*nm*): la reprise des **bombardements** (*bombing raid*)

bombarder (*vt*): [*fam*] **être bombardé** ministre de l'enseignement supérieur (*be catapulted [into a job]; be nominated unexpectedly*)

bonification (*nf*): départ à 55 ans avec **bonifications d'ancienneté** (*long-service bonus*)

bonus (*nm*): deux accidents entraînent la suppression du **bonus** (*no-claims bonus*)

boom (*nm*): l'économie britannique est **en plein boom** (*expanding, in a period of expansion*); pendant le **boom immobilier** des années 70 (*real estate/property boom*)

bordereau (*nm*): le **bordereau** annuel de renouvellement d'adhésion au club (*slip, counterfoil*); les retenues marquées sur le **bordereau de salaire** (*salary advice, wages slip*)

bouc (*nm*): transformant la minorité grecque en **bouc émissaire** (*scapegoat*)

bouclage (*nm*): l'allégement du **bouclage** de Gaza et de la Cisjordanie (*sealing off; cordoning off*)

boucler (*vt*): le dossier doit être **bouclé** avant la fin de l'année (*complete, close*); la difficulté de **boucler un budget** (*balance a budget*); tout le quartier **fut bouclé par les forces de l'ordre** (*was sealed off by the police*)

bouclier (*nm*): SEE **levée**

bouder (*vt*): beaucoup de jeunes immigrés **boudent** ces activités communautaires (*want nothing to do with; stay away from*); le Canada menace de **bouder** le sommet de la francophonie (*refuse to attend*)

bourg (*nm*): Parthenay, gros **bourg** rural de 11 000 habitants (*[market] town*)

bourgade (*nf*): une petite **bourgade** de 815 habitants dans le Puy-de-Dôme (*village, [small] town*)

bourgeois, -e (*adj/nm,f*): un **grand bourgeois**, né dans le Pas-de-Calais (*member of the upper middle class*)

bourgeoisie (*nf*): originaire de la **bourgeoisie** bordelaise de la fin du siècle dernier (*middle class; bourgeoisie*)

bourse (*nf*): pouvoir s'acheter des médicaments **sans bourse délier** (*without any outlay of funds*); la reprise a été confirmée à la **Bourse de Londres** (*London Stock Exchange*); les retraités CGT d'Orléans, réunis à la **Bourse du travail** (*trades' council*); SEE ALSO **coter, introduction**

boursier, -ière (*adj/nm,f*): les **gains boursiers** sont imposables (*Stock market gains/profits*); des **boursiers** dont les études sont financées par l'État (*student in receipt of grant*); SEE ALSO **krach, raid**

bout (*nm*): SEE **venir**

box (*nm*): dans le **box [des accusés]**, la jeune femme s'est défendue vaillamment (*dock*)

boycottage (*nm*): les appels au **boycottage** de produits français (*boycotting*); son parti appelle au **boycottage des élections** (*electoral boycott*)

boycotter (*vt*): un scrutin **boycotté** par le Syndicat de la magistrature (*boycott*)

bradage (*nm*): l'opposition crie au **bradage** du patrimoine national (*selling off*); le **bradage** de ces territoires (*abandoning*)

brader (*vt*): [*fig*] accusé de **brader** l'héritage du général de Gaulle (*abandon; squander*); des exportations **à des prix bradés** sur le marché mondial (*at rock-bottom prices*); en pleine crise de surproduction, l'aluminium **se bradait** à 1 000 dollars la tonne (*be sold off cheaply*)

braderie (*nf*): [*fig*] l'Opposition dénonce la grande **braderie** de l'industrie de la défense (*clearance sale; selling off*)

branche (*nf*): les **branches** les plus touchées par la crise (*industrial sector*); la **branche politique** de l'IRA (*political wing/arm*)

bras (*nm*): l'agriculture manque de **bras** et d'engrais (*manpower*); **bras droit** du Premier ministre japonais (*right-hand man*); la menace que représente le FIS et son **bras armé** (*armed wing [of political movement]*); [*fig*] le **bras de fer** continue entre la direction et les grévistes (*deadlock; trial of strength*)

bretelle (*nf*): prendre la **bretelle de raccordement** avec l'autoroute (*connecting/linking section of road*); l'aéroport est relié par une **bretelle d'accès** à l'autoroute A42 (*access road*)

brevet (*nm*): décrocher son **brevet** (*French school-leaving certificate*); après deux ans d'études il a décroché son **brevet de technicien** (*technical training diploma*); payer une redevance pour l'utilisation de **brevets [d'invention]**; la protection des **brevets** (*patent*)

breveter (*vt*): faire **breveter** un nouveau procédé (*patent, take out a patent for*)

briguer (*vt*): Hachette **brigue** le troisième rang mondial de l'édition (*make a bid for*); avoir la ferme intention de **briguer l'Élysée** aux prochaines élections (*stand for the presidency of France*)

brochure (*nf*): diffuser une **brochure** à l'intention des électeurs immigrés (*booklet, pamphlet, brochure*)

brouille (*nf*): dans la **brouille** qui oppose la Russie et l'Ukraine (*quarrel, disagreement*)

brûlant, -e (*adj*): l'un des sujets **brûlants** évoqués; autre dossier **brûlant**: le projet d'autoroute (*controversial, ticklish [issue]*)

brut, -e (*adj/nm*): le **salaire brut** recouvre les versements aux salariés et les cotisations et autres retenues (*gross salary/pay*); le prix du **[pétrole] brut** est en chute libre (*crude oil; crude*); SEE ALSO **produit**

budget (*nm*): le **budget d'austérité** norvégien est vivement contesté (*austerity budget*); le **budget de la défense** en augmentation pour la troisième année consécutive (*defence budget/spending*); SEE ALSO **boucler, insuffisance, misère**

budgétaire (*adj*): SEE **collectif, dépassement**

bulletin (*nm*): déposer dans l'urne son **bulletin de vote** (*vote; voting paper*); l'accroissement des **bulletins blancs** ou **nuls** (*blank/spoiled ballot paper*); pour avoir un **bulletin de naissance**, il faut s'adresser à la mairie (*birth certificate*); SEE ALSO **élire**

buraliste (*nm*): un préposé, ou **buraliste**, de la Poste (*clerk, [counter] clerk*); la vignette auto est en vente chez les **buralistes** (*tobacconist [licensed to sell stamps, etc.]*)

bureau, *pl* **-x** (*nm*): la décision a été annoncée au cours du **bureau national** de la centrale syndicale (*national congress*); le **bureau exécutif** du PS, réuni mercredi soir (*executive board*); les timbres fiscaux s'achètent au **bureau de tabac** (*tobacconist*); SEE ALSO **immeuble, placement**

bureaucratie (*nf*): l'énorme **bureaucratie** des organismes sociaux (*bureaucracy, bureaucratic machine; officialdom*)

but (*nm*): SEE **lucratif**

buter (*vi*): [*fig*] les négociations **butent sur** des problèmes de souveraineté nationale (*founder, come to grief*); les obstacles sur lesquels **butent** les négociations syro-israéliennes (*the obstacles to/in the way of*)

butin (*nm*): en vue de l'importance du **butin dérobé** (*goods stolen; haul*)

butoir (*nm*): SEE **date**

butte (*nf*): [*fig*] se trouver en **butte à** l'incompréhension de l'opinion (*be the object/victim of*); il **est en butte à** une grave crise au sein de sa majorité (*be faced with*)

C

cabale (*nf*): la **cabale** montée contre lui par l'aile gauche du parti (*plot; intrigue*)

cabinet (*nm*): former un nouveau **cabinet** (*ministry, government*); le ministre de l'énergie du **cabinet fantôme** (*shadow cabinet*); un **cabinet** composé des collaborateurs directs du ministre (*advisers; private secretariat*); des **cabinets immobiliers** anglais installés dans le Pas-de-Calais (*estate agent's office*); un important **cabinet d'audit** de Londres (*accountancy firm*); l'étude de délocalisation a été menée par un **cabinet conseil** (*consulting firm, consultancy*)

cachet (*nm*): à partir de la date du **cachet de la poste** (*postmark*)

cacique (*nm*): son projet de réforme a heurté les **caciques du parti** (*party bosses*)

cadastral, -e, *pl* **-aux** (*adj*): le **plan cadastral** de la commune (*land register*)

cadastre (*nm*): consulter le **cadastre** pour établir les limites exactes de la commune; le **cadastre** est "l'état-civil" de la propriété foncière (*land register*)

cadence (*nf*): les syndicats dénoncent les **cadences trop élevées** à l'usine de Selongey (*excessive production rates; high-speed assembly lines*); diminuer ses effectifs **à la cadence de** 8 000 emplois par an (*at the rate of*)

cadre (*nm*): 400 **cadres** seront embauchés l'an prochain (*managerial/ executive staff*); tous les employés, et pas seulement les **cadres supérieurs** (*top manager/management*); l'amélioration du **cadre de vie** rural ou urbain (*environment*); **dans le cadre de** la lutte contre le terrorisme (*in the context/within the framework of*); SEE ALSO **accord, hors**

caduc, caduque (*adj*): un traité jugé **caduc** à Jérusalem (*null and void*); l'OPA **devient caduque** ce vendredi (*expire; lapse*)

cahier (*nm*): la stricte contrainte des **cahiers des charges** (*schedule of conditions; specifications*); présenter son **cahier des doléances** au nouveau ministre (*[list of] complaints; demands*)

caisse (*nf*): l'expansion actuelle apporte d'abondantes recettes fiscales dans les **caisses de l'État** (*the coffers of the state*); un médecin contrôleur de la **caisse d'assurances sociales** (*social security fund/office*); des organismes comme les **caisses d'allocations familiales** (*child benefit office*); des achats financés par la **caisse noire** (*slush fund*); SEE ALSO **alimenter, facilité, renflouer**

calendrier (*nm*): aucun accord sur un **calendrier** du retrait des forces d'intervention (*timetable*); **fixer le calendrier** des travaux de la session (*set a timetable*); **tenir le calendrier** qu'on s'est fixé (*keep to a timetable*); SEE ALSO **accorder**

calomnie (*nf*): se poser en victime de la **calomnie**; la diffamation orale ou **calomnie** est un délit (*slander, calumny*)

calomnier (*vt*): un avocat condamné pour avoir **calomnié** un magistrat (*slander; libel*)

cambiste (*nm*): d'après les **cambistes**, la baisse de la devise américaine continuera (*foreign exchange dealer*)

camouflet (*nm*): la Chine essuie un **camouflet** à Hongkong (*snub, insult*); le Bundestag a **infligé un camouflet** au gouvernement (*deliver a snub; insult*)

camp (*nm*): les fauteurs de guerre **des deux camps** (*on both sides*)

campagne (*nf*): la sur-représentation des **campagnes** dans l'assemblée départementale (*rural areas*); la **campagne électorale** bat son plein (*election campaign*); **mener une campagne personnelle** contre l'implantation de nouvelles grandes surfaces (*fight a one-man campaign*); SEE ALSO **référendaire**

canaliser (*vt*): tenter de **canaliser** le mécontentement populaire (*channel, give expression to; contain*)

candidat, -e (*nm,f*): deux fois il **fut candidat à la présidence** (*run for president*); **candidat à sa propre succession** pour la présidentielle de 1996 (*seeking re-election*); SEE ALSO **pressenti**

candidature (*nf*): le premier à **faire acte de candidature** (*stand/apply for election*); il va **poser sa candidature** pour le poste devenu vacant (*apply, make application*); SEE ALSO **pluralisme**

canton (*nm*): le **canton** a perdu beaucoup de son importance (*[in France] administrative subdivision of* arrondissement); le **canton**, circonscription pour les élections au conseil général (*[in France] constituency/district [for local elections]*); dans les **cantons** francophones de la Suisse (*canton*)

cantonal, -e, *pl* **-aux** (*adj*): leurs chances d'emporter les **[élections] cantonales** (*[in France] elections to the council of the* département); la contribution **cantonale** pour les étudiants dans les universités suisses (*pertaining to a [Swiss] canton*); SEE ALSO **consultation**

cantonner [se] (*vpr*): la France **se cantonne** dans un rôle de gendarme (*confine oneself*)

capacité (*nf*): la **capacité** de l'Europe à résister à la compétition américaine (*ability*); réduire les **capacités de production** dans la CE (*manufacturing capacity*); sans réduire les **capacités de défense** de la France (*defence capability*)

capital, *pl* **-aux** (*nm*): prendre 51% du **capital social** d'une entreprise (*share capital*); rassembler un **capital de départ** de 2 millions de francs (*start-up capital*); Honda **entre dans le capital** de Rover à hauteur de 20% (*buy into; take a stake in*); des **sociétés à capitaux mixtes**, montées avec les Soviétiques (*joint venture*); SEE ALSO **hémorragie, recomposition**

capitalisation (*nf*): les entreprises françaises souffrent d'une trop faible **capitalisation** (*capital base*)

capoter (*vi*): dispute qui risque de faire **capoter** les négociations (*collapse, fall through, fail*)

caractérisé, -e (*adj*): il estime qu'il s'agissait là de **dumping caractérisé** (*a clear case of dumping*)

carcéral, -e *pl* **-aux** (*adj*): pour mieux faire connaître l'**univers carcéral** (*prison life*); les **conditions carcérales** déplorables des détenus (*prison conditions*); SEE ALSO **surpeuplement**

carence (*nf*): la **carence** des pays socialistes dans ce domaine (*deficiency*); à cause des **carences** de notre législation (*shortcomings*); ces pays n'ignorent pas la **carence alimentaire** (*food shortages*)

caritatif, -ive (*adj*): des opérations **caritatives** ou humanitaires (*charitable*); SEE ALSO **association**

carnet (*nm*): tant que les **carnets de commandes** restent à moitié vides; l'amélioration des **carnets** ne saurait tarder (*order book*)

carrière (*nf*): les grévistes réclament une augmentation de 1 500F et des **améliorations de carrière** (*better career prospects*); SEE ALSO **déroulement, évolution**

carte (*nf*): avoir sa **carte d'adhérent** (*membership card*); l'obtention d'une **carte de séjour** (*residence permit*); pour réduire le trafic de **cartes grises** d'épaves (*car registration papers; log book*); SEE ALSO **horaire**

cartel (*nm*): l'**office des cartels**, chargé de faire respecter la libre concurrence (*monopolies board*)

cas (*nm*): les questions se règlent **au cas par cas** (*one by one; as they arise*); son **cas** a été réexaminé par la cour d'appel de Colmar (*case*); depuis 1860, ce **cas de figure** s'est présenté huit fois (*case, instance*); un centre de réinsertion pour **jeunes cas sociaux** (*underprivileged children*); SEE ALSO **statuer**

caser (*vt*): il n'est pas facile de **caser** un jeune Maghrébin (*place in a job*); [se] (*vpr*): les diplômés ont moins de problèmes pour **se caser** (*obtain employment*)

caserne (*nf*): les gendarmes sont rentrés à leur **caserne** (*barracks*)

casier (*nm*): son **casier judiciaire** est déjà fourni (*criminal record*); il a un **casier judiciaire vierge** (*clean record*)

casque (*nm*): incidents entre **Casques bleus** et Chypriotes turcs (*United Nations peace-keeping force*)

cassation (*nf*): dans la perspective d'une éventuelle **cassation**, et donc d'un nouveau procès (*quashing [of a verdict]*); la **Cour de cassation**, la juridiction suprême de l'institution judiciaire (*Supreme Court of Appeal*); SEE ALSO **pourvoi, pourvoir**

casse (*nf*): deux jeunes Algériens arrêtés pour **casse** et expulsés (*vandalism*)

casser (*vt*): la Cour de cassation **cassa** le verdict (*overturn, quash*); **casser les prix** pour rester compétitif (*slash prices*)

casse-tête (*nm*): ce dossier est un vrai **casse-tête** pour le ministre (*brain-teaser; delicate problem*)

casseur (*nm*): la présence de **casseurs** dans un défilé pacifique (*rioting demonstrator*); voter la **loi anti-casseur** (*legislation against rioting demonstrators*); les **casseurs de prix** venus d'Allemagne (*hard-discounter*)

cassure (*nf*): la **cassure** entre les syndicats et la base (*split*)

catégoriel, -ielle (*adj*): SEE **revendication**

cause (*nf*): l'avenir de la démocratie **est en cause** (*is at stake; is under attack*); l'enquête risque de **mettre en cause** des personnalités importantes (*implicate; incriminate*); l'éventuelle **mise en cause** du banquier suisse (*implicating*); cette agitation va **remettre en cause** la croissance de l'économie (*jeopardize, put at risk*); Paris semble incapable de **remettre en cause** son soutien à Alger (*call into question, reconsider*); la CGT refuse toute **remise en cause** du SMIC (*reconsideration; attack [on]*); SEE ALSO **commun, fait, gain**

caution (*nf*): verser une **caution** de 250F (*deposit, down payment*); votre débiteur, ou la personne qui **porte caution** pour lui (*stand surety*); [fig] la France voudrait **apporter sa caution** à un éventuel compromis (*give support/backing*); **être laissé en liberté sous caution** pendant toute la durée du procès (*be freed on bail*); SEE ALSO **libérer, sujet**

cautionnement (*nm*): chaque candidat paye un **cautionnement** de 10 000F; le **cautionnement** dans le cadre d'une opération de crédit mobilier (*surety; guarantee*)

cautionner (*vt*): se refuser à **cautionner** la politique du maire (*back, support*); ne pas vouloir **cautionner** une manifestation anti-républicaine (*give approval to; support*)

céder (*vt*): le groupe Perrier vient de **céder** sa filiale suisse (*dispose of, sell*); **ne rien céder** sur la sécurité extérieure (*concede nothing, make no concession*); le titre a **cédé** 0,75 à 1 067F (*fall back, lose*)

ceinture (*nf*): la progression du Front national dans la **ceinture** parisienne (*peripheral area; belt*); la **ceinture verte** du Val-de-Marne (*green belt*); il a grandi dans la **ceinture rouge** des Hauts-de-Seine (*Communist belt*)

célibataire (*adj/nmf*): les enfants majeurs **célibataires** (*single, unmarried*); **célibataire**, divorcé ou séparé (*single person*); SEE ALSO **mère**

cellule (*nf*): une **cellule d'urgence** a été mise en place (*crisis team*); les cinq **cellules de réflexion** ont mis en place un plan d'action (*think-tank*); la situation matérielle de la **cellule familiale** (*family unit*)

censure (*nf*): le gouvernement italien menacé de **censure** (*vote of no-confidence*); SEE ALSO **assouplissement, motion**

central, -e, *pl* **-aux** (*adj/nm,f*): lors du plasticage du **central [téléphonique]** de Bastia (*telephone exchange*); quatre prisonniers évadés de la **centrale** de Colmar (*county prison; [in France] prison for offenders serving a sentence of more than 12 months*); les **centrales [syndicales]** réclament une hausse du pouvoir d'achat (*confederation of trade unions*)

centralisme (*nm*): le trop grand **centralisme** de l'Éducation nationale (*centralism, control from the centre*)

centre (*nm*): SEE **hébergement, ouverture, redressement, réinsertion, urbain, urgence**

cessation (*nf*): la **cessation** des combats et Tchétchénie (*suspension; cessation*); recourir à la **cessation de travail** pour appuyer une revendication (*stoppage*); joindre à la demande une attestation de **cessation d'activité** (*ceasing work/employment; termination of business*); **en cessation de paiements** depuis un mois, la société dépose son bilan (*having suspended all payments; unable to meet its financial obligations*)

cesser (*vt*): les salariés ont **cessé le travail** (*stop work, down tools*)

cession (*nf*): la **cession** à la Russie de la flotte ukrainienne (*transfer, handing-over, handover*); la **cession** de leurs activités minières (*sale, selling-off; disposal*); la **cession au privé** de neuf entreprises publiques (*privatization*); l'ensemble des **cessions d'actifs** (*disposal of assets*)

chaîne (*nf*): la suppression du **travail à la chaîne** est l'objectif prioritaire (*assembly-line production*)

chambre (*nf*): la **Chambre haute** du parlement anglais (*Upper Chamber/House*); les 172 sièges à pourvoir à la **Chambre basse** du parlement (*Lower House*); l'instruction terminée, le dossier est transmis à la **chambre d'accusation** (*[in France] court of criminal appeal*); devant la première **chambre pénale** du tribunal de Paris (*criminal division*)

chance (*nf*): des **chances égales** en matière d'emploi (*equal opportunity*); SEE ALSO **égalité**

chancelier (*nm*): le **chancelier de l'Échiquier**, le ministre anglais des Finances (*[UK] Chancellor of the Exchequer*)

chancellerie (*nf*): discorde entre la **Chancellerie** et Matignon (*[in France] Ministry of Justice*); le candidat à la **Chancellerie** du Parti social-démocrate (*post of Chancellor*); dans les **chancelleries** occidentales, on s'inquiète (*foreign ministry; chancellery*)

change (*nm*): SEE **agent, contrôle, réserve, taux**

changement (*nm*): mettre en place une politique de **changement** (*change*); SEE ALSO **mobiliser, réticent**

chantier (*nm*): le nombre de logements **mis en chantier** (*start, commence*); les **mises en chantier** s'élèvent à 310 000 logements cette année (*building start*); [*fig*] la **mise en chantier** des réformes annoncées l'an dernier (*carrying out; implementation*); de nombreux **grands chantiers** comme celui de la Bibliothèque de France (*major building project*); les **chantiers navals** de Hambourg et de Brême (*shipyard*)

chapeauter (*vt*): il **chapeautait** l'éducation spéciale dans le Vaucluse (*oversee; be at the head of*)

chapelle (*nf*): SEE **querelle**

chapitre (*nm*): le rapport comporte neuf **chapitres** (*chapter; item*)

charbonnages (*nmpl*): l'opération entraînerait la fermeture de 41 **charbonnages** sur 74 (*coal mine, colliery*)

charcutage (*nm*): procéder à un véritable **charcutage de la carte électorale** (*radical redrawing of electoral boundaries*)

charge (*nf*): un transfert de responsabilités et de **charges** (*responsibility*); faire la même **charge de travail** (*work, work load*); s'acheter une **charge de notaire** (*lawyer's practice*); aucune **charge** n'a été retenue contre lui (*charge, accusation*); l'ensemble des **charges sociales** qui pèsent sur les entreprises (*overheads [esp. social security contributions]*); en bénéficiant de **charges salariales** deux fois moins élevées (*wage costs*); qui va **prendre en charge** les frais de déménagement? (*pay; take on*); la **prise en charge** par l'État des frais de justice et des honoraires d'avocat (*paying the cost*); le coût du repas est **à la charge des parents** (*payable by/the responsibility of the parents*); SEE ALSO **cahier, enfant, locatif, plan, témoin**

chargé, -e (*adj/nm,f*): quand celui-ci était ministre, **chargé de l'environnement** (*in charge of environmental affairs*); **chargé de mission** au cabinet du ministre de la Ville (*person holding special responsibility/with special duties*)

charger (*vt*): les autorités ont **chargé** un comité d'experts d'enquêter sur cette affaire (*ask, instruct*)

chassé-croisé (*nm*): un véritable **chassé-croisé** entre Tokyo et Washington (*toing and froing, coming and going*)

chaud, -e (*adj*): dans un quartier réputé **chaud** de la banlieue d'Alger (*dangerous*); la rentrée risque d'être **chaude** (*difficult, turbulent*); SEE ALSO **annoncer**

chef (*nm*): le **chef de la diplomatie italienne** en visite à Kiev (*Italian foreign minister*); les prérogatives d'un **chef d'État** (*head of state*); **chef de file** du principal parti de l'opposition (*[political] leader*); malgré les réticences des **chefs d'entreprise** (*company head/manager*); 40% des **chefs d'exploitation** ont plus de 55 ans (*farm owner*); les **chefs d'établissement** dans les collèges et lycées (*head, principal*); deux **chefs de mise en examen** sont retenus contre lui (*charge, count*); SEE ALSO **opposition**

chef-lieu, *pl* **-x** (*nm*): les décisions sont prises au **chef-lieu du département** (*administrative centre of French* département)

cheminot (*nm*): semaine agitée dans le secteur public: les **cheminots** en grève (*railway worker*)

chèque (*nm*): payer des achats au moyen de **chèques sans provision** (*bad/bounced cheque*); SEE ALSO **endosser, opposition**

cher, chère (*adj*): SEE **vie**

cherté (*nf*): se plaindre de la **cherté de la vie** (*high cost of living*); une prime que la **cherté des prix** dévorera en quelques mois (*high prices*)

chevronné, -e (*adj*): tous militants politiques **chevronnés**; parlementaire **chevronné** et plusieurs fois ministre (*experienced, seasoned*)

chicane (*nf*): une source de **chicane** dans les copropriétés (*dispute; quibbling, wrangling*)

chiffrage (*nm*): un **chiffrage** exact reste difficile à établir (*costing; figure*)

chiffre (*nm*): enregistrer une croissance à **deux chiffres** (*two-figure, in two figures*); un bénéfice de 3 MF pour un **chiffre d'affaires** de 22 millions (*turnover*)

chiffrer (*vt*): le coût global n'a pas été **chiffré** (*assess; estimate*); [se] (*vpr*): les morts **se chiffrent en milliers** (*are estimated at several thousand*)

choc (*nm*): le **choc** de deux nationalismes (*conflict; collision*); depuis le premier **choc pétrolier** en 1973 (*oil crisis*)

chômage (*nm*): Renault décide des mesures de **chômage partiel** à Douai (*short-time working*); la grève risque de **mettre au chômage technique** de nombreux salariés (*lay off*); SEE ALSO **inscrit, montée, pointer, résorption, traitement**

chômé, -e (*adj*): une **journée chômée** par semaine dans l'usine d'Angers (*compulsory rest day; day off*); le gouvernement a **décrété jour chômé** le jeudi 14 mars (*designate as a public holiday*)

chômer (*vi*): la Bourse **chôme** en raison de la fête de la Toussaint (*close, shut; be at a standstill*); **chômer** à raison de trois heures par semaine (*be idle; be on reduced working hours*)

chômeur, -euse (*nm,f*): les **chômeurs de longue durée**, une catégorie exclue des allocations (*long-term unemployed*); les plus déshérités: **chômeurs en fin de droits** ou familles en difficulté (*person no longer qualifying for basic unemployment benefit*); SEE ALSO **embaucher, réinsertion**

chronique (*nf*): la **chronique** boursière (*rubric, column, page*); SEE ALSO **défrayer**

chute (*nf*): la **chute** brutale du prix du pétrole (*fall, collapse*); les recettes pétrolières **sont en chute libre** (*are plummeting*)

chuter (*vi*): les résultats semestriels ont **chuté** de 35% (*fall*); faisant **chuter** le tourisme au Maroc de plus de 20% (*bring down, reduce*)

ciblage (*nm*): le message doit être clair et son **ciblage** précis (*target audience; targeting*)

cibler (*vt*): l'annonce **est ciblée sur** les lecteurs du *Point* (*targets; is aimed at*); des secteurs **bien ciblés** de l'économie (*[precisely] targeted*)

circonscription (*nf*): le député de la quatrième **circonscription** du Vaucluse (*electoral constituency*)

circonstance (*nf*): en l'absence de **circonstances atténuantes** (*mitigating/ extenuating circumstances; a plea in mitigation*); des **circonstances aggravantes** sont prévues par le nouveau Code pénal (*aggravating circumstances/factors*)

circulaire (*nf*): une **circulaire** qui porte sur les conditions de l'emploi obligatoire de la langue française (*circular; official instruction*)

circulation (*nf*): le droit à la **libre circulation** est un droit universel; la **libre circulation des personnes** en Europe (*[person's] freedom of movement*)

citadin, -e (*adj/nm,f*): la France est de plus en plus **citadine** (*town-dwelling; urban*); créer de nouvelles relations entre les **citadins** et les ruraux (*city/town dweller*)

citation (*nf*): une sommation, ou **citation [à comparaître]** en justice (*court summons*); recevoir une **citation d'huissier** (*bailiff's summons*)

cité (*nf*): adjoint au maire de la **cité** de Bayonne (*municipality; city; town*); une **cité** de 200 logements répartis en huit bâtiments; le désespoir de ces **cités [ouvrières]** peuplées d'exclus (*housing estate*); Sarcelles, **cité-dortoir** de la banlieue parisienne (*dormitory town*)

citer (*vt*): il fut **cité comme témoin** (*call as witness*); toute personne trouvée en possession de drogue sera **citée devant les tribunaux** (*prosecute, take before the courts*)

citoyen, -enne (*nm,f*): un jury d'assises est formé de trois magistrats et de neuf **citoyens** tirés au sort (*citizen; member of the public*)

citoyenneté (*nf*): faciliter l'accession à la **citoyenneté** de certains jeunes étrangers (*citizenship*); celui qui aspire à **prendre la citoyenneté française** (*acquire French citizenship*)

civil, -e (*adj/nm*): la mort de deux **civils** après l'attentat à la bombe hier (*civilian*); SEE ALSO **code, partie, procédure**

civique (*adj*): SEE **droit**

civisme (*nm*): la conscription, considérée comme un outil d'intégration et de **civisme** (*sense of civic duty; public-spiritedness*)

clair, -e (*adj*): ceci veut dire **en clair** la fermeture de l'usine (*in simple language, put clearly*); une prépondérance de programmes **en clair** (*not scrambled [TV broadcast]*)

clandestin, -e (*adj/nm,f*): la répression du travail **clandestin** (*illegal; undeclared*); un **[travailleur] clandestin** en situation irrégulière (*illegal [immigrant] worker*); SEE ALSO **expulsion, immigration, rétention**

clandestinité (*nf*): le chef des rebelles, aujourd'hui **en clandestinité** (*underground; in hiding*)

classe (*nf*): l'accès de 80% d'une **classe d'âge** au baccalauréat (*age group*); une élite fortement intégrée à la **classe dirigeante** (*ruling class*); seules les **classes possédantes** en profiteront (*owning class*); la **classe politique**, des conservateurs aux travaillistes, s'interroge (*political community*)

classer (*vt*): l'affaire a été **classée** pour manque de preuves (*dismiss*); le dossier sera-t-il **classé sans suite**, faute d'éléments? (*close a file on a legal case; decide there is no case to answer*)

clause (*nf*): des contrats comportant des **clauses abusives** (*unfair clause*)

clé, clef (*nf*): la consommation, la **clé** de la reprise tant attendue (*key*); trois **personnages-cléfs** de l'affaire Péchiney (*key figure/personality*); la présence de femmes à des **postes-clés** (*key post*); l'usine sera livrée, **clés en main**, fin mai (*ready for occupation; with vacant possession*); la firme de Rennes **met la clé sous la porte** (*cease trading*); [*fig*] avec **à la clé** une pression fiscale en hausse de 8% (*as a consequence*); ce pacte, **clé de voûte** de l'équilibre stratégique en Asie-Pacifique (*linchpin, cornerstone*)

client, -e (*nm,f*): le premier **client** de l'Espagne (*customer; client*); SEE ALSO **exportation**

clientèle (*nf*): sa **clientèle électorale** se trouve dans les banlieues ouvrières (*electorate, electoral support*); SEE ALSO **fidéliser, séduire**

clientélisme (*nm*): le **clientélisme**, la corruption et la violence politique (*vote-catching gimmicks; populism*)

clignotant (*nm*): [*fig*] tous les **clignotants** sociaux sont au rouge (*warning light; key indicator*)

clivage (*nm*): [*fig*] accentuant le **clivage** entre les deux communautés (*split, rift; divide*); la décentralisation dépasse les **clivages politiques** (*political divisions*)

clochardisation (*nf*): les universités sont au bord de la **clochardisation** (*beggary; impoverishment*)

clocher (*nm*): [*fig*] une campagne marquée par des **rivalités de clocher** (*parochial/petty rivalries*); stratégies industrielles et **esprit de clocher** (*parochialism*)

clore (*vt*): l'Assemblée **clôt** sa session ordinaire en adoptant une loi sur la presse (*close, terminate*); décider de **clore le dossier**, faute d'éléments (*close a file*)

clos, -e (*adj*): l'instruction est **close** (*finished, complete*); SEE ALSO **huis clos**

clôture (*nf*): **clôture** des candidatures: le 30 juin (*closing/final date*); dès la **clôture** de la Bourse (*close of trading*); les cours de la Bourse **en clôture** (*at close of trading*)

clôturer (*vi*): à la Bourse de Paris, l'indice CAC a **clôturé** à 523,9 (*close; register at close of trading*); [se] (*vpr*): l'exercice qui vient de **se clôturer** (*come to an end, close*)

club (*nm*): fondateur de l'Union des **clubs** pour le renouveau de la gauche; le délégué général des **clubs** Perspectives et Réalités (*political club/association*)

coalisé, -e (*adj/nm*): le rejet par les **coalisés** du plan de paix soviétique (*members of a coalition; allies*)

coalition (*nf*): SEE **gouvernement**

code (*nm*): selon le **code civil** (*civil code*); le **code pénal**, le recueil des lois définissant les infractions (*penal code*); SEE ALSO **contrevenant, déontologie**

coefficient (*nm*): le **coefficient** qui est appliqué aux disciplines au moment des épreuves (*weighting*); la baisse du **coefficient d'occupation** des avions (*occupancy rate*)

coercitif, -ive (*adj*): des mesures plus **coercitives** pour combattre la violence à l'école (*coercive, firm*)

coercition (*nf*): recourir à la **coercition** (*coercion; force*); s'exposer à des **mesures de coercition** par la force des armes (*coercive measures*)

cogestion (*nf*): dans la **cogestion**, les travailleurs participent aux prises de décisions (*joint management, co-management*)

cohabitation (*nf*): la **cohabitation** des époux; des jeunes qui prolongent la **cohabitation** avec leurs parents (*cohabitation, living under the same roof*); la période de **cohabitation** qui s'ouvre en mars 1986 (*situation where French president rules with an opposition majority in the National Assembly*)

cohabiter (*vi*): le président socialiste, obligé de "**cohabiter**" avec une majorité parlementaire conservatrice (*rule with an opposition parliamentary majority*)

cohérence (*nf*): la **cohérence** de la politique gouvernementale (*coherence, consistency*)

cohérent, -e (*adj*): poursuivre une stratégie économique **cohérente** dans la durée (*coherent, consistent*)

cohésion (*nf*): le Premier ministre appelle la majorité à la **cohésion** (*solidarity; unity*); agir pour la justice et la **cohésion nationale** (*national unity*); reconstituer la **cohésion sociale** dans les banlieues (*social harmony*)

coiffer (*vt*): le même ministre **coiffe** à la fois l'aménagement du territoire et l'urbanisme (*head, have overall responsibilty for*); [fig] la liste du PCF **fut coiffée sur le fil** par celle du PS (*was narrowly defeated*)

col (*nm*): augmentation du nombre de **cols blancs** et des emplois féminins (*white-collar worker*); SEE ALSO **délinquance**

colistier, -ière (*nm,f*): la tête de liste, mais aussi l'ensemble des **colistiers** (*candidate on same electoral list*)

collaborateur, -trice (*nm,f*): un ancien **collaborateur**, licencié, et toujours au chômage (*colleague*); la firme recrute de nouveaux **collaborateurs** à l'étranger (*member of staff; staff*)

collaborer (*vi*): il avait **collaboré** *à* plusieurs journaux, dont *Le Monde* (*contribute to; write for*)

collecte (*nf*): des **collectes** pour venir en aide aux sinistrés (*collection*); le rôle du fisc, c'est la **collecte de l'impôt** (*tax-collecting*); la propagande et la **collecte de fonds** (*fund-raising*)

collecter (*vt*): les agences de presse **collectent** et diffusent les informations (*collect, assemble*); **collecter** l'impôt sur le revenu pour le compte du trésor (*collect [esp. taxes]*)

collectif, -ive (*adj/nm*): les divers réseaux **collectifs** d'eau, d'électricité et de téléphone (*shared; public*); un **collectif** regroupant une dizaine d'organisations politiques (*joint organization; action group*); le **collectif budgétaire** ou projet de loi de finances rectificative (*mini budget*); SEE ALSO **convention, crèche, équipement, habitat**

collectivité (*nf*): son dévouement au service de la **collectivité** (*community; society as a whole*); la région, élevée au statut de **collectivité territoriale** en 1982 (*local government authority [with a measure of autonomy]*); certaines **collectivités locales** contrôlées par le Labour (*local authority*)

collège (*nm*): désigné par un **collège** de notables (*college; body of electors*); SEE ALSO **principal**

collimateur (*nm*): [*fig*] les médecins sont **dans le collimateur du gouvernement** (*under government scrutiny*)

collusion (*nf*): la **collusion** entre classe politique et clans mafieux (*collusion*)

colombe (*nf*): [*fig*] il est à classer parmi les **colombes** de l'Administration (*dove*)

colon (*nm*): les **colons** juifs dans les territoires occupés (*settler*)

colonie (*nf*): évacuer les **colonies de peuplement** en Cisjordanie (*settlement*)

colonne (*nf*): **sur quatre colonnes** à la une de l'édition dominicale (*across four newspaper columns*)

combinaison (*nf*): une lutte pour le contrôle de la municipalité sur fond de **combinaisons** et d'âpres rivalités (*conspiracy; plot*)

combler (*vt*): pour **combler** le déficit (*make up, make good*)

comité (*nm*): des discussions **en comité restreint**; se rencontrer **en petit comité** au Kremlin (*in a small group; in private*); réunir un **comité d'experts** (*group of experts*); des candidats au **comité directeur**, le "parlement" du Parti socialiste (*executive committee*); les projets de licenciements furent révélés au cours d'un **comité d'entreprise** (*works committee, works council*); SEE ALSO **constituer**

commande (*nf*): [*fig*] il a montré qu'il est toujours **aux commandes** (*in charge, at the controls*); les **prises de commandes** ont été très flatteuses (*order; placing of an order*); SEE ALSO **baisser, levier**

commanditaire (*nm*): les tueurs présumés et **leurs commanditaires** possibles (*the people behind them*)

commandite (*nf*): former une **société en commandite simple** (*[simple] partnership*); la transformation de la SA en **société de commandite par actions** renforcera l'indépendance des dirigeants (*form of limited partnership*)

commanditer (*vt*): accusé d'avoir **commandité** la tentative d'assassinat (*finance/organize [esp. terrorist activity]*)

commerçant, -e (*adj/nm,f*): la Grande-Bretagne, vieille **nation commerçante** (*trading nation*); le **petit commerçant** est-il condamné à disparaître? (*small shopkeeper/trader*)

commerce (*nm*): dans le monde du **commerce** (*business, commerce*); malgré un mauvais résultat du **commerce extérieur** (*foreign trade*); un texte condamnant le **commerce des armes** (*arms trade*); les milieux criminels **faisant commerce de drogues dures** (*dealing in hard drugs*); conserver le **fonds de commerce** mais céder les locaux (*business [with goodwill]*); SEE ALSO **détail, dominical, libéraliser, voyageur**

commercer (*vi*): pour **commercer** avec les pays du Proche-Orient (*trade, do business*)

commercial, -e, *pl* **-aux** (*adj/nm,f*): avoir des notions d'**anglais commercial** (*business English*); il faudra embaucher une trentaine de **commerciaux** (*sales executive*); SEE ALSO **négociation**

commercialisation (*nf*): Renault prévoit la **commercialisation** de ce modèle au Brésil (*marketing*)

commercialiser (*vt*): ses marques sont **commercialisées** dans 70 pays (*market; sell*)

commis (*nm*): plusieurs **grand commis de l'État** étaient présents (*senior civil servant*)

commissaire (*nm*): le **commissaire** européen à l'agriculture (*commissioner*); un **commissaire [de police]** a été mis en examen (*[police] superintendent*); le **commissaire aux comptes** présente son rapport aux actionnaires (*auditor*); le **commissaire-priseur** adjuge les marchandises au plus offrant (*auctioneer*)

commissariat (*nm*): être conduit au **commissariat [de police]** (*police station*); le **haut commissariat** aux Réfugiés de l'ONU (*High Commission*)

commission (*nf*): la **commission** des affaires culturelles, familiales et sociales (*committee*); des **commissions permanentes**, chacune traitant d'un problème particulier (*standing committee*); la **commission d'enquête** vient de publier son rapport (*committee of enquiry; fact-finding committee*); des investigations, sur **commission rogatoire** du juge d'instruction (*commission to take evidence*); le **versement de commissions douteuses** dans des marchés d'exportation (*paying illegal commission*); faire obstacle à la **commission d'un crime** (*committing of a crime*); SEE ALSO **paritaire, réflexion, sénatorial, urbanisme**

commode (*adj*): l'absence de moyens de transport **commodes** (*convenient; handy*)

commodité (*nf*): par souci d'efficacité et de **commodité** (*convenience*); (*pl*): une absence de **commodités** [voirie, eau potable, évacuation des eaux usées]; à louer, studio avec **commodités** (*services; facilities*)

commun, -e (*adj*): la **déclaration commune** de Londres et Dublin (*joint declaration*); sur cette question, la France et l'Italie **font cause commune** (*make common cause*); SEE ALSO **droit, tronc**

communal, -e, *pl* **-aux** (*adj*): l'espace **communal** reste l'élément de base de la communauté (*communal, pertaining to the commune*)

communautaire (*adj*): dans un **local communautaire** (*community hall/room*); l'Europe **communautaire** avait rendez-vous hier à Strasbourg (*pertaining to the European Community*); l'irruption du **droit communautaire** dans le droit national (*[European] Community law*); SEE ALSO **acquis**

communauté (*nf*): une charge sur la **communauté** (*general public, community*); l'ensemble des 27 communes de la **communauté urbaine** de Bordeaux (*grouping of urban communes*); un couple **marié sous un régime de communauté [des biens]** (*married under a contract establishing joint ownership of goods and chattels*); l'avantage de la **communauté réduite aux acquêts** (*communal estate comprising only property acquired after marriage*)

commune (*nf*): une petite **commune** rurale du Doubs (*commune, administrative district*)

compagne (*nf*): expulsé de France avec sa **compagne** (*companion, partner [esp. common-law wife]*)

compagnon (*nm*): il faut un diplôme [CAP, **compagnon**, apprentissage artisanal] (*apprentice; member of trade guild*); ceux qu'on appelait les **compagnons de route** de Staline (*fellow traveller*)

comparaître (*vi*): la première fois qu'il **comparaît** devant un tribunal; les sept détenus ont **comparu** devant la chambre correctionnelle (*appear [before a court of law]*); SEE ALSO **assignation, citation, délit, mandat**

comparution (*nf*): en attendant une **comparution** devant le conseil de discipline (*appearance before tribunal/court of law*); interpellations de jeunes casseurs et **procès en comparution directe** (*summary court proceedings*)

compère (*nm*): les deux **compères** n'en étaient pas à leur première escroquerie (*accomplice, partner [in crime]*)

compétence (*nf*): les **compétences** professionnelles d'un candidat (*skill, competence*); une nouvelle répartition des **compétences** entre départements et régions (*area of responsibility*); la santé **relève de la compétence de l'État** (*is the responsibility of the state*); on estimait que le ministre **sortait de sa compétence** (*exceed one's powers; go beyond one's remit*)

compétent, -e (*adj*): l'absence de personnel formé et **compétent** (*competent, skilled*); les régions **sont compétentes** en matière d'urbanisme (*be competent/have authority to act*); s'adresser au **service compétent** (*appropriate/relevant department*)

compétitif, -ive (*adj*): vendre à des tarifs très **compétitifs** (*competitive*)

compétition (*nf*): l'entreprise, soumise à une **compétition accrue** (*increased competition*)

compétitivité (*nf*): la nécessité d'améliorer la **compétitivité** de l'usine (*competitiveness*)

complaire (*vt*): pour **complaire à** la France en particulier (*please, satisfy*)

complaisance (*nf*): le gouvernement, accusé de **complaisance à l'égard de l'immigration clandestine** (*condoning illegal immigration*); soupçonné de **complaisance à l'égard de l'extrême droite** (*having a soft attitude towards right-wing extremists*); SEE ALSO **pavillon**

complaisant, -e (*adj*): une attitude **complaisante** à l'égard du pouvoir (*uncritical; indulgent*)

complément (*nm*): toucher le **complément familial** et une aide au logement (*means-tested family allowance*); avoir droit à un **complément de retraite** (*supplementary pension*); le juge **demanda un complément d'information** (*ask for further information*)

complicité (*nf*): avec la **complicité** de la communauté internationale (*complicity; collusion*); inculpé de **complicité d'escroquerie** (*conspiracy to defraud*)

composante (*nf*): un peuple corse, **composante** du peuple français; la **composante** d'extrême droite de la majorité (*element, component*)

composer (*vt*): les dix pays qui **composent** l'Afrique australe (*form, make up*); (*vi*): même s'il doit **composer avec** une Assemblée hostile à ses idées (*come to terms with*)

compréhension (*nf*): Bonn compte sur la **compréhension** de Paris (*sympathy; understanding*)

compression (*nf*): une réduction de salaires et des **compressions des effectifs**; le plan de restructuration conduira à une **compression du personnel** (*cuts in manpower; redundancies*)

compris, -e (*adj*): le taux de chômage reste **compris** entre 12% et 20% de la population active (*within a range*)

compromettre (*vt*): sa femme, également **compromise**, fut blanchie par la commission (*implicated, involved*); [se] (*vpr*): un diplomate qui se **compromet** dans une affaire d'espionnage (*compromise oneself*)

compromis (*nm*): un **compromis**, intervenu après treize heures de discussions (*compromise*); l'offre d'achat en Angleterre n'est pas la même chose que le **compromis de vente** français (*preliminary contract/agreement to sell*)

compromission (*nf*): il avait perdu toute crédibilité par ses **compromissions** avec l'ancien pouvoir (*[shady] deal; dishonourable behaviour*)

comptabiliser (*vt*): de nombreuses dépenses sont **comptabilisées** dans d'autres rubriques (*post, enter [in ledger]*); les années d'ancienneté sont loin d'être intégralement **comptabilisées** (*count [in], take into consideration*)

comptabilité (*nf*): les enquêteurs ont **épluché la comptabilité** de la firme d'armements (*go through the accounts*)

comptable (*adj/nm*): compte tenu de l' **échéance comptable** de 1993 (*end of the accounting year*); les experts-comptables et les **comptables** agréés (*accountant*); SEE ALSO **expertise**

comptage (*nm*): des erreurs ont été commises dans le **comptage des voix** (*counting of votes*)

comptant (*adj*): une remise sera accordée sur tout achat **comptant** (*cash; in cash*); (*adv*): une réduction de 10% pour **règlement au comptant** (*payment in cash*); SEE ALSO **payer**

compte (*nm*): approuver les **comptes** de l'exercice 1991 (*financial accounts*); retirer de l'argent d'un **compte de dépôt** (*deposit account*); les sommes sont virées automatiquement sur un **compte sur livret** (*savings account*); il veut **se mettre à son compte** sans tarder (*set up in business*); chargé de l'aménagement de la ZAC **pour le compte** de la Ville de Paris (*on behalf of*); trois éléments doivent être **pris en compte** (*take into account*); la **prise en compte** du temps de service dans le calcul de la retraite (*counting; taking into account*); un **compte rendu** de la gestion financière (*report*); le **compte rendu de la réunion** permettra de le savoir avec précision (*report on a meeting; minutes of a meeting*); la manière peu objective dont les médias **rendaient compte de l'affaire** (*reported the matter/ case*); SEE ALSO **commissaire, équilibrer, établir, installer, règlement, relevé**

compter (*vt*): la flotte de la mer Noire qui **compte** 300 bâtiments (*comprise, consist of, number*); **on compte** 80 sociétés françaises représentées à Taipei (*there are in all . . .*); la ville d'Angoulême **compte 44 000 habitants** (*has a population of 40,000*); [se] (*vpr*): les morts et les blessés **se comptent par dizaines de milliers** (*there are tens of thousands of . . .*)

concentration (*nf*): le secteur agro-alimentaire poursuit sa **concentration** (*integration; merging into large groups*); une loi limitant les **concentrations** dans l'audiovisuel et dans la presse (*merger*)

concertation (*nf*): une **concertation** franco-britannique sur la sécurité européenne (*dialogue, discussions*); la réforme sera précédée d'une **large concertation** (*wide consultation*)

concerté, -e (*adj*): l'Europe et l'OTAN: vers une discussion **concertée** (*concerted, joint*); SEE ALSO **ZAC**

concerter [se] (*vpr*): après **s'être concertés**, ils ont rejeté l'accord (*confer [with each other]*)

conciliateur, -trice (*adj/nm,f*): le **conciliateur** est chargé de faciliter le règlement amiable des différends; nommé **conciliateur** par le ministre dans le conflit de la RATP (*conciliator; mediator*)

conciliation (*nf*): la **conciliation** de la vie familiale et de la vie professionnelle (*reconciling; compatibility*); dans ces cas, une **conciliation** est prévue par des accords collectifs (*mediation, conciliation procedure*); soumettre un litige à une **commission de conciliation**, pour éviter la grève (*conciliation board*)

conclure (*vt*): le sommet israélo-palestinien devant **conclure un accord** sur Hébron (*reach an agreement*); le jury **a conclu au meurtre** (*returned a verdict of murder*)

conclusion (*nf*): la **conclusion d'un traité** sur l'interdiction des essais nucléaires (*signing of a treaty*)

concordant, -e (*adj*): des témoignages partiels, mais **tous concordants** (*all in agreement; which all tally*)

concours (*nm*): avec le **concours** de la Ville de Paris (*assistance, help, support*); l'admission est **par [voie de] concours**, sur titres, ou sur épreuves (*by competitive examination*); SEE ALSO **avis, prêter, recruter**

concret, -ète (*adj*): aboutir rapidement à des résulats **concrets** (*concrete, tangible*); acquérir une **formation concrète** (*practical training*)

concrétisation (*nf*): l'emploi dépend de la **concrétisation** éventuelle de commandes en cours de négociation (*confirmation; coming into being*)

concrétiser (*vt*): sa visite permettra de **concrétiser** des projets de coopération entre les deux pays (*give practical effect to; bring to fruition*); [se] (*vpr*): si le plan **se concrétise**, ce sera la catastrophe (*materialize; come into effect*)

concubin, -e (*nm,f*): **concubins** et mariés toujours inégaux face à l'impôt (*cohabitant, co-habitee*); la **concubine** bénéficie des mêmes droits que la femme mariée (*common-law wife*); SEE ALSO **couple**

concubinage (*nm*): un couple **vivant en concubinage notoire** (*[openly] cohabit, contract a common-law marriage*)

concurrence (*nf*): ils sont plutôt sous-payés par rapport à la **concurrence** (*competitor; competition*); l'État n'encourage ni le monopole ni la **concurrence sauvage** (*unregulated/unrestricted competition*); la **concurrence déloyale** des grandes surfaces vis-à-vis du petit commerce (*unfair competition*); pratiquer des **prix défiant toute concurrence** (*unbeatable prices*); une majoration de 1 000F pour le premier enfant et **jusqu'à concurrence de 2 000F** par enfant à partir du deuxième (*up to 2,000F*); SEE ALSO **face, fausser, jeu, libre, subir**

concurrencer (*vt*): le tunnel va **concurrencer** le trafic trans-Manche (*compete against*)

concurrent, -e (*adj/nm,f*): la SNCF et Air Inter sont deux entreprises désormais **concurrentes** (*rival, competing*); racheter un de ses principaux **concurrents** (*competitor*)

concurrentiel, -ielle (*adj*): demeurer **concurrentiel** sur un marché agressif (*competitive*)

concussion (*nf*): la **concussion** ou la perception illicite par un agent public de sommes qu'il sait ne pas être dues (*misappropriation of public funds*)

condamnation (*nf*): avoir trois **condamnations** à son actif; cette **condamnation** pourra faire jurisprudence (*conviction; sentence*)

condamné, -e (*nm,f*): un droit d'appel inconditionnel qui sera ouvert au **condamné** comme au parquet (*convicted person*)

condamner (*vt*): être **condamné** pour détournement de fonds; la société a été **condamnée** pour fraude fiscale (*find guilty; convict*); Damas a **condamné sans appel** l'accord du Caire (*condemn unreservedly*)

condition (*nf*): la somme de 362F, versée jusqu'à 16 ans **sous condition de ressources** (*subject to means-testing*); SEE ALSO **carcéral, libérer, trêve**

conditionnel, -elle (*adj*): SEE **libération**

conditionner (*vt*): les pouvoirs publics **conditionnent** ce type d'aide à la réalisation de nouveaux investissements (*make as a condition for*)

conduire (*vt*): c'est ce qu'ont confirmé des expériences **conduites** en Israël (*carry out; conduct*); il **conduisait le pays** pendant ces quinze années difficiles (*govern a country*); les Verts choisissent un inconnu pour **conduire leur liste** (*head an electoral list*)

conduite (*nf*): la **conduite** de la politique étrangère (*conduct, operation*); SEE ALSO **écart**

confédération (*nf*): le 700e anniversaire de la **Confédération** (*confederation of States*); deux des grandes **confédérations syndicales** [CGT, CFDT] (*trade union confederation*)

confiance (*nf*): le manque de **confiance** des consommateurs et des entreprises (*confidence*); l'Assemblée nationale a **voté la confiance** au gouvernement (*pass a vote of confidence*); SEE ALSO **crise, question**

confirmer (*vt*): la cour d'appel de Paris **confirme** le jugement du TGI (*uphold, confirm*); [se] (*vpr*): la reprise économique, si elle **se confirme** (*is confirmed*)

confiscation (*nf*): la **confiscation** des terres palestiniennes à Jérusalem (*seizure, confiscation*); **il y a eu confiscation de la révolution** par les néo-communistes (*the revolution was taken over*)

confisquer (*vt*): ni le Premier ministre ni le chef de l'État ne peut **confisquer la politique extérieure** (*take sole control of foreign policy*); le Premier ministre fit arrêter le roi et **confisqua le pouvoir** (*take over power*)

conflictuel, -elle (*adj*): les relations **conflictuelles** entre les houillères et la commune (*conflictual*); les grévistes ont obtenu raison sur deux **sujets conflictuels** (*subject of disagreement/dispute*)

conflit (*nm*): il faut essayer d'empêcher de futurs **conflits sociaux**; mettre fin aux **conflits du travail** (*labour/industrial dispute*); SEE ALSO **enjeu, issue, radicalisation**

confondre (*vt*): les partis, **toutes tendances confondues**, sont d'accord là-dessus (*without exception; across the whole political spectrum*); le pouvoir d'achat du salaire net moyen [secteurs privé et public **confondus**] (*without distinction; taken together*)

conforme (*adj*): ce qu'il a fait est **conforme à** la Constitution (*in accordance with*); SEE ALSO **copie**

conformément (*adv*): **conformément aux** dispositions de l'article 15 de la loi (*in accordance with*)

conformer [se] (*vpr*): le juge, **se conformant aux** réquisitions du parquet, fait arrêter le jeune homme; **se conformer aux** conventions internationales (*abide by; conform to*)

conformité (*nf*): **être en conformité avec** les exigences imposées par la compagnie d'assurance (*comply with, respect*)

conforter (*vt*): les entreprises soucieuses de **conforter** leurs parts de marché (*consolidate; increase*); chiffre qui vient **conforter** les craintes du Premier ministre (*reinforce; confirm, justify*)

confusion (*nf*): un texte qui **prête à confusion** (*be open to misinterpretation*); le système de la **confusion des peines** permet de ne prendre en compte que la condamnation la plus lourde (*concurrent prison sentences*)

congé (*nm*): le plan social offre à tout licencié 24 mois de **congé-conversion**; se voir proposer des **congés-formation** (*paid retraining course*); le droit des salariés à des **congés payés** (*paid holiday*); prendre plusieurs jours de **congé sans solde** (*unpaid leave, time off without pay*); si votre propriétaire vous a **notifié votre congé** (*give notice to leave/quit*); **être mis en congé** du Parti socialiste (*be expelled*); la Lituanie **prit congé de** l'URSS (*leave, quit*); SEE ALSO **maternité, parental, sabbatique**

congédier (*vt*): le Premier ministre a **congédié** les commissions mises en place par son prédécesseur (*sack, dismiss*)

52

conjoint, -e (*adj/nm,f*): une offensive **conjointe** de patrons et de syndicats (*joint; combined*); le **conjoint** de l'assuré est aussi couvert; quel que soit le **conjoint** qui est décédé (*spouse, partner*)

conjointement (*adv*): lancer **conjointement** un appel au calme (*jointly*)

conjoncture (*nf*): la **conjoncture** ou l'ensemble des variations à court terme de l'activité économique (*general economic climate*); conséquence de la **conjoncture euphorique** alors (*buoyant economic conditions*); le ralentissement de la **conjoncture du logement** (*housing market*); SEE ALSO **retournement**

conjoncturel, -elle (*adj*): l'**environnement conjoncturel** était plutôt bon (*economic conditions*); cette spirale inflationniste est bien évidemment **conjoncturelle** (*short-term; cyclical*)

conjoncturiste (*nm*): les **conjoncturistes** prédisent une reprise de l'activité économique (*economic forecaster*)

conjugal, -e, *pl* **-aux** (*adj*): SEE **réintégrer**

conjugué, -e (*adj*): la chute **conjuguée** des prix du pétrole, du café et du cacao (*combined*)

conjuguer (*vt*): dans le domaine des transports, la Ville et l'État **conjuguent leurs efforts** (*co-operate, combine their efforts*)

conscience (*nf*): la **conscience** qu'on a de l'importance du nucléaire (*awareness*); la **prise de conscience** progressive de ce que le renouveau de l'Europe passe par la coopération (*realization*); la **liberté de conscience** est garantie par la constitution (*freedom of conscience*); SEE ALSO **prisonnier**

conscription (*nf*): l'abandon pur et simple de certaines formes de la **conscription** (*conscription*); une armée professionnelle moins nombreuse que l'actuelle **armée de conscription** (*conscript army*); SEE ALSO **dérober**

conscrit (*nm*): une armée allemande de **conscrits** (*conscript*)

consécutif, -ive (*adj*): hausse des carburants **consécutive** à celle du baril du pétrole (*following [upon]*)

conseil (*nm*): bon vendeur, mais aussi **conseil**, et homme de marketing (*consultant; adviser*); exercer la profession de **conseil juridique** (*legal adviser; solicitor [UK]*); le projet sera discuté en **conseil des ministres** (*cabinet, cabinet of ministers*); le projet fut accepté par le **conseil d'administration** (*board of directors*); le comité exécutif, ou **conseil de gérance** (*management committee*); le jour même où la Bundesbank avait son **conseil directeur** (*board meeting*); SEE ALSO **cabinet, surveillance**

conseil (*nm*) **général**: le **conseil général** est élu par tous les électeurs du canton; président du **conseil général** de la Sarthe (*[elected] council of a French* département)

conseiller, -ère (*nm,f*): un proche **conseiller** du président bosniaque (*adviser*); proposer un poste de **conseiller technique** (*technical adviser/consultant*); le maire, avec le **conseiller général** du canton (*councillor in French* département); les **conseillers municipaux** procèdent à l'élection du maire (*local/town councillor*)

conseiller (*vt*): **conseiller** la caution (*advise, counsel*)

conseil (*nm*) **municipal**: les membres du **conseil municipal** élisent le maire (*town/city/borough council*); lors du dernier **conseil municipal** de Colmar (*meeting of town/city/borough council*)

conseil (*nm*) **régional**: le **conseil régional** ou l'administration locale qui se situe au niveau de la Région (*regional council*)

consensuel, -elle (*adj*): l'image **consensuelle**, centriste, du Premier ministre (*consensual, seeking the middle ground*); un des thèmes les plus **consensuels** (*consensual, where there is a degree of consensus*)

consensus (*nm*): le **consensus** sur le recours à un prélèvement sur tous les revenus (*consensus; general agreement*); il s'agit de sauvegarder le **consensus social** allemand (*social harmony*); sur cette question **un consensus s'est dégagé** (*a consensus emerged*)

consentement (*nm*): le divorce **par consentement mutuel** (*by consent*)

consentir (*vt*): on voit les commerçants **consentir d'énormes rabais** pour attirer la clientèle (*offer large discounts*); chez eux, **un effort important est consenti** pour la formation (*a considerable effort has been made*)

conservateur, -trice (*adj/nm,f*): l'émergence d'un puissant sentiment **conservateur**; la droite **conservatrice** (*conservative*); les **Conservateurs** remportent les élections (*Conservative [party]*)

consigne (*nf*): il ne donne pas de **consignes de vote** (*voting recommendations*); la **consigne de grève** a été largement suivie (*strike call*)

consolidation (*nf*): le retrait des troupes et la **consolidation** de la paix (*reinforcing, consolidation*)

consolider (*vt*): Nestlé SA décide de **consolider** ses filiales d'aliments et de boissons (*consolidate*); [se] (*vpr*): le dollar **s'est consolidé** au cours des dernières séances (*strengthen, become firmer*)

consommateur, -trice (*nm,f*): où sont donc passés les **consommateurs**? (*consumer; customer*); SEE ALSO **défense**

consommation (*nf*): la **consommation** a augmenté d'environ 50% (*consumption*); le refus de la **société de consommation** (*consumer society*); la **consommation des ménages** a tendance à se tasser (*consumer/domestic spending*); SEE ALSO **bien, inciter**

consommer (*vt*): si les Français préfèrent épargner plutôt que **consommer** (*spend [on consumer goods]*)

constant, -e (*adj*): SEE **franc**

constat (*nm*): la commission dressa un **constat** très sévère (*report, conclusion, finding*); les Douze se sont donc quittés **sur un constat d'échec** (*having to admit failure*); la police est venue **faire un constat** sur les lieux (*draw up a report*); faire procéder à un **constat d'huissier** (*bailiff's report*)

constatation (*nf*): deux **constatations** s'imposent (*observation, remark*); selon les **premières constatations** de la commission d'enquête (*initial/preliminary findings*); les policiers ont **procédé aux constatations d'usage** (*carry out routine investigations*)

constater (*vt*): avec 275 000 crimes et délits **constatés** en 1996 (*record*); il est alors souhaitable de **constater un état des lieux** (*draw up an inventory*); l'obligation de **constater le décès** (*certify that death has occurred*); SEE ALSO **avarie**

constituer [se] (*vpr*): les habitants **se sont constitués en comité de défense** (*form an action committee*); il a décidé de **se constituer prisonnier** (*give himself up, surrender*); la famille **s'est constituée partie civile** (*take civil action; sue for damages*)

constitution (*nf*): la **constitution** de la future équipe présidentielle (*setting-up, forming*); la **constitution** de ghettos ethniques et la crise des banlieues (*formation*); SEE ALSO **non conforme**

consultance (*nf*): spécialiste dans la **consultance** économique (*consultancy*)

consultation (*nf*): la **consultation** du peuple par référendum (*consulting*); l'échec de la majorité lors des **consultations cantonales** de mars 1985 (*French departmental elections*); la revalorisation des honoraires de **consultation médicale** (*doctor's surgery/consultation*)

contenir (*vt*): essayer de **contenir** le pouvoir d'achat (*contain, control*)

contentieux, -ieuse (*adj/nm*): la recherche d'une issue au **contentieux** communautaire (*dispute, disagreement*); s'adresser au **service des contentieux** (*legal department*); SEE ALSO **apurer, liquider, solder**

contenu (*nm*): on n'a pas de détails sur le **contenu** des conversations (*content, substance*); les **contenus** des diplômes professionnels sont négociés avec les branches patronales (*course content; curriculum*)

contestation (*nf*): la **contestation** prend de l'ampleur dans les ghettos noirs (*protest movement*); l'ensemble des mesures fait l'objet d'une vive **contestation syndicale** (*trade-union resistance*); SEE ALSO **larvé**

contester (*vt*): **contesté** même au sein de son propre parti (*challenged*); l'avocat parisien qui avait **contesté le verdict** (*challenge the verdict*); (*vi*): vous pouvez **contester** (*appeal [against a decision]*)

continent (*nm*): les fonctionnaires attirent l'attention du **continent** sur le malaise corse (*[mainland] France*)

contingent (*nm*): chaque formation a reçu un **contingent** strict d'invitations (*number, quota*); le **contingent** cubain, estimé à 55 000 soldats (*contingent, unit*); les **soldats du contingent** ont été envoyés pour rétablir la paix (*conscript troops*); SEE ALSO **appelé, recrue**

contingentement (*nm*): des **contingentements** imposés par le GATT (*[setting of] quotas*)

contingenter (*vt*): les exportations de fruits et légumes, longtemps **contingentées** (*subject to quotas*)

contournement (*nm*): le **contournement** est très attendu par les habitants du village; création d'une **voie de contournement** de la RN52 (*bypass; ring road*); SEE ALSO **rocade**

contourner (*vt*): la Lituanie tente de **contourner** le blocus économique (*get round, circumvent*)

contracter (*vt*): **contracter un emprunt** pour acheter un bien immobilier (*arrange a loan*)

contractuel, -elle (*adj/nm,f*): avoir recours à des [agents] **contractuels**, non statutaires (*unestablished civil servant; contract staff*); s'adresser au **contractuel de service** (*staff on duty*)

contraignant, -e (*adj*): des règles de procédure beaucoup plus **contraignantes** et précises; des mesures très **contraignantes** pour le régime de Bagdad (*restrictive*)

contraindre (*vt*): un troisième ministre **contraint à la démission** (*forced to resign*)

contrat (*nm*): signer un **contrat** (*deed, contract, agreement*); les **contrats à durée déterminée [CDD]** sont devenus la règle (*fixed-term contract*); de nouveaux types de **contrats emploi-formation** sont adoptés dès 1982 (*[in France] government-sponsored skills training initiative*); la signature d'un **contrat de plan État-Région** (*[in France] economic development contract between state and region*); SEE ALSO **décrocher, inexécution, juteux**

contravention (*nf*): les faits lui reprochés ne relèvent pas du délit mais de la simple **contravention** (*minor offence*); **être en contravention** totale avec les textes (*contravene; be in breach of*); les **contraventions** impayées (*parking fine/ticket*)

contrecoup (*nm*): l'industrie **subit le contrecoup** d'un quasi-doublement de la TVA (*feel the effects*); une forte montée du mark et, **en contrecoup**, une faiblesse relative du franc (*as an indirect consequence*)

contrefaçon (*nf*): la **contrefaçon** sera plus sévèrement réprimée (*forgery*); la **contrefaçon des marques**, assimilée dorénavant à la contrebande (*imitation of branded goods*)

contremaître (*nm*): suivre un apprentissage pour passer **contremaître** (*foreman, supervisor*)

contre-performance (*nf*): une véritable **contre-performance** qui ne se reproduira plus (*bad result; poor performance*)

contre-pied (*nm*): il n'a pas hésité à **prendre le contre-pied** de la politique définie par le gouvernement précédent (*take the opposite course; do the opposite*)

contrer (*vt*): pour **contrer** la propagande du Parti travailliste; Air France tente de **contrer** Air Liberté en Afrique (*counter*)

contreseing (*nm*): le **contreseing** du Premier ministre est requis (*counter-signature*)

contresigner (*vt*): les actes du Président sont **contresignés** par un ministre (*countersign*)

contrevenant, -e (*nm,f*): aucune sanction n'est prévue contre les **contrevenants** (*offender*); les **contrevenants à la loi** de 1975 (*person in breach of a law*); du grand criminel au simple **contrevenant au Code de la route** (*person guilty of a traffic offence*)

contrevenir (*vt*): les pays ayant **contrevenu** à l'embargo pétrolier (*contravene*); les pays riches n'hésitent pas à **contrevenir aux règles** qu'ils se sont données (*break/contravene rules*)

contre-vérité (*nf*): dire des **contre-vérités**, sinon des mensonges (*untruth, falsehood*)

contribuable (*nm*): chaque **contribuable** estime qu'il paie trop d'impôts locaux (*taxpayer; ratepayer*); le déficit public est supporté par le **petit contribuable** (*low taxpayer*); les **gros contribuables** bénéficieront autant que les cadres moyens des allégements fiscaux (*high taxpayer*)

contribution (*nf*): le principe 'à revenu égal, **contribution** égale' (*taxes, taxation*); les **contributions indirectes** sont en France moins onéreuses (*indirect taxation*); la **contribution patronale** vient de passer à 12,3% (*employer's contribution to National Insurance scheme*); travailler aux **contributions** (*[in France] tax office, tax-collection department*)

contrôle (*nm*): les **contrôles** de fin de trimestre (*[school] test/assessment*); instaurer des **contrôles à l'entrée dans le pays** (*immigration/customs checks*); procéder à un démantèlement des **contrôles des changes** (*exchange controls*); le juge le laisse libre, mais **sous contrôle judiciaire** (*under a supervision order; under legal restrictions*); la **prise de contrôle** de Lesieur par Ferruzzi (*taking control/majority interest*); SEE ALSO **probatoire**

contrôler (*vt*): on ne **contrôle** plus les passeports (*examine, check*); **contrôler** les opérations (*control, supervise*)

contumace (*nf*): juger **par contumace**, c'est-à-dire en l'absence des accusés (*[proceedings] in the absence of the accused*)

conurbation (*nf*): dans la **conurbation** londonienne (*conurbation*)

convaincre (*vt*): leur raisonnement ne l'a pas **convaincu** (*convince, persuade*); être **convaincu** de participation à l'attentat; le nombre de sportifs **convaincus** d'avoir consommé du cannabis (*convicted/found guilty*)

convenir (*vi*): les deux pays ont **convenu de** mettre davantage l'accent sur ce qui les rapproche (*agree*); (*v impers*): le **traitement qu'il conviendra d'appliquer** aux sociétés privatisées (*appropriate treatment*)

convention (*nf*): la nouvelle **convention** d'assurance-chômage (*agreement, contract*); patronat et syndicats représentatifs signent une **convention collective** (*collective labour agreement*); tenir une **convention** sur l'environnement (*hold a convention/conference*); SEE ALSO **extradition**

conventionné, -e (*adj*): les **médecins conventionnés** ne sont pas concernés par ce train de mesures (*[in France] state-approved doctor*)

conversion (*nf*): SEE **congé, pôle, zone**

convivial, -e, *pl* **-iaux** (*adj*): un ordinateur muni d'un logiciel **convivial** (*user-friendly*)

convivialité (*nf*): les foyers socio-éducatifs et autres lieux de rencontre et de **convivialité** (*friendliness, friendly relations*)

convocation (*nf*): faire obstacle à la **convocation** d'une telle réunion (*convening; convoking*); en refusant de répondre à la **convocation** du juge (*summons*)

convoquer (*vt*): le chef de l'État **convoque des élections** pour l'automne (*call elections*); il va falloir **convoquer les membres** (*call/convene a meeting of members*)

coopérant (*nm*): travailler au Gabon en qualité de **coopérant**; mort de deux **coopérants** français en Algérie (*young person doing national service in a non-military capacity in a developing country*)

coopératif, -ive (*adj/nf*): les avatars des **coopératives** de consommation en 1985-6 (*cooperative*)

coopération (*nf*): la tendance à la **coopération** entre les industriels (*collaboration, cooperation*); la **coopération** prend la forme d'aides financières et d'assistance technique (*[in France] cultural or technical aid; form of national service involving working abroad on aid project*); SEE ALSO **titre**

coopérer (*vi*): l'industrie de l'armement est condamnée à **coopérer** (*collaborate*)

coordination (*nf*): une **coordination** des efforts vers une plus grande efficacité (*coordinating*); une **coordination interministérielle** pour faciliter les contacts (*joint committee*); une **coordination** permet de revendiquer sans passer par les syndicats traditionnels (*joint action committee*)

coordonner (*vt*): pour **coordonner** la politique des deux pays (*co-ordinate*); [se] (*vpr*): Français et Américains semblent maintenant décidés à se **coordonner** (*co-ordinate their efforts, work together*)

copie (*nf*): l'original ou la **copie conforme** d'un document (*certified true copy*); des journalistes **en mal de copie** (*short of a story*)

copropriété (*nf*): l'acquisition d'un appartement **en copropriété** (*jointly owned*)

coquille (*nf*): une version dactylographiée pleine de **coquilles** et de fautes de frappe (*misprint; typo*)

corbeille (*nf*): du côté de la **corbeille**, les actions grimpent en flèche (*Paris Stock Exchange trading floor, Bourse*)

corps (*nm*): en attendant la décision du **corps électoral** (*electorate; the voters*); devant le **corps diplomatique** au grand complet (*diplomatic corps*); l'ensemble du **corps médical** est hostile au projet (*medical profession*); l'envoi d'un **corps expéditionnaire** (*task force*); SEE ALSO **séparation, supplétif**

correction (*nf*): la production a diminué de 1,9% après **correction des variations saisonnières** (*taking into account seasonal adjustments*)

correctionnel, -elle (*adj*): le renvoi des malfaiteurs présumés devant la [cour] **correctionnelle**; le **tribunal correctionnel** statue sur les délits (*magistrates' court*)

cotation (*nf*): la **cotation** reprendra lundi le 8 février (*share-price quotation*); demander une **cotation** à la bourse de Tokyo (*Stock Exchange listing/quotation*)

cote (*nf*): le Premier ministre améliore sa **cote de popularité** (*popularity rating*); la **très faible cote** du président (*unpopularity*); lorsque la **cote d'alerte** est dépassée (*danger point*)

coter (*vi*): le Mark valait 3F40, aujourd'hui il **cote** 3F46 (*be worth*); (*vt*): la société vient d'**être cotée en Bourse** (*be listed/quoted on the Stock Exchange*)

cotisant, -e (*nm,f*): la réduction du nombre de **cotisants** est due au chômage (*person paying Social Security contributions; subscriber, paid-up member*)

cotisation (*nf*): la **cotisation** des adhérents d'un syndicat (*membership due, contribution*); une augmentation de la seule **cotisation patronale** (*employer's [social security] contribution*); supprimer la **cotisation-maladie** et la remplacer par un nouveau prélèvement (*sickness-benefit contribution*)

cotiser (*vi*): **cotiser** à une caisse de retraite (*pay contributions*)

coulisse (*nf*): des contacts **en coulisse** entre les deux pays (*secret, discreet*); un habitué des **coulisses du pouvoir** (*corridors of power*)

coup (*nm*): après des rumeurs de **coup de force** à Moscou (*coup*); **un coup dur** pour les Socialistes (*a heavy blow*); à la faveur d'un **coup d'État** militaire sans effusion de sang (*coup, coup d'état*); traiter les revendications catégorielles **au coup par coup** (*as they occur; one by one, individually*); étrangers, donc **sous le coup d'une mesure d'expulsion** (*liable to expulsion; under an expulsion order*); **tomber sous le coup de** la nouvelle loi anti-fraude (*fall foul of [a law]*); inculpé pour **coups et blessures** (*aggravated assault*); risquer dix ans d'emprisonnement pour **coups et blessures volontaires** (*malicious wounding*); SEE ALSO **filet, inculpation, pouce**

coupable (*adj/nmf*): il a été jugé **coupable** du meurtre de sa patronne (*find guilty, convict*); SEE ALSO **plaider, reconnaître**

coupe (*nf*): les **coupes** drastiques opérées dans le budget militaire (*cut-back, reduction*); **coupe claire** dans la fonction publique: 37 000 emplois supprimés (*drastic staff cut-backs*)

couple (*nm*): l'avantage fiscal dont bénéficient les **couples non mariés** (*unmarried couple*); la disparition de l'avantage fiscal des **couples concubins** (*cohabiting couple*); la **vie en couple** en dehors du mariage se banalise (*living together; cohabitation*)

coupon (*nm*): il vous suffit de remplir le **coupon-réponse** ci-joint (*detachable reply coupon*)

coupure (*nf*): la **coupure** de l'île de Chypre en deux parties (*division*); la **coupure** entre la base et la direction du parti (*gap, gulf*); plusieurs **coupures** de 1 000F ont disparu (*banknote, bill*)

cour (*nf*): la **cour d'assises** seule peut juger les crimes (*Assize Court; Crown Court*); la Chambre des lords, **cour d'appel ultime** en Angleterre (*court of final appeal*)

courant, -e (*adj/nm*): l'existence de **courants** au sein du parti; il existe bel et bien un **courant** centriste (*tendency, trend; group*); SEE ALSO **expédier, franc**

courbe (*nf*): les **courbes** de l'épargne et de la consommation (*curve; graph*)

courir (*vi*): un attentat dont les auteurs **courent encore** (*be on the run; run free*)

couronne (*nf*): une commune de la **couronne parisienne** (*outer suburbs of Paris*); dans les trois départements de la **petite couronne** (*inner ring of départements within the Paris region*); les départements périphériques de l'Ile-de-France, la **grande couronne** (*outer ring of* départements *within the Paris region*)

cours (*nm*): les **cours des produits alimentaires** ont dégringolé (*food prices*); la faiblesse actuelle des **cours** (*share price*); le franc est près de son **cours plancher** (*floor, bottom rate*); le DMark est à son **cours plafond** (*ceiling rate*); **suivre des cours** à la faculté (*attend classes, follow courses*); SEE ALSO **affaissement, rattrapage, repli**

course (*nf*): [*fig*] la **course aux rendements** dans l'agriculture moderne (*maximizing yields*); la **course aux armements** entre les deux grandes puissances (*arms race*)

court, -e (*adj*): la **courte** expérience du pluralisme politique (*brief, short*); une **courte victoire** pour le président sortant (*narrow victory*); (*adv*) la grève générale **prend de court** les dirigeants du pays (*take by surprise*); les négociations ont **tourné court** très rapidement (*be cut short; come to a premature end*); SEE ALSO **vue**

courtage (*nm*): à la Bourse de New York, le **courtage** est informatisé (*share brokerage*); les grandes **firmes de courtage** (*brokerage firm*)

courtier (*nm*): pour les **courtiers** et agents d'assurance (*broker*); servir de **courtier** dans une affaire (*broker, agent, intermediary*)

coût (*nm*): le **coût élevé** de la main-d'œuvre (*high cost*); les entreprises essayent de réduire les **coûts salariaux** (*salary/wage costs*); loin de couvrir les **coûts de fabrication** (*production costs*); en provenance de **pays à bas coût de revient** (*low-cost producer*); SEE ALSO **réduction**, **serrer**

coûteux, -euse (*adj*): rendant ces produits aussi **coûteux** que ceux produits en France (*dear, expensive, costly*)

coutume (*nf*): le texte prévoit le maintien des **coutumes** islamiques (*custom, tradition*); SEE ALSO **us**

couverture (*nf*): la **couverture** de tous les risques (*cover, insurance*); assurer à tous une bonne **couverture médicale** (*medical cover/insurance*); des millions d'Américains sont privés de **couverture sociale** (*social security cover*); le **taux de couverture** des importations par les exportations reste assez faible (*cover ratio*)

couvre-feu (*nm*): lever le **couvre-feu** imposé il y a une semaine (*curfew*); un camp de réfugiés a été placé **sous le régime du couvre-feu** (*under curfew*)

couvrir (*vt*): comparaître pour avoir **couvert** le versement de pots-de-vin (*cover up; accept after the fact*); **être couvert** par une assurance médicale personnelle (*have [insurance] cover*)

créance (*nf*): exiger le remboursement de ces **créances** (*money owed, debt*); la banque a accumulé une série de **créances douteuses**; avec 40 milliards de francs de **mauvaises créances** (*bad debt*); SEE ALSO **lettre**, **recouvrement**, **souffrance**

créancier, -ière (*nm,f*): les **créanciers** de Varsovie commencent à serrer la vis (*creditor*); les principales **banques créancières** acceptent l'étalement des remboursements (*creditor banks*)

création (*nf*): avec la **création**, en 1971, du Bangladesh (*creation, coming into existence*); on annonce la **création d'impôts nouveaux** (*new taxes*); il s'agit d'une **création de poste** (*new post/job*); la **création de 200 postes** sur quatre ans (*200 new jobs*); sans avoir recours à la **création monétaire** (*printing of money*)

crèche (*nf*): les enfants qui sont gardés dans des **crèches collectives** (*day nursery*); multiplier les halte-garderies et relancer les **crèches [à domicile]** (*day nursery [run by parents in their own home]*); SEE ALSO **inexistant**

crédibilité (*nf*): le terrorisme avait **porté atteinte à la crédibilité** de l'OLP (*damage the credibility of*); SEE ALSO **entamer**

crédible (*adj*): aucune dissuasion purement conventionnelle n'est **crédible** en Europe (*credible*); ces révélations tardives sont **peu crédibles** (*hardly convincing, unconvincing*)

crédit (*nm*): obtenir un **crédit** du FMI de 650 millions de dollars (*loan*); des mesures pour alléger le **coût du crédit** (*cost of borrowing*); outre-Manche un **crédit immobilier** se prend sur 25 ans (*mortgage loan*); tous les **crédits-formation** étaient épuisés pour 1995 (*training money/ funds*); SEE ALSO **débloquer, encadré, encadrement, remboursement**

créditer (*vt*): son parti est **crédité** de 20% des intentions de vote (*credit*)

créditeur, -trice (*adj/nm,f*): un compte **créditeur** (*in credit*); la centaine de banques **créditrices** (*creditor*)

créer (*vt*): **créer** de nouveaux postes (*create*); [se] (*vpr*): 3 000 nouvelles associations **se créent** chaque année (*are set up/founded*) SEE **pièce, zizanie**

créneau, pl -x (*nm*): préserver l'emploi dans un **créneau** industriel qui participe de la sécurité nationale (*sector*); leader sur certains **créneaux du marché** (*market sector*); l'écologie devrait constituer un **créneau porteur pour l'emploi** (*sector providing good job prospects*); le ministre **monte au créneau** et exige des éclaircissements (*go onto the attack*)

creusement (*nm*): **creusement du déficit** français des échanges de marchandises (*increasing deficit*)

creuser (*vt*): ceci contribue à **creuser** davantage les inégalités entre Français (*increase, accentuate*); la Sécurité sociale **creuse son déficit** (*go further into the red*); SEE ALSO **écart**

creux, creuse (*adj/nm*): octobre à décembre, les **mois creux** de l'année (*slack months*); une bonne année, puis le **creux** de 1993 (*slack period*)

criant, -e (*adj*): les carences dans ce domaine apparaissent **criantes** (*flagrant*)

crier (*vt*): SEE **haro**

crime (*nm*): les **crimes** sont des infractions graves (*crime, [criminal] offence*); plus d'un tiers de l'ensemble des **crimes et délits** (*offences*); SEE ALSO **banalisation, commission, lieu**

criminalité (*nf*): on a constaté depuis une **baisse de la criminalité** (*fall in the crime rate*); le succès du gouvernement dans la lutte contre la **petite criminalité** (*petty crime; small crimes*); SEE ALSO **fléchissement, montant, répression**

criminel, -elle (*adj/nm,f*): lors du procès des **criminels de guerre** (*war criminal*); un projet de loi introduisant un appel **en matière criminelle** (*in criminal cases*); SEE ALSO **procès, réclusion**

crise (*nf*): la **crise** qui secoue la majorité (*crisis*); une **crise de confiance** en l'avenir (*crisis of confidence*); chacun a ressenti les effets de la **crise** dans sa vie quotidienne (*[economic] crisis, slump*); hausse des prix, **crise du logement** (*housing shortage*); SEE ALSO **dénouement, endiguer, frais**

crispation (*nf*): traiter ce dossier sans **crispations** inutiles (*conflict, tension*); malgré la **crispation dogmatique** de ce gouvernement (*inflexibility, unbending attitude*)

crisper [se] (*vpr*): ces dernières semaines, les **relations se sont crispées** (*tension has mounted between them*)

croissance (*nf*): globalement la **croissance** se maintient (*growth*); les **entreprises à forte croissance** semblent à l'abri de la crise (*growth industries*); des difficultés nées de la **croissance urbaine** (*urban growth/development*); une très forte **croissance démographique** (*population growth*); SEE ALSO **laissé-pour-compte, prévaloir, tirer**

croissant, -e (*adj*): l'écart **croissant** entre riches et pauvres (*growing, increasing*); à cause des **besoins croissants** en sources d'énergie (*growing need/requirement*)

croître (*vi*): la dette extérieure de l'Asie ne cesse de **croître**; la production **croît** à un rythme soutenu (*grow*)

croupion (*nm*): un **gouvernement croupion** dirigé par le chef de l'armée (*rump government*); la grande inconnue, c'est l'attitude de ce **parlement croupion** (*rump parliament*)

culpabilité (*nf*): une inculpation n'implique nullement la **culpabilité** de la personne inculpée (*guilt*)

cumul (*nm*): grâce au **cumul** de leurs salaires, ils touchent 15 000 francs par mois (*accumulated total*); grâce au **cumul des peines**, il passera 12 ans en prison (*adding together prison sentences*); le **cumul des mandats** locaux et nationaux (*multiple office-holding, plurality of offices*)

cumulé, -e (*adj*): des magazines spécialisés, dont le **tirage cumulé** se chiffre en centaines de milliers d'exemplaires (*accumulated/combined circulation*)

cumuler (*vt*): il devient député, poste qu'il **cumule** avec la mairie de Châteauroux (*hold concurrently/simultaneously*); le fonctionnaire ne peut **cumuler deux emplois** (*hold two jobs concurrently*)

cure (*nf*): la **cure d'austérité** se poursuit (*austerity policy/measures*)

cursus (*nm*): l'école propose des **cursus** de trois ou quatre ans (*course [of study]*); le **cursus scolaire** des candidats n'est pas déterminant (*course of school study*)

D

danger (*nm*): l'enfance **en danger** est devenue le domaine des départements (*in danger; at risk*); SEE ALSO **non-assistance**

date (*nf*): se donner une **date limite** pour aboutir; la **date butoir** pour la conclusion d'un accord (*deadline, final date*); la Chine et son antagonisme **de longue date** contre l'URSS (*long-standing*)

dauphin (*nm*): le président choisissait personnellement son **dauphin** (*heir apparent*)

débauchage (*nm*): le **débauchage** des quinze ouvriers alimente la chronique locale (*laying-off; making redundant*)

débat (*nm*): SEE **houleux**

débaucher (*vt*): les entreprises ont tendance à **débaucher**; il a fallu **débaucher** du personnel fixe (*lay off staff, make staff redundant*)

débit (*nm*): réduire le **débit** du pétrole exporté par oléoduc (*flow, rate of flow*); la fermeture d'un grand nombre de **débits d'alcool** (*bar*); un timbre fiscal peut se procurer dans n'importe quel **débit de tabac** (*tobacconist*)

débiter (*vt*): créditer son compte et **débiter** celui de son créancier (*debit*); une machine qui peut **débiter** jusqu'à 60 stères de bois à l'heure (*deliver, turn out*)

débiteur, -trice (*adj/nm,f*): le compte de la société est **débiteur** de 50 000F (*overdrawn*); les quinze États les plus fortement **débiteurs** (*in debt*); lorsque le **débiteur** ne respecte pas ses engagements (*debtor*)

déblocage (*nm*): le **déblocage** de 500 000F et la création de deux postes d'enseignement (*unfreezing, release [of funds]*); le probable **déblocage de la crise serbe** (*end of the deadlock in Serbia*)

débloquer (*vt*): de part et d'autre, on veut **débloquer la négociation** (*get talks back on course*); **débloquer l'impasse** au Conseil de sécurité (*break the deadlock*); **débloquer les crédits** nécessaires (*release/make available funds*); le rectorat refuse de **débloquer des postes** (*create/finance new [teaching] posts*)

déboires (*nmpl*): connaître des **déboires** politiques (*set-back, disappointment*); l'idéologie libérale **connaît de sérieux déboires** (*experience a grave set-back*)

débordement (*nm*): le gouvernement craint des **débordements** lors de la manifestation paysanne (*disturbance, violence*); les pouvoirs publics craignent des **débordements violents** (*explosion of violence*)

débouché (*nm*): le Botswana, privé de tout **débouché** sur la mer (*outlet*); un **débouché** pour les armes soviétiques (*outlet, market*); les **débouchés des baccalauréats** (*career opening for person having passed the baccalauréat*)

déboucher (*vi*): [*fig*] ces négociations pourraient **déboucher sur** des coopérations solides (*lead to, result in*)

débouter (*vt*): dans 50% des cas, **le plaignant est débouté** (*the plaintiff's case is dismissed*); les **déboutés** du droit d'asile (*person whose application/appeal has been rejected*)

débrayage (*nm*): **débrayage** d'une heure hier à l'usine Peugeot (*stoppage; walkout*)

débrayer (*vi*): les ouvriers ont **débrayé** pour protester contre l'agression (*down tools, walk out*)

débridé, -e (*adj*): la menace d'un interventionnisme **débridé** (*unbridled, unfettered*)

deçà (*prep*): légèrement **en deçà** de ses objectifs pour l'année; les investissements engagés restent très **en deçà** des besoins (*below; less than, inferior to*)

décalage (*nm*): avec un **décalage** d'un an (*gap; delay*); **être en décalage** avec les vrais problèmes des Français (*be out of step/out of touch*); il y a six heures de **décalage horaire** avec la France (*difference with local time; time gap*)

décalé, -e (*adj*): être un peu **décalé par rapport avec l'opinion** (*out of step with public opinion*)

décennie (*nf*): 4 500 emplois ont disparu en une **décennie** (*period of ten years, decade*); lors des restructurations de la **décennie 90** (*the Nineties*)

décentralisation (*nf*): le débat sur la **décentralisation** (*devolution; decentralization of decision-taking responsibilities*)

décerner (*vt*): le titre d'ingénieur est **décerné** à l'issue de quatre années de formation (*award, confer*); SEE ALSO **satisfecit**

décharge (*nf*): supprimer les **décharges** sauvages (*dump, rubbish tip*); SEE ALSO **arguer, témoin**

décharger (*vt*): certaines firmes **sont déchargées** en partie de leurs impôts (*be exempt*); [se] (*vpr*): le département devra **se décharger** de certaines de ses fonctions sur les communes (*hand over, relinquish*)

déchet (*nm*): les usagers de **déchets recyclables** (*recyclable waste*); enterrer des **déchets nucléaires** (*nuclear waste*)

déchetterie (*nf*): une **déchetterie** où il est possible d'apporter tout ce qui est recyclable ou toxique (*waste collection centre*)

déchirer (*vt*): le Liban est **déchiré** depuis 1970 (*torn apart*); [se] (*vpr*): les Libanais **se déchirent** devant une opinion publique impuissante (*tear each other apart*)

déchoir (*vt*): la fiancée française d'un étranger est menacée d'**être déchue de ses droits civiques** (*be deprived of her civil rights*); le militant nationaliste **déchu de sa nationalité soviétique** (*stripped/deprived of his Soviet citizenship*)

déchu, -e (*adj*): le président **déchu** a été conduit à l'aéroport militaire (*deposed*)

décideur (*nm*): la rubrique économique, lue par tous les **décideurs**; les **décideurs** économiques de la région (*decision-maker*)

décision (*nf*): le tribunal **rendra sa décision** le 8 novembre (*give its ruling/verdict*); quelle que soit la **décision de justice**; il a fait appel de la **décision des juges** (*decision of the court*); disposer d'un réel **pouvoir de décision** (*decision-taking powers*); SEE ALSO **révoquer, surseoir**

décisionnel, -elle (*adj*): il faut repenser le système **décisionnel** concernant l'économie du pays (*decision-making*); SEE ALSO **organe**

déclaration (*nf*): remplir un formulaire de **déclaration de sinistre** (*insurance claim notification*); le montant de ses **déclarations fiscales** (*declaration of income*)

déclaré, -e (*adj*): beaucoup ont recours aux petits boulots **non déclarés** (*undeclared*)

déclarer (*vt*): il n'avait pas à **déclarer ses revenus** en France (*declare his income*); [se] (*vpr*): **un incendie s'est déclaré** hier en fin d'après-midi (*a fire broke out*)

déclenchement (*nm*): le **déclenchement** de la guerre civile (*outbreak*)

déclencher (*vt*): l'offensive a été **déclenchée** dès 8 heures du matin (*set off, trigger*); cette mesure a **déclenché un véritable tollé** (*provoke an outcry of protest*)

déclin (*nm*): la production industrielle **est en déclin** depuis le premier choc pétrolier de 1973 (*be in decline*)

décliner (*vt*): le président a **décliné** son invitation au sommet de Lyon (*decline, turn down*); refuser de **décliner son identité** (*give one's name*)

décloisonnement (*nm*): faire le pari du **décloisonnement** et de l'ouverture (*removal of barriers*)

décloisonner (*vt*): dans le but de **décloisonner les rapports** à l'intérieur de l'entreprise (*break down barriers*)

décollage (*nm*): [*fig*] le **décollage** de l'économie du Sud-Ouest (*take-off; getting off the ground*)

décoller (*vi*): sans apport massif de crédits, l'économie ne **décollera** pas (*get off the ground; take off*)

décommander (*vt*): la visite a été **décommandée** (*call off, cancel*); [se] (*vpr*): un empêchement l'a obligé à **se décommander** (*cancel a visit/ appearance*)

décomposer (*vt*): permettant de **décomposer** le prix du voyage (*break down, analyse*)

décomposition (*nf*): la **décomposition** de la société russe (*disintegration, breaking-up*); la **décomposition** des coûts d'exploitation de la société (*detailed breakdown*)

décompte (*nm*): selon un **décompte** arrêté dimanche (*count; calculation*); en attendant l'ultime **décompte des voix** (*counting of votes*)

décompter (*vt*): déduire ou **décompter** les voix frauduleuses (*subtract, deduct*)

déconcentration (*nf*): une plus grande **déconcentration** des services de l'emploi (*devolving, decentralizing*)

déconcentrer (*vt*): **déconcentrer** l'autorité gouvernementale (*devolve, decentralize*); la réorganisation des **services déconcentrés** de l'État (*decentralized public services*)

déconfiture (*nf*): la spectaculaire **déconfiture** du gouvernement (*defeat, rout*); se porter acquéreur d'une **entreprise en déconfiture** (*failed company*); rétablir une situation économique et sociale **en pleine déconfiture** (*catastrophic; hopeless*)

déconvenue (*nf*): une **déconvenue** pour le président socialiste (*disappointment; disaster*)

décote (*nf*): le titre étant coté à 68p, la **décote** atteint donc 28% (*fall in value/price*); le DMark **a subi une décote** de 16% par rapport au dollar (*has fallen in value*)

découpage (*nm*): procéder à un nouveau **découpage électoral** (*redrawing of constituency boundaries*)

découper (*vt*): **découper** un canton en trois circonscriptions électorales (*divide, cut up*)

découplage (*nm*): le **découplage** entre les États-Unis et l'Europe (*uncoupling, separation, divergence*)

découpler (*vt*): le danger de **découpler** ainsi les États-Unis de l'Europe (*detach*)

décousu, -e (*adj*): la politique africaine **décousue** pratiquée par le gouvernement (*incoherent*)

découvert (*nm*): il se trouve avec un **découvert bancaire** de 10 000F; le montant du **découvert** qui a été consenti (*bank overdraft*); (*adv*) son compte en banque est **à découvert** (*overdrawn*)

décret (*nm*): selon le **décret** paru vendredi au *Journal officiel* (*decree, edict, order*); le SMIC a été augmenté **par décret** sur décision du gouvernement (*by decree*); SEE ALSO **édicter**

décréter (*vt*): la décision de **décréter** un embargo sur les livraisons d'armes (*decree, order*); le président mexicain **décrète la trêve** (*call/order a cease-fire*); SEE ALSO **blocus**

décrispation (*nf*): un nouveau signe de la **décrispation Est-Ouest** (*improved East-West relations*)

décrisper (*vt*): leur libération va **décrisper la situation** (*ease/defuse the situation*); une France **décrispée** sur le plan politique et social (*less tense/conflict-ridden; more relaxed*)

décrochage (*nm*): assister à un **décrochage** international de l'industrie française (*falling behind; failure to keep up with*); le **décrochage** d'une partie de la population (*dropping-out*); le taux de **décrochage scolaire** (*dropping-out of the school system; persistent truancy*)

décrocher (*vt*): **décrocher un gros contrat** en Chine (*win a large order*); (*vi*): quand les salaires **décrochent de l'inflation** (*fail to keep up with inflation*); le PCF a **décroché de la société française** (*lose touch with the French people*)

décroître (*vi*): la ville de Paris a continué à voir sa population **décroître** (*decrease*)

décuplement (*nm*): le **décuplement** en dollars du prix du pétrole (*tenfold increase; great increase*)

décupler (*vt*): la crise eut pour effet de **décupler** le prix du brut (*increase/multiply tenfold*); (*vi*): la population de Lagos a **décuplé** en 30 ans (*increase tenfold*)

dédommagement (*nm*): condamné à verser 5 000F de **dédommagement** à chacun des locataires (*compensation, indemnity*)

dédommager (*vt*): **dédommager** partiellement les pieds-noirs de la perte de leurs biens (*compensate; indemnify*); pour **dédommager** le préjudice subi (*make compensation for*)

déductible (*adj*): les intérêts d'emprunt sont **déductibles de l'impôt** (*tax-deductible; deductible against tax*)

déduction (*nf*): la **déduction fiscale** d'une partie des cotisations syndicales (*deduction from taxable income*); SEE ALSO **bénéficier**

défaillance (*nf*): les **défaillances** du tissu industriel (*breakdown; collapse*); une **défaillance** du système de fermeture des portes (*failure, malfunctioning*); le nombre des **défaillances d'entreprises** a progressé de 10% (*company collapse/failure*)

défaillant, -e (*adj*): le nombre des **entreprises défaillantes** a progressé de 9% (*failed company/business*)

défaillir (*vi*): si la société venait à **défaillir** (*collapse, fold [company]*)

défalcation (*nf*): crédité de 1 000 voix d'avance, après **défalcation** des voix frauduleuses (*deduction*)

défalquer (*vt*): il a fallu **défalquer** les 2 000 voix suspectes (*deduct, subtract*)

défaut (*nm*): le **défaut** majeur de ces propositions, c'est leur coût (*fault, drawback*); être arrêté par la police pour **défaut de port de casque** (*failure to wear a helmet*); les exportateurs, assurés contre les **défauts de paiement** (*default on payment*); SEE ALSO **jurisprudence**

défavorable (*adj*): SEE **avis**

défavorisé, -e (*adj/nm,f*): dans les zones urbaines et rurales **défavorisées** (*poor; disadvantaged*); un plan d'action pour le logement des **personnes défavorisées** (*the underprivileged*)

défection (*nf*): la **défection** d'une partie de son électorat (*defection; desertion*); **faire défection** et demander le droit d'exil (*defect*)

défendeur, -eresse (*nm,f*): le **défendeur**, la personne contre laquelle est engagé un procès civil (*defendant*)

défendre [se] (*vpr*): **se défendre** d'être un néo-libéral (*deny*)

défense (*nf*): la **défense** a jusqu'au 19 novembre pour faire appel (*[counsel for] the defence*); une association de **défense des consommateurs** (*consumer protection/rights*); il est pour la **défense de fumer** dans les lieux publics (*ban on smoking*); SEE ALSO **budget, capacité, constituer, légitime**

défenseur (*nm*): les **défenseurs** des inculpés demandent la relaxe de leurs clients (*defence lawyer; counsel*); l'infatigable **défenseur** des droits de l'homme (*defender*)

déférer (*vt*): les parlementaires de l'opposition **déférent** la nouvelle loi au Conseil constitutionnel (*submit; refer*); 13 personnes ont été **déférées au parquet** (*refer for trial*); l'accusé a refusé de **déférer** à une citation à comparaître (*defer to; obey*)

défi (*nm*): les **défis** posés aux agriculteurs européens (*challenge*); SEE ALSO **relever**

défiance (*nf*): la cohabitation suscite la **défiance** de 47% des personnes interrogées (*distrust, hostility*); subir un **vote de défiance** à l'Assemblée (*vote of no confidence*)

déficit (*nm*): l'aggravation du **déficit extérieur** (*external trade deficit*); le **déficit d'exploitation** du groupe ne cesse de s'alourdir (*operating loss*); [*fig*] le problème du **déficit démocratique** (*absence/lack of democracy*); SEE ALSO **creusement, creuser**

déficitaire (*adj*): les comptes lourdement **déficitaires** de la société fin 1995 (*showing a deficit*); la société **est déficitaire** depuis 1990 (*is making a loss*); SEE ALSO **solde**

défilé (*nm*): en province, **défilés** spontanés et affrontements (*[protest] march*)

défiler (*vi*): lycéens et étudiants ont de nouveau **défilé** hier (*march [in protest]*)

défiscalisation (*nf*): la **défiscalisation** totale est un attrait certain de ces propositions (*exemption from tax*)

défiscaliser (*vt*): des rémunérations en partie **défiscalisées** et dispensées de charges sociales (*exempt from tax*)

défrayer (*vt*): la déconfiture de cette société a **défrayé la chronique** locale (*make the headlines; be in the news*)

défunt, -e (*adj/nm,f*): les héritiers du **défunt** PC hongrois (*defunct*)

dégagement (*nm*): les conséquences du **dégagement** jordanien de Cisjordanie (*withdrawal, disengagement*)

dégager (*vt*): la police a mis deux heures pour **dégager** les rues des manifestants (*clear*); la firme a enfin **dégagé un bénéfice** (*make a profit*); [se] (*vpr*): deux tendances **se dégagent** de l'étude de l'OCDE (*emerge; be revealed*); SEE ALSO **consensus**

dégât (*nm*): l'ampleur des **dégâts** (*damage, destruction*); la protection contre le **dégât des eaux** (*flooding; flood damage*); SEE ALSO **limiter, subir**

dégel (*nm*): [*fig*] le **dégel** dans les relations sino-soviétiques (*thaw, détente*)

dégradation (*nf*): les destructions et **dégradations** volontaires de biens privés (*material damage, destruction*); emploi industriel: la **dégradation** se poursuit (*deterioration*); la **dégradation de la situation** en Algérie (*worsening situation*)

dégradé, -e (*adj*): un climat social **dégradé** (*[which has] got worse/ deteriorated*)

dégrader (*vt*): **dégradant** la compétitivité des entreprises (*do damage to*); [se] (*vpr*): la situation commerciale commence à **se dégrader** (*worsen, deteriorate*)

dégraissage (*nm*): une vente massive d'actifs, et un **dégraissage des effectifs** (*slimming-down of staffing levels; laying-off of staff*)

dégraisser (*vt*): la firme doit **dégraisser** 1 000 postes supplémentaires (*cut back; shed [jobs]*); avec un appareil de production **dégraissé** (*leaner; slimmed down*)

degré (*nm*): franchir un nouveau **degré** dans l'escalade de la tension (*step*); la Cour de cassation, trop souvent considérée comme un troisième **degré** de juridiction (*tier*); le syndicat national des **enseignants du second degré** (*secondary school teachers*)

dégressif, -ive (*adj*): le montant sera **dégressif** dans le temps; trente mois à taux plein, puis douze mois à **taux dégressif** (*on a reducing scale*)

dégrèvement (*nm*): dans certains cas il y a des exonérations et des **dégrèvements [fiscaux]** (*tax relief*)

dégrever (*vt*): ces gains sont **dégrevés d'impôts** (*exempt from tax*)

dégringolade (*nf*): la **dégringolade** du marché (*rapid fall; slump*)

dégringoler (*vi*): sa cote de popularité a brutalement **dégringolé** (*fall sharply, slump*); les prix **dégringolent** (*fall sharply, tumble*)

déjouer (*vt*): il a dû **déjouer** plusieurs tentatives de coup d'état (*foil*)

délabrement (*nm*): compte tenu du **délabrement de l'économie** (*run-down/poor state of the economy*); le **délabrement urbain** partout présent dans ces villes du nord du pays (*urban blight/decay*)

délai (*nm*): avant l'expiration des **délais** fixés par les ravisseurs (*deadline*); il faut faire vite si l'on veut **tenir les délais** (*keep the deadline*); suspendre **sans délai** l'importation d'ivoire (*immediately, forthwith*); un **délai de réflexion** suffisant pour trouver un compromis (*time to think; period for thought*); respecter les **délais de livraison** (*delivery time*)

délégation (*nf*): envoyer une **délégation** auprès du ministre (*delegation*); décider de renoncer à sa **délégation** (*authority, mandate*); **agir par délégation** pour le président (*act as proxy*); refuser toute **délégation de souveraineté** (*handing over/delegation of sovereignty*)

délégué, -e (*adj/nm,f*): représentant syndical CGT et **délégué du personnel** (*workers' representative on works committee*); le **délégué syndical** a communiqué la décision patronale aux travailleurs (*union representative; shop steward [UK]*); SEE ALSO **ministre**

déléguer (*vt*): **déléguer** l'autorité parentale (*delegate*)

délibéré (*nm*): lors du **délibéré**, il a surtout été question du premier des deux chefs d'inculpation (*deliberation by a court*); le tribunal a **mis son jugement en délibéré** au 26 juin (*adjourn for further deliberation*)

délicatesse (*nf*): Elf Aquitaine **en délicatesse avec** les autorités nigérianes; **être en délicatesse avec** le fisc (*be in dispute with*)

délictueux, -euse (*adj*): la vente et l'importation du hachisch restent **délictueuses** (*a criminal offence*); on les soupçonnait fortement d'autres **activités délictueuses** (*criminal activities*)

délinquance (*nf*): la **délinquance** "quotidienne" a fait plus que doubler en 20 ans (*crime*); la **grande délinquance** a beaucoup décru (*serious crime*); une étude met en valeur l'importance de la **délinquance en col blanc** (*white-collar crime*)

délinquant, -e (*adj/nm,f*): durcir la répression contre les **jeunes délinquants** (*juvenile delinquent; young offender*); SEE ALSO **enfance, mineur**

déliquescence (*nf*): une nation **en pleine déliquescence** (*in rapid decline*)

délit (*nm*): coupable du **délit** de recel (*offence, misdemeanour*); dans le cas d'un **délit mineur** (*summary offence*); l'avortement n'est plus un **délit sanctionné par les tribunaux** (*indictable offence*); un automobiliste coupable du **délit de fuite** (*failure to report an accident; hit-and-run offence*); purger une peine de prison pour **délit de presse** (*violation of laws governing the press*); la COB enquête pour décider s'il y a eu **délit d'initié** (*insider dealing*); SEE ALSO **opinion**

délivrance (*nf*): la **délivrance** de plein droit d'une carte de séjour (*issue*); ces études aboutissent à la **délivrance d'un diplôme** (*award of a diploma*)

délivrer (*vt*): le pouvoir de **délivrer** les permis de construire (*grant, issue*); une centaine d'Africains **se verront délivrer un titre de séjour** (*will be granted residence permits*); le collège ne **délivre** aucun diplôme (*award*)

délocalisation (*nf*): la **délocalisation** des unités de production dans des pays à bas salaires (*relocation; transfer*); la **délocalisation des capitaux** américains au Brésil (*exporting capital/investment*)

délocaliser (*vt*): les industriels qui **délocalisent** leur production hors Hexagone (*relocate; transfer*); [se] (*vpr*): les entreprises qui désirent **se délocaliser en province** (*transfer operations to the provinces*)

demande (*nf*): la **demande** est largement supérieure à l'offre (*demand*); l'offre n'arrive pas à **rattraper la demande** (*catch up with demand*); un quart du taux de croissance était expliqué par la **demande intérieure** (*domestic demand*); SEE ALSO **approvisionner, gonflement**

demandeur, -eresse (*nm,f*): le **demandeur** a obtenu gain de cause (*plaintiff; complainant*)

demandeur, -euse (*nm,f*): les **demandeurs d'emploi** représentent 15% de la population active (*job-seeker, person looking for work*); le **demandeur d'asile** se verra retirer son passeport (*asylum seeker*)

démantèlement (*nm*): procéder au **démantèlement des droits de douane** prévu par le traité (*removal of customs duties*)

démanteler (*vt*): il est question de **démanteler** le monopole public de l'électricité (*dismantle*); Bruxelles: trafic de drogue **démantelé** (*break up*)

démarchage (*nm*): **faire du démarchage** pour vendre des contrats d'assurance-vie (*do door-to-door selling*)

démarche (*nf*): multiplier les **démarches** pour sauvegarder la paix (*move, initiative*); leur **démarche** consiste à faire élire un Québécois à la tête du Canada (*policy, strategy*); les **démarches [administratives]** à accomplir sont les mêmes (*formalities*)

démarcher (*vt*): il **démarche** systématiquement les sociétés déjà implantées en Europe (*canvass; make approaches to*)

démarcheur, -euse (*nm,f*): se méfier des **démarcheurs** peu scrupuleux (*door-to-door salesperson; canvasser*)

démarrage (*nm*): [*fig*] la campagne électorale a connu un **démarrage** hésitànt (*start, beginning*)

démarrer (*vt*): [*fig*] **démarrer une affaire** avec très peu d'argent; (*vi*): celui qui veut **démarrer en affaires** (*set up in business*)

démêlé (*nm*): les **démêlés** publics de Pékin et de Londres à propos de Hongkong (*wrangle, dispute*)

démenti (*nm*): **apporter un démenti** aux rumeurs de désunion (*deny*)

démentir (*vt*): Pékin **dément** la préparation d'une attaque contre Taïwan (*deny*); [se] (*vpr*): un boom de la consommation qui **ne se dément pas** (*continue unabated*)

démettre (*vt*): le roi a **démis** son ministre **de ses fonctions** (*sack, dismiss, remove from office*); [se] (*vpr*): les 12 élus **se sont démis** en bloc (*resign from office*)

demeure (*nf*): **mettre en demeure** les autorités de se prononcer sans délai (*instruct, order*); recevoir une **mise en demeure** d'un créancier (*notice to pay*)

demeurer (*vi*): SEE **attente**

démission (*nf*): il a **donné sa démission** au Président (*resign, tender one's resignation*); [*fig*] la conséquence de la permissivité et de la **démission des parents** (*abdication of parental responsibility*); SEE ALSO **contraindre, lettre, remettre**

démissionnaire (*adj/nmf*): le premier ministre turc **démissionnaire** a sauvé sa coalition (*outgoing; having tendered his resignation*)

démissionner (*vi*): le chef du service de sécurité intérieure a **démissionné** (*tender one's resignation*); (*vt*): les ministre vient d'**être démissionné** par le Président (*be dismissed*)

démobiliser (*vt*): c'est un sale coup et qui va **démobiliser** le personnel (*demotivate*)

démuni, -e (*adj*): les femmes **démunies** et sans emploi (*impoverished, destitute*); les peuples les plus **démunis** (*deprived*); [*fig*] face à la fraude fiscale, la justice se trouve souvent **démunie** (*powerless*)

dénégation (*nf*): en dépit des **dénégations** de Matignon (*denial*)

déni (*nm*): le **déni de justice** fait aux Palestiniens (*denial of justice, injustice*)

denier (*nm*): la population la plus déshéritée, habituée à **vivre des deniers publics** (*live off the state/on public funds*)

dénier (*vt*): la Russie **dénie** à l'OTAN le droit de décider des raids aériens (*deny*)

dénombrer (*vt*): **on dénombre** plus de 20 différents taux de TVA; **on en dénombre** plus de deux millions en 1990 (*there are . . . altogether*)

dénomination (*nf*): la nouvelle entité prend comme **dénomination sociale** Toulouse Sanitaire (*trading name*)

dénouement (*nm*): le **dénouement** tragique de la prise d'otages (*outcome, conclusion*); le principal obstacle au **dénouement de la crise actuelle** (*solving the present crisis*)

dénouer (*vt*): réussir à **dénouer** un conflit (*resolve, end*); [se] (*vpr*): alors que la crise tarde à **se dénouer** (*come to an end; be resolved*)

dénoyautage (*nm*): le projet de loi sur le **dénoyautage** des entreprises privatisées (*breaking-up of a hard-core group of shareholders*)

dénoyauter (*vt*): le ministre de l'économie veut **dénoyauter** les entreprises privatisées par l'ancien gouvernement (*buy out hard-core shareholders*)

denrée (*nf*): une **denrée** très recherchée (*commodity*); le riz y reste la **denrée de base** (*staple food*)

dénuement (*nm*): pour ceux qui vivent dans le **dénuement le plus complet** (*utter deprivation*)

déontologie (*nf*): c'est une question de **déontologie** et de morale (*ethics*); un **code de déontologie** fixé par la profession (*code of professional ethics*)

déontologique (*adj*): cette solution poserait de graves problèmes **déontologiques** (*ethical, of professional ethics*)

départ (*nm*): demander le **départ** du président (*resignation*); il faudrait hâter les **départs à la retraite**, surtout en cas d'invalidité (*retirement*); le rythme des **départs en préretraite** se réduit (*early retirement*); une prime de 50 000F en cas de **départ volontaire** (*voluntary retirement, redundancy*); SEE ALSO **capital, incitatif, indemnité, prime**

département (*nm*): la Corse est formée de deux **départements** (*[administrative] department, one of the 95 main administrative divisions of France*)

dépassement (*nm*): les pénalités pour **dépassement** de quotas laitiers (*exceeding, overshooting*); le **dépassement budgétaire** est évalué à 10 milliards de francs (*overspending, overspend*)

dépasser (*vt*): la demande a largement **dépassé** l'offre (*exceed*); le médecin peut **dépasser ces tarifs** pour certains soins (*charge higher fees*)

dépêcher (*vt*): la décision de **dépêcher** dans la région des dragueurs et chasseurs de mines (*dispatch, send*)

dépénalisation (*nf*): le débat sur la **dépénalisation** des drogues douces (*decriminalizing*)

dépénaliser (*vt*): un projet de loi qui **dépénalise** la pratique de l'euthanasie; devrait-on **dépénaliser** l'usage des drogues douces? (*decriminalize*)

dépendance (*nf*): le développement de la toxicomanie et la **dépendance à l'égard de l'aide sociale** (*dependency culture*)

dépendant, -e (*adj*): des personnes âgées **dépendantes** (*dependent*); l'aide à domicile pour **personnes dépendantes** (*dependent persons*)

dépens (*nmpl*): acquitté, il a été **condamné aux dépens** (*order to pay costs of court action*)

dépense (*nf*): la maîtrise des **dépenses publiques** (*public expenditure*); le transfert aux collectivités locales de certaines **dépenses d'équipement** (*capital expenditure*); les **dépenses des ménages** se sont quelque peu augmentées (*domestic spending*); SEE ALSO **allouer**

dépensier, -ière (*adj*): les Français sont parmi les plus **dépensiers** pour leur santé (*spendthrift, extravagant*)

dépeuplement (*nm*): le **dépeuplement** dont souffrent la Creuse et la Lozère (*depopulation*)

dépeupler [se] (*vpr*): les départements du Centre **se dépeuplent** progressivement (*become depopulated*)

dépistage (*nm*): le **dépistage** du sida (*detection*)

dépister (*vt*): **dépister** des abus (*track down*)

déplacé, -e (*adj*): Liban: réintégration des **personnes déplacées**; quelques milliers de **déplacés** campent à la frontière iranienne (*displaced person*)

déplacement (*nm*): le **déplacement** annoncé du Premier ministre en Chine (*journey, trip*); il y a eu des **déplacements de voix** considérables (*voting/electoral swing*)

déplafonnement (*nm*): le projet de **déplafonnement** des allocations familiales (*removal of ceiling/upper limit*)

déplafonner (*vt*): en abaissant et en **déplafonnant** le taux des cotisations familiales (*remove ceiling/upper limit*)

déploiement (*nm*): le **déploiement** de forces onusiennes au Koweït (*deployment*)

déployer (*vt*): le contingent italien **déployé** en Bosnie (*deployed*); [se] (*vpr*): l'immense activité qui **se déploie** actuellement en océan Indien (*be deployed*); Total va **se déployer dans la chimie** (*move into the chemical industry*)

déposant (*nm*): un krach ne toucherait pas les **petits déposants** (*small depositor/saver*)

déposer (*vt*): une trentaine d'amendements ont été **déposés** (*table, put down [bill/motion]*); au moment de **déposer** officiellement sa candidature (*submit [application]*); la société vient de **déposer son bilan** (*file for bankruptcy; go into [voluntary] liquidation*); (*vi*): il refusa de **déposer** devant la commission enquêtant sur l'affaire (*testify, give evidence*); SEE ALSO **pourvoi, recours**

déposition (*nf*): tout au long du procès, il a maintenu sa **déposition** (*statement, evidence*); au lendemain de la **déposition** du président (*deposing*)

dépôt (*nm*): le **dépôt** est au maximum de 25% (*deposit*); la date limite de **dépôt des dossiers de candidature** (*submission of applications*); le **dépôt** des ordures ménagères sur la voie publique (*depositing*); en garde à vue **au dépôt** de la préfecture de police (*in the cells/in prison*); beaucoup de PME sont au bord du **dépôt de bilan** (*bankruptcy*); SEE ALSO **banque, compte, mandat**

dépouillement (*nm*): le **dépouillement** des dossiers prendra du temps (*analysis, scrutiny*); après le **dépouillement des suffrages** (*counting of votes*)

dépouiller (*vt*): le temps requis pour **dépouiller un scrutin** (*count the votes*)

dépoussiérer (*vt*): [*fig*] il est temps, en France, de **dépoussiérer** le concept de laïcité (*blow the cobwebs from, bring up to date*)

dépression (*nf*): la **dépression** du marché automobile; la récession prend des allures de **dépression** (*depression, slump*)

déprime (*nf*): la Bourse a eu un nouvel accès de **déprime** mercredi (*gloom; depressed trading conditions*); le boom économique, sur fond de **déprime du prix du pétrole** (*fall in oil prices*)

déprimé, -e (*adj*): une activité économique **déprimée** et une forte dégradation de l'emploi (*depressed*)

déprimer (*vt*): le nouveau reflux du dollar a **déprimé** le franc (*depress, force down*); (*vi*): le yen s'effondre, la bourse **déprime** (*slump; be depressed*)

députation (*nf*): candidat à la **députation** (*post of deputy; having a seat in the French National Assembly*)

député, -e (*nm,f*): **député** socialiste et président du conseil général (*deputy, member of the French National Assembly*); membre de la SFIO, et **député-maire** de Marseille (*deputy and mayor*); see also **non-inscrit**, **suppléance**

dérapage (*nm*): il est vital qu'il n'y ait pas **dérapage de l'inflation** (*spiralling inflation*); on s'inquiète des **dérapages** que pourrait entraîner l'application de ce décret (*abuse, excess*)

déraper (*vi*): les prix ne **déraperont** pas l'an prochain (*soar, rise sharply*); [*fig*] la Nouvelle-Calédonie **dérape!** (*get/go out of control*)

déréglementation (*nf*): la **déréglementation** mondiale de la communication; la **déréglementation** du marché du travail (*decontrolling, deregulation*)

dérégulation (*nf*): la **dérégulation** ou la suppression du monopole exercé par les entreprises publiques (*deregulation*)

déréguler (*vt*): il faut libéraliser la formation des prix, il faut **déréguler** (*deregulate*)

dérisoire (*adj*): les **dérisoires** retraites des agriculteurs, commerçants et artisans (*derisory; absurdly low*)

dérive (*nf*): [*fig*] l'évolution des finances publiques, ou plutôt leur **dérive** (*drifting off course/out of control*); à gauche, on craint une possible **dérive centriste** du Parti socialiste (*drift to the centre*); pour empêcher une **dérive terroriste** de l'islamisme (*drift towards terrorism*)

dérobade (*nf*): la **dérobade** du gouvernement éclaire les relations du pouvoir et des milieux financiers (*equivocation, evasion*)

dérober (*vt*): coupable d'avoir **dérobé** des objets de valeur (*steal, remove*); [se] (*vpr*): tenter de **se dérober à la conscription** (*avoid/evade conscription*); see also **butin**

dérogation (*nf*): l'octroi d'une **dérogation** à la fermeture de dimanche (*exemption, dispensation*); on l'a autorisé, **par dérogation spéciale**, à consulter les archives privées (*by special dispensation*)

dérogatoire (*adj*): le **régime dérogatoire** actuel est supprimé (*exceptional regime/arrangements*)

déroger (*vi*): ce serait **déroger à la règle établie** (*depart from custom/ established practice*); le scrutin d'aujourd'hui **ne dérogera pas à la règle** (*will be no exception*)

déroulement (*nm*): le **déroulement** de l'enquête (*progress, development*); gêner les **déroulements de carrière** (*career development*); établir formellement **le déroulement des faits** (*the facts; the sequence of events*)

dérouler [se] (*vpr*): les négociations de paix qui **se déroulent** à Genève; des affrontements **se sont déroulés** à Beyrouth (*take place*)

déroute (*nf*): une humiliante **déroute** pour le parti au pouvoir (*defeat, reverse*); les conservateurs **subissent une véritable déroute** (*suffer a heavy defeat*)

désaccord (*nm*): **désaccord** sur l'avenir politique de la communauté (*disagreement*); les deux pays sont **en plein désaccord** à ce sujet (*in total disagreement*)

désaffecté, -e (*adj*): disposer d'un ancien atelier **désaffecté**; une mine à ciel ouvert **désaffectée** (*disused, abandoned*)

désaffection (*nf*): la **désaffection** de l'opinion américaine envers l'OTAN (*disaffection, loss of interest*); la **désaffection** qui menace le Parti conservateur (*loss of favour; unpopularity*)

désarmer (*vi*): le refus de l'IRA de **désarmer** (*lay down arms; give up weapons*); [*fig*] les opposants **ne désarment pas** (*do not give up the fight*); l'opposition des syndicats **ne désarme pas** (*is unrelenting*)

désarroi (*nm*): après le sommet raté, c'est le **désarroi** dans le camp occidental (*disarray; confusion*)

désaveu, *pl* **-x** (*nm*): le **désaveu** de sa politique par le peuple (*rejection*); pour le Président, le **désaveu** est cinglant (*rebuff*)

désavouer (*vt*): le ministre, **désavoué** par son parti, a été acculé à la démission (*disown; repudiate*)

désenclavement (*nm*): le **désenclavement** de la façade maritime, avec le projet autoroutier (*opening up*); sans **désenclavement routier**, plus d'investissements! (*improved road access*)

désenclaver (*vt*): se battre pour **désenclaver** la capitale de la Picardie (*open up; make less isolated*)

désendetter (*vt*): soucieux de **désendetter** l'État, le ministre maintient le cap choisi par son prédécesseur (*get out of debt*)

désengagement (*nm*): un **désengagement** total de Moscou sur la scène internationale (*withdrawal, retreat*)

désengager [se] (*vpr*): le gouvernement a décidé de **se désengager** de l'opération; AEG entend **se désengager** entièrement de l'électronique (*withdraw*)

déséquilibre (*nm*): corriger les grands **déséquilibres** structurels (*imbalance*); l'apparition d'un nouveau **déséquilibre** au centre de l'Europe (*instability*)

désertification (*nf*): un département agricole **en voie de désertification** (*losing population*); les problèmes liés à la **désertification rurale** en France (*population drain; rural depopulation*)

désertifier [se] (*vpr*): l'espace rural continue à **se désertifier** (*become depopulated*)

77

désescalade (*nf*): Londres-Pékin: la **désescalade** (*reduction of tension*); la poursuite de la **désescalade** des taux d'intérêt (*fall, reduction*)

désétatiser (*vt*): partout on cherche à **désétatiser** un secteur public tentaculaire (*denationalize; remove from state control*)

déshérité, -e (*adj/nm,f*): les problèmes dans les banlieues **déshéritées** (*underprivileged, deprived*); les **déshérités**, les plus durement touchés par la crise (*the underprivileged, the have-nots*)

désignation (*nf*): la **désignation** d'un successeur (*appointment*); l'organisation de primaires pour la **désignation** d'un candidat unique (*nomination; selection*)

désigner (*vt*): dimanche, les électeurs vont **désigner** leurs députés (*choose, vote for*)

désistement (*nm*): peu de **désistements**, beaucoup de candidats se maintiennent (*withdrawal in favour of a better placed candidate*)

désister [se] (*vpr*): le candidat socialiste **s'était désisté** en faveur du communiste (*withdraw, stand down*)

désobéissance (*nf*): l'opposition appelle à la **désobéissance civile** (*civil disobedience*)

désolidariser [se] (*vpr*): la classe politique **s'est désolidarisée** du président colombien (*dissociate oneself; withdraw one's support*)

dessaisir (*vt*): **dessaisir un juge** pour incompétence (*remove a judge from a case*); [se] (*vpr*): **se dessaisir de ses fonctions** d'adjoint au maire (*resign/ relinquish office*)

dessaisissement (*nm*): le **dessaisissement** de l'État au profit d'autres niveaux de pouvoir (*taking/removal of power*); son avocat demande et obtient le **dessaisissement du juge** (*removal of a judge [from a case]*)

desserte (*nf*): améliorer la **desserte** du site par les transports en commun (*service [esp. by public transport]*); Swissair suspend la **desserte d'Alger** (*Algiers route, [air] service to Algiers*); le problème de la **desserte autoroutière** vers Paris (*motorway link*)

desservir (*vt*): le port de Dunkerque **dessert** tout le nord-ouest du continent européen (*serve*)

dessous (*nm*): les **dessous** de la guerre entre service secret et gouvernement (*hidden aspect, shady side*); [*fig*] admettre des [versements de] **dessous-de-table** à des partis politiques (*back-hander, under-the-counter payment*)

dessus (*nm*): l'armée du gouvernement **reprend le dessus** (*regain the upper hand*)

destituer (*vt*): les Républicains allemands **destituent** leur président (*dismiss*); le Congrès américain peut **destituer** le Président (*depose*)

destitution (*nf*): il protesta contre la **destitution** du gouvernement (*dismissal*); la **destitution** du président brésilien (*deposing, removal from office*)

désuni, -e (*adj*): SEE **famille**

détaché, -e (*adj*): le personnel français **détaché** à l'étranger (*on secondment; on temporary assignment*)

détacher (*vt*): être **détaché** à Athènes après la guerre (*be seconded*)

détail (*nm*): dans le **commerce de détail** l'emploi reste un gros point noir (*retail sector; retailing*); SEE ALSO **prix**

détaillant, -e (*nm,f*): les **détaillants** vont répercuter cette hausse sur le consommateur (*retailer*)

détaxe (*nf*): **détaxe** sur le prix imposé pour livres scolaires (*removal/reduction of tax*)

détaxer (*vt*): l'État peut **détaxer** la partie du revenu consacrée à l'épargne (*reduce/abolish tax on*)

détenir (*vt*): l'État **détient** 45% du capital de la firme (*hold, possess*); la police pourra **détenir** tout suspect pendant une durée de sept jours (*detain*)

détente (*nf*): la **détente** entre les deux super-puissances (*detente, improvement in relations*); la **détente des taux d'intérêt** se poursuit à Paris (*fall in interest rates*)

détenteur, -trice (*nm,f*): les **détenteurs** d'un passeport britannique (*holder*); **détenteur** des plus vastes réserves de pétrole (*possessor of*)

détention (*nf*): une tentative de vol de voiture et la **détention** de faux papiers (*being in possession of*); coupable de **détention illégale d'armes** (*unlawful possession of arms*); sa **détention** n'a duré que six mois (*detention; imprisonment*); il avait effectué plus de quatre ans de **détention provisoire** (*custody [pending trial]*); SEE ALSO **ordonnance**

détenu, -e (*adj/nm,f*): le nombre de **détenus** le 1er juillet s'élevait à 50 000 personnes (*prisoner, prison inmate*)

déterminant, -e (*adj*): cette victoire, **déterminante** pour l'avenir du parti (*crucial, decisive*); un témoignage qui pourrait **s'avérer déterminant** (*prove decisive*)

déterminé, -e (*adj*): SEE **contrat**

détournement (*nm*): une affaire de **détournement** de subventions municipales (*misuse of funds, embezzlement*); la nouvelle du **détournement de l'avion** (*hijacking*); inculpé de **détournement de mineur** (*abduction of a minor; corruption of a minor*)

détourner (*vt*): accusé d'avoir **détourné** des fonds qu'il avait fait voter en conseil municipal (*embezzle*)

dette (*nf*): la **dette extérieure** de l'Asie ne cesse de croître (*foreign debt*)

dévalorisation (*nf*): la progression du nombre des enseignants a facilité la **dévalorisation** de leur traitement (*devaluation; depreciation*)

dévaloriser [se] (*vpr*): le métier d'enseignant **se dévalorise** au fil des réformes (*lose prestige; be devalued*)

devancer (*vt*): le maire, **devancé** au premier tour, se retira en faveur du socialiste (*head, lead*); certains jeunes Français **devancent l'appel** dès dix-huit ans (*enlist before draft/call-up*)

déviance (*nf*): l'homosexualité était considérée comme une **déviance** (*deviant behaviour*)

déviant, -e (*adj*): réduire les comportements **déviants** (*deviant*)

déviation (*nf*): les travaux de la future **déviation** de Châteaudun ont débuté (*bypass*)

devis (*nm*): il demanda un **devis** pour la réfection de la maison (*estimate*); faire établir un **devis** pour les travaux (*estimate, quote*)

devise (*nf*): Travail, Famille, Patrie: la **devise** de Vichy (*motto, slogan*); la **devise** américaine, le billet vert, est très demandée en ce moment (*currency*)

devoir (*nm*): les fonctionnaires, statutairement tenus par un **devoir de réserve** (*duty of confidentiality*)

dévolu, -e (*adj*): les nouvelles compétences qui **sont dévolues** à la région (*fall to; devolve upon*)

dévolution (*nf*): des **dévolutions** successives de souveraineté au profit d'institutions internationales (*devolution, transfer*)

dialogue (*nm*): cette lettre poursuit le **dialogue de sourds** entamé avec le PS (*dialogue of the deaf*); SEE ALSO **approfondissement, renouer**

dialoguer (*vi*): l'opposition s'est déclarée prête à **dialoguer** avec le gouvernement (*have talks/discussions*)

diffamation (*nf*): porter plainte pour **diffamation** (*slander; libel*); les **procès en diffamation** se multiplient en Grande-Bretagne (*libel action*); SEE ALSO **attaquer**

diffamatoire (*adj*): des propos **diffamatoires** et mensongers (*slanderous, defamatory; libellous*)

diffamer (*vt*): une personne qui s'estime **diffamée** peut attaquer la presse (*libel*)

différend (*nm*): avant sa démission et son éclatant **différend** avec le Premier ministre (*difference of opinion, disagreement*); ce **différend frontalier** est vieux de cinquante ans (*frontier dispute*)

différer (*vt*): la Belgique **diffère** sa décision sur l'achat de l'avion français (*defer, postpone*)

difficile (*adj*): SEE **annoncer, quartier**

difficulté (*nf*): ancien délégué à l'insertion des **jeunes en difficulté** (*children with behavioural problems*); regrouper dans la même classe des **élèves en difficulté** (*pupils with learning problems*); SEE ALSO **insertion**

diffuser (*vt*): son portrait a été **diffusé** dans tous les aéroports (*distribute; circulate*); selon un nouveau bilan **diffusé** hier (*publish, put out*); une émission **diffusée en direct** (*broadcast live*)

diffusion (*nf*): après la **diffusion** du communiqué (*broadcasting, putting out*); c'est la seconde **diffusion** qui a été la plus suivie (*broadcast*); le magazine, qui subit une **baisse de sa diffusion** (*fall in circulation*)

dilapidation (*nf*): la lutte contre la **dilapidation** des fonds publics (*waste, squandering*)

dilapider (*vt*): les contribuables ont le sentiment que l'État **dilapide** leurs deniers (*fritter away, squander*); l'Occident **dilapide son crédit de confiance** auprès des pays arabes (*endanger her good standing*)

diligenter (*vt*): l'ONU souhaite **diligenter une enquête** sur les massacres (*carry out an urgent enquiry*)

diminuer (*vt*): on propose de **diminuer les effectifs** dans l'usine de Caen (*cut back on staff/numbers*); (*vi*): l'activité devra **diminuer** d'autant l'an prochain (*slow down; decrease, fall*)

diminution (*nf*): tabler sur une **diminution** de l'impôt direct; le temps partiel et la **diminution** du temps de travail (*reduction, fall*)

diplomatie (*nf*): la récente évolution de la **diplomatie russe** (*Russian foreign policy*); SEE ALSO **chef**

diplomatique (*adj*): SEE **appui, ballet, corps, froid, rupture**

diplôme (*nm*): quitter l'école **sans diplôme** (*without qualifications*); **l'obtention d'un diplôme** reste une protection contre le chômage (*obtaining qualifications*); SEE ALSO **délivrance**

diplômé, -e (*adj/nm,f*): **diplômé** d'une grande école d'ingénieurs (*graduate*); les jeunes **diplômés** condamnés au chômage (*person with qualifications*); l'embauche des jeunes, **diplômés ou non**, à 80% du SMIC (*with or without qualifications*)

directeur, -trice (*adj/nm,f*): le **directeur** du quotidien *Le Monde* (*editor-in-chief*); le président et le **directeur général** ont été renouvelés (*managing director*); SEE ALSO **comité, conseil**

direction (*nf*): conserver la **direction** du parti (*leadership*); une rencontre entre **direction** et syndicats (*management*); avec le concours de la **Direction** des affaires culturelles (*section, department*); SEE ALSO **assurer, douane, équipement, surveillance**

directive (*nf*): Bruxelles prépare une **directive** bien plus souple que la législation française (*directive, instruction*); la **directive communautaire** sur les marchés publics (*[European] community directive*)

directoire (*nm*): l'établissement d'un **directoire** mondial en matière de sécurité (*directorate*); être nommé président du **directoire** (*directorate; board of directors*)

dirigeant, -e (*adj/nm*): deux **dirigeants** de la société ont été arrêtés (*director*); les **dirigeants** socialistes s'y sont opposés en bloc (*leadership; leader*); SEE ALSO **classe, instance**

diriger (*vt*): **diriger** une société industrielle (*manage, run*); celui qui **dirigeait** le pays jusqu'alors (*govern, rule*)

dirigiste (*adj*): un gouvernement, qu'il soit libéral ou **dirigiste** (*in favour of a planned economy*)

discours (*nm*): prononcer un **discours** devant l'ONU (*speech*); il **tenait un discours** bien plus ferme (*adopt a tone/attitude*); le **discours** d'extrême droite sur l'immigration (*rhetoric, discourse*); SEE ALSO **outrance**

discrimination (*nf*): abolir les **discriminations** en matière d'emploi (*discrimination*); lutter contre la **discrimination liée à l'âge** (*age discrimination*); l'élimination des **discriminations à l'encontre des femmes** (*discrimination against women*); l'absence de toute **discrimination fondée sur le sexe** (*sexual discrimination*)

discriminatoire (*adj*): des lois contre des **pratiques discriminatoires** (*discrimination, discriminatory practices*)

disette (*nf*): passer d'une situation de **disette** à l'autosuffisance (*scarcity; famine, food shortages*); la sécheresse a entraîné une **disette de légumes frais** (*shortage of fresh vegetables*); la **disette de logements** à vendre et à acheter (*shortage/scarcity of housing*)

dispendieux, -euse (*adj*): des programmes sociaux jugés **dispendieux** (*costly, extravagant*)

dispense (*nf*): bénéficier d'une **dispense** du service militaire (*exemption*); **accorder une dispense** pour des motifs graves (*grant a dispensation*)

dispenser (*vt*): des journées de formation **dispensées** par les cadres de l'INSEE (*give, dispense*); 8% des jeunes gens **sont dispensés** du service national (*be exempted/excused*)

disponibilité (*nf*): de bonnes **disponibilités en logements** pour les employés (*availability of housing*); la firme possède plus de 30 milliards de **disponibilités** (*available funds, liquid assets*); tenu pour responsable, il a été **mis en disponibilité** (*suspend from duty*); demander sa **mise en disponibilité** (*leave of absence*)

disponible (*adj*): le **revenu disponible** par habitant, après impôts et cotisations sociales (*disposable income*)

disposer (*vt*): ce dernier **dispose de 15 jours pour former un gouvernement** (*has two weeks to form a government*); il affirme **le droit des peuples à disposer d'eux-mêmes** (*the right of nations to self-determination*)

dispositif (*nm*): le gouvernement approuve deux améliorations au **dispositif** actuel (*scheme*); la France renforce son **dispositif naval** dans cette zone (*naval deployment/force*); au milieu d'un impressionnant **dispositif de sécurité** (*security operation*)

disposition (*nf*): le Conseil constitutionnel annule deux **dispositions** de la loi des finances (*clause*); la police va **prendre les dispositions nécessaires** (*take all necessary measures*); des locaux **mis à disposition** par la municipalité (*made available; provided*); la **mise à disposition** de personnel en nombre suffisant (*provision, supply*)

disputer (*vt*): Belfort **dispute** à Besançon le monopole universitaire (*compete/fight over; vie for*); [se] (*vpr*): le Cachemire, territoire que **se disputent** le Pakistan et l'Inde; **se disputer** un marché très réduit (*contest, compete for*)

dissension (*nf*): le projet suscite des **dissensions profondes** au sein du cabinet (*considerable differences of opinion*)

dissidence (*nf*): l'Église américaine est au bord de la **dissidence** (*rebellion, breakaway*); les dirigeants de l'ancienne **dissidence** communiste (*breakaway movement*)

dissident, -e (*adj/nm,f*): les rénovateurs communistes **dissidents** du PCF (*breakaway, dissident*); le plus connu des **dissidents** chinois (*dissident*)

dissolution (*nf*): la **dissolution** de l'Assemblée nationale (*dissolving*); dans des situations de **dissolution de la cellule familiale** (*breaking-up/break-up of the family unit*)

dissoudre (*vt*): les conseils locaux ont été **dissous** par la junte en 1993 (*dissolve; break up*); le nouveau Président **dissoudra le Parlement** (*dissolve Parliament*)

dissuasif, -ive (*adj*): la peine de mort **est dissuasive** pour les terroristes (*is a deterrent*); en vente **à un prix dissuasif** (*at a prohibitive price*)

dissuasion (*nf*): le facteur de **dissuasion** le plus important (*dissuasion; deterrence*); le refus de la **dissuasion nucléaire** (*nuclear deterrent*)

distance (*nf*): les partis de l'opposition désirent **prendre leurs distances** par rapport aux indépendantistes (*dissociate/distance oneself*)

distancer (*vt*): les communistes ont largement **distancé** les socialistes (*lead; outstrip*)

district (*nm*): le regroupement de petites communes en **districts** (*syndicate [of small communes]*); dans le **district urbain** du pays de Montbéliard (*urban district*)

divers, -e (*adj*): les listes **divers droite** et FN ont fusionné (*mixed Right-wing*); SEE ALSO **fait divers**

diversification (*nf*): quelques initiatives de **diversification** industrielle ont été prises à temps (*diversification*); grâce à la **diversification des cultures** (*growing new crops*)

diversifier (*vt*): la crise conduit la région Champagne-Ardennes à **diversifier ses activités** (*diversify*); [se] (*vpr*): il a fait fortune dans l'immobilier, et **s'est diversifié** dans l'agro-alimentaire (*diversify; branch out*)

dividende (*nm*): payer aux actionnaires un **dividende** confortable (*share dividend*); le **dividende intérimaire** a été fixé à 76 pence (*interim dividend*)

doléance (*nf*): les **doléances** exprimées par les jeunes (*grievance*); SEE ALSO **cahier**

domicile (*nm*): l'emploi d'une **personne à domicile** donne droit à une réduction d'impôt (*domestic help*); le nombre de **sans domicile fixe [SDF]** s'accroît (*person of no fixed abode*); SEE ALSO **aide, élire, inviolabilité, porter, réintégrer, violation**

domicilier (*vi*): il **s'était fait domicilier** à Paris (*give as one's address [for official purposes]*)

dominical, -e, *pl* **-aux** (*adj*): ce quotidien à grand tirage, dans son **édition dominicale** (*Sunday edition*); autoriser le **commerce dominical** (*Sunday trading*); SEE ALSO **ouverture, repos**

dommage (*nm*): l'indemnisation des **dommages** subis (*damage, prejudice*); les installations portuaires ont subi de **graves dommages** (*serious/heavy damage*); une assurance qui vous permet de vous assurer contre de nombreux **dommages** (*risk*); il demande 10 000 francs de **dommages et intérêts** (*damages*)

dommageable (*adj*): ce blocage est **dommageable** à l'ensemble de l'économie mondiale (*prejudicial, harmful*)

DOM-TOM (*nmpl*): les départements et territoires d'outre-mer **[DOM-TOM]** dépendent d'un ministre délégué auprès du Premier ministre (*French overseas departments and territories*)

don (*nm*): des **dons** à des organismes agréés (*gift, donation*); les **dons** des entreprises aux partis politiques (*[political] donation*)

donation (*nf*): signer une **donation** en usufruit de tous ses biens (*settlement*)

donne (*nf*): [*fig*] la poussée des écologistes change **la donne politique** (*the balance of political power*); cette **nouvelle donne diplomatique** imposée par le conflit en Bosnie (*new diplomatic situation*)

donnée (*nf*): ceci complique un peu plus les **données** du conflit israélo-arabe (*facts; situation*); copier des **données informatiques** (*computer data*); le chômage a augmenté de 0,7% **en données corrigées des variations saisonnières** (*according to seasonally adjusted figures*); SEE ALSO **banque, base**

donner (*vt*): les sondages **donnent un net avantage aux Libéraux** (*give the Liberals a clear lead*); **être donné largement battu** par tous les sondages (*be expected to lose heavily*); SEE ALSO **lecture**

doper (*vt*): [*fig*] les exportations japonaises **dopées** par la baisse du yen (*make artificially high; boost*)

dos (*nm*): ne pas **se mettre à dos** une partie de ses sympathisants (*antagonize, make an enemy of*); les jeunes **tournent le dos** aux activités syndicales (*reject; turn one's back on*)

dossier (*nm*): 12 000 **dossiers** ont été déposés par des demandeurs d'emploi (*application*); les **dossiers d'inscription** sont à retirer jusqu'au 13 mai (*application/registration form*); les syndicats restent divisés sur les **grands dossiers sociaux** (*major social questions*); SEE ALSO **clore, instruction, instruire, placard, retrait, sensible**

dotation (*nf*): la faiblesse de la **dotation** de la Comédie-Française (*grant, subsidy*); la **dotation globale de fonctionnement** que l'État verse aux collectivités locales (*grant from central to local government*)

doter (*vt*): une Hongkong **dotée d'institutions démocratiques** (*democratically administered*); les missiles **dotés de** charges conventionnelles (*equipped with*); [se] (*vpr*): Amman veut **se doter** d'un réacteur nucléaire expérimental (*acquire, obtain*)

douane (*nf*): abolition progressive des **droits de douane** (*customs duties*); le rôle de la **direction des douanes** dans la lutte contre ce trafic (*Customs and Excise [UK]*); SEE ALSO **passage, préposé**

douanier, -ière (*adj/nm,f*): SEE **barrière, tarif**

double (*nm*): ses exportations **atteignent le double** de celles du Japon (*be double/twice as large*); deux armes dont on peut penser qu'elles **feront double emploi** (*be redundant; be surplus to requirements*); SEE ALSO **vocation**

doublement (*nm*): Washington annonce le **doublement** de son aide à l'Ukraine (*doubling*)

doubler (*vt*): les élèves qui **doublent** leurs classe de troisième (*repeat [a year]*); (*vi*): les exportations de produits finis ont **doublé** (*double*)

doute (*nm*): ces révélations **mettent en doute** les affirmations des autorités françaises (*cast doubt upon; challenge, question*); l'adoption du texte **ne semble pas faire de doute** (*seems assured*)

doyen, -enne (*nm,f*): le **doyen** de la nouvelle Assemblée (*most senior/oldest member*)

draconien, -ienne (*adj*): des **mesures draconiennes** de rétorsion furent prises (*very severe/draconian measures*)

drainage (*nm*): l'irrigation, le **drainage** et l'entretien des digues (*drainage*)

drainer (*vt*): [*fig*] les collectivités locales **drainent** 12% des revenus fiscaux (*syphon off*); les charges sociales **drainent** des sommes folles (*use up*)

drapeau, *pl* **-x** (*nm*): le Nicaragua, avec plus de 100 000 hommes **sous les drapeaux** (*doing military service*); SEE ALSO **appel**

drastique (*adj*): une diminution **drastique** des visas de sortie accordés aux juifs (*drastic*); le **drastique plan d'austérité** du ministre des Finances suédois (*drastic austerity measures*)

dresser (*vt*): SEE **procès-verbal**

droit (*nm*): l'Écosse a un **droit** distinct du droit anglais (*legal system; system of law*); le mouvement pour les **droits civiques** aux États-Unis (*civil rights*); l'ivresse publique, par exemple, **relève du droit commun** (*be a common-law offence*); empêcher l'exercice des **droits de la personne humaine** (*human rights*); manifester pour les **droits des femmes** [avortement, contraception, emploi] (*women's rights*); une infraction qui relève du **droit pénal** (*criminal law*); le **droit du travail** anglais ne prévoit pas de période d'essai (*labour/employment law*); la part de la succession qui revient **de droit** à ces héritiers (*as of right, rightfully*); être membre **de [plein] droit** de la commission (*ex-officio, as of right*); leurs produits d'exportation sont frappés de **droits** anti-dumping (*duty, tax*); SEE ALSO **allocation, ayant droit, chômeur, communautaire, douane, égalité, État, préemption, privation, règle, sol, succession, valoir, véto**

droit, -e (*adj/nf*): flattant les sensibilités **de droite** (*right-wing*); se réclamer de **la droite** conservatrice (*the Right [wing]*); SEE ALSO **basculement, divers, extrême, virer**

dumping (*nm*): l'assouplissement des **règles anti-dumping** (*anti-dumping laws*)

duplicata (*nm*): en aucun cas il ne sera délivré de **duplicata** (*[duplicate] copy*)

dur, -e (*adj/nm,f*): tous sauf les **durs** du parti (*hardliner; the hard core*); SEE ALSO **coup, grève, ligne, pur, tendance**

durcir (*vt*): la junte **durcit** sa politique de répression (*harden, intensify*); le Premier ministre **durcit ses positions** (*toughen his stance*); Pékin **durcit le ton** contre Taïwan (*take a harder line*); [se] (*vpr*): [*fig*] la révolte **se durcit** au fil des jours (*harden; gain strength*)

durcissement (*nm*): un **durcissement** de la politique monétaire américaine (*hardening*); il y eut un net **durcissement à la base** (*hardening of grass-roots opinion*)

durée (*nf*): la **durée** de la garantie (*duration, length*); la **durée de vie** moyenne de la femme (*life expectancy*); à la recherche d'un **poste salarié à temps plein et à durée indéterminée** (*full-time permanent position*); SEE ALSO **chômeur, contrat, hebdomadaire**

dysfonctionnement (*nm*): une table ronde sur le **dysfonctionnement** de l'économie corse (*dysfunction, malfunctioning*); il faut traquer les **dysfonctionnements** et les abus (*flaw, defect*)

E

eau, *pl* **-x** (*nf*): à la limite des **eaux territoriales françaises** (*French territorial waters*); les **eaux usées**, traitées dans des stations d'épuration (*waste water; effluent*); les **eaux ménagères** et les eaux d'origine industrielle (*waste [household] water*); SEE ALSO **adduction, dégât, évacuation, voie**

ébauche (*nf*): cette **ébauche** de relations diplomatiques entre les deux pays (*first steps/moves towards*); le projet d'autoroute **n'est qu'à l'état d'ébauche** (*is only at the drawing-board stage*)

ébranler (*vt*): une nouvelle affaire de corruption **ébranle** le pouvoir (*shake; weaken, undermine*); le parti **sort durement ébranlé** de ce scrutin (*emerge in a much weakened state*)

écart (*nm*): un accroissement de l'**écart des revenus** entre les riches et les pauvres (*wage differential/gap*); l'**écart de prix** peut aller du simple au double (*difference in price*); le moindre **écart de conduite** est lourdement sanctionné (*misdemeanour*); les deux hommes, **mis à l'écart** en 1989 (*sideline; sack*); des fautes sanctionnées par mutations ou **mises à l'écart** (*dismissal*); l'**écart s'est creusé** entre l'Est et l'Ouest (*the gap has widened*)

écarter (*vt*): cette décision visait à **écarter** un homme jugé dangereux (*exclude, eliminate*); une coalition **écartée du pouvoir** au bout d'un an (*remove from power*); la police **écarte l'hypothèse d'un meurtre** (*rule out murder*)

échange (*nm*): la bonne tenue des **échanges** avec le Japon (*trade, commerce*); le volume des **échanges** à la Bourse de Paris a doublé (*transaction*); SEE ALSO **barrière, libéralisation**

échanger [s'] (*vpr*): le Mark **s'échangeait** hier à 4,90F; plus de 10% des actions de la société **se sont échangées** hier (*change hands; be traded*)

échangeur (*nm*): un **échangeur** au cœur de l'agglomération lilloise (*road interchange*)

échantillon (*nm*): l'enquête portait sur un **échantillon** de 3 699 personnes (*sample; specimen*)

écharpe (*nf*): l'**écharpe tricolore** que porte le maire (*[mayor's] sash*); le maire sortant RPR a réussi à **garder son écharpe** (*be re-elected mayor*)

échauffourée (*nf*): à Paris hier, **échauffourées** au cours d'une manifestation de mineurs (*brawl, skirmish*)

échéance (*nf*): cette **échéance** va obliger les deux antagonistes à s'entendre (*deadline; due date*); incapable de faire face aux **échéances** d'une dette de 30 milliards de dollars (*repayment*); [*fig*] à la veille de l'**échéance électorale** de 1995 (*election/polling day*); un grand nombre de baux **parviennent à échéance** cette année (*mature; fall due*); son mandat **vient à échéance** fin décembre (*come to an end, terminate*); l'arrêté devrait entrer en vigueur **à brève échéance** (*soon, shortly*); SEE ALSO **comptable**

échéancier (*nm*): le programme se poursuit selon l'**échéancier** fixé (*timetable*); effectuer les remboursements selon l'**échéancier** prévu (*agreed schedule [of repayments]*)

échec (*nm*): les **échecs** régulièrement subis par les Travaillistes (*defeat*); le ministre a **fait échec à l'amendement socialiste** (*block/defeat the socialist amendment*); le mouvement anti-avortement **mis en échec** aux États-Unis (*foil; defeat*); la **mise en échec** de l'opération de commando (*foiling*); réduire l'**échec scolaire** (*academic failure; underperforming at school*); SEE ALSO **constat**

échelle (*nf*): à l'**échelle de l'entreprise** ou de l'établissement (*at company level*); l'influence de la France est ressentie à l'**échelle du globe** (*worldwide; on a global scale*); SEE ALSO **économie, fabriquer**

échelon (*nm*): on gravit les **échelons [hiérarchiques]** largement à l'ancienneté (*grade, rung on the [promotion] ladder*); des émissions locales, à l'**échelon des villes** (*at the urban/city level*)

échelonnement (*nm*): demander un **échelonnement de la dette** (*payment of a debt by instalments; spreading out of repayments*)

échelonner (*vt*): avoir la faculté d'**échelonner les paiements** (*pay by instalments*); [s'] (*vpr*): les versements peuvent **s'échelonner sur** plusieurs mois (*be spread over [a period of time]*)

échiquier (*nm*): [*fig*] notre influence **sur l'échiquier international** est en nette régression (*on the international scene*); une troisième force au centre de l'**échiquier politique** britannique (*political scene*); SEE ALSO **chancelier**

écho (*nm*): les critiques dont ce journal a **fait l'écho** (*report; repeat*)

échoir (*vi*): le délai de livraison vient d'**échoir** (*expire*); la présidence de la commission **échoit à un Anglais** (*fall to an Englishman*)

échouer (*vi*): une tentative de cessez-le-feu et de dialogue a **échoué** (*fail; come to nothing*); **échouer** à prendre le contrôle du conglomérat allemand (*fail, be unsuccessful*)

éclabousser (*vt*): face aux scandales qui **éclaboussent** son gouvernement (*tarnish/sully the good name of*)

éclaircir (*vt*): ses explications permettent d'**éclaircir la question** (*shed light on the matter*); le mystère a été enfin **éclairci** (*clear up, solve*)

éclaircissement (*nm*): l'**éclaircissement** du massacre se fait toujours attendre (*explanation*)

éclaté, -e (*adj*): un secteur très **éclaté** [81 000 salariés dans 350 entreprises] (*fragmented*)

éclatement (*nm*): l'**éclatement** d'une crise au sein du Parti communiste (*outbreak*); au moment de l'**éclatement** de la fédération yougoslave (*break-up, split-up*); les conflits parents-enfants et l'**éclatement des familles** (*break-up of the family unit*)

éclater (*vi*): avec la crise, de plus en plus de familles **éclatent** (*break up*); SEE ALSO **guerre**

école (*nf*): pour défendre l'**école libre** contre le gouvernement de gauche (*private-sector school; denominational schooling*); les défenseurs de l'**école privée** (*private school; independent education*); les partisans de l'**école publique** (*state educational sector*); SEE ALSO **laïc, mixité**

économie (*nf*): la recherche d'**économies d'échelle** (*economies of scale*); partisan de l'**économie libérale** (*free-market economy*); dans l'ex-URSS, l'**économie parallèle** est florissante (*unofficial/black economy*); SEE ALSO **assistance, fructifier, surchauffe**

économique (*adj*): SEE **éventuel, poumon**

économiquement (*adv*): on ne fait rien pour les **économiquement faibles** (*lower-income groups*)

écoper (*vt*): il a **écopé de six mois de mise à pied** (*get six months' suspension*)

écot (*nm*): verser son **écot** (*contribution, share [of bill]*)

écoulement (*nm*): pour l'**écoulement** de ses produits manufacturés (*selling, disposal*)

écouler (*vt*): avoir du mal à **écouler** sa production; **écouler** les invendus et les fins de série (*sell; dispose of*)

écoute (*nf*): des **écoutes téléphoniques** illégales opérées depuis 1983 (*telephone tapping*); SEE ALSO **indice**

écrasement (*nm*): depuis l'**écrasement** de l'insurrection communiste (*crushing*)

écraser (*vt*): la Commission européenne ne veut pas qu'on **écrase les prix** (*reduce prices drastically*); [s'] (*vpr*): touché par un missile, l'appareil **s'écrase** en flammes (*crash*)

écritures (*nfpl*): SEE **faux**

écrouer (*vt*): un policier et ses complices **écroués** pour extorsion de fonds (*imprison*)

écroulement (*nm*): la fatalité d'un **écroulement** du totalitarisme (*collapse*)

écrouler [s'] (*vpr*): Albanie, le dernier des régimes communistes à l'Est à **s'écrouler** (*collapse*)

édicter (*vt*): l'interdiction, **édictée** par Bruxelles, d'importer de la viande de bœuf (*decree*); le droit d'**édicter des décrets** pour s'attaquer à la crise (*enact/pass a decree*)

édulcorer (*vt*): réussir à **édulcorer** la résolution sur l'abandon des centrales nucléaires (*water down, tone down*)

effectif, -ive (*adj/nm*): sont prises en compte les périodes de **travail effectif** (*actual work*); les **effectifs** ont été réduits d'un tiers (*staffing levels; work force*); l'augmentation des **effectifs scolaires** (*number of pupils; pupil rolls*); SEE ALSO **dégraissage, diminuer, pléthorique**

effectuer (*vt*): il a **effectué** une étude approfondie auprès de 1 500 usagers (*carry out*); **effectuer** un raid dans les faubourgs de la ville (*carry out, execute*); [s'] (*vpr*): la rentrée **s'est effectuée** dans le calme (*take place*); SEE ALSO **préavis**

effondrement (*nm*): l'**effondrement** de plusieurs bâtiments publics; l'**effondrement** de la monnaie italienne (*collapse*); l'**effondrement du marché** a surpris les spécialistes (*slump in the market*)

effondrer [s'] (*vpr*): des sociétés bien cotées ont vu leurs cours **s'effondrer** (*collapse*); depuis Noël, **le marché s'est effondré** (*the bottom has fallen out of the market*)

effraction (*nf*): il est **entré par effraction** dans la nuit de jeudi à vendredi (*break into premises*); en effet 75% des chéquiers volés le sont par **effraction de véhicules** (*breaking into a vehicle*); SEE ALSO **vol**

effritement (*nm*): l'**effritement** de nombreuses monnaies par rapport au franc suisse (*erosion*); nouvel **effritement des voix socialistes** (*erosion of the Socialist vote*)

effriter [s'] (*vpr*): les monnaies européennes **se sont effritées** vis-à-vis du dollar (*lose value*)

effusion (*nf*): une prise de pouvoir **sans effusion de sang** (*without bloodshed*)

égal, -e, *pl* **-aux** (*adj*): il faut que la justice soit **égale pour tous** (*equal/the same for all*); SEE ALSO **chance**

égalitaire (*adj*): la Suède, royaume réputé si **égalitaire** (*egalitarian*)

égalité (*nf*): la justice sociale, et l'**égalité des chances** (*equal opportunity*); le combat pour l'**égalité des droits** (*equal rights*); les femmes demandent l'**égalité des salaires** (*equal pay*); la pleine **égalité d'accès au travail** entre femmes et hommes (*equal employment opportunities*)

égide (*nf*): un cessez-le-feu **sous l'égide syrienne** (*under the aegis/control of Syria*)

égratigner (*vt*): [*fig*] les administrateurs, dans leur rapport, **égratignent** les syndicats comme la direction (*criticize; have a dig at*)

élargi, -e (*adj*): Bercy pourrait disposer de **pouvoirs élargis** (*wider powers*)

élargir (*vt*): on **élargit** les catégories d'étrangers bénéficiant de la carte de résident (*extend, widen*); **élargir** un détenu avant qu'il n'ait purgé la moitié de sa peine (*discharge, release from prison*); [s'] (*vpr*): dans une Europe appelée à **s'élargir** (*expand; become larger*)

élargissement (*nm*): un futur **élargissement** de l'UE à six pays de l'Est (*enlargement*); un **élargissement** de la gamme de peines fixées par la loi (*extension*); l'**élargissement**, puis l'expulsion, des trois hommes (*release, freeing*)

électeur, -trice (*nm,f*): dimanche l'**électeur** français se rend aux urnes (*voter*); les **électeurs** font confiance à leur député (*electorate; constituents*); 2 708 **grands électeurs** se réunissent pour les sénatoriales (*[in France] member of restricted electoral college*); SEE ALSO **indécis**

électif, -ive (*adj*): conquérir son premier **mandat** électif; briguer des **fonctions électives** (*elected office*)

élection (*nf*): on annonce des **élections anticipées** pour le 11 juillet (*early elections*); son intention est de provoquer des **élections générales** (*general election*); SEE ALSO **annulation, arbitrer, cantonal, convoquer, issu, partiel, pluraliste, présidentiel, primaire, prud'homal**

électoral, -e, *pl* **-aux** (*adj*): SEE **assise, clientèle, corps, découpage, échéance, fichier, fief, fraude, liste, participation, période, plate-forme, redécoupage, tripotage**

électorat (*nm*): partir à la conquête de l'**électorat** (*electorate, voters*); ce sont les **électorats flottants** qui décident des élections (*floating voters*)

élément (*nm*): aucun **élément** n'a pu être retenu contre lui (*[piece of] evidence*); et pourtant des **éléments accablants** plaident contre eux (*damning evidence*)

élévation (*nf*): cette évolution, surtout due à l'**élévation** des taux d'imposition (*raising, putting up*); l'**élévation** générale du niveau scolaire (*rise*)

élevé, -e (*adj*): quatre fois **plus élevé** que la moyenne nationale (*higher*)

élever (*vt*): **élever des barrières douanières** contre les importations (*erect tariff barriers*); [s'] (*vpr*): le bilan des victimes **s'élevait** à 129 morts (*total, add up to*); les autorités **s'élèvent contre** les accusations de torture (*protest against*)

éligibilité (*nf*): accorder le droit de vote et d'**éligibilité** aux femmes (*eligibility*)

éligible (*adj*): le militaire est **éligible**, mais doit choisir entre sa fonction et son mandat (*eligible for election/office*); on lui a promis une **place d'éligible** sur la liste socialiste (*place on electoral list giving a realistic chance of election*)

élire (*vt*): **élire** un député (*elect*); **élire à bulletin secret** un nouveau comité central (*elect by secret ballot*); en 1992, il a **élu domicile** à Paris (*adopt as one's official address*)

élu, -e (*adj/nm,f*): une délégation d'**élus** lorrains (*elected member, deputy, representative*); SEE ALSO **vacation**

élucider (*vt*): huit affaires ont été **élucidées** par les services de police (*solve*); les faits étaient restés **non élucidés** pendant 20 ans (*unexplained; unsolved*)

Élysée (*nprm*): SEE **briguer**

élyséen, -éenne (*adj*): le Premier ministre porte ombrage aux desseins **élyséens**; soucieux de ménager les susceptibilités **élyséennes** (*[in France] from the Élysée Palace, presidential*)

emballage (*nm*): l'**emballage** peut constituer lui-même un moyen de publicité (*packaging; wrapping*); reprendre les **emballages vides** (*container [esp. bottle, can]*)

emballement (*nm*): l'économie donnait déjà des signes d'**emballement** (*going out of control*)

emballer [s'] (*vpr*): le crédit à la consommation risque de s'**emballer** (*rise steeply; shoot up*)

embargo (*nm*): en raison d'un **embargo à l'encontre de Tripoli** (*embargo against Tripoli*); Paris assouplit l'**embargo pétrolier** vis-à-vis de Téhéran (*oil embargo*)

embauche (*nf*): le projet initial prévoit l'**embauche** de 50 salariés (*employment, taking on labour*); le nombre des **embauches fermes** augmente sensiblement (*firm offer of employment*); SEE ALSO **entretien, frilosité, monopole, salaire**

embaucher (*vt*): les firmes recommencent à investir et à **embaucher** (*take on/recruit labour*); l'insertion ne se limite pas à **embaucher des chômeurs** (*offer jobs to the unemployed*)

embellie (*nf*): l'**embellie** provoquée par la baisse du prix du pétrole; après la courte **embellie** des premiers mois de 1996 (*temporary/short-lived improvement*)

émettre (*vt*): la chaîne nationale, seule à encore **émettre** (*broadcast*); les Postes **émettent** une nouvelle série de timbres commémoratifs (*issue*); **émettre un emprunt** d'un milliard de francs (*float a loan*); SEE ALSO **avis**

émeute (*nf*): les **émeutes** hier ont fait 18 morts (*riot, rioting*); lors des **émeutes urbaines** de l'été (*urban riots*)

émeutier, -ière (*nm,f*): le procès des **émeutiers** passionne l'opinion publique (*rioter*)

émission (*nf*): augmenter son capital par l'**émission de nouvelles actions** (*issue of new shares*); condamnés pour **émission frauduleuse de chèques** (*writing dud cheques*)

émoi (*nm*): alors que l'**émoi** suscité par sa défaite inattendue était encore vif (*surprise; confusion*); le retour de l'OLP **suscite l'émoi** en Israël (*cause concern/emotion/anger*)

émoluments (*nmpl*): les **émoluments** d'un notaire (*remuneration, emolument*)

émouvoir (*vt*): l'annulation de la visite a **ému** les Autrichiens (*upset; arouse indignation of*); [s'] (*vpr*): le Président s'**est ému des** propos de son ministre (*express concern/displeasure*); le gouvernement belge s'**en est ému** (*was roused to action*)

empiètement (*nm*): le chef de l'État met en garde contre tout **empiètement** sur la fonction présidentielle (*encroachment*)

empiéter (*vt*): le Premier ministre **empiète** sur le terrain présidentiel (*encroach*)

empirer (*vi*): la tendance **empire** à la fin des années 1970; la crise ne fait qu'**empirer** (*get worse*)

emploi (*nm*): le projet de loi sur l'**emploi de la langue française** (*the use of French*); l'**emploi** s'améliore, le chômage diminue (*employment/job situation*); continuer à chercher un **emploi fixe**; trouver un **emploi définitif** à l'issue de son stage (*permanent job*); quand on est **sans emploi** (*unemployed, out of work*) SEE also **atypique, bassin, contrat, cumuler, familial, insécurité, offre, perspective, plein, précaire, précarité, raréfier, sécurité, suppression, supprimer**

employé, -e (*nm,f*): le notaire américain est un **employé d'État** (*public officer, state employee*); des ménages qui prennent un **employé de maison** (*domestic help; servant*)

employer [s'] (*vpr*): l'Égypte se dit disposée à **s'y employer** (*work to that end*); Moscou **s'emploie à resserrer ses liens** avec Téhéran (*work to establish closer links*)

emporter (*vt*): la liste emmenée par l'ancien maire a **emporté** cette élection partielle (*win*); c'est le parti arrivé en tête qui **emporte le siège** (*win the seat*); la droite **l'a emporté** le 16 mars (*win, come out on top*); l'intérêt du pays **l'emporte sur** toute autre considération (*override; come before*)

emprise (*nf*): Moscou confirme son **emprise** sur les États indépendants (*hold, influence*)

emprunt (*nm*): le remboursement d'**emprunts** (*loan*); le vif succès du dernier **emprunt gouvernemental** de 4 milliards de DMarks à 10 ans (*government loan*); SEE ALSO **contracter, émettre**

emprunter (*vt*): **emprunter** à la banque pour se faire construire une maison (*borrow, take out/contract a loan*)

énarque (*nm*): une direction composée de 200 fonctionnaires, la plupart **énarques** (*graduate of the ENA*)

encadré, -e (*adj*): les HLM, très **encadrés** par l'État (*regulated, controlled*); à l'époque, **le crédit était encadré** (*credit restrictions were in force*)

encadrement (*nm*): l'**encadrement** est assuré par des officiers d'expérience (*training*); les femmes sont sous-représentées dans les **postes d'encadrement** (*managerial posts*); avec la levée de l'**encadrement du crédit** (*restriction on borrowing; credit controls*); l'**encadrement des loyers**, instauré à l'automne 1989 (*rent controls*)

encadrer (*vt*): les syndicats ont du mal à **encadrer** ces mouvements spontanés (*organize, control*)

encaisser (*vt*): il a **encaissé** de substantiels bénéfices (*receive; collect*)

encart (*nm*): faire paraître un **encart publicitaire** dans la presse régionale (*promotional insert*)

encarté, -e (*adj/nm,f*): le candidat des militants **encartés** (*card-holding [member]*); premier département en nombre d'adhérents, avec 4 000 **encartés** (*card-holder; card-holding member*)

encarter [s'] (*vpr*): le refus de **s'encarter** (*take out membership [of political party]*)

enchère (*nf*): après une dernière **enchère** de 250F (*bid [at auction]*); SEE ALSO **adjuger**

enchérir (*vi*): les produits de première nécessité **enchérissent** au fil des semaines (*become dearer, go up in price*); refusant d'**enchérir sur son offre** de vendredi (*make a higher bid, up a bid*)

enchérissement (*nm*): par crainte d'un **enchérissement** des importations (*rise in cost*)

enclave (*nf*): l'**enclave** musulmane sécessionniste est tombée (*enclave*)

enclavement (*nm*): ceci accentue l'**enclavement** actuel de l'est du pays, dépourvu de TGV; cet **enclavement** relatif de la région est un handicap essentiel (*isolation; hemmed-in situation*)

enclaver (*vt*): le Lesotho, un petit royaume complètement **enclavé** en Afrique du Sud (*landlocked*); malgré son aérodrome récent, Albi est **enclavé** (*isolated, cut off*)

encombrement (*nm*): l'**encombrement des prisons** est un grand sujet de préoccupation (*prison overcrowding*)

encontre (*prep*): les mesures prises **à l'encontre des syndicats** (*against the unions*); **aller à l'encontre de** l'évolution constatée dans les autres pays d'Europe (*run counter to*); **à l'encontre de** leurs homologues français (*unlike; in contrast to*)

encourir (*vt*): le principal prévenu **encourt** dix ans d'emprisonnement (*incur, be liable to*); lorsque la **peine encourue** n'excède pas cinq ans (*sentence incurred*)

endetté, -e (*adj*): expulsant les locataires **endettés** (*in debt; owing rent*); la commune est **fortement endettée** (*heavily in debt*)

endettement (*nm*): en raison d'un **endettement** trop lourd (*debt; level of debt*); le problème de l'**endettement du tiers-monde** (*Third World debt*)

endetter [s'] (*vpr*): **s'endetter** auprès d'établissements de crédit (*contract debts; go into debt*)

endiguement (*nm*): la **politique d'endiguement** préconisée par les Américains (*policy of containment*)

endiguer (*vt*): **endiguer** la chute du dollar (*check, arrest*); un plan destiné à **endiguer la crise** qui sévit dans ce pays (*contain the crisis*)

endos (*nm*): retourner un chèque à ordre, faute d'**endos** (*endorsement [esp. on back of cheque]*)

endossement (*nm*): une lettre de change peut être transmise à un tiers par **endossement** (*endorsement*)

endosser (*vt*): il a dû **endosser** la responsabilité des activités de ses collègues (*take on, accept*); **faire endosser par les États-Unis** son projet d'élections dans les territoires occupés (*get American endorsement for*); **endosser un chèque** à l'ordre du client (*endorse a cheque*)

énergétique (*adj*): conquérir son indépendance **énergétique** en dix ans (*in energy resources*); la fourniture par Alger de 40% de nos **besoins énergétiques** (*energy requirements*)

énergie (*nf*): le **prix de l'énergie** reste bas et a tendance à baisser (*energy prices*); SEE ALSO **renchérissement**

enfance (*nf*): des structures d'accueil pour la **petite enfance** (*infants; early childhood*); une institution pour **enfance inadaptée** (*maladjusted children*); un projet de loi sur l'**enfance délinquante** (*juvenile crime*); un service d'accueil téléphonique pour **enfance maltraitée** (*[cases of] child abuse*)

enfant (*nmf*): la CGT réclame 200F par mois par **enfant à charge** (*dependent child*); SEE ALSO **garde, juge, maltraitance, scolariser, traitement, tribunal**

enfreindre (*vt*): **enfreindre la loi** sur l'importation de l'ivoire (*transgress/be in breach of the law*)

engagé, -e (*adj/nm,f*): un journal **engagé**, mais non militant (*committed [to a cause/party]*); mobiliser davantage d'appelés pour remplacer les **engagés** (*enlisted soldier*); les **engagés volontaires** et autres personnels de métier (*volunteer [for military service]*)

engagement (*nm*): l'**engagement** définitif d'un salarié est précédé d'une période d'essai (*taking on, engaging*); le faible **engagement** de l'État (*involvement; contribution*); il faut rassurer les Allemands sur l'**engagement européen** de la France (*commitment to Europe*); ne pas **tenir ses engagements** (*keep a pledge/promise*); SEE ALSO **exécuter, violer**

engager (*vt*): les super-puissances viennent d'**engager un timide dialogue** (*begin exploratory talks*); **[s']** (*vpr*): de jeunes intellectuels désireux de **s'engager** (*become [politically] involved*); c'est une triple bataille qui **s'engage** à Washington (*start, begin*); la lutte contre le terrorisme **s'engage dans une nouvelle phase** (*enter a new phase*); SEE ALSO **poursuite**

engin (*nm*): l'**engin** a explosé faisant dix morts (*[explosive] device*); un bâtiment porteur d'**engins nucléaires** endommagé par un incendie (*nuclear weapon*); SEE ALSO **fabrication**

englober (*vt*): ces projets doivent **englober** les autres pays européens (*include*)

engorgement (*nm*): les investisseurs redoutent un **engorgement du marché** (*glut in the market*)

engouement (*nm*): la privatisation a confirmé l'**engouement** nouveau des petits épargnants pour la Bourse (*passion, craze, enthusiasm*); l'assurance-vie **bénéficie toujours de l'engouement** des Français (*is still a favourite with the French*)

engrenage (*nm*): la répression est responsable de l'**engrenage de la violence** (*increasing/spiralling violence*); le Yémen **est entré dans l'engrenage de la guerre civile** (*is caught up in the vicious circle of civil war*)

énième (*adj*): après une **énième** tentative de conciliation (*nth, umpteenth*)

enjeu, *pl* -**x** (*nm*): se trouver face à un **enjeu** considérable (*challenge; task*); le pays, l'**enjeu des rivalités** de ses puissants voisins (*focus of rivalry*); ne pas être d'accord sur l'**enjeu du conflit actuel** (*what is at stake in this conflict*); dans les discussions à Bonn, l'**enjeu sera de taille** (*there will be a lot at stake*)

enlever (*vt*): les Islamistes **enlèvent** 31 sur 80 sièges; bien placé pour **enlever** l'appel d'offres (*capture; win*); une lutte entre Washington et Paris pour **enlever un marché** de 26 milliards de pesetas (*win a contract*)

enlisement (*nm*): comment sortir l'Europe de l'**enlisement**? (*rut, impasse*)

enliser [s'] (*vpr*): cette stratégie marque le pas, et les négociations **s'enlisent** (*fail to advance; get bogged down*); SEE ALSO **enquête**

énoncé (*nm*): après l'**énoncé du verdict** (*pronouncement of the verdict*)

enquête (*nf*): la police a **ouvert une enquête** (*start an investigation*); au cours d'une longue **enquête policière** (*police investigation*); selon la police, l'**enquête s'enlisait** (*the investigation was making little progress*); lors d'une **enquête d'opinion** effectuée début mars (*survey; opinion poll*); le projet **sera soumis à enquête publique** (*will be the subject of a public enquiry*); SEE ALSO **commission, diligenter, piétinement**

enquêter (*vi*): la commission qui **enquête** sur cette affaire (*investigate*)

enquêteur, -**trice** (*nm,f*): envoyer une équipe d'**enquêteurs** sur le terrain (*investigator*); les **enquêteurs** cherchent toujours un mobile au meurtre (*person carrying out a [police] investigation*)

enracinement (*nm*): la gauche compte sur son **enracinement** pour garder la majorité dans le Nord (*[strong] local roots*)

enrayement (*nm*): contribuer à l'**enrayement de la hausse de la délinquance** (*checking/curbing the rise in crime*)

enrayer (*vt*): comment espérer **enrayer** la crise des vocations?; l'objectif est d'**enrayer** toute spirale inflationniste (*arrest; bring under control*)

enregistrer (*vt*): le chiffre le plus bas **enregistré** depuis vingt ans (*record; register*); le parti a **enregistré un revers** aux élections (*suffer a defeat/setback*)

ensanglanter (*vt*): le drame qui **ensanglante** l'ex-Yougoslavie (*bring bloodshed to*); un nouvel attentat a **ensanglanté le pays** (*bring bloodshed to the country*)

enseigne (*nf*): Monoprix [280 magasins, en incluant les **enseignes** Uniprix et Inno] (*trading name*); [*fig*] tous les pays ne sont pas **logés à la même enseigne** (*in the same situation, similarly placed*)

ensemble (*nm*): un projet de résorption des **grands ensembles** de banlieues (*high-density housing estate*); réunir **l'ensemble des membres du gouvernement** (*the whole government*); **l'ensemble de la production agricole** est en recul (*agricultural production as a whole*)

entamer (*vt*): **entamer** la lutte contre ce fléau (*begin, initiate*); une défaite qui va largement **entamer sa crédibilité** (*damage one's credibility*)

entendre (*vt*): les auteurs présumés du vol ont été **entendus** par le juge (*hear, interview*); l'opposition travailliste **entend** s'y opposer (*intend, be determined*); [s'] (*vpr*): Paris et Alger **s'entendent sur** un prix pour le gaz algérien (*come to an agreement on; agree*)

entente (*nf*): une amende infligée aux deux firmes pour **entente illicite**; il y a bien eu **entente sur un marché** (*illicit [trade] agreement*); SEE ALSO **terrain**

entériner (*vt*): une réforme doit être **entérinée** par tous les États membres; les Croates désirent **entériner** le statu quo actuel (*confirm, ratify*)

enterrement (*nm*): autre sujet de mécontentement: **l'enterrement de la réforme agraire** (*shelving/abandoning of agrarian reform*)

enterrer (*vt*): il refuse que le dossier des "affaires" soit **enterré** (*forget about; put on ice, shelve*); le nouveau texte **enterre le projet de réforme fiscale** (*shelve proposed tax reforms*)

entier, -ière (*adj/nm*): SEE **membre**

entorse (*nf*): une **entorse aux règlements** du libéralisme (*bending the rules*)

entourage (*nm*): des malades dont **l'entourage** ne peut plus assumer la souffrance (*family; [close] friends and relations*); **dans l'entourage du maire**, on minimise l'importance du scandale (*among those people close to the mayor*)

entraîner (*vt*): l'évolution technologique **entraîne** un besoin croissant de personnel qualifié (*cause, bring about; bring in its train*)

entrave (*nf*): une action en justice pour **entrave** au droit syndical (*obstruction*); pour **le droit de circuler sans entrave** au sein de l'Union (*freedom of movement*)

entraver (*vt*): la cherté du crédit **entrave** effectivement le commerce (*be a barrier to; hinder, impede*)

entrée (*nf*): SEE **vigueur, visa**

entremise (*nf*): reste un seul recours: **l'entremise** du Président (*intervention; mediation*); amorcer un dialogue **par l'entremise des États-Unis** (*with the mediation of the United States*)

entreprenant, -e (*adj*): parmi les plus instruits, les plus **entreprenants** (*enterprising, dynamic*)

entreprendre (*vt*): avant d'**entreprendre** une importante réduction des forces armées (*set about, carry out*); une incitation à **entreprendre** (*set up a business*)

entrepreneur (*nm*): un **petit entrepreneur** et qui gagne bien sa vie (*small businessman; tradesman*)

entreprise (*nf*): hésiter entre l'**entreprise** et la finance (*business, a career in business*); dans cette **entreprise familiale** de Rouen (*family business*); une **PME [petite ou moyenne entreprise]** d'Orléans qui se développe en élargissant la gamme de ses produits (*small/medium-sized company*); SEE ALSO **chef, comité, échelle, juriste, libre, public, rapprochement, stage**

entrer (*vi*): SEE **application, capital, vigueur**

entretenir (*vt*): l'illusion **entretenue** par la classe dominante (*foster, maintain, promote*); [s'] (*vpr*): il désire **s'entretenir** avec eux du rôle du Conseil constitutionnel (*discuss*)

entretien (*nm*): leur **entretien** est à la une de tous les quotidiens (*conversation; talks*); passer un **entretien d'embauche** (*job interview*); l'**entretien de la voirie** relève du maire (*highway repairs and maintenance*)

enveloppe (*nf*): fixer à 15 milliards de francs l'**enveloppe d'allégements fiscaux** (*package of tax cuts*); prévoir une **enveloppe d'investissements** de 450 millions pour 1993 (*investment budget*)

envenimer (*vt*): cela ne peut manquer d'**envenimer les rapports** entre les deux États (*poison relations*); [s'] (*vpr*): les relations sino-soviétiques **s'enveniment** (*grow more acrimonious*)

envergure (*nf*): l'Europe a des problèmes, et ils sont **d'envergure!** (*considerable, sizeable*); un homme **de grande envergure** (*high-calibre*); une **action d'envergure** est prévue par la RATP pour le 5 janvier (*large-scale [industrial] action*); une entreprise qui a **pris de l'envergure** (*expand, develop*)

environnement (*nm*): un tramway, considéré comme une **atteinte à l'environnement** (*environmentally harmful*); SEE ALSO **conjoncturel, nuisance**

envol (*nm*): le dollar poursuit son **envol** (*rise*)

envolée (*nf*): les gains réalisés grâce à l'**envolée des cours** (*steep rise in share prices*); l'**envolée des prix** inquiète le gouvernement (*soaring prices; price explosion*)

envoler [s'] (*vpr*): la pression fiscale **s'est envolée** en 1993; les prix **se sont envolés** à Paris hier (*soar, rise steeply*)

envoyé, -e (*nm,f*): l'**envoyé spécial** belge est attendu dans les prochains jours (*special envoy*); reportage de notre **envoyé spécial** en Nouvelle-Zélande (*special correspondent*)

épargnant, -e (*nm,f*): une bonne partie des **petits épargnants** risque de vendre ses actions (*small saver/investor*)

épargne (*nf*): on s'enrichit plus facilement par l'**épargne** que par le travail (*saving/s*); Consommation: réduction de l'**épargne des ménages** (*domestic savings*); accéder à la propriété grâce au **plan d'épargne logement** (*savings scheme offering low-interest mortgages*); SEE ALSO **peser**

épargner (*vt*): consommer plutôt qu'**épargner** (*save; put money aside*)

épauler (*vt*): le ministre est venu de Paris **épauler** le candidat dans sa campagne (*support, back*)

épingle (*nm*): cette affaire, **montée en épingle** par la presse de gauche (*blown up [out of all proportion]*); la firme a pu **tirer son épingle du jeu** grâce à sa compétitivité (*emerge unscathed/successfully*)

épingler (*vt*): [*fam*] un rapport **épingle** la gestion des hôpitaux; le Nigéria **épingle** l'ingérence française dans son différend avec le Cameroun (*single out for criticism; take to task*)

éplucher (*vt*): les experts **épluchent** les données économiques (*dissect, examine closely*); SEE ALSO **comptabilité**

éponger (*vt*): la maison mère a dû débourser 160 milliards de DMarks pour **éponger les dettes** (*pay off debts*)

épouvantail (*nm*): brandissant l'**épouvantail** de la natalité galopante (*bogy; scare*)

épreuve (*nf*): on doit passer un certain nombre d'**épreuves facultatives** (*optional test/examination/paper*); une peine de 18 mois de prison avec sursis et **mise à l'épreuve pendant deux ans** (*a 2-year probationary period*); les forces serbes **mettent à l'épreuve** la communauté internationale (*put to the test*); la poursuite de l'**épreuve de force** entre le pouvoir militaire et l'opposition (*trial of strength, confrontation*); les élections: une **épreuve de vérité** pour le gouvernement (*acid/litmus test*)

éprouvé, -e (*adj*): reprenant une formule déjà **éprouvée** aux États-Unis (*tried and tested*)

épuration (*nf*): les travaux d'assainissement et d'**épuration** des collectivités locales (*water treatment*); l'**épuration ethnique** perpétrée par des escadrons gouvernementaux (*"ethnic cleansing"*)

épurer (*vt*): **épurer** l'eau usée avant de la rendre au milieu naturel; un tiers seulement des rejets urbains est actuellement **épuré** (*purify; treat*)

équilibre (*nm*): le respect de l'**équilibre** entre logements et emplois (*balance, equilibrium*); permettre un retour à l'**équilibre financier**; seul un **équilibre d'exploitation** est espéré fin 1997 (*balanced [financial] budget*); SEE ALSO **métropole**

équilibré, -e (*adj*): un partage des responsabilités **plus équilibré** (*fairer, more even*)

équilibrer (*vt*): les PTT sont tenues d'**équilibrer** leurs recettes et leurs dépenses (*balance*); la SNCF s'est fixé pour objectif d'**équilibrer ses comptes** avant deux ans (*be in balance, break even*)

équipe (*nf*): les **équipes** qui travaillent en 2 × 8 (*shift, shift workers, team*); le **personnel en équipe** travaillera 28 heures par semaine (*staff on shift work*)

équipement (*nm*): pour une meilleure utilisation des **équipements** (*plant, machinery*); les divers **équipements** culturels, sociaux ou sportifs (*[recreational] amenities; facilities*); préserver un équilibre entre emplois, logements et **équipements collectifs** (*public facilities*); les 28 000 agents employés par la **direction départementale de l'équipement** (*road maintenance department*); SEE ALSO **bien, dépense**

équiper [s'] (*vpr*): les entreprises se déclarent prêtes à **s'équiper** (*invest in plant and machinery, tool up*)

équité (*nf*): juger un impôt sur son **équité** et sur son efficacité (*fairness, equitableness*)

équivoque (*nf*): c'est ici que l'**équivoque** peut s'entretenir! (*misunderstanding*); Tunisie: **lever les équivoques** entre Paris et le nouveau pouvoir (*remove misunderstandings*); rejeter **sans équivoque** la thèse du porte-parole de la droite (*unequivocally*)

escalade (*nf*): nouvelle **escalade** dans la course aux armements (*escalation*)

escale (*nf*): faire une courte **escale** à Brazzaville; Cathay Pacific va suspendre ses **escales** à Bahrein (*stopover*)

escarmouche (*nf*): les premières **escarmouches** sérieuses ont éclaté en fin de journée (*skirmish*)

escompte (*nm*): **faire un escompte** de 6% pour paiement au comptant (*allow a discount*); SEE ALSO **taux**

escompté, -e (*adj*): la fin **escomptée** des hostilités entre gouvernement et rebelles (*expected*); loin d'**avoir l'effet escompté** (*have the expected effect*)

escompter (*vt*): les personnes dont on **escompte** la coopération (*rely/count on; hope for*)

escroquer (*vt*): accusé d'avoir voulu **escroquer** son assureur (*defraud; swindle*); ils auraient agi pour **escroquer les assurances** (*defraud an insurance company*)

escroquerie (*nf*): être victime d'une **escroquerie** (*fraud, deception*); une peine de prison pour **escroquerie aux chèques volés** (*issuing stolen cheques*); SEE ALSO **complicité**

espace (*nm*): créer des emplois et **maintenir la vie dans les espaces ruraux** (*preserve rural life*); SEE ALSO **vert**

espèce (*nf*): exiger d'être payé **en espèces** (*in cash*); on peut effectuer des **retraits en espèces** dans toutes les agences de la banque (*cash withdrawals*)

espérance (*nf*): démographie: l'**espérance de vie** augmente encore (*life expectancy*); étant donné l'**allongement de l'espérance de vie** (*increased life expectancy*)

esquisse (*nf*): les **premières esquisses** du Xe Plan (*first sketch, outline draft*)

esquisser (*vt*): **esquisser** un rapprochement avec la Chine (*initiate*); un discours dans lequel il tente d'**esquisser** le paysage social de l'automne (*outline, sketch out*)

essai (*nm*): nouvel **essai nucléaire** français à Mururoa (*nuclear test*); SEE ALSO **ballon, période**

essor (*nm*): les ventes de magnétoscopes connaissent un **essor** fulgurant (*boom, expansion*); l'apprentissage **est en plein essor** (*is growing fast; is flourishing*)

essoufflement (*nm*): [*fig*] miser sur l'**essoufflement** du mouvement de protestation (*running out of steam*)

essouffler [s'] (*vpr*): le miracle économique allemand **s'essouffle** (*run out of steam; lose momentum*)

essuyer (*vt*): le parti au pouvoir **essuya de lourds revers** lors des élections (*suffer heavy losses*); le fourgon **a essuyé une rafale d'arme automatique** (*come under automatic fire*)

établir (*vt*): on a pu **établir** sa participation à l'attentat (*establish with certainty*); [s'] (*vpr*): son ambition: **s'établir à son compte** (*set up in business on one's own account*)

établissement (*nm*): il est pour l'**établissement** d'une liste d'union pour les élections (*setting up*); l'**établissement** normand est un des leaders français des appareils ménagers (*firm, company*); les **établissements scolaires**, lycées et collèges (*school, educational establishment*); SEE ALSO **chef**

étalement (*nm*): ceci impliquerait un **étalement** de certains grands programmes militaires (*lengthening*); l'**étalement des vacances** est loin d'être la règle en France (*staggering holiday periods*); le blocage de l'**étalement suburbain** (*urban spread/sprawl*)

étaler (*vt*): les pays arabes **étalent** leurs divisions face à Israël (*display, reveal*); [s'] (*vpr*): un programme économique **s'étalant sur trois ans** (*spread over three years*)

étape (*nf*): une nouvelle **étape** a été franchie; les **étapes** du processus de décentralisation (*stage*); une diminution **par étapes** de la durée du travail (*in stages, staged*)

état (*nm*): publier un **état** assez détaillé des forces armées (*account, statement*); un **état des lieux** établi par un expert immobilier (*inventory; survey*); voter un texte **en l'état** (*as it stands, in its present form*); des témoins **font état de massacres** (*report massacres*); le roi **fait état de** ses prérogatives constitutionnelles (*cite; put forward*); le maire reste agent de l'État pour l'**état-civil** (*civic status; registry office dealing with civil status*); malgré les **états d'âme** de plusieurs députés (*doubts; qualms; soul-searching*); SEE ALSO **remise, urgence**

État (*nm*): la fin de l'**État de droit** et le retour à la jungle (*rule of law; legally constituted state*); le **tout-État** fabrique un peuple d'assistés (*excessive state control/aid*); les plus défavorisés tiennent à l'**État-providence** (*Welfare State*); SEE ALSO **agent, appointer, chef, commis, sûreté**

état-major (*nm*): les **états-majors** ont rejeté l'accord avec le patronat (*leadership, leading members*); **dans les états-majors**, on craint le pire (*at headquarters*)

étatique (*adj*): un système **étatique** de retraite (*state; of the state*); les **dépenses étatiques** n'ont progressé que de 5% (*public expenditure*)

étatisation (*nf*): l'**étatisation** de toutes les filiales du groupe; l'**étatisation** du système de santé (*taking under state control*)

étatiser (*vt*): le gouvernement a **étatisé** les grandes entreprises (*take/bring under state control*)

étendre [s'] (*vpr*): la célèbre firme anglaise **s'étend** aux États-Unis (*expand, enlarge its presence*)

étendu, -e (*adj*): le nouveau statut **confère des pouvoirs étendus** à l'exécutif local (*give wide-ranging powers*)

étiquette (*nf*): se présenter aux élections sous l'**étiquette** du Parti socialiste; les **étiquettes politiques** n'ont pas joué dans cette élection (*political label*); SEE ALSO **valse, valser**

étouffer (*vt*): leurs efforts pour **étouffer** l'enquête (*cover up/hush up*)

étranger, -ère (*adj/nm,f*): 65% de la population active est **étrangère** (*foreign*); l'**étranger** ne comprend pas toujours nos réticences (*foreigners; foreign countries*); les commandes **émanant de l'étranger** (*from abroad; foreign*); SEE ALSO **fournisseur, irrégulier, mainmise, provenance**

étrennes (*nfpl*): sombres **étrennes** pour des milliers de licenciés en puissance (*Christmas box; New Year's present*)

étroit, -e (*adj*): grâce à l'**étroite collaboration** des polices des deux côtés de la frontière (*close co-operation*)

étroitesse (*nf*): réaffirmant l'**étroitesse de la coopération** entre les deux pays (*close links/co-operation*)

étude (*nf*): l'**étude sur le terrain** révèle l'ampleur du problème (*on-site study*); l'heure est au lancement des **études d'impact** (*impact study*); une loi-cadre sur l'exclusion **est à l'étude** (*is under consideration; is in preparation*); SEE ALSO **faisabilité, sanction**

étudié, -e (*adj*): la politique des prix chez eux est **très étudiée** (*keen*); ils sont vendus **à des prix très étudiés** (*at lowest possible prices*)

euphorie (*nf*): finie l'**euphorie** des années de plein emploi (*euphoria, confidence*); le **mouvement d'euphorie** a touché les bourses de Londres et de Tokyo (*mood of confidence; euphoria*)

euphorique (*adj*): Wall Street **euphorique** hier (*bullish, buoyant*); SEE ALSO **conjoncture**

évacuation (*nf*): les techniques d'**évacuation des eaux de ruissellement** (*drainage*)

évacuer (*vt*): il n'est pas question d'**évacuer** la zone de sécurité (*evacuate, withdraw from*); le ministre a **évacué** deux questions importantes (*evade; shrug off*); accusé de contourner l'obstacle et d'**évacuer les vrais problèmes** de la Sécurité sociale (*fail to deal with the real problems*)

évasion (*nf*): l'accroissement des possibilités d'**évasion fiscale** (*tax avoidance*)

éventail (*nm*): [*fig*] des personnes d'un large **éventail** socio-économique (*range, spread, spectrum*); l'**éventail des salaires** s'est élargi aussi en Suède (*salary range*)

éventualité (*nf*): l'**éventualité** d'élections anticipées (*possibility*); sans écarter toutefois l'**éventualité de licenciements** (*possible redundancies*)

éventuel, -elle (*adj*): lors de l'ouverture d'**éventuelles** négociations de paix (*future, possible*); dresser une liste d'**éventuelles représailles économiques** (*possible economic reprisals/sanctions*)

éventuellement (*adv*): la région parisienne et **éventuellement** la province (*possibly; perhaps*)

éviction (*nf*): deux heures après son **éviction du pouvoir** (*removal from power/office*)

évidence (*nf*): le vote de censure **met en évidence** les divisions de l'opposition (*reveal, bring out*); SEE ALSO **nier**

évincement (*nm*): des élections aboutissant à l'**évincement** des communistes du parlement (*ousting*)

évincer (*vt*): il a été **évincé** de la direction (*oust, eliminate*); **évincé** en mai dernier du gouvernement socialiste (*sack, expel*)

évoluer (*vi*): il est nécessaire de **faire évoluer** les bas salaires (*raise, increase*); à l'époque il **évoluait dans les milieux d'extrême droite** (*he moved in extreme right-wing circles*)

évolutif, -ive (*adj*): un poste passionnant et **évolutif** (*with good promotion prospects*); avec une **rémunération évolutive** [70% du SMIC la première année] (*progressive pay scale*)

évolution (*nf*): s'inquiéter de l'**évolution de la situation** (*the way things are developing*); les **évolutions** à la hausse ou à la baisse (*price movements*); cet accord vise à favoriser une meilleure **évolution de carrière** pour les ouvriers (*improved career development*)

exacerbation (*nf*): il redoute une **exacerbation de la guerre des prix** (*a hotting-up of the price war*)

exacerber [s'] (*vpr*): les antagonismes entre les deux camps **s'exacerbaient** (*become more acute*); la situation risque de **s'exacerber** (*get worse, deteriorate*)

exactions (*nfpl*): de nombreuses **exactions**, commises par des militaires, ont été signalées (*atrocities; acts of violence*)

exactitude (*nf*): le ministère conteste l'**exactitude** de certains de ces chiffres (*accuracy*)

examen (*nm*): un projet de loi **en cours d'examen** (*under discussion*); le juge chargé de l'**examen** de la plainte déposée en 1992 (*investigation [into]*); convoquer, **mettre en examen**, et puis incarcérer (*charge with an offence*); cinq **mises en examen** ont déjà été prononcées dans cette affaire (*charge, indictment*); l'inculpé ou le **mis en examen** (*person charged with a crime, accused*); SEE ALSO **chef, lecture**

examiner (*vt*): le Conseil d'État va **examiner** ce litige (*examine, consider; investigate*)

excédent (*nm*): résoudre le problème des **excédents laitiers** (*dairy surpluses*); l'**excédent commercial** du prêt-à-porter français a atteint deux milliards de francs (*trade surplus*); à son départ, il laisse la Sécurité sociale **en excédent** (*in the black; in surplus*)

excédentaire (*adj*): le commerce extérieur de la France est **excédentaire** (*in surplus*)

excéder (*vt*): la demande **excède** l'offre (*exceed*)

exception (*nf*): hostile au rétablissement de la législation **d'exception** (*special, exceptional [laws/rule]*)

exclu, -e (*adj/nm,f*): les immigrés, déjà largement **exclus** (*marginalized; excluded, left out*); défenseur du prolétariat et des **exclus** (*the marginalized; social outcasts*); aider les **exclus du monde du travail** en leur redonnant le sentiment d'être utiles à la société (*jobless*)

exclure (*vt*): l'accord **exclut** l'agriculture (*exclude*); le gouvernement **exclut** toute négociation avec les chefs indépendantistes (*rule out*); les dirigeants **excluent** que des emplois soient supprimés (*rule out [a possibility]*); une nouvelle flambée de violence **n'est pas à exclure** (*cannot be ruled out*); le vice-président, **exclu de son poste** il y a quinze jours (*sacked, dismissed*)

exclusif, -ive (*adj/nf*): éviter toute **exclusive**, tout esprit de chapelle (*exclusion; debarment*); il faut rassembler, **sans exclusives** (*with nobody excluded*)

exclusion (*nf*): la lutte contre la misère et l'**exclusion** (*marginalization; alienation*); 1,4 million de Français **s'enfoncent dans la grande exclusion** (*be relegated to the outer fringes of society*); après l'**exclusion** des 22 jeunes musulmanes voilées (*expulsion [from school]*); une **exclusion** figurant sur un contrat d'assurance (*exclusion clause*); SEE ALSO **zone**

exclusivité (*nf*): British Telecom n'a plus l'**exclusivité du téléphone** en Grande-Bretagne (*monopoly of telephone services*); on lui a confié l'**exclusivité** des exportations de diamants (*exclusive rights*)

exécutant, -e (*nm,f*): un des **exécutants** présumés de l'attentat (*person carrying out a deed*)

exécuter (*vt*): avoir trois mois pour **exécuter** la décision du Conseil de la concurrence et des prix (*carry out*); dès qu'ils auront **exécuté leurs engagements** (*carry out a promise*)

exécutif, -ive (*adj/nm*): le maire est l'**agent exécutif** de la commune (*executive officer*); Premier ministre et Président partagent le **[pouvoir] exécutif** (*executive power*); SEE ALSO **bureau**

exécution (*nf*): une conférence internationale chargée de l'**exécution** des accords (*implementation*); un ajournement de l'**exécution de la sentence** (*carrying out of the sentence*); un projet qu'on n'a jamais **mis à exécution** (*carry out, put into operation*); SEE ALSO **surseoir, sursis**

exemplaire (*nm*): le livre s'est vendu à plus de 30 000 **exemplaires** (*copy*); Delhi a commandé mille **exemplaires de cet avion** (*aircraft of this type*)

exempt, -e (*adj*): les hommes de Berlin-Ouest étaient **exempts de service militaire** (*exempted from military service*); ces importations sont **exemptes de taxe** (*duty-free*)

exempter (*vt*): cette loi **exempte** les fermiers de taxes et d'impôts pendant cinq ans (*exempt*)

exemption (*nf*): les **exemptions** au service national (*exemption*); l'**exemption de TVA** serait souhaitable (*exemption from value-added tax*)

exercer (*vt*): la famille adoptive **exerce** l'autorité parentale (*exercise, administer*); perdre un pouvoir qu'il **exerçait** depuis 16 ans (*exercise, wield*); (*vi*): un avocat **exerçant** dans un cabinet privé (*practise, be in practice*)

exercice (*nm*): l'**exercice** du droit syndical (*exercising [right, power]*); les actionnaires ont approuvé les comptes de l'**exercice [fiscal]** (*financial year; accounting period*); parmi les ministres **de plein exercice** (*full; fully-fledged*); SEE ALSO **avocat**

exonération (*nf*): l'**exonération des charges sociales** accordée aux entreprises embauchant des jeunes (*exemption from paying social-security contributions*); huit milliards de francs d'**exonération [d'impôts]** sont encore accordés au patronat (*tax exemption*)

exonérer (*vt*): la Suisse **exonère de droits de douane** les produits importés de la CE (*exempt from customs duty*); sont **exonérés d'impôts** les intérêts du livret de Caisse d'épargne (*tax-free*)

exorbitant, -e (*adj*): le pouvoir **exorbitant** de quelques responsables (*inordinate, exorbitant*); une revendication jugée **exorbitante** (*excessive; outrageous*)

expectative (*nf*): habillement: les fabricants **dans l'expectative** (*adopting a wait-and-see attitude*)

expédient (*nm*): obligé, à l'approche des élections, d'utiliser tous les **expédients** (*short-term measures*); SEE ALSO **vivre**

expédier (*vt*): le gouvernement en fin de mandat se contente d'**expédier les affaires courantes** (*deal with day-to-day business*)

expéditif, -ive (*adj*): pour venir à bout de la guérilla, il faut des solutions **expéditives** (*quick, expeditious*)

expédition (*nf*): un nouveau Premier ministre a été désigné **pour l'expédition des affaires courantes** (*to deal with day-to-day business/matters*)

expérience (*nf*): l'**expérience** d'ouverture hebdomadaire en nocturne (*experiment*); il s'agit d'une **expérience-pilote** de lutte contre le chômage féminin (*experimental scheme*); forts de leur **expérience de terrain** (*practical experience*)

expérimental, -e, *pl* **-aux** (*adj*): un système d'imagerie radar **expérimental** (*experimental*); un service mis en place **à titre expérimental** (*as an experiment*)

expérimenté, -e (*adj*): du personnel formé et **expérimenté**; un homme politique **expérimenté**, ayant servi dans plusieurs cabinets (*experienced*)

expérimenter (*vt*): la formule sera **expérimentée** dans plusieurs régions de France; 200 villes vont **expérimenter** de nouveaux rythmes scolaires (*try out, test*)

expert, -e (*adj/nm*): une réunion d'**experts** présidée par le secrétaire d'État américain (*expert, specialist*); un rapport fait par un **expert immobilier** (*chartered surveyor*); SEE ALSO **comité, onusien**

expertise (*nf*): procéder à des **expertises** (*evaluation; appraisal*); le **rapport d'expertise** est formel; l'**expertise** a conclu à une erreur de pilotage (*finding by an expert*); une **expertise comptable** fait découvrir un détournement de fonds important (*financial audit*)

expiration (*nf*): lors de l'**expiration** de la période d'essai (*expiry, coming to an end*); son mandat ne **vient à expiration** qu'au mois d'août (*expire, come to an end*)

expirer (*vi*): son OPA sur la maison d'édition américaine **expire** lundi 12 septembre (*expire, lapse*)

exploit (*nm*): par lettre recommandée ou **exploit d'huissier** (*writ*)

exploitant, -e (*nm,f*): les **exploitants** des salles de cinéma (*owner, manager*); 2 000 **petits exploitants** font le siège du ministère de l'Agriculture (*small farmer, smallholder*)

exploitation (*nf*): une autorisation d'**exploitation** de salles de jeux (*operating, running*); il déplorait l'**exploitation médiatique** de l'affaire (*media exploitation/hype*); les **grandes exploitations** dominent dans la Beauce (*large farming unit*); SEE ALSO **chef, déficit, équilibre, perte, résultat**

exploiter (*vt*): **exploiter un petit fonds de commerce** dans le centre ville (*run a small business*); ils **exploitent** 35 hectares dans l'Aveyron (*farm*)

exportation (*nf*): la Chine, son premier **client à l'exportation** (*export customer/market*); en dépit des faibles **aides à l'exportation** (*export subsidies*); SEE ALSO **marché, recette**

exporter (*vt*): **exporter** le surplus de la production (*export*); **exporter** la culture française (*spread abroad*); SEE ALSO **interdiction**

exposé (*nm*): après l'**exposé** du ministre sur ce sujet (*presentation; talk*); un **exposé** clair et lucide (*exposition, account*); la réforme est justifiée par l'**exposé des motifs** suivant (*preamble [to bill], explaining grounds for its adoption*)

exprès, -esse (*adj*): à la demande **expresse** de Bonn (*formal, express*)

expression (*nf*): SEE **liberté**

exprimer (*vt*): les réticences **exprimées** hier par le ministre (*express, voice*); [s'] (*vpr*): le Premier ministre, invité à **s'exprimer** devant la commission (*speak; express an opinion, have one's say*)

expropriation (*nf*): la construction de l'autoroute entraînera l'**expropriation** de centaines de familles (*expropriation; compulsory purchase*)

expulser (*vt*): tenter d'**expulser** les clandestins (*expel; deport; evict*)

expulsion (*nf*): un locataire menacé d'**expulsion** (*eviction*); partisan de l'**expulsion des clandestins** (*expulsion/deportation of illegal immigrants*); SEE ALSO **arrêté, coup**

exsangue (*adj*): [*fig*] **le pays est exsangue**, ruiné par douze années de guerre (*the country has been bled white*)

extension (*nf*): **extension** de l'agitation sociale en Algérie (*spread; growth*); à cause de l'**extension du travail à temps partiel** (*increased part-time working*)

extérieur, -e (*adj/nm*): la dépendance de l'économie vis-à-vis de l'**extérieur** (*the outside world*); en cas d'événements graves à l'**extérieur** (*abroad*); SEE ALSO **aide, commerce, déficit, dette**

extorquer (*vt*): avoir recours à la torture pour **leur extorquer des aveux** (*get them to confess*)

extorsion (*nf*): ils accusent le commissaire d'**extorsion de fonds** (*extortion*)

extrader (*vt*): un ressortissant turc **extradé** des Pays-Bas (*extradite*)

extradition (*nf*): la France et l'Argentine ne sont pas tenues par une **convention d'extradition** (*extradition agreement*)

extraire (*vt*): il ne reste plus de charbon à **extraire** (*extract, mine*)

extrait (*nm*): un **extrait de compte** est envoyé à la fin du mois (*bank statement*); le bulletin de naissance est remplacé par l'**extrait [d'acte] de naissance** (*birth certificate*)

extrême (*adj*): les militants **d'extrême droite** (*of the extreme/far right*)

extrémisme (*nm*): l'Iran s'enfonce de nouveau dans l'**extrémisme** religieux (*extremism*); la montée de l'**extrémisme islamiste** (*Islamic fundamentalism*)

extrémiste (*adj/nmf*): il faudra choisir entre lui et les **extrémistes** palestiniens (*extremist*)

F

fabricant (*nm*): le troisième **fabricant** mondial d'équipements sportifs (*manufacturer, producer*); des contrats mirobolants en perspective pour les **fabricants d'armes** (*arms manufacturer*)

fabrication (*nf*): après avoir informatisé la **ligne de fabrication** (*production line*); une forte explosion produite par un **engin de fabrication artisanale** (*home-made bomb/explosive device*); SEE ALSO **coût**, **procédé**

fabriquer (*vt*): **fabriquer** des meubles (*manufacture, produce*); un article qu'il compte **fabriquer sur une grande échelle**; la décision de les **fabriquer en série** (*mass-produce*)

face (*nf*): **faire face à la concurrence** des hypermarchés (*face the competition of, compete with*); ne plus pouvoir **faire face à ses remboursements** (*keep up one's repayments*)

face-à-face (*nm*): lors de leur récent **face-à-face** télévisé (*one-to-one debate; encounter, confrontation*)

facilité (*nf*): nous pouvons consentir des **facilités de paiement** (*easy [re]payment terms*); la **facilité de caisse** consentie par la banque (*overdraft facilities*)

faction (*nf*): les diverses **factions** qui composent l'opposition au régime en place (*faction, group*); entre **factions rivales** sunnite et chiite (*rival factions*); les policiers **en faction** devant la porte du ministère (*on [guard] duty*)

facturation (*nf*): exiger une **facturation** en dollars (*billing; invoicing*)

facture (*nf*): Gaz: Paris et Alger d'accord sur la **facture** (*bill*); la **facture pétrolière** est payée en dollars (*oil bill*); faire transiter des fonds sous couvert de **fausses factures** (*false accounting/invoicing*)

facturer (*vt*): les compagnies pétrolières sont **facturées** en fin de mois (*invoice, bill*)

facultatif, -ive (*adj*): l'heure de religion **facultative** dans les écoles (*optional*); SEE ALSO **épreuve**

faculté (*nf*): les députés **ont la faculté** d'introduire une motion de censure (*have the right*); **avoir la faculté de vendre**, en tant que propriétaire du terrain (*have the option of selling*)

faible (*adj*): on s'inquiète du **faible niveau de la production** (*low production levels*); le **faible volume** des transactions (*low volume, small number*); toutes les études montrent le **faible coût** du transport fluvial (*cheapness, low cost*); SEE ALSO **économiquement, inflation**

faiblement (*adv*): le commerce extérieur a **faiblement** augmenté en volume (*very slightly*); SEE ALSO **rémunérer**

faiblesse (*nf*): la **faiblesse du franc** représente une occasion à saisir pour les exportateurs français (*weakness of the franc*); la **faiblesse des moyens** consacrés à l'Université (*inadequate funding/spending*); SEE ALSO **force**

faiblir (*vi*): demande et production **faiblissent**, mais on continue à embaucher (*fall, drop, dwindle*)

faille (*nf*): les **failles** du système (*weakness, defect, flaw*)

faillite (*nf*): le fabricant belge est au bord de la **faillite** (*bankruptcy*); le système d'assurances sociales sera **en faillite** avant la fin du siècle (*bankrupt*); [*fig*] on déplore la **faillite des valeurs traditionnelles** (*collapse of traditional values*); contre la Mafia, toutes les solutions ont **fait faillite** (*fail, come to nothing*)

faisabilité (*nf*): la Banque mondiale va financer une **étude de faisabilité** (*feasibility study*)

fait (*nm*): la mesure **entrait dans les faits**, malgré la contestation des syndicats (*be implemented, come into effect*); les Américains **prennent fait et cause pour** les rebelles (*give total backing to*); SEE ALSO **avouer, fait divers, nier, reconnaître, reprocher**

fait (*nm*) **divers**: chaque fois qu'un **fait divers** frappe l'opinion (*[short] news story; trivial event*); un entrefilet **dans la rubrique "faits divers"** (*in the "news in brief" column*)

familial, -e, *pl* **-aux** (*adj*): les **emplois familiaux** [garde d'enfants, assistance aux personnes âgées] (*domestic employment*); SEE ALSO **allocation, cellule, entreprise, planification, planning, prestation, quotient, regroupement, rupture, valeur**

famille (*nf*): les difficultés d'une **famille monoparentale** (*one/single-parent family*); les aides sont réservées aux **familles nombreuses** (*family with more than two children*); deux garçons de **familles désunies** des faubourgs de la ville (*broken home*); mettre en place un réseau de **familles d'accueil** (*host family*); SEE ALSO **éclatement, salaire**

fantoche (*adj/nm*): le gouvernement **fantoche** mis en place par l'Irak (*puppet [government/regime]*)

fantôme (*adj/nm*): véritable **ville-fantôme** depuis la fermeture de la mine (*ghost town*); SEE ALSO **cabinet**

farouche (*adj*): l'enjeu d'une **farouche** bataille commerciale (*fierce, bitter*); le scrutin majoritaire conserve ses **farouches partisans** (*staunch supporter/advocate*)

farouchement (*adv*): il était **farouchement opposé** à l'entrée de son pays dans le Marché commun (*bitterly opposed*)

fascicule (*nm*): ce **fascicule** ne peut être vendu séparément (*booklet; manual*)

faste (*adj*): depuis lors, le parti vit une période **faste** (*successful*); une **année faste** pour les Postes et Télécommunications (*good/profitable year*)

faucon (*nm*): [*fig*] les **faucons** sont majoritaires dans le cabinet (*hawk, hard-liner*)

fausser (*vt*): de grosses unités industrielles susceptibles de **fausser** les échanges européens (*distort*); pour éviter de **fausser la concurrence** (*distort competition*)

faute (*nf*): être licencié **pour faute professionnelle** (*for professional misconduct*); en cas de **faute grave** du salarié (*grave misconduct*); s'il s'agit d'une **faute lourde**, l'employeur peut licencier sur-le-champ (*gross misconduct [often leading to immediate dismissal]*); les chantiers navals licencient, **faute de commandes** (*for lack of orders*); SEE ALSO **licenciement**

fauteuil (*nm*): les socialistes ont donné leur accord pour qu'il conserve son **fauteuil** (*[local government] seat*); des **fauteuils du maire** très convoités (*mayoral seat*)

fauteur, -trice (*nm,f*): ils ont arrêté des **fauteurs de troubles** (*trouble-maker; agitator*); la police réagit sévèrement contre tout **fauteur de violence** (*perpetrator of violence*); il dénonce les **fauteurs de guerre** dans le camp occidental (*warmonger*)

fautif, -ive (*adj/nm,f*): l'automobiliste **fautif** s'est vu confisquer son permis de conduire et son véhicule (*at fault, guilty*)

faux, fausse (*adj/nm*): en possession d'un **faux passeport** (*false/forged passport*); sous le coup d'une inculpation pour **faux et usage de faux** (*forgery and use of forged documents*); inculpé pour **faux en écritures** (*false accounting*); SEE ALSO **facture, inscrire, témoignage**

fédéral, -e, *pl* **-aux** (*adj*): secrétaire **fédéral** du PC de Seine-Saint-Denis (*federal; of a federation*)

fédération (*nf*): lors de la constitution de la **fédération** de Russie (*federation [of states]*); la **fédération** socialiste des Bouches-du-Rhône; les syndicats des métaux, qui forment la **fédération départementale** de la métallurgie (*local federation of trade unions representing a single trade*)

fédérer (*vt*): cet impôt qui divise la gauche et **fédère** l'opposition (*unite, bring together*); les cinq Länder [**États fédérés**] sur le territoire de l'ex-RDA (*federated state*)

féliciter [se] (*vpr*): les syndicats **se félicitent** de la décision du gouvernement (*be very pleased; express satisfaction*)

féminin, -e (*adj*): la population active **féminine** (*female*)

femme (*nf*): le code civil ne connaît que la **femme mariée** (*married woman*); **femme au foyer** depuis son mariage (*[unemployed] housewife*); venir en aide aux **femmes isolées** [veuves, divorcées, séparées] (*woman living on her own*); SEE ALSO **discrimination, droit, policier**

féodalité (*nf*): empêcher la constitution de **féodalités** et restaurer l'autorité de l'État (*powerful [semi-autonomous] group*)

férié, -e (*adj*): les **jours fériés**, y compris le dimanche (*[public] holiday*)

ferme (*adj*): condamné à seize mois de prison dont quatre **fermes** (*with no remission*); SEE ALSO **embauche**

fermer (*vt*): une usine de confection qui vient de **fermer ses portes** (*close down, go out of business*)

fermeté (*nf*): une plus grande **fermeté** de Tokyo à l'égard de Pékin (*firmness*); encouragé par la **fermeté** de la place new-yorkaise hier (*firmness/stability [of prices]*)

fermeture (*nf*): de nouvelles **fermetures de sites** sont annoncées (*plant/ factory closure*)

feuille (*nf*): recevoir sa **feuille d'impôts locaux** (*council tax demand [UK]*); rédiger sa **feuille d'imposition**, case par case (*income tax return*); l'assuré doit fournir à la caisse primaire les trois dernières **feuilles de paie** (*pay slip*)

fiabilité (*nf*): la publicité met en avant la **fiabilité** du produit; un taux de **fiabilité** de 95,6% (*reliability, dependability*)

fiable (*adj*): ces statistiques sont jugées **peu fiables** par les experts occidentaux (*unreliable*)

fichage (*nm*): la réglementation relative au **fichage informatique** (*putting on computer file/record*)

fiche (*nf*): retourner la **fiche d'inscription**, dûment remplie (*enrolment form*); les retenues sont portées sur la **fiche de paie** (*pay slip*)

ficher (*vt*): ces huit personnes, **fichées** en France au grand banditisme (*on police record/file*)

fichier (*nm*): avoir accès aux **fichiers** des services de l'État (*files; records*); en l'absence de tout **fichier électoral** (*electoral register*)

fidèle (*adj/nmf*): **fidèle** et ami de toujours du Président (*loyal supporter*); traditionaliste, **fidèle à lui-même** (*unchanging; consistent*)

fidéliser (*vt*): conserver des services peu rentables pour **fidéliser la clientèle** (*retain one's customers*)

fief (*nm*): fils d'un parlementaire dont il a hérité le **fief électoral** (*electoral stronghold*)

figure (*nf*): il **faisait figure** d'homme providentiel (*appear [as/to be]*); les Français **font figure de parents pauvres** dans ce domaine (*appear the poor relations*); SEE ALSO **cas**

figurer (*vi*): **faire figurer** une exclusion sur un contrat d'assurance (*include, insert*)

filature (*nf*): les **filatures** du Nord ne connaîtront plus leur prospérité d'antan (*textile mill*); **pris en filature par la police**, il les a menés à la cache (*tailed/shadowed by the police*)

file (*nf*): SEE **chef**

filet (*nm*): la police a procédé à un **coup de filet** dans les milieux islamistes (*[police] raid*)

filiale (*nf*): le groupe, qui a des **filiales** à Genève et à Bruxelles (*subsidiary [company]*); **filiale à 100%** de la compagnie suisse (*wholly owned subsidiary*)

filialiser (*vt*): Sandoz France **filialise** ses activités chimie et agrochimie (*hive off into subsidiary companies*)

filière (*nf*): de **nouvelles filières** ont été mises en place dans les lycées (*new subjects*); plusieurs **filières** mènent aux métiers de l'immobilier (*pathway [educational/career]*); la crise de la **filière papetière** (*paper-making sector/industry*); les **filières** d'immigration clandestine en provenance du sud-est de l'Asie (*network, connection*); SEE ALSO **scolariser**

fin (*nf*): l'utilisation des pistes militaires **à des fins civiles** (*for civilian purposes*); SEE ALSO **allocation, locatif**

finance (*nf*): le monde de la **finance** (*finance*); une réforme des **finances publiques** s'avère urgente (*public finances*); SEE ALSO **loi**

financement (*nm*): la loi sur le **financement** des partis politiques (*financing, funding*); le problème du **financement occulte** des campagnes électorales (*secret funding*); avec l'aide de **financements publics** (*public funds/funding*)

financer (*vt*): comment **financer** un tel investissement? (*finance, fund*); **faire financer sa formation** par l'entreprise (*have one's training funded*)

financier, -ière (*adj/nm*): SEE **milieu, montage, rubrique**

firme (*nf*): SEE **courtage**

fisc (*nm*): le **fisc** estime le bénéfice qu'il a pu faire sur son chiffre d'affaires; les concubins sont mal vus par le **fisc** (*tax authorities; taxman*)

fiscal, -e, *pl* **-aux** (*adj*): SEE **abattement, allégement, déclaration, déduction, évasion, foyer, fraude, incitation, paradis, ponction, pression, recette, redressement**

fiscalité (*nf*): la **fiscalité** y est plus lourde qu'en France (*taxation; tax burden*); une réduction de la **fiscalité des plus-values** (*tax on capital gains*); la **fiscalité s'est alourdie**, notamment depuis 1988 (*the burden of taxation has increased*); SEE ALSO **peser**

fixation (*nf*): avec la **fixation** de sommets à un rythme désormais régulier (*fixing*); la **fixation** à 60 ans de l'âge de la retraite (*fixing, setting*)

fixe (*adj/nm*): outre les commissions, on touche un **fixe** mensuel (*basic/fixed salary*); [*fig*] les relations franco-algériennes **sont au beau fixe** (*are on an excellent footing*); SEE ALSO **domicile, emploi, idée, poste, rendement**

fixer (*vt*): SEE **calendrier, objectif**

flambée (*nf*): [*fig*] la **flambée terroriste** du mois de juin (*sharp rise in terrorist activity*); ce qui n'a pas empêché une **flambée des loyers** (*steep rent increases*)

flamber (*vi*): les prix des produits agricoles **flambent** cette année (*rise sharply, soar*); spéculation qui risque de **faire flamber le titre** (*make a share price rise sharply*)

flanc (*nm*): il ne veut pas **prêter le flanc aux critiques** de ses ennemis (*invite/lay oneself open to criticism*)

fléau, *pl* **-x** (*nm*): [*fig*] un véritable **fléau social** (*blight on society*)

flèche (*nf*): les cours du pétrole avaient **monté en flèche** (*rise sharply*)

fléchir (*vi*): le nombre des sans-travail a **fléchi** pour la deuxième année consécutive (*fall, come down*); les Européens tentent de faire **fléchir** le leader bosniaque (*yield, give way; relent*)

fléchissement (*nm*): construction: **fléchissement** de la demande (*fall, drop*); le **net fléchissement de la criminalité** enregistré en 1994 (*significant fall in crime*)

fleuron (*nm*): Boeing redevient le **fleuron** de l'industrie américaine (*jewel in the crown*)

florissant, -e (*adj*): grâce à une activité touristique **florissante** (*flourishing, thriving*)

flottant, -e (*adj*): SEE **électorat**

flottement (*nm*): après deux semaines de **flottement**, les choses commencent à se préciser (*uncertainty; wavering*)

flou, -e (*adj/nm*): profitant d'un **flou juridique** total (*absence of a clear legal precedent*)

flux (*nm*): immigration: contrôle des **flux migratoires** (*immigration; influx of immigrants*)

focaliser (*vt*): en **focalisant l'attention** sur les plus superficielles apparences (*focus attention*); [se] (*vpr*): notre action **s'est focalisée** sur l'équilibre régional (*focus, concentrate*)

foi (*nf*): selon certaines sources **dignes de foi** (*reliable, trustworthy*); son avocat **plaida la bonne foi** (*claimed his client acted in good faith*)

foncier, -ière (*adj/nm*): une nouvelle politique **foncière** est nécessaire (*relating to land ownership*); le coût du **foncier** est un lourd handicap pour les jeunes qui veulent s'installer (*land*); la **taxe sur le foncier bâti** est payée par les propriétaires (*property tax paid on buildings*); la **taxe sur le foncier non-bâti** est un impôt qui frappe les terres (*land tax*); SEE ALSO **propriétaire**

fonction (*nf*): il a pris ses **fonctions** fin août (*position, post*); les dirigeants ont été écartés 18 mois après **leur entrée en fonctions** (*taking up their duties*); après la **prise de fonctions** du Premier ministre (*taking office*); il serait prêt à **quitter ses fonctions** (*resign*); les **hautes fonctions** auxquelles il aspirait (*high office*); faire carrière dans la **fonction publique** (*civil service; public service*); 710 000 **agents de la fonction publique** sur un total de 4,9 millions (*civil servant, state employee*); SEE ALSO **électif, logement, reconduire, relever, titulariser, valorisant**

fonctionnaire (*nm*): on entend par **fonctionnaire** les agents des services civils de l'État (*civil servant*); **haut fonctionnaire** au ministère de la Défense (*senior civil servant*)

fonctionnement (*nm*): le **fonctionnement** de la Communauté (*functioning, operating*); SEE ALSO **frais**

fond (*nm*): cela ne touche pas aux **questions de fond** que se posent les Français (*basic/fundamental questions*); des **divergences de fond** divisent les deux partis (*fundamental differences of opinion*); SEE ALSO **article**

fondamentalisme (*nm*): le **fondamentalisme** islamique menace les sociétés occidentales (*[religious] extremism; fundamentalism*)

fondamentaliste (*adj/nmf*): les **fondamentalistes** hindouistes l'emporteraient si l'on votait aujourd'hui (*fundamentalist*)

fondateur, -trice (*nm,f*): membre **fondateur** du comité (*founder*)

fondation (*nf*): lors de la **fondation** de l'État d'Israël en 1948 (*founding, setting-up*)

fondé, -e (*adj/nm*): les États-Unis **sont fondés à intervenir** à tout moment (*would be justified in intervening*); les bruits qui courent, sont-ils **fondés**? (*justified; well founded*); envoyer un **fondé de pouvoirs** pour traiter avec la délégation chinoise (*authorized representative*)

fondement (*nm*): les accusations sont absolument **sans fondement** (*groundless, without basis*)

fonder (*vt*): la société, **fondée** en 1958 (*founded, set up*); le désir de **fonder un foyer** (*start a home and family*); [se] (*vpr*): le juge **se fonde sur** la loi Besson de 1990 (*base one's judgment on*)

fonds (*nm*): **récolter des fonds** en faveur des familles des grévistes (*collect funds*); on a prétendu que des **fonds publics** serviront à financer la campagne électorale (*public money/funds*); les sept milliards de **fonds propres** qu'apportera l'État (*capital, funding*); une diminution du **fonds de roulement** (*working/trading capital*); chaque employé cotise au **fonds de garantie** (*reserve fund*); gagner 1,2 milliard pour une **mise de fonds** de 600 MF (*capital outlay*); un dealer en **fonds d'État** britanniques (*gilt-edged stock*); SEE ALSO **bailleur, collecte, commerce, exploiter, extorsion, retrait**

force (*nf*): heurts entre manifestants et **forces de l'ordre** (*the forces of law and order; the police*); la **force de frappe** nucléaire française (*strike force*); **les forces et les faiblesses** de notre système judiciaire (*the strengths and weaknesses*); SEE ALSO **coup, épreuve, interposition, usage**

forfait (*nm*): le **forfait** comprend le prix de l'achat et d'éventuelles réparations (*all-in price*); le **forfait hébergement** reste à la charge du patient (*[standard] accommodation fee*); commettre d'autres **forfaits** (*[heinous] crime*)

forfaitaire (*adj*): soit une **somme forfaitaire**, fixée par avance, soit une prime variable (*standard/all-in charge*); SEE ALSO **abattement**

forfaiture (*nf*): accusé de **forfaiture** dans l'affaire des ventes d'armes; la **forfaiture** ou un manquement grave dans l'exercice de ses fonctions (*abuse of authority; malfeasance*)

formaliser (*vt*): un accord a peu de chances d'être **formalisé** avant le 18 juin (*formalize*)

formation (*nf*): la **formation** d'écoles pour immigrés islamiques (*founding*); les autres **formations de l'opposition** préféraient s'abstenir (*opposition party*); assurer la **formation** des apprentis (*training*); des cours de **formation permanente** proposés au personnel enseignant (*continuing education*); l'obligation de consacrer 1,2% de la masse salariale à la **formation continue** (*in-service training*); la mise en place de **stages de formation professionnelle alternés** avec les entreprises (*block release vocational training; sandwich course*); SEE ALSO **congé, crédit, financer**

forme (*nf*): SEE **vice**

former (*vt*): on embauche d'abord, on **forme** après (*train*); un animater social **formé sur le tas** (*trained on the job/in the field*); **se former** pendant son service militaire (*be trained; acquire a skill*)

formulaire (*nm*): le **formulaire d'inscription** dûment rempli doit impérativement arriver avant le 15 septembre (*registration form*); SEE ALSO **viser**

fort, -e (*adj*): **forte augmentation** des loyers à Paris (*big/swingeing rise*); la minorité grecque, **forte de 60 000 membres** (*numbering 60,000*); SEE ALSO **franc, homme, perte, place**

fortune (*nf*): **faire fortune** dans l'immobilier (*make a fortune, get rich*); SEE ALSO **impôt**

foudroyant, -e (*adj*): son ascension a été **foudroyante** (*extremely rapid, meteoric*)

fouet (*nm*): la pêche française **touchée de plein fouet** par la baisse des cours (*hard-hit*)

fouille (*nf*): la police pratique des **fouilles** impromptues sur des individus qu'elle suspecte (*search*)

fourchette (*nf*): le taux de syndicalisation se situe **dans une fourchette** comprise entre 12 et 16% (*within a range*); les articles proposés sont dans une **fourchette de prix** assez restreinte (*price range*); la **fourchette des rémunérations** a été jusqu'ici très étroite (*wage differential*)

fournisseur (*nm*): principal pays **fournisseur**: la Chine (*supplier; dealer*); un contrat conclu avec un **fournisseur étranger** (*foreign supplier*)

fourniture (*nf*): la France a signé un contrat pour la **fourniture** d'une usine de retraitement nucléaire (*supply*); la **fourniture** de services sociaux et éducatifs (*provision*)

foyer (*nm*): la construction d'un **foyer** pour personnes âgées (*hostel; [residential] home*); l'intégration du jeune dans son **foyer d'accueil** (*foster home; home for children*); les principaux **foyers de l'industrie manufacturière** (*manufacturing/industrial centre*); conflits armés et **foyers de tension** en Europe (*centre of unrest*); un **foyer fiscal** sur deux est exonéré de l'impôt sur le revenu (*household [for tax purposes]*); SEE ALSO **femme, fonder, monoparental, violence**

fracassant, -e (*adj*): les déclarations **fracassantes** d'un porte-parole (*sensational*)

fracture (*nf*): sensible à son discours sur la **fracture sociale** en France (*profound division within society*)

fragile (*adj*): les populations les plus **fragiles** (*at risk*); des PME **fragiles**, touchées de plein fouet par la crise (*vulnerable*)

fragiliser (*vt*): les acquisitions **fragilisent** certainement les entreprises à court terme; la société française est aujourd'hui **fragilisée** et vulnérable (*weaken, make vulnerable*)

fraîchement (*adv*): accueillir très **fraîchement** une proposition (*coolly*)

frais (*nm*): leurs **frais** leur sont remboursés (*expenses*); les marges ont baissé et les **frais généraux** sont très lourds (*overheads*); les **frais d'exploitation** sont très élevés; absence de contrôle financier, **frais de fonctionnement** excessifs (*running/operating costs*); devoir régler intégralement les **frais de justice**; il fallait payer les **frais de procédure** (*[court/legal] costs*); les petits commerçants risquent de **faire les frais de la crise** (*bear the brunt of the recession*); SEE ALSO **menu, note, scolarité**

frais, fraîche (*adj*): SEE **argent**

frais (*adv*): **frais émoulu** de la faculté de droit (*recently graduated*)

franc, franche (*adj*): l'accord a reçu un oui **franc et massif** (*unequivocal; unanimous*); des marchandises livrées **franc de port** (*postage paid*); SEE ALSO **jour**

franc (*nm*): le maintien de la politique du **franc fort** (*a strong franc*); soit 100 milliards de plus qu'en 1995 **en francs courants** (*in francs at current rate*); le coût réel, c'est-à-dire en **francs constants**, est bien supérieur (*in inflation-adjusted francs*); il décida de vendre la société **pour un franc symbolique** (*for a nominal sum*)

franchise (*nf*): les correspondances avec les services publics bénéficient souvent de la **franchise postale** (*exemption from postal charges*); réaliser un achat **en franchise d'impôt** (*tax-free*); une **franchise**, ou droit d'enseigne et de marque accordé par une entreprise à une autre (*franchise*); une **franchise** de 5 000F reste à la charge de l'assuré (*[insurance] excess*)

franco-français, -e (*adj*): le problème est moins une affaire Est-Ouest qu' **une affaire franco-française** (*a specifically French matter*)

francophone (*adj/nmf*): une école **francophone** de droit (*French-language*); la population **francophone** de Bruxelles (*French-speaking*)

francophonie (*nf*): la **francophonie** ou la communauté de langue des pays francophones (*the French-speaking world*); la vivacité de la **francophonie** en Roumanie (*French as a world language*)

franc-tireur (*nm*): quelques **francs-tireurs** centristes tenaient à montrer leur indépendance (*independent; maverick*)

frappe (*nf*): Paris réclame des **frappes aériennes** (*air strike*); les missiles **de première frappe** (*first strike*); SEE ALSO **force**

frapper (*vt*): l'ensemble de la fiscalité qui **frappe** le patrimoine des Français (*be levied on*); toute personne **frappée d'une mesure de reconduite à la frontière** (*made the subject of an expulsion order*)

fraude (*nf*): les **fraudes** à la vignette automobile (*fraud*); des accusations de **fraude électorale** (*electoral fraud*); la persistance d'une forte **fraude fiscale** (*tax evasion*); SEE ALSO **arguer**

frauder (*vt*): les contribuables salariés ne pourront plus **frauder** (*cheat; defraud [the tax authorities]*)

fraudeur, -euse (*nm,f*): la chasse aux **fraudeurs** s'est intensifiée (*swindler, defrauder*)

frauduleux, -euse (*adj*): la **gestion frauduleuse** de l'ancien maire (*corrupt administration*); SEE ALSO **agissement, émission**

freiner (*vt*): le souci aussi de **freiner** la hausse des prix (*curb; put a brake on*)

fréquentable (*adj*): quelques dictateurs **peu fréquentables** (*politically not very respectable*)

fréquentation (*nf*): la **fréquentation** des transports en commun est en baisse (*number of people using a [public] facility]*); la **fréquentation** en classes maternelles est faible (*[school] attendance*); il compte dans ses **fréquentations** de nombreuses personnalités politiques (*acquaintance, friend*)

fréquenter (*vt*): les élèves qui **fréquentent** les écoles primaires publiques (*attend [esp. school]*); les touristes **fréquentant la capitale** (*visiting the capital*)

friche (*nf*): la **mise en friche** d'une partie des terres agricoles en France (*leaving fallow*); transformer les **friches industrielles** en zone d'activité (*industrial waste land*)

frileux, -euse (*adj*): la tentation d'un repli **frileux** (*overcautious*); l'**attitude frileuse** de la Grande-Bretagne vis-à-vis les institutions européennes (*suspicious/cautious attitude*)

frilosité (*nf*): critiqué pour sa **frilosité** en politique étrangère (*over-cautiousness, lack of adventure*); la **frilosité** des employeurs à l'embauche (*reluctance to take on labour*)

froid, -e (*adj/nm*): sa visite met fin à une période de **froid diplomatique** entre la France et la Syrie (*strained diplomatic relations*); SEE ALSO **guerre**

fronde (*nf*): la **fronde** des "eurosceptiques" conservateurs (*revolt; rebellion*)

fronder (*vi*): certains députés de la majorité **frondent** (*revolt; rebel*)

frondeur, -euse (*adj/nm,f*): ces initiatives **frondeuses** sont réprouvées par les inconditionnels du parti (*rebellious; insubordinate*)

front (*nm*): aborder le problème **de front** (*head-on, directly*); il se garde bien de l'**attaquer de front** (*attack head-on*)

frontalier, -ière (*adj/nm,f*): un **incident frontalier** fait dix morts (*border incident*); 30 000 **frontaliers** vont travailler en Allemagne (*person living close to border*); SEE ALSO **différend**

frontière (*nf*): s'infiltrant à travers la **frontière septentrionale** du pays (*northern border*); **le tracé actuel de la frontière** entre les deux pays (*the present-day border*); SEE ALSO **reconduite, verrouiller**

fructifier (*vi*): 200F qui auront beaucoup **fructifié** depuis (*yield a profit*); le meilleur moyen de **faire fructifier ses économies** (*make one's savings grow*)

fuite (*nf*): 11 000 **fuites de cerveaux** par an vers les États-Unis (*brain-drain*); une **fuite en avant** qui reporte à plus tard la solution des problèmes (*reluctance to take necessary action; ill-considered action*); SEE ALSO **délai**

fuseau (*nm*): Londres, dont le **fuseau horaire** permet de traiter dans la journée avec New York et Tokyo (*time zone*)

fusion (*nf*): cette **fusion** entraînera des suppressions d'emplois; cette année ont été conclues 163 **opérations de fusion** ou de prises de participation (*merger, merger by amalgamation*); le **projet de fusion** des deux départements alsaciens (*proposal to merge*); SEE ALSO **monopole**

fusionner (*vt*): le groupe français va **fusionner** les activités de sa filiale avec celles du constructeur américain; (*vi*): contraindre les entreprises à **fusionner** ou à se rapprocher (*amalgamate; merge*)

fustiger (*vt*): le ministre **fustigea** l'attitude de l'opposition; les socialistes parisiens **fustigent** le "conservatisme" de leur maire (*censure, denounce*)

G

gabegie (*nf*): Bruxelles dénonce la **gabegie** de l'aide au tiers-monde (*muddle, mess; inefficiency*); mettre de l'ordre dans une société où régnait une **gabegie financière** (*squandering of financial resources*)

gâchis (*nm*): le **gâchis** financier et humain est immense (*waste, squandering [of resources]*)

gage (*nm*): Londres réclame des **gages** supplémentaires à Dublin; une monnaie forte, **gage** d'une France forte (*guarantee*)

gageure (*nf*): **c'est une véritable gageure** que de vouloir en six mois redresser la situation (*it is quite a challenge; it is attempting the impossible*)

gain (*nm*): le **gain** de quatre sièges (*winning, gaining*); négocier avec les syndicats des **gains de productivité** (*productivity increases*); **obtenir gain de cause** dans une action en justice (*win a lawsuit*); la cour **donne gain de cause** à la société Peugeot (*find in favour of*); SEE ALSO **boursier**

galère (*nf*): [*fam*] la **galère** des jeunes peu diplômés (*hard grind; hassle*); suivent des **années de galère** (*years of struggle*)

galérer (*vi*): [*fam*] **galérer** toute une journée, sans résultat tangible (*slave away; struggle, have a hard time*)

gamme (*nf*): le produit le plus populaire de la **gamme** (*range*); une firme spécialisée dans les matériels **haut de gamme** (*top-of-the-range; up-market*)

garant, -e (*adj/nm,f*): les **puissances garantes** du statut de l'Allemagne (*guarantor powers*); le créancier peut alors réclamer au **garant** l'intégralité de la dette (*guarantor*); **se porter garant** n'est pas un acte anodin (*stand guarantor/vouch for [a person]*)

garantie (*nf*): pour un chômeur de plus de 60 ans, on applique la **garantie de ressources** (*top-up of social security benefit for the out-of-work*); SEE ALSO **fonds**

garantir (*vt*): les libertés **garanties** par la Constitution (*guarantee, safeguard*); la marque NF **garantit** la conformité des produits à des normes de qualité (*guarantee, ensure*)

garde (*nm*): les 8 000 **gardes champêtres** exercent dans les communes de moins de 2 000 habitants (*rural policeman ([in France]*); le **garde des Sceaux** fait le bilan de ses deux années à la tête du ministère de la Justice (*[French] Minister of Justice*); (*nf*): obtenir la **garde** de ses enfants (*custody*); confier ses enfants à une **garde d'enfants** (*childminder*); la présence d'un avocat pendant les **gardes à vue** (*period of police custody*); **mettre en garde** contre tout optimisme déplacé (*warn*); lancer une **mise en garde** aux syndicats enseignants (*warning*)

garde-fou (*nm*): [*fig*] mettre en place de nécessaires **garde-fous** (*safeguard*)

garder (*vt*): **faire garder** ses enfants (*have [child/sick/elderly person] looked after*); SEE ALSO **anonymat, écharpe**

garderie (*nf*): la mise en place de **garderies** et de jardins d'enfant (*child-minding facilities*); SEE ALSO **halte-garderie**

gardien, -ienne (*nm,f*): des **gardiens de la paix** du commissariat voisin (*police officer, policeman*); emmener ses enfants en bas âge chez la **gardienne [d'enfants]** (*childminder*)

gauche (*adj/nf*): **la gauche** a toutes les chances de l'emporter (*the Left [wing]*); SEE ALSO **ancrage, sensibilité**

gel (*nm*): un long **gel** des relations avec Paris (*freezing*); le **gel des avoirs albanais** en Grèce (*freezing of Albanian assets*); le **gel des salaires** a conduit directement à la chute du gouvernement (*wage freeze*); un plan de **gel des terres** (*taking land out of cultivation*)

geler (*vt*): on va **geler** les salaires et les revenus (*freeze*); le ministre **gèle son** projet de réforme fiscale (*suspend/put on hold tax reforms*); la France **gèle** ses relations avec Pékin (*suspend*); l'État veut **geler les terres** (*take land out of cultivation*)

gendarme (*nm*): les **gendarmes** ont établi rapidement la réalité des faits (*the police*); laissant aux États-Unis le soin de **jouer les gendarmes du monde** (*act the role of global policeman*)

gendarmerie (*nf*): les militaires de la **gendarmerie** (*[in France] police force, gendarmerie*); s'adresser à la **gendarmerie**, place d'Armes (*police station [in small town/rural area]*)

gêne (*nf*): limiter la **gêne** des riverains; la **gêne** des usagers du Métro devrait être limitée (*inconvenience; discomfort*)

général, -e, *pl* **-aux** (*adj*): SEE **assemblée, avocat, conseil général, conseiller, élection**

généralisé, -e (*adj*): les scandales et la corruption **généralisée** (*widespread*)

généraliser (*vt*): la CNPF souhaite **généraliser** cette mesure (*extend; generalize*); [se] (*vpr*): le mouvement de mécontentement se **généralise** (*spread; become widespread*)

généraliste (*adj/nmf*): en France, on a une chaîne de télévision **généraliste** de trop (*general; general interest*); les [**médecins**] **généralistes** sont les parents pauvres de la profession (*doctor in general practice*)

gérance (*nf*): **pendant leur gérance**, l'affaire a périclité (*under their management*); SEE ALSO **conseil**

gérant, -e (*nm,f*): **gérant** d'un complexe touristique en Corse (*manager*); une Sàrl est administrée par un **gérant** (*administrator*)

gérer (*vt*): 93% des citoyens estiment que leur ville est **bien gérée** (*well administered*); trop jeune pour pouvoir **gérer un portefeuille ministériel** (*hold ministerial office*)

gestion (*nf*): confier la **gestion** à un entrepreneur du privé (*running; management, administration*); les erreurs de la **gestion socialiste** (*socialist administration*); la **gestion des stocks** est cruciale dans le commerce (*stock control; inventory management*); SEE ALSO **frauduleux, paritaire, quotidien, trésorerie**

giratoire (*adj*): un grand [**sens**] **giratoire** ouvrira des prolongements vers l'Est et l'Ouest (*roundabout*)

girondin, -e (*adj/nm,f*): [*fig*] les **thèses girondines** commencent à s'imposer (*federalist ideas/policies*)

glissade (*nf*): la **glissade** du dollar devient inquiétante (*slide*)

glissement (*nm*): le **glissement** constaté vers la répression (*shift*); en dépit d'un **glissement à droite** aux élections municipales (*swing to the right*); à la fin mai, le **glissement** des prix était déjà de 0,4% (*fall, slide*)

glisser (*vi*): les sondages indiquent que l'électorat **glisse à gauche** (*shift leftwards/to the left*); le pays tout entier **glisse vers l'anarchie** (*slide into anarchy*)

global, -e, *pl* **-aux** (*adj*): le **résultat global** est satisfaisant (*overall result*); 70% du **montant global du contrat** (*total contract price*); SEE ALSO **dotation**

globalement (*adv*): le bilan est **globalement** positif; **globalement** la fécondité a continué de baisser en France (*on the whole; taken as a whole*)

globe (*nm*): SEE **échelle**

gonflement (*nm*): le **gonflement de la demande** suivra obligatoirement (*increase in demand*)

gonfler (*vt*): le taux de participation aurait été largement **gonflé** (*exaggerate, inflate*); SEE ALSO **masse**

goulet (*nm*): SEE **goulot**

goulot (*nm*): perdre des ventes en raison de **goulots d'étranglement** dans la production (*bottleneck*)

gouvernant, -e (*adj/nm,f*): l'incapacité des **gouvernants** à réduire des inégalités criantes (*government; those in power*)

gouvernement (*nm*): la démission du **gouvernement** ne saurait tarder (*government*); le **gouvernement de coalition** nippon mis en échec (*coalition government*); SEE ALSO **croupion, transition**

grâce (*nf*): bénéficier d'une **grâce** présidentielle (*pardon; reprieve*); SEE ALSO **recours**

gracier (*vt*): condamné à mort, mais **gracié** par décision du Président (*pardon, reprieve*)

gracieusement (*adv*): notre bulletin de liaison vous sera envoyé **gracieusement** (*free of charge*)

gracieux, -euse (*adj*): il avait obtenu un prêt **gracieux** de 20 000F (*free [of charge]*)

grade (*nm*): l'obtention d'un **grade universitaire** (*university degree/qualification*)

gradué, -e (*adj*): un processus **gradué** et négocié (*progressive, step-by-step*)

grand, -e (*adj*): SEE **bourgeois, commis, ensemble, muet, public, puissance, surface, travail**

grandeur (*nf*): le Japon, autre puissance économique **de première grandeur** (*of the first order/magnitude*)

graphique (*nm*): un **graphique** permet de visualiser facilement ce genre de données (*graph*)

gratuit, -e (*adj*): SEE **santé**

gratuité (*nf*): la **gratuité** pour les chômeurs et les personnes âgées (*exemption [from charge]*); il n'est pas question de toucher à la **gratuité des soins médicaux** (*free medical care*); un local mis à leur disposition **avec la gratuité du loyer** pendant trois ans (*rent-free*)

gratuitement (*adv*): un annuaire est envoyé **gratuitement** à tout abonné (*without charge*)

grave (*adj*): SEE **faute**

gré (*nm*): les cours du baril fluctuent **au gré des événements dans le pays** (*as the domestic situation dictates*); amener l'employeur, **de gré ou de force**, à payer des salaires plus élevés (*willingly or otherwise*)

greffe (*nm*): extrait des minutes du **greffe** de la Cour d'appel de Paris (*registry; Office of Clerk to the Court*)

greffier (*nm*): les notes d'audience prises par le **greffier** (*clerk to the court*)

grève (*nf*): les syndicats ont **appelé à la grève** (*call for a strike*); le centre de tri est paralysé par une **grève illimitée** (*indefinite strike*); RATP: **grève dure**, sans mobile apparent (*all-out strike*); les aiguilleurs du rail, **en grève perlée** depuis des mois (*using go-slow tactics*); la seule arme de la direction: la **grève patronale** (*lockout*); faire pression sur l'employeur au moyen de **grèves sauvages** (*wild-cat strike*); des **grèves tournantes** qui affectent les ateliers à tour de rôle (*strike by rota; staggered strike*); la **grève bouchon** entraîne déjà des licenciements chez les fournisseurs de General Motors (*partial strike*); la **grève du zèle** a contraint le patron à fermer l'usine (*work-to-rule*); des **grèves sur le tas** qui arrêtent la production (*sit-down strike*); SEE ALSO **consigne, mot d'ordre, mouvement, piquet, préavis**

grever (*vt*): les lourdes charges sociales qui **grèvent** les PME en France (*cripple, place a heavy burden on*); les virements **sont grevés de frais de transferts** (*incur [high] transfer costs*)

griffe (*nf*): articles et vêtements portant la **griffe** Cardin (*maker's label; couturier's name/signature*)

griffé, -e (*adj*): vendus 30% moins cher que des produits **griffés** (*bearing a famous name/label*)

grille (*nf*): l'émission a été supprimée de la **grille des programmes** (*programme schedule*); les salariés de base s'alignent sur la **grille de salaires** de la Banque de France (*salary structure, pay scale*)

grogne (*nf*): devant la montée de la **grogne** syndicale en France (*dissatisfaction, discontent*); ce projet risque de **provoquer quelques grognes** (*cause discontent*); SEE ALSO **venir**

grogner (*vi*): les Allemands **grognent** contre l'effort fiscal qui leur est demandé (*grumble, complain*)

gros, grosse (*adj/nm*): un avenir **gros de périls** (*perilous*); **le gros des manifestants** s'est regroupé plus loin (*the main body of protesters*); **les gros** semblent à l'abri de la crise (*the wealthy, the rich*); SEE ALSO **contribuable, négociant, prix, rapporter**

grossir (*vt*): ils ne veulent pas **grossir** les deux millions de chômeurs (*increase, swell*); (*vi*): et le chiffre pourrait **grossir** encore (*rise*)

grossiste (*nm*): le **grossiste** ou intermédiaire achète au producteur (*wholesaler*)

groupe (*nm*): deux filiales français de **groupes** américains (*group, conglomerate*); un **groupe de travail** sur la toxicomanie fut mis en place (*working party*); les interventions des divers **groupes d'intérêt** (*interest group*); les **groupes de pression**, comme le lobby noir américain (*pressure group, lobby*)

groupuscule (*nm*): un **groupuscule** d'extrême droite (*small group; faction*)

guéguerre (*nf*): une **guéguerre** dérisoire face aux vrais problèmes du pays (*squabble; squabbling*)

guérilla (*nf*): les massacres de civils perpétrés par la **guérilla** (*guerrilla force*); un nouveau **mouvement de guérilla** au Mexique (*guerrilla movement*); [*fig*] la **guérilla** parlementaire des partis de l'opposition (*guerrilla tactics*); SEE ALSO **recrudescence**

guerre (*nf*): la **guerre éclata** entre le Tchad et la Libye (*war broke out*); le seul État issu de **la guerre froide**, la RDA, a disparu (*cold war*); la **guerre d'usure** entre gouvernement et opposition (*war of attrition*); dans la **guerre des prix** engagée sur les vols transatlantiques (*price war*); SEE ALSO **criminel, exacerbation, fauteur, sanglant**

guichet (*nm*): le nombre de **guichets** du réseau Barclays (*service point; counter [esp. of bank]*)

guigner (*vt*): deux groupes financiers puissants **guignent** la célèbre chaîne d'hôtels (*have designs upon*)

H

H (*nm*): à **l'heure H** du jour J (*at zero hour*)

habilitation (*nf*): la **loi d'habilitation** autorisant le gouvernement à prendre par ordonnances des mesures économiques (*law empowering government to legislate by decree*)

habiliter (*vt*): les lois **habilitent** le gouvernement à recourir aux ordonnances (*empower, entitle*); seul le Congrès **est habilité** à démettre le Président (*be authorized/entitled*)

habitant, -e (*nm,f*): SEE **autochtone**

habitat (*nm*): vivre dans **une région où l'habitat est dispersé** (*a region of scattered housing*); des opérations d'aménagement de **l'habitat ancien** (*older housing*); les **habitats collectifs** et notamment les logements sociaux (*apartment block, block of flats*); SEE ALSO **marché**

habitation (*nf*): la distance entre le **lieu d'habitation** et le lieu de travail (*place of residence, home*); vivre en **HLM [habitation à loyer modéré]** (*[in France]cheap municipal housing*); SEE ALSO **immeuble, taxe**

halte-garderie (*nf*): la **halte-garderie** accueille les enfants de moins de six ans (*short-stay child-care facilities*)

handicap (*nm*): aider les régimes pauvres à surmonter leurs **handicaps** (*handicap*)

handicapé, -e (*adj/nm,f*): des aides aux personnes dépendantes âgées ou **handicapées** (*handicapped, disabled*); une maison d'accueil pour **handicapés adultes** (*disabled adult*)

harcèlement (*nm*): le **harcèlement** dont il s'estime la cible (*harassment; pestering*); victime de **harcèlement sexuel**, elle porta plainte (*sexual harassment*)

harki (*nm*): hommage aux **harkis** soldats de la France (*Algerian soldier who fought on the French side during the Algerian war*)

haro (*excl*): PS: **haro sur** les privatisations (*outcry against*); les centristes **crient haro sur** le projet de réforme de la fiscalité (*rail/inveigh against*)

hausse (*nf*): la **hausse des impôts** ne dépassera pas 2,9% (*tax increases*); entraîner des **hausses de tarif** de 10 à 15% (*prices increases*); **la tendance est à la hausse** sur les marchés des changes (*upward trend; "bullish" conditions*); SEE ALSO **moduler, orienter, réévaluation, rémunération, revoir**

hausser (*vt*): il propose de **hausser** le plafond à 150 000F (*raise, increase*)

haussier, -ière (*adj*): le marché reste **haussier** (*rising, bullish*); aucun mouvement **haussier** n'est prévisible à la Bourse de Paris (*rising/ "bullish" trend*)

haut, -e (*adj*): dénoncer la corruption **en haut lieu** (*in high places*); (*adv*): les prix du pétrole **au plus haut** depuis 13 ans (*at their highest*); SEE ALSO **chambre, commissariat, fonction, fonctionnaire, gamme, niveau, rang**

hauteur (*nf*): des réductions de capacités **à hauteur de** 20 millions de tonnes (*up to; of the order of*); les résultats ne sont pas **à la hauteur de nos espoirs** (*on a par with expectations*)

hebdomadaire (*adj/nm*): fixer la **durée hebdomadaire de travail** à 36 heures (*working week*); *Unité*, **hebdomadaire** du Parti socialiste (*weekly newspaper*); *Spiegel*, le grand **hebdomadaire d'information** allemand (*news weekly*); SEE ALSO **presse**

hébergement (*nm*): en plus, il existe des facilités d'**hébergement** (*housing, shelter*); un **centre d'hébergement** pour les SDF (*hostel*)

héberger (*vt*): **héberger** des vieux qui ne sont plus capables de vivre seuls chez eux (*house, accommodate*)

hégémonie (*nf*): la double **hégémonie** de la France et de la Grande-Bretagne au Proche-Orient; le souci de la Russie d'affirmer son **hégémonie régionale** (*regional hegemony*)

hémicycle (*nm*): dans l'**hémicycle** du palais Bourbon, les parlementaires sont répartis en groupes (*benches of the French National Assembly; semicircular Chamber*)

hémorragie (*nf*): [*fig*] taxe qui lui fait craindre une **hémorragie des capitaux** hors d'Europe (*flood/outflow of capital*)

hériter (*vt*): **hériter d'**une grande fortune (*inherit*); (*vi*) la question de savoir qui va **hériter** (*inherit, come into an inheritance*)

héritier, -ière (*nm,f*): les **héritiers** en ligne directe (*heir*); l'**héritier présomptif** du président syrien (*heir apparent*)

heure (*nf*): l'Espagne **à l'heure de la morosité** (*in a gloomy mood*); **l'heure est à la concertation** (*it is a time for consultation/dialogue*); les **heures supplémentaires** sont rémunérées au même taux (*overtime*); SEE ALSO **H**

heurt (*nm*): des **heurts** ont éclaté pendant un meeting électoral (*clash, fight*); la transition s'est faite **sans heurts** (*smoothly*)

heurter (*vt*): une décision qui a vivement **heurté** l'opinion publique en Allemagne (*offend, upset*); [se] (*vpr*): la foule **se heurtait à l'armée** (*clashed with the army*)

hexagonal, -e, *pl* **-aux** (*adj*): enfin sorti d'un gaullisme trop **hexagonal** (*gallocentric*); ils restent trop **hexagonaux** par rapport à leurs concurrents (*inward-looking; parochially French*)

hexagone (*nm*): l'**Hexagone** compte quelque 400 000 sans-domicile-fixe; l'ambiguïté des rapports entre la Corse et l'**Hexagone** (*metropolitan France*)

hiérarchie (*nf*): l'ensemble de la **hiérarchie des salaires** (*wage scales*); se conformer aux instructions de la **hiérarchie** (*top brass; higher echelons*); la question a toujours partagé la **hiérarchie ecclésiastique** (*church/religious hierarchy*)

hiérarchique (*adj*): il dut céder à son **supérieur hiérarchique** (*superior*); il est fortement conseillé de **suivre la voie hiérarchique** (*go through the correct channels*)

holà (*excl*): Dublin **y a mis le holà**, par une loi imposant un séjour minimum de 48 heures (*put a stop/an end to it*)

holding (*nm or nf*): le groupe zurichois va prendre la forme juridique d'un **holding** (*holding company*); reverser 25% de sa filiale dans une **holding commune** (*joint-owned holding*)

homicide (*nm*): condamné à deux ans de prison pour **homicide involontaire** (*manslaughter*); inculpé d'**homicide volontaire** et écroué (*murder*)

homme (*nm*): le nouvel **homme fort** du pays depuis le coup de force (*key figure*); des **hommes de main** qui manipulent en réalité leurs commanditaires (*collaborator; agent*)

homologue (*adj/nmf*): chez les femmes cadres, comme chez leurs **homologues** masculins; le Premier ministre, comme son **homologue** anglais (*opposite number; counterpart*)

homologuer (*vt*): les nouveaux tarifs ont été **homologués** et seront appliqués dès janvier (*ratify, approve*)

honoraires (*nmpl*): les **honoraires d'avocat** sont très élevés (*lawyer's fees*); SEE ALSO **libre**

honorifique (*adj*): le roi, dont les fonctions sont essentiellement **honorifiques** (*honorary*); garder un **poste honorifique** au conseil d'administration (*honorary post/position*)

horaire (*adj/nm*): le SMIC **horaire** sera porté à 34F (*hourly, per hour*); avec du retard sur l'**horaire prévu** (*agreed timetable*); choisir entre un système d'**horaires modulables** et un temps partiel; les **horaires à la carte** sont également pratiqués au Crédit Lyonnais (*flexible working hours; flexitime*); SEE ALSO **décalage, fuseau, non-respect, plage**

hors (*prep*): **hors** pétrole, la hausse des prix à la consommation n'accélère pas (*excluding, with the exception of*); nommé préfet **hors cadre** en 1984 (*on secondment*); SEE ALSO **loi**

hôte (*nmf*): [*fig*] l'**hôte** actuel de la Maison Blanche (*incumbent, occupant*)

hôtel (*nm*): ses chances de reconquérir l'**hôtel de ville** sont minces (*town hall; mayoral office*); dans un élégant **hôtel particulier**, quai Branly (*town house, mansion*)

houille (*nf*): le charbon britannique revient plus cher que la **houille** importée (*coal*)

houiller, -ère (*adj/nf*): compressions de personnel dans l'industrie **houillère** (*coal-mining*); la fermeture récente des **houillères** de Provence (*colliery, coal-mine*)

houlette (*nf*): [*fig*] un groupe de travail, **sous la houlette de** l'ancien ministre (*under the leadership of*)

houleux, -euse (*adj*): à l'issue d'une assemblée générale **houleuse** (*rowdy, noisy*); **débat houleux** à l'Assemblée (*stormy/rowdy debate*)

huis (*nm*) **clos**: l'audience a eu lieu **à huis clos** (*in camera, behind closed doors*)

huissier (*nm*): un **huissier** posté à l'entrée de l'hémicycle (*usher*); l'**huissier [de justice]** est venu saisir les biens et expulser les locataires (*bailiff*); SEE ALSO **citation, constat, exploit**

huit (*adj/nm*): SEE **trois**

huitaine (*nf*): l'affaire a été **remise à huitaine** (*postpone for one week*); un comité d'experts se réunira **sous huitaine** (*within a week*)

humain, -e (*adj*): SEE **ressource**

humanitaire (*adj*): les **organisations humanitaires** s'inquiètent (*aid organization*); SEE ALSO **ingérence**

hussarde (*nf*): **voté à la hussarde**, le nouveau texte veut limiter les abus (*rushed through parliament [esp. legislation]*)

hygiène (*nf*): s'adresser aux **services d'hygiène** départementaux (*public health department*); des secteurs tels que l'**hygiène et la sécurité** (*public health and safety*)

hypothécaire (*adj*): mesures en faveur des **sociétés de crédit immobilier hypothécaire** (*building society offering mortgages [UK]*); SEE ALSO **prêt**

hypothèque (*nf*): le **contrat d'hypothèque** est obligatoirement un acte notarié (*mortgage agreement*); ce qui entraînait une **mise sous hypothèque** de ses biens immobiliers (*mortgaging*); [*fig*] un mouvement social-démocrate débarrassé de l'**hypothèque socialiste** (*the socialist threat*)

hypothéquer (*vt*): vendre ou **hypothéquer** tout ce qu'on possède (*mortgage*); ceci avait un temps **hypothéqué** la stratégie d'Israël (*endanger; put at risk*)

hypothèse (*nf*): l'**hypothèse** de sa candidature aux élections semble assez fantaisiste (*hypothesis*); **dans l'hypothèse** d'une unification des deux Corées (*in the event of*); **dans l'hypothèse contraire**, il n'est pas exclu qu'il se représente (*if the contrary is true; otherwise*); SEE ALSO **écarter**

hypothétique (*adj*): attendre un **hypothétique** redressement (*hypothetical*); la rentabilité **hypothétique** du tunnel sous la Manche (*uncertain; doubtful*)

I

idée (*nf*): retenons-en quelques **idées-forces** (*key idea; central theme*); la sécurité est une **idée fixe** de la droite (*obsession*); SEE ALSO **prévaloir**

identitaire (*adj*): ranimer le **sentiment identitaire** de la communauté (*sense of identity*); SEE ALSO **revendication**

identité (*nf*): SEE **décliner, justifier, pièce, vérification**

ignorer (*vt*): l'industrie de l'agro-alimentaire, **ignore** la crise actuelle (*be untouched by; be unaffected by*); les États socialistes **ignorent le chômage** (*have no experience of unemployment*)

illégal, -e, *pl* **-aux** (*adj*): le financement **illégal** des partis politiques (*illegal*); SEE ALSO **détention, immigrant**

illégalité (*nf*): les nouvelles centrales syndicales **agissent dans l'illégalité** (*be in breach of the law*)

illicite (*adj*): le lock-out préventif est **illicite** (*unlawful*); le travail **illicite** ou clandestin (*illegal*); SEE ALSO **entente, trafic**

illisible (*adj*): [*fig*] le système juridique est devenu largement **illisible** pour le citoyen (*incomprehensible*)

îlot (*nm*): dans certains **îlots** frappés par la délinquance (*[housing] block; urban area*)

îlotage (*nm*): dans les quartiers "chauds", l'**îlotage [policier]** sera mis en place; l'**îlotage**, c'est aussi développer le dialogue avec la population (*area surveillance; community policing*)

îlotier (*nm*): le policier, **îlotier** du commissariat du 4e arrondissement; dans la Seine-Saint-Denis, 300 **îlotiers** se partagent le terrain (*policeman on the beat; community policeman*)

image (*nf*): la nécessité de redorer son **image de marque** (*brand image; corporate identity*); les hommes politiques **soignent leur image de marque** (*look after their public image*)

immatriculation (*nf*): les **immatriculations** devraient peu diminuer l'an prochain (*registration [especially of new vehicle]*); SEE ALSO **plaque**

immatriculer (*vt*): une voiture **immatriculée** dans le Vaucluse (*register*)

immeuble (*nm*): la construction de huit **immeubles de bureaux** en banlieue parisienne (*office block*); un **immeuble [d'habitation]** de la rue du Dragon (*apartment block*); SEE ALSO **bien**

immigrant, -e (*adj/nm,f*): la plupart sont des **immigrants illégaux** (*illegal immigrant*)

immigration (*nf*): les familles étrangères ou **issues de l'immigration** (*immigrant, of immigrant stock*); la lutte contre l'**immigration clandestine** (*illegal immigration*)

immigré, -e (*adj/nm,f*): SEE **taux**

immiscer [s'] (*vpr*): Amman n'a pas l'intention de **s'immiscer** dans les affaires intérieures de Bagdad (*interfere, meddle*); la France ne tolérera pas qu'un pays étranger **s'immisce dans ses affaires** (*interfere in her affairs*)

immixtion (*nf*): l'**immixtion** croissante de la justice dans la vie politique italienne (*interfering; meddling*)

immobilier, -ière (*adj/nm*): le **[marché] immobilier** est en pleine expansion (*housing/property market*); la montée des prix de l'**immobilier** (*property, real estate*); SEE ALSO **arnaque, boom, cabinet, crédit, expert, prêt**

immobiliser (*vt*): éviter ainsi d'**immobiliser** un argent rare (*tie up [capital]*)

immobilisme (*nm*): la Roumanie: entre réforme et **immobilisme**; l'**immobilisme** des partis traditionnels (*opposition to change*); l'Europe semble décidée à **jouer l'immobilisme** (*maintain the status quo; resist change*)

impact (*nm*): Pékin s'inquiète de l'**impact social** des réformes (*social impact*); SEE ALSO **étude**

impasse (*nf*): [*fig*] les problèmes économiques compliquent l'**impasse politique** (*political deadlock*); le conflit **est dans l'impasse** (*be deadlocked*); prévoir une **impasse [budgétaire]** de 40 milliards de Marks pour la fin de l'année (*budget deficit*); SEE ALSO **débloquer**

impayé, -e (*adj/nm*): les **impayés** de la contribution américaine à l'ONU (*unpaid instalment*); la saisie, la procédure extrême en cas d'**impayés de loyer** (*arrears of rent*)

impératif, -ive (*adj/nm*): des besoins **impératifs** (*imperative, urgent*); l'**impératif** d'économies budgétaires (*urgency; necessity*)

impéritie (*nf*): la corruption générale et l'**impéritie** de l'État (*incompetence*); la montée de la pauvreté et l'**impéritie** gouvernementale à y faire face (*inability*)

implantation (*nf*): la société poursuit sa stratégie d'**implantations** en Asie (*setting up [business/factory]*); Liban: vive polémique sur l'**implantation** de réfugiés palestiniens (*establishment of settlements [in occupied land]*)

implanter (*vt*): les entreprises françaises **implantent** des filiales dans les pays de la CE (*set up, locate*); [s'] (*vpr*): le premier hôtelier occidental à **s'implanter** à Moscou (*set up business*); beaucoup d'immigrants polonais **s'implantèrent** dans le Nord (*settle*)

implication (*nf*): condamné pour son **implication** dans l'assassinat de l'ancien ministre; il nie toute **implication** dans l'escroquerie (*involvement*)

impliquer (*vt*): des incidents violents **impliquant** les forces de l'ordre (*involve*); **impliqué** dans une affaire de pots-de-vin (*implicated*); [s'] (*vpr*): l'armée algérienne est prête à **s'impliquer** davantage; **s'impliquer** dans le comité de gestion (*become/get involved*)

importance (*nf*): en raison de leur **importance** stratégique (*importance*); l'**importance** des effectifs envoyés indique la gravité de la situation (*size, number*); une entreprise **de moyenne importance** (*middle-sized*)

important, -e (*adj*): l'**importante** minorité hongroise en Roumanie (*sizeable*); un pays confronté à d'**importants** problèmes politiques et sociaux (*major; serious*); la récolte a été **moins importante** que prévu (*smaller, less*)

importation (*nf*): SEE **quota**

imposable (*adj*): à condition que le **revenu imposable** ne dépasse pas 20 000F (*taxable income*)

imposer (*vt*): en aucune manière la religion ne serait **imposée** (*impose, make obligatory*); le nouveau système **impose** chaque adulte d'un montant égal (*tax, assess for tax*); [s'] (*vpr*): les efforts d'économies **s'imposent** autant aujourd'hui qu'hier (*be necessary*); le PS **s'est imposé** au second tour (*win; come out on top*); la difficulté pour les femmes de **s'imposer** dans un secteur peu féminisé (*make an impact*)

imposition (*nf*): l'**imposition** du vote à bulletin secret avant chaque grève (*imposing*); les plus-values réalisées ne font l'objet d'aucune **imposition** (*taxation*); SEE ALSO **feuille, seuil, tranche**

impôt (*nm*): tous sont égaux devant l'**impôt** (*tax*); les Britanniques payent un fort **impôt sur le revenu** (*income tax*); un **impôt local** prélevé sur chaque citoyen et égal pour tous (*local tax*); l'**impôt sur les grandes fortunes [IGF]** frappe un nombre croissant de personnes (*wealth tax*); l'**impôt sur les sociétés** doit descendre à 40% (*corporation tax*); SEE ALSO **alourdir, arriéré, assiette, assujetti, collecte, création, dégrever, exonérer, feuille, franchise, hausse, recette, réduction, soumis**

imprévoyance (*nf*): subir les conséquences de son **imprévoyance** (*lack of foresight*); l'incohérence et l'**imprévoyance des politiques** du gouvernement (*shortsighted policies*)

imprévoyant, -e (*adj*): le conseil de surveillance était-il **imprévoyant** ou incompétent? (*lacking in foresight*)

imprévu, -e (*adj/nm*): une visite **imprévue** par le député de la circonscription (*unexpected, surprise*); **sauf imprévu**, il assistera à la réunion (*barring accidents/unforeseen circumstances*)

imprimé (*adj/nm*): remplir un **imprimé** (*printed form*); les **imprimés** sont expédiés à un tarif réduit (*printed matter*)

impuissance (*nf*): l'**impuissance** des gouvernements à réduire le chômage (*powerlessness, inability*)

impulsion (*nf*): il faudrait **donner une impulsion nouvelle** à la construction européenne (*give new impetus*)

impunité (*nf*): dans la plus totale **impunité** (*impunity*); les auteurs de l'attentat **ont obtenu l'impunité** (*go unpunished*)

inactif, -ive (*adj/nm,f*): familles défavorisées, parents **inactifs**, échec scolaire (*out-of-work*); sans compter les **inactifs** (*non-working population; out-of-work, unemployed*)

inaction (*nf*): les erreurs et l'**inaction** du gouvernement; tenter de justifier son **inaction** (*failure to act; lack of initiative*)

inactivité (*nf*): retourner à l'**inactivité** ou au chômage (*inactivity; unemployment*)

inadaptation (*nf*): il explique le chômage par l'**inadaptation de l'éducation nationale à l'entreprise** (*failure of the educational system to prepare the young for the world of work*); chez ces jeunes, le chômage s'ajoute à l'**inadaptation sociale** (*inability to cope with life in society*)

inadapté, -e (*adj*): le Bac, cet examen **inadapté** aux besoins contemporains (*unsuitable; ill-suited*); SEE ALSO **enfance**

inadéquation (*nf*): une **inadéquation** entre l'offre et la demande (*discrepancy*); lutter contre l'**inadéquation** de notre système de formation (*inadequacy; failings, shortcomings*)

inamical, -e, *pl* **-aux** (*adj*): une tentative de prise de contrôle **inamicale** du groupe textile (*unwelcome, hostile*); la Turquie, entourée de pays avec lesquels **elle entretient des relations inamicales** (*she is on bad terms*); SEE ALSO **offre**

inapte (*adj*): l'héritier est considéré comme **inapte** à devenir roi (*unfit, unsuited*); ceux qui sont **inaptes au travail** (*unfit for work*)

incapacité (*nf*): son **incapacité** apparente à enrayer cette évolution (*inability*); pour répondre à d'éventuelles **incapacités de remboursement** d'un prêt immobilier (*inability to make repayments*); ses blessures lui valent trois mois d'**incapacité de travail** (*industrial disability; unfitness for work*)

incarcérer (*vt*): inculpé de coups et blessures et **incarcéré** à la maison d'arrêt (*imprison, lock up*)

inchangé, -e (*adj*): CE: taux de chômage **inchangé** (*unchanged*)

incidence (*nf*): avoir de lourdes **incidences** sur la rentabilité de l'opération (*effect, repercussion*)

incitatif, -ive (*adj*): Air France proposerait au personnel des **mesures incitatives de départ** (*early retirement incentives*)

incitation (*nf*): **incitation** à la haine et à la violence (*incitement*); cette réduction se fera par **incitations** à la retraite et mutations (*inducement, incentive*); des **incitations fiscales** qui comprennent des abattements de 100% pour dépenses d'équipement (*tax incentive*)

inciter (*vt*): **inciter** les jeunes à prendre part à la vie politique (*encourage*); la publicité **incitant à la consommation du tabac** (*which encourages smoking*)

incivisme (*nm*): délinquance de masse et **incivisme** renforcent le sentiment d'insécurité (*general lawlessness*)

incohérence (*nf*): les **incohérences** de la gestion socialiste de la ville (*inconsistency; incoherence*); le président du Conseil italien est handicapé par les **incohérences** de sa coalition (*disunity*)

incomber (*vt*): les responsabilités qui lui **incombent** dans cette affaire (*devolve, fall to*)

incompressible (*adj*): le parquet demande une **peine incompressible** de 30 ans (*sentence without remission*)

inconnue (*nf*): une **inconnue** demeure: le taux de participation (*unknown factor*)

incontesté, -e (*adj*): il devient en 1978 le maître **incontesté** du pays (*unchallenged*)

incontournable (*adj*): la guérilla des Khmers rouges en fait un élément **incontournable** de tout règlement (*unavoidable; which cannot be ignored*)

inconvénient (*nm*): ces réformes cumulent trois sortes d'**inconvénient** (*drawback*)

incorporation (*nf*): l'étudiant peut repousser son **incorporation** à 24 ans (*military draft, call-up*); SEE ALSO **report, sursis**

incorporer (*vt*): tout le régiment qui vient d'être **incorporé** (*draft, call up*)

incriminer (*vt*): les personnes **incriminées** (*accuse; incriminate*); **incriminés** déjà dans des affaires de drogues (*involved, implicated*)

inculpation (*nf*): la détention, sans **inculpation** ni jugement, de prisonniers politiques (*formal charge*); **être sous le coup d'une inculpation** pour proxénétisme aggravé (*face criminal charges*)

inculpé, -e (*adj/nm,f*): le seul **inculpé** toujours détenu dans cette affaire (*person charged with offence*)

inculper (*vt*): mort d'un manifestant: un deuxième policier **inculpé** (*charge, bring charge against, indict*)

incurie (*nf*): aidé par l'**incurie** de l'État; l'**incurie** des gestionnaires travaillistes (*carelessness, negligence*)

indécis, -e (*adj/nm,f*): rarement les **[électeurs]** **indécis** ont été aussi nombreux (*floating voter, "don't know"*)

indélicat, -e (*adj*): des fonds détournés par des intermédiaires **indélicats** (*dishonest, unscrupulous*)

indélicatesse (*nf*): accusé d'**indélicatesse**, il fut démis de ses fonctions; chacun est à la merci d'une **indélicatesse** ou d'une tromperie (*dishonesty*)

indemne (*adj*): ne pas sortir **indemne** des élections du 4 novembre (*emerge unscathed*)

indemnisation (*nf*): le gouvernement instaura l'**indemnisation** à 90% pour les chômeurs (*compensation, indemnity*)

indemniser (*vt*): des victimes du tabac **indemnisées** aux États-Unis (*indemnify, compensate*); le nombre de chômeurs **indemnisés** a légèrement baissé (*in receipt of benefit*)

indemnité (*nf*): une hausse des **indemnités** de chauffage (*allowance*); l'**indemnité de logement** versée aux instituteurs (*housing allowance*); toucher des **indemnités d'arrêt-maladie** égales à 80% du salaire brut (*sick pay*); être licencié **sans indemnité** (*without redundancy pay*); une **indemnité de départ** égale à un mois de salaire par année d'ancienneté (*severance pay*)

indépendance (*nf*): l'autonomie, première étape vers l'**indépendance** (*[political] independence*)

indépendant, -e (*adj/nm,f*): le grand parti des **[travailleurs]** **indépendants** et des paysans (*self-employed person*)

indépendantiste (*adj/nmf*): comment contenir la fièvre **indépendantiste** des républiques soviétiques? (*separatist*); les **indépendantistes** veulent négocier en position de force (*separatist; member of independence movement*)

indéterminé, -e (*adj*): SEE **durée**

indexation (*nf*): mettre fin à l'**indexation** des salaires sur les prix (*indexing*)

indexer (*vt*): les pensions seront **indexées sur les prix** (*index-linked to prices*)

indice (*nm*): la police ne dispose d'aucun **indice** sérieux (*clue*); l'**indice de l'INSEE** permet de constater l'évolution des prix pendant une période donnée (*retail price index*); l'**indice d'écoute** a baissé (*TV/radio audience rating*)

indigent, -e (*adj/nm,f*): même les **indigents** seront tenus de s'acquitter du nouvel impôt (*destitute; poor*)

indiscuté, -e (*adj*): un monopole longtemps **indiscuté** (*undisputed, unchallenged*)

individu (*nm*): les relations de l'**individu** avec l'État (*private individual*)

indu, -e (*adj*): cette société aurait perçu des commissions **indues** (*unjustified, unwarranted*)

indûment (*adv*): occuper **indûment** un lit hospitalier (*without justification*); on lui reproche d'avoir **indûment** touché plus de 13 000F (*wrongfully; fraudulently*)

inédit, -e (*adj*): selon un sondage **inédit** de la SOFRES (*unpublished*); des élections pluralistes, **inédites** dans l'histoire du pays (*unprecedented, totally new*)

inégalité (*nf*): une politique de redressement des **inégalités** (*inequality; disparity*); il y dénonçait les **inégalités sociales** (*social injustice*)

inéluctable (*adj*): la fermeture du quotidien semble **inéluctable** (*unavoidable, inevitable*); la hausse des prélèvements sociaux **n'est pas inéluctable** (*is not inevitable; can be avoided*)

inemploi (*nm*): un statut qui garantit un revenu minimum en cas d'**inemploi** (*unemployment*)

inexécution (*nf*): réclamer des dommages et intérêts en cas d'**inexécution du contrat** (*failure to honour agreement/contract*)

inexistant, -e (*adj*): le chômage, **inexistant** sous les régimes communistes (*nonexistent*); **les crèches sont inexistantes,** les femmes peuvent difficilement travailler (*there are hardly any day nurseries*)

inexistence (*nf*): l'**inexistence** d'une véritable opposition politique (*lack; absence*); des problèmes réels, comme l'**inexistence d'une politique de la jeunesse** (*the total absence of a policy for young people*)

inféoder [s'] (*vpr*): une radio totalement **inféodée au pouvoir** (*in government hands*); ils accusent le PCF d'**être inféodé** à Moscou (*be pledged to, have an allegiance to*)

infirmer (*vt*): **infirmer** un jugement; la chambre d'accusation **infirme** les ordonnances prises par le juge d'instruction (*overturn, quash*)

inflation (*nf*): un **niveau faible d'inflation** justifie l'optimisme général (*low levels of inflation*)

infléchir (*vt*): les constructeurs commencent à **infléchir** leur publicité dans le sens de la sécurité (*slant, direct*); un comportement que les politiques démographiques ont peu de chances d'**infléchir** (*influence, affect*); [s'] (*vpr*): la production décline, les exportations s'**infléchissent** (*slump, fall*)

infléchissement (*nm*): nouvel **infléchissement** de la position des Douze (*adjustment, shift, reorientation*); un **infléchissement** du trafic aérien (*slight drop/fall*)

inflexion (*nf*): toute **inflexion** de la politique de rigueur aurait une incidence sensible sur l'économie du pays (*change*); une **inflexion de la politique française** est donc amorcée (*shift in French policy*)

influence (*nf*): SEE **trafic**

influent, -e (*adj*): le journal le plus **influent** de Serbie (*influential*)

infondé, -e (*adj*): des critiques totalement **infondées** (*unjustified, groundless*)

information (*nf*): cette **information** n'a pas encore été confirmée (*report; news*); après la fin de l'enquête de la police, le parquet **ouvrit une information** (*start a preliminary investigation*); des projets d'**autoroutes de l'information** (*information highways*); SEE ALSO **complément, hebdomadaire, presse**

informatique (*adj/nf*): SEE **donnée, fichage, piratage, saisie**

informatisé, -e (*adj*): un système **informatisé** d'enregistrement du cheptel (*computerized*)

informé, -e (*adj*): le quotidien algérien, généralement **bien informé** (*well informed*)

infraction (*nf*): les **infractions** à la législation sur les stupéfiants; toute **infraction** aux dispositions du présent article sera punie d'une amende de 50 000F (*offence, breach [of the law]*); SEE ALSO **pluralité**

infrastructure (*nf*): le groupe brésilien renforce ainsi son **infrastructure** européenne (*base; organization*); l'avantage de posséder déjà une **infrastructure portuaire** (*port facilities*)

infructueux, -euse (*adj*): après des mois de discussions **infructueuses** (*fruitless*)

ingérence (*nf*): une **ingérence** dans les affaires intérieures du pays (*interference*); les limites de l'**ingérence humanitaire** (*interference for humanitarian reasons*); sous le coup d'une inculpation pour **délit d'ingérence** (*criminal mismanagement of funds*); SEE ALSO **non-ingérence**

initiative (*nf*): **lancer une initiative** contre le service militaire obligatoire (*make policy proposals*); le parlement **a l'initiative des lois** (*can propose legislation*)

initié, -e (*nm,f*): lors du rachat de la firme américaine, des **initiés** ont gagné des millions de dollars (*insider trader/dealer*); SEE ALSO **délit**

injonction (*nf*): obtenir une **injonction du tribunal** interdisant la reprise de sa maison (*injunction*); le tribunal **rend une ordonnance d'injonction** de payer (*issue an injunction*)

injure (*nf*): les textes de loi qui répriment l'**injure raciale** (*racial abuse/insults*)

innocence (*nf*): démontrer l'**innocence** de son client (*innocence*); il continuait de **clamer son innocence** (*protest his innocence*); SEE ALSO **présomption**

innocent, -e (*adj*): **innocent** du meurtre (*innocent, not guilty*)

innocenter (*vt*): accusé de vol, mais **innocenté** par la cour d'appel (*clear, pronounce innocent*)

innovant, -e (*adj*): une entreprise dynamique, performante, **innovante** (*innovative*)

innovation (*nf*): les entreprises veulent valoriser l'**esprit d'innovation** de leurs salariés (*creativity*)

innover (*vi*): la loi de 1982 **innove** sur un point essentiel (*innovate; break new ground*)

inobservation (*nf*): l'**inobservation** des normes de sécurité (*failure to observe; non-compliance with*)

inopérant, -e (*adj*): les remèdes s'avèrent **inopérants** (*ineffective*)

inopiné, -e (*adj*): à moins d'un retournement de situation **inopiné** (*unexpected, surprise*); des contrôles sont faits, à grande échelle et de **façon inopinée** (*in a random manner*)

inopinément (*adv*): il a dû démissionner **inopinément** la semaine dernière (*unexpectedly*)

inquiéter [s'] (*vpr*): **s'inquiéter** des conséquences (*express concern/disquiet*)

inquiétude (*nf*): l'OCDE manifeste sur ce point de réelles **inquiétudes** (*anxiety, concern*)

insalubre (*adj*): la démolition de **logements insalubres** (*slum housing*)

insatisfaction (*nf*): leur **insatisfaction** vis-à-vis du président sortant (*dissatisfaction*)

inscription (*nf*): le directeur d'une école refuse l'**inscription** de sept enfants marocains (*[school] registration*); SEE ALSO **dossier, fiche, formulaire**

inscrire [s'] (*vpr*): **s'inscrire** à la faculté des Lettres (*register/enrol [esp. for course]*); il tenait à **s'inscrire en faux** contre ces allégations (*strongly deny, refute*); ses propositions **s'inscrivent dans un plan d'ensemble** parfaitement cohérent (*be part of an overall scheme*); SEE ALSO **liste**

inscrit, -e (*adj/nm,f*): le nombre d'**inscrits au chômage** a augmenté de 12% (*registered jobless*); SEE ALSO **non-inscrit**

insécurité (*nf*): la lutte contre l'**insécurité** (*climate of fear; fear syndrome*); le manque d'enseignants et l'**insécurité des locaux** (*unsafe condition of the buildings*); les risques de faillite ou d'**insécurité d'emploi** (*lack of job security*)

insérer (*vt*): un programme qui vise à **insérer** 15 000 jeunes **dans les entreprises** (*place in work/employment*); [s'] (*vpr*): des jeunes qui ne sont pas parvenus à **s'insérer socialement** (*become socially integrated*)

insertion (*nf*): les **difficultés d'insertion [professionnelle]** expliquent la poursuite d'études après le Bac (*difficulty in finding employment*); pour faciliter l'**insertion dans le monde du travail** (*integration into a work environment*); SEE ALSO **revenu, stage**

insolvabilité (*nf*): en état d'**insolvabilité** notoire, la procédure de redressement judiciaire a été ouverte à leur égard (*insolvency*)

insolvable (*adj*): une forte augmentation du nombre de foyers **insolvables** (*insolvent*)

inspecteur, -trice (*nm,f*): l'**inspecteur d'Académie**, au niveau départemental (*education officer; inspector of schools*)

inspection (*nf*): la nomination d'un instituteur par l'**inspection académique** (*schools inspectorate*); l'**inspection du travail**, sise au chef-lieu du département (*Health and Safety Executive [UK]*)

installation (*nf*): optimiser les nouvelles **installations** (*equipment, plant*)

installer [s'] (*vpr*): les jeunes ménages qui cherchent à **s'installer** (*set up home/in business*); une entreprise qui vient **s'installer** dans la zone industrielle (*set up [a business]*); quitter le cabinet pour **s'installer à son compte** (*set up on one's own*)

instance (*nf*): les plus hautes **instances** irakiennes (*authority, body*); des reproches sont adressés par des militants à leurs **instances dirigeantes** (*governing body, authority*); condamné **en première instance**, puis en appel, il avait formé un pourvoi en cassation (*in a court of first instance*); des dossiers **en instance** s'empilent dans les bureaux (*awaiting a decision, pending*); SEE ALSO **régulation, séparation, tribunal**

instauration (*nf*): partisan de l'**instauration de quotas** (*fixing quotas*); malgré l'**instauration de l'état d'urgence** (*declaration of a state of emergency*)

instaurer (*vt*): avoir l'intention d'**instaurer** une démocratie réelle (*set up*); [s'] (*vpr*): l'ordre nouveau qui **s'instaure** en Afrique australe (*come about; be established*)

instituer (*vt*): le SMIC, **institué** en 1968; **instituer** de nouveaux règlements (*set up, establish*)

instituteur, -trice (*nm,f*): l'indemnité de logement versée aux **instituteurs** (*primary-school teacher*)

institution (*nf*): l'**institution** d'un pouvoir dominé par l'armée (*setting-up*); les **institutions politiques** de la nouvelle République (*political institutions*); SEE ALSO **doter**

instructeur, -trice (*adj/nm,f*): SEE **magistrat**

instruction (*nf*): une **instruction** a été ouverte; l'**instruction du dossier** a été confiée au juge Dupont (*preliminary examination of the case [by an examining magistrate]*); une centaine d'arrêtés, circulaires et **instructions** ont été publiés (*directive*); SEE ALSO **juge**

instruire (*vt*): le juge chargé d'**instruire la plainte** (*investigate a complaint*); un juge d'instruction de Rennes va **instruire le dossier** (*conduct an investigation; prepare a case for judgment*)

insuccès (*nm*): l'**insuccès** de 1988 semble bien lointain (*failure; defeat*)

insuffisance (*nf*): les **insuffisances** du système de santé (*deficiencies; defects*); l'**insuffisance des traitements** offerts aux professeurs (*inadequate level of pay*); l'**insuffisance du budget** consacré à la justice (*inadequate level of spending*); SEE ALSO **provision**

insuffisant, -e (*adj*): estimant **insuffisantes** les peines prévues par la loi; juridiquement les preuves étaient **insuffisantes** (*inadequate; insufficient*)

insurgé, -e (*nm,f*): les **insurgés** se sont emparé des bases militaires (*insurgent, rebel*)

insurger [s'] (*vpr*): l'association **s'est insurgée contre** cette attitude (*protest against; condemn*)

intangibilité (*nf*): insister sur l'**intangibilité** de la frontière occidentale de la Pologne; la réaffirmation de l'**intangibilité** de l'unité italienne (*inviolability*)

intégral, -e, *pl* **-aux** (*adj*): le texte **intégral** de son discours (*whole, complete*)

intégralité (*nf*): Téhéran exporte l'**intégralité de son brut** via le Golfe (*all her oil production*)

intégrant, -e (*adj*): SEE **partie**

intégration (*nf*): le nouveau ministre de l'**intégration** et de la lutte contre l'exclusion (*[social] integration*); l'**intégration** des primes dans le salaire (*inclusion*); l'**intégration** de la Géorgie dans la CEI (*entry; admission*)

intégrer (*vt*): **intégrer** la fonction publique (*join, enter*); le Premier ministre voulait l'**intégrer** dans son cabinet (*include, admit*); [s'] (*vpr*): la volonté de **s'intégrer** en milieu rural (*integrate; settle*); ce projet **s'intègre dans** un vaste projet régional (*be a part of*)

intégrisme (*nm*): la montée de l'**intégrisme** dans ce pays en majorité musulman; l'**intégrisme** chiite est venu bouleverser les données de la situation (*fundamentalism*)

intégriste (*adj/nmf*): les **intégristes**, partisans de la stricte application des dogmes et des pratiques musulmanes (*fundamentalist*); il va falloir faire taire les **intégristes** des deux camps (*extremist*)

intégrité (*nf*): préserver l'**intégrité** de la petite république balte (*[territorial] integrity*)

intempestif, -ive (*adj*): les remarques **intempestives** du ministre (*untimely; ill-timed, inopportune*)

intenable (*adj*): c'est peu dire que la position française était **intenable** (*untenable; indefensible*)

intendance (*nf*): l'**intendance** commence à se mettre en place (*administrative services*); [*fig*] au Premier ministre l'**intendance**, au Président la diplomatie (*day-to-day matters*)

intendant (*nm*): un **intendant** de collège tue le principal, et se suicide (*bursar*)

intenter (*vt*): il **intenta un procès** contre les autorités françaises (*institute proceedings*)

intention (*nf*): un sondage lui donne 52% des **intentions de vote** (*promised/intended vote*); pourquoi **faire un procès d'intention** à l'Allemagne? (*blame on the basis of presumed motives*)

interdiction (*nf*): depuis l'**interdiction** de la publicité pour l'alcool et le tabac (*ban, prohibition*); la **levée de l'interdiction** des activités politiques (*lifting of the ban*); l'**interdiction d'exporter** qui frappe animaux vivants et viande (*export ban*)

interdire (*vt*): le seul quotidien indépendant du pays **a été interdit de publication** (*be banned [esp. newspaper]*); l'étranger risque d'être expulsé ou d'**être interdit de séjour** (*be refused a residence permit*); [s'] (*vpr*): Paris **s'interdit** d'apporter une aide logistique aux Tchadiens (*refuse*)

interdit (*nm*): la levée des **interdits** concernant la consommation d'alcool (*ban, restriction*); les rares jeunes qui osent **braver les interdits** (*defy a taboo/ban*)

intéressant, -e (*adj*): proposer des conditions très **intéressantes**; cette formule d'épargne n'est **intéressante** que pour certaines catégories de personnes (*attractive; profitable*)

intéressé, -e (*adj/nm,f*): cette perspective fut très bien accueillie par les **intéressés** eux-mêmes (*interested party*)

intéressement (*nm*): une réduction des salaires avec **intéressement aux résultats** de la société (*profit-sharing; profit-related pay scheme*); SEE ALSO **prime**

intéresser (*vt*): la réforme **intéressera** 1,5 million de familles; tous les départements **intéressés** par ces mesures (*concern*); il faut les **intéresser** directement aux résultats de l'entreprise (*give a share [esp. in profits]*)

intérêt (*nm*): Pechiney cède ses **intérêts** aux Japonais (*stake; operation*); SEE ALSO **abaisser, groupe, taux, travail**

interférer (*vi*): nous n'avons pas à **interférer** dans leur politique d'investissement (*interfere; involve oneself*)

intérieur, -e (*adj*): SEE **affaire, demande, politique, règlement**

intérim (*nm*): l'**intérim** de la présidence (*interim office*); **assurer l'intérim** de la direction financière (*deputize for; cover for*); s'adresser à une **société d'intérim** (*temping agency*); SEE ALSO **mission**

intérimaire (*adj/nmf*): la composition d'un gouvernement **intérimaire** (*interim, caretaker*); embaucher des **[travailleurs] intérimaires** (*temporary employee; "temp"*); SEE ALSO **dividende**

interjeter (*vt*): les dirigeants ont la possibilité d'**interjeter appel** de la décision (*lodge an appeal*)

interlocuteur, -trice (*nm,f*): les Russes, seuls **interlocuteurs** des Serbes (*negotiating partner*); chercher dans le camp adverse **un interlocuteur valable** (*an acceptable negotiating partner*)

intermédiaire (*adj/nm*): les ventes d'armes dégagent des commissions énormes pour les **intermédiaires** (*go-between, middleman*); se proposer pour **servir d'intermédiaire** (*mediate*)

intermittent, -e (*adj/nm,f*): les dockers mensualisés et les **intermittents** (*contract worker; casual labour*)

interne (*adj*): une coalition en proie à des dissensions **internes** (*internal*); SEE ALSO **promotion**

interpellation (*nf*): **il y a eu 15 interpellations** jeudi lors des manifestations (*15 people were detained for questioning*); les ministres n'ont plus à redouter les **interpellations** (*oral question [in parliament]*)

interpeller (*vt*): six jeunes **ont été interpellés** et placés en garde à vue (*be stopped for questioning [by police]*); **interpeller** directement le ministre sur un dossier (*question; challenge*)

interposer [s'] (*vpr*): les Casques bleus **s'interposent** aux quatre coins du monde; **s'interposer** dans le déchirement yougoslave (*intervene [to keep the peace]*)

interposition (*nf*): constituer une **force d'interposition** (*intervention force*)

interprète (*nmf*): **se faire l'interprète de** l'ensemble des travailleurs (*represent, speak for*)

interrogatoire (*nf*): subir 12 heures d'**interrogatoires** (*questioning*)

interroger (*vt*): après avoir été **interrogé**, il a été écroué (*question*); [s'] (*vpr*): l'Angola **s'interroge sur** les véritables intentions de Pretoria (*wonder/speculate about*)

intersyndicale (*nf*): l'**intersyndicale** justice, regroupant magistrats, avocats et fonctionnaires (*inter-union committee*)

intervenant, -e (*nm,f*): les discours des divers **intervenants** (*speaker [in debate]*)

intervenir (*vi*): des reclassements de personnel pourraient **intervenir** (*occur, take place*); la communauté internationale semble disposée à **intervenir** militairement au Burundi (*intervene*); **intervenant** devant les assises du parti (*speak, intervene [in debate/discussion]*); le rôle des syndicats est d'**intervenir** dans la gestion de l'entreprise (*play a part, participate*); **faire intervenir** les comités d'entreprise (*bring/call in, involve*); SEE ALSO **fondé**

intervention (*nf*): à la veille de l'**intervention** militaire en Tchétchénie (*intervention*); consacrant son **intervention** aux questions européennes (*speech; contribution [to a debate]*); la nécessité de la relance de l'**intervention** pour la viande bovine (*fixing of an intervention price*)

intestin, -e (*adj*): SEE **querelle**

intimité (*nf*): inculpé pour atteinte à l'**intimité de la vie privée** (*privacy of the individual*)

intoxication (*nf*): le mensonge et l'**intoxication**; dénoncer une campagne d'**intoxication** (*disinformation; propaganda*)

intraitable (*adj*): la base demeure **intraitable** sur sa revendication principale (*uncompromising, inflexible*)

introduction (*nf*): remettre à plus tard son **introduction en bourse** (*going public; listing on the stock market*)

invalider (*vt*): la Cour suprême a **invalidé** hier cette décision (*quash*)

invalidité (*nf*): SEE **pension**

inverser (*vt*): ne rien faire qui pourrait **inverser la tendance** (*reverse the trend*)

investir (*vt*): le candidat **investi** par l'UDF (*appoint, select*); des sans-papiers **investissent** une église parisienne (*occupy, take over [building]*); persuader les entreprises à **investir** et les ménages à consommer (*invest*); [s'] (*vpr*): **s'investir dans** la vie associative (*put a lot of effort into; involve oneself fully in*)

investissement (*nm*): un gros effort d'**investissement** doit être fait (*investment*); l'**investissement se maintient**, le chômage cesse de progresser (*investment remains steady*); SEE ALSO **amortir**

investiture (*nf*): briguer l'**investiture** du parti en vue des élections (*nomination [as candidate]; investiture*)

inviolabilité (*nf*): quant à l'**inviolabilité** des frontières (*intangibility, inviolability*); la protection de la vie privée, notamment l'**inviolabilité du domicile** (*right to privacy in one's own home*)

irrecevabilité (*nf*): l'objet de l'exercice d'**irrecevabilité**, c'est de faire admettre que le texte proposé est contraire à la constitution (*inadmissibility [of proposed legislation/bill]*)

irrecevable (*adj*): 13% des dossiers ont été jugés **irrecevables** (*inadmissible*); le tribunal de grande instance a **déclaré irrecevable** la requête (*reject as inadmissible*)

irréductible (*adj/nmf*): l'opposition **irréductible** de plusieurs députés libéraux (*out-and-out, implacable*); les **irréductibles** refusent tout compromis (*diehard, hardliner*)

irrégularité (*nf*): des élections tachées d'**irrégularité** (*irregularity*); le problème de l'**irrégularité de ses rentrées d'argent** (*irregular income*)

irrégulier, -ière (*adj*): l'État continue à combattre le séjour **irrégulier** des étrangers (*illegal; unauthorized*); la prolifération d'**étrangers en situation irrégulière** (*illegal immigrants*)

irresponsabilité (*nf*): son **irresponsabilité** lui évite toute poursuite judiciaire (*unimpeachability*); l'**irresponsabilité politique** du Parlement européen n'est plus à démontrer (*[political] non-accountability*)

irresponsable (*adj*): le Président était **irresponsable**, mais le gouvernement était responsable devant le Parlement (*not accountable for its actions before a higher authority*)

isolé, -e (*adj*): le PCF se retrouve **isolé** sur la monnaie unique (*isolated*); SEE ALSO **femme, parent**

isolement (*nm*): l'aggravation de l'**isolement** économique du pays (*economic isolation*)

isoloir (*nm*): les déserteurs de l'**isoloir** expliquent leur comportement par la faiblesse des enjeux (*voting booth*)

issu, -e (*adj*): la révolte, **issue du mécontentement populaire** (*caused by popular discontent*); un gouvernement **issu d'élections libres** (*democratically elected*); SEE ALSO **immigration**

issue (*nf*): quelle que soit l'**issue** du scrutin (*result, verdict*); chercher une **issue au conflit** (*solution to the conflict*)

J

J (*nm*): SEE **jour**

jachère (*nf*): imposer la **jachère**, et casser la course aux rendements; instaurer un programme limité de **mise en jachère** des terres cultivables (*taking land out of cultivation; leaving land fallow*)

jacobin, -e (*adj/nm,f*): l'État centralisateur et **jacobin** renforce son emprise sur la société; une politique d'inspiration **jacobine** (*Jacobinic*)

jacobinisme (*nm*): le **jacobinisme** centralisateur d'une certaine gauche (*Jacobinism*); passer du régionalisme au **jacobinisme** (*state centralism*)

jacquerie (*nf*): le populiste ultraconservateur poursuit sa **jacquerie** contre le Parti républicain (*Jacquerie, uprising, revolt*)

jaune (*adj/nm*): le **métal jaune**, et la pierre: deux valeurs refuges (*gold*); on les traitait de **jaunes** et de vendus (*blackleg, strikebreaker*)

jet (*nm*): **jets de pierres** sporadiques et charges de CRS (*stone-throwing [esp. by demonstrators]*)

jeter (*vt*): SEE **base**

jeu, *pl* **-x** (*nm*): être en faveur du **libre jeu de la concurrence** (*free/unrestricted competition*); Autriche: la crise **fait le jeu de** l'extrême droite (*play into the hands of, benefit*); aucun intérêt matériel n'**est en jeu** (*be at stake*); une crise qui **met en jeu** les intérêts de la France (*put at risk, threaten*); le gouvernement **calme le jeu** en retirant son projet de loi (*cool/calm a situation down*); SEE ALSO **épingle**

joint-venture (*nm*): former une **société en joint-venture** [ou entreprise commune] avec British Aerospace; un accord de **joint-venture** avec un partenaire indien (*joint venture*)

jouir (*vt*): le président, qui **jouissait** toujours de sondages favorables (*enjoy*); le peuple haïtien doit pouvoir **jouir de la sécurité** (*feel safe*)

jouissance (*nf*): maison à vendre **avec jouissance immédiate** (*with immediate possession*); l'**entrée en jouissance** du nouveau propriétaire (*coming into possession of property*)

jour (*nm*): Privatisations: Elf-Aquitaine à la veille du **jour J** (*D-Day; the big day*); la durée maximale est de huit **jours francs** (*clear day*); les atrocités commises en Bosnie sont peu à peu **mises au jour** (*reveal, bring to light*); la **mise à jour** de la programmation réclamerait 20 MF (*updating; bringing up to date*); SEE ALSO **chômé, férié, ouvrable, ouvré**

journal, *pl* -**aux** (*nm*): dans une ordonnance publiée dans le **Journal officiel** du 21 mars (*French government publication containing details of new acts, laws, etc.*); les images du **journal télévisé** (*television news bulletin*); SEE ALSO **un**

journée (*nf*): une **journée ouvrée** par semaine (*working day*); la mise en place de la **journée continue** (*remaining open over lunch hour/all day [office, shop]*); les syndicats se mobilisent et organisent des **journées d'action** (*day of industrial action*); SEE ALSO **chômé**

jouxter (*vt*): la dernière maison d'Avon **jouxte** la première de Fontainebleau (*adjoin, be adjacent to*)

judiciaire (*adj*): le **[pouvoir] judiciaire**, en vertu du principe de la séparation des pouvoirs, est indépendant (*judicial power, judiciary*); SEE ALSO **administrateur, administration, antécédent, casier, contrôle, liquidateur, police, poursuite, procédure, redressement**

juge (*nm*): les **juges** appartiennent à la magistrature assise (*judges; the Bench [UK]*); une plainte déposée devant un **juge de paix** (*Justice of the Peace, magistrate*); le **juge d'instruction**, à la fois juge et enquêteur (*[in France] examining magistrate*); passer devant le **juge des enfants** (*juvenile magistrate*); SEE ALSO **décision, suppléant**

jugement (*nm*): le **jugement** sera rendu le 4 juin (*verdict, judgment*); le tribunal a **rendu son jugement** (*give/hand down a verdict*); SEE ALSO **délibéré, prévenu**

juger (*vt*): le tribunal d'instance **juge** les délits peu graves (*judge/try [a case]*); quatre ans de détention sans **être jugé** (*be brought to trial*); c'est à l'ONU de **juger** ce différend (*arbitrate [in a dispute]*); SEE ALSO **coupable**

juguler (*vt*): réussir à **juguler** le chômage; comment **juguler** l'inflation? (*arrest, halt, stop*)

junte (*nf*): la **junte militaire** qui est au pouvoir (*military junta*)

juré (*nm*): pour être **juré d'assises**, il faut être citoyen français (*juror, jury member*); les **jurés** ont conclu à une mort naturelle (*the jury*)

juridiction (*nf*): le Conseil d'État, la plus haute **juridiction** administrative; une **juridiction** créée pour statuer sur des affaires d'espionnage (*court, tribunal*); SEE ALSO **assise**

juridique (*adj*): la réforme des **professions juridique et judiciaire** (*legal profession*); SEE ALSO **conseil, statut, vide**

jurisprudence (*nf*): la source principale du droit était la **jurisprudence**; l'importance de la **jurisprudence** en droit anglais (*case law, jurisprudence*); l'arrêt pourrait **faire jurisprudence** (*set/establish a precedent*); dans cette situation, **la jurisprudence fait défaut** (*there is no legal precedent*)

juriste (*nm*): un **juriste** spécialiste en droit du travail (*jurist, legal expert*); un poste de **juriste d'entreprise** (*company lawyer*)

jury (*nm*): un **jury** comprenant douze jurés (*jury*)

jusqu'au-boutisme (*nm*): il risque de payer très cher son **jusqu'au-boutisme** (*hard-line stance, extremism*)

jusqu'au-boutiste (*adj/nm*): connu pour ses vues **jusqu'au-boutistes** (*extreme, hard-line*); les **jusqu'au-boutistes**, partisans de la répression aveugle (*hard-liner; extremist*)

justice (*nf*): une aspiration à une plus grande **justice sociale** (*social justice*); transmettre un dossier à la **justice** (*the courts; the law, legal system*); les associations de consommateurs peuvent **aller en justice** (*go to court*); il menace de les **attaquer en justice** (*take to court*); les **justices de paix**, disparues en 1958 (*court presided over by* juge de paix); celui qui prétend **se faire justice** (*take the law into one's own hands*); SEE ALSO **action, décision, déni, palais, plainte, poursuite, saisir, témoigner, traduire**

justiciable (*adj/nmf*): un délit **justiciable d'**une peine de prison (*punishable by*); la nécessité d'une justice qui soit plus proche du **justiciable** (*person accused of a crime/on trial*)

justificatif, -ive (*adj/nm*): fournir un **justificatif** (*written proof, documentary evidence*); SEE ALSO **pièce**

justification (*nf*): une **justification** de son nouveau domicile, par exemple une quittance de loyer; sur **justification** de sa qualité de salarié (*[documentary] evidence; proof*)

justifier (*vt*): les étrangers souhaitant séjourner en France doivent **justifier** leur moyen d'existence (*furnish proof of*); sur son refus de **justifier de son identité** (*show proof of identity*)

juteux, -euse (*adj*): faire une **juteuse** opération financière (*lucrative*); décrocher de **juteux contrats** (*lucrative contract*); réaliser de **juteuses plus-values** boursières (*considerable/juicy profits*)

K

kiosque (*nm*): disponible dans tous les **kiosques à journaux** (*news-stand, newspaper kiosk*)

krach (*nm*): depuis le **krach boursier** d'octobre dernier (*stock-market crash*)

kyrielle (*nf*): on annonça **toute une kyrielle de mesures** (*a whole range of measures*); débiter **une kyrielle de mensonges** (*a pack of lies*)

L

Labour (*nm*): le **Labour** a toutes les chances de gagner les élections; le **Labour** se pose en alternative aux conservateurs (*[British] Labour Party*)

lâche (*adj*): une conception plus **lâche** du fédéralisme (*loose*)

laïc, -que (*adj/nm,f*): pays **laïc** et ouvert à l'Occident (*secular*); l'affaire du foulard islamique à l'**école laïque** (*secular [state] school*); l'**éducation laïque** est sur la défensive face aux attaques du secteur privé (*[in France] the state educational sector*)

laïcité (*nf*): il défend la conception républicaine de la **laïcité** en France (*secularity; secularism*); la **laïcité de l'enseignement** est toujours son crédo (*secular education*)

laissé-pour-compte (*nm*): comment venir en aide aux **laissés-pour-compte de la croissance**? (*victim/casualty of economic growth*)

laminer (*vt*): [*fig*] le pouvoir d'achat des salariés **est laminé** (*be eroded*); la concurrence a **laminé les marges** (*squeeze profit margins*); les centristes, **laminés** entre les blocs antagonistes (*crushed, squeezed*)

langue (*nf*): il possède à merveille la **langue de bois** des politiciens (*cliché-ridden language; [political] cant*)

larcin (*nm*): quinze jours de préventive pour un **larcin** de 125 francs (*petty theft*); SEE ALSO **menu**

large (*adj*): entamer de **larges** consultations (*wide-ranging, extensive*); bénéficier d'un **large soutien** (*wide support*); SEE ALSO **concertation**

largement (*adv*): être **largement** vainqueur (*by a comfortable margin*)

larvé, -e (*adj*): Nouvelle-Calédonie: **crise sociale larvée** et divisions politiques (*latent social unrest*); confronté à une **contestation larvée** au sein de la rédaction (*simmering revolt*); la **guerre civile larvée** qui ravage ce pays centraméricain (*state of undeclared civil war*)

laxisme (*nm*): accusé de **laxisme** dans la lutte contre la mafia (*being soft; permissiveness*); SEE ALSO **orienter**

laxiste (*adj*): la politique **laxiste** en matière de délinquance juvénile (*lax, permissive*)

leader (*nm*): le **leader** extrémiste allemand lavé d'une accusation de racisme (*leader*); 50 entreprises **leader sur leur marché** cherchent des candidats vendeurs (*market leader*)

lecteur, -trice (*nm,f*): les **lecteurs** de la presse magazine (*readers; readership*)

lectorat (*nm*): la fidélité d'un **lectorat** important (*readership; readers*)

lecture (*nf*): adopter un texte de loi en première **lecture** (*reading of a parliamentary bill*); l'**examen en seconde lecture** d'une proposition de loi (*second reading of a bill*); **donner lecture** d'un communiqué (*read [aloud]*)

légal, -e, *pl* **-aux** (*adj*): **légal**, car conforme à la loi française (*legal, lawful*)

légaliser (*vt*): une signature **légalisée** (*authenticated, certified*); **légaliser** ou dépénaliser les drogues aurait des conséquences graves (*legalize*)

légalité (*nf*): violer la **légalité** constitutionnelle (*law*); agir tout en **restant dans la légalité** (*keeping within the law*)

légataire (*nmf*): le **légataire**, ou le bénéficiaire d'un legs (*legatee*)

légiférer (*vi*): il ne reste plus au législateur qu'à **légiférer**; comment **légiférer** sur une question si personnelle? (*legislate; lay down the law*)

législateur, -trice (*nm,f*): il faut que le **législateur** fasse preuve d'imagination (*parliament, legislature*)

législatif, -ive (*adj/nm*): le **[corps] législatif** jadis avait trop de pouvoir face à l'exécutif (*legislature; legislative body*); dans les **[élections] législatives** de mars, la droite est revenue au pouvoir (*parliamentary elections*)

législation (*nf*): la mise en œuvre de **législations** écologiques (*laws, legislation*); spécialiste dans la **législation du travail** (*labour legislation/law*); SEE ALSO **trust**

législature (*nf*): la durée actuelle d'une **législature** est de cinq ans (*term of office; life of a parliament*); le mandat d'une **législature** peut être écourté en cas de dissolution (*legislature, legislative body*)

légitime (*adj*): il estime **légitimes** les revendications étudiantes (*legitimate, justified*); sa tactique: **plaider la légitime défense** (*plead self-defence*)

légitimer (*vt*): les couples choisissant de **légitimer** leur union (*legitimize; regularize*)

légitimité (*nf*): la **légitimité** des revendications de l'Armée zapatiste de libération (*legitimacy*); le gouvernement de transition, **sans légitimité populaire** (*without a mandate from the people*)

legs (*nm*): un **legs** qui est contesté par les héritiers (*legacy; bequest*)

léguer (*vt*): avoir un patrimoine à **léguer** (*hand down, pass on*); **léguer par testament** sa fortune à une organisation caritative (*bequeath*)

lèse-majesté (*nf*): un crime de **lèse-majesté** aux yeux des purs et durs (*treason*)

lettre (*nf*): l'ambassadeur présente ses **lettres de créance** (*credentials*); envoyer une **lettre de démission** (*letter of resignation*); des **lettres de licenciement** envoyées aux salariés (*letter of dismissal; redundancy notice*); sachant que leurs décisions **resteront lettre morte** (*go unheeded*); SEE ALSO **revendicateur, sollicitation**

levée (*nf*): la **levée** de l'état d'urgence a été annoncée (*lifting, suspension*); la première phase du financement prévoit la **levée** de 75 milliards en capital (*raising [esp. of funds/capital]*); l'accord a déclenché une **levée de boucliers** du côté protestant (*strong opposition; outcry*); SEE ALSO **interdiction**

lever (*vt*): l'état d'urgence sera bientôt **levé** (*lift, end*); Péchiney s'apprête à **lever** plus de cinq milliards de francs (*raise [capital]*); SEE ALSO **équivoque**

levier (*nm*): le secteur public doit jouer un rôle de **levier** (*lever*); c'est lui dorénavant qui **est aux leviers de commande** de l'État (*be in control/ command*)

liaison (*nf*): la nouvelle **liaison** Sarre-Moselle (*link*); les **liaisons routières** trans-Pyrénées (*road link*); la **liaison 2 × 2 voies** entre ici et Boulogne (*dual-carriageway road link*); Taïwan propose des **liaisons maritimes** entre l'île et le continent (*sea link*)

libellé (*nm*): le **libellé** du texte de révision de la Constitution (*wording [esp. of a legal text]*)

libeller (*vt*): le chèque devrait être **libellé à l'ordre de** notre société (*draw up, make out to*); acheter des avoirs **libellés en dollars** (*payable in dollars*)

libéral, -e, *pl* **-aux** (*adj/nm,f*): la politique économique est d'orientation **libérale** (*non-interventionist*); les **libéraux** préconisent la liberté des changes (*free- marketeer, liberal economist*); SEE ALSO **économie, projet**

libéralisation (*nf*): ouvrir les frontières, et multiplier la **libéralisation des échanges** dans tous les domaines (*easing of restrictions on trade*); quand les Russes se sont lancés dans la **libéralisation des prix** (*removal of price controls*)

libéraliser (*vt*): le ciel européen sera bientôt intégralement **libéralisé** (*liberalize, deregulate*); **libéraliser le commerce** et diminuer l'intervention de l'État (*ease/lift restrictions on trade*)

libéralisme (*nm*): le **libéralisme** anglais s'oppose à l'interventionnisme français; dans un monde en crise, le **libéralisme** intégral est dangereux (*free-market system; liberalism*)

libération (*nf*): sa **libération** ne saurait tarder (*freeing; discharge*); bénéficier d'une **libération conditionnelle** (*release on parole*); la prison à perpétuité sans possibilité de **libération anticipée** (*early release*); la **libération des prix** pourrait être la cause d'abus (*removal of price controls*); la loi sur la **libération des loyers** (*lifting of rent controls*)

libérer (*vt*): obligé de **libérer** un appartement (*vacate*); le prix des carburants a été entièrement **libéré** (*deregulate*); dans ces conditions, comment **libérer les prix**? (*remove price controls*); il est **libéré sous condition** en 1970 (*release conditionally*); **libérer sous caution** un prévenu (*release on bail*)

liberté (*nf*): une charte des **libertés** fondamentales (*freedom; liberty*); sa demande de **mise en liberté** conditionnelle fut rejetée (*release; discharge*); l'auteur présumé du crime a été **mis en liberté provisoire** (*[release on] parole*); une période de **liberté surveillée** sous le contrôle d'un éducateur (*[release on] probation*); revenir à la **liberté des prix**, et laisser jouer la concurrence (*freedom from price controls*); la **liberté de réunion** et d'association (*freedom of assembly*); la **liberté de presse** ne sera pas remise en cause (*freedom of the press*); garantir la **liberté d'expression**; la **liberté d'opinion** est leur revendication principale (*freedom of speech, free speech*); SEE ALSO **caution, conscience**

libre (*adj*): dans la profession médicale, **les honoraires sont libres** (*there are no restrictions on the fees that can be charged*); une entorse à la règle générale de la **libre concurrence** (*free competition*); des contraintes qui entravent la **libre entreprise** (*free enterprise*); SEE ALSO **accès, école**

libre-échange (*nm*): le **libre-échange** avec les États-Unis créera 200 000 emplois (*[policy of] free trade*); la nouvelle **zone de libre-échange** économique nord-américaine (*free-trade area*)

libre-échangiste (*adj*): la dérive **libre-échangiste** de l'Europe (*free-market, free-trade*)

librement (*adv*): SEE **administrer**

lice (*nf*): deux candidats **sont en lice** (*are in the lists/in contention*)

licence (*nf*): se voir octroyer une **licence exclusive** de production et de distribution (*sole/exclusive licence*); être présent dans 80 pays via des **accords de licence** (*licensing agreement*)

licencié, -e (*adj/nm,f*): **licencié** en droit privé de la faculté d'Alger (*graduate*); un club qui a démarré avec une vingtaine de **licenciés** (*registered member [esp. of sports federation]*); aux **licenciés [économiques]** sera versée une allocation spéciale pendant un an (*employee made redundant*)

licenciement (*nm*): cent vingt suppressions d'emploi, dont quinze **licenciements secs** (*compulsory redundancy*); les demandeurs d'emploi qui s'inscrivent à l'ANPE pour **licenciement [économique]** (*redundancy; lay-off*); des cas de **licenciements abusifs** (*unfair dismissal*); le **licenciement pour faute** doit être fondé sur une mauvaise conduite de l'employé (*dismissal*); SEE ALSO **éventualité, lettre, prime**

licencier (*vt*): on parle de **licencier** 500 employés (*make redundant, lay off*); **licencié** pour faute grave (*dismissed*)

licite (*adj*): le lock-out consécutif à une grève est **licite** (*lawful, within the law*)

lien (*nm*): **renforcer les liens** entre l'Europe et le Canada (*strengthen ties/links*); SEE ALSO **employer**

lier (*vt*): un marchand d'armes syrien **serait lié à l'attentat** (*is alleged to be involved in the terrorist attack*)

lieu, *pl* **-x** (*nm*): aller enquêter **sur les lieux du crime** (*at the site of the crime*); le développement de la démocratie **sur les lieux de travail** (*in the workplace*); SEE ALSO **état, haut, occuper**

lieu-dit (*nm*): le hameau a été ravalé au rang de **lieu-dit** (*[named] place, locality*)

ligne (*nf*): suivant aveuglément la **ligne du parti** (*party line*); partisan d'une **ligne dure** vis-à-vis du Japon (*hard-line [approach]*)

lignée (*nf*): il est à cet égard **dans la lignée des** autres Présidents de la République (*in the tradition of*)

limite (*nf*): quatre ans avant la **limite d'âge** (*age limit*); SEE ALSO **date**

limiter (*vt*): parvenir à **limiter** les effets de la pollution (*limit, restrict*); le retour d'un temps sec a permis de **limiter les dégâts** (*minimize the damage; stop things getting any worse*)

limitrophe (*adj*): Aquitaine, Poitou-Charentes, Auvergne, les pays **limitrophes** du Limousin (*bordering, neighbouring*); l'Île-de-France et ses sept **régions limitrophes** (*neighbouring/surrounding regions*)

limogeage (*nm*): après son **limogeage** de la direction du Parti communiste; une vague de **limogeages** a suivi les troubles dans le Caucase (*dismissal, sacking*); SEE ALSO **série**

limoger (*vt*): le président **limogea** le chef d'état-major de l'armée; **limogé** de son poste de premier secrétaire (*sack, dismiss*)

liquidateur (*nm*): le **liquidateur judiciaire** vend les actifs de la société pour payer les créanciers (*official receiver*)

liquidation (*nf*): le tribunal de commerce de Pontoise prononce la **liquidation judiciaire** de la société (*winding-up [by decision of court]*); la **liquidation** d'avril termine sur une hausse de 9% (*Stock exchange settlement day*); *[fig]* après la **liquidation de la crise ministérielle** (*settling of the ministerial crisis*)

liquide (*adj/nm*): SEE **payer**

liquider (*vt*): Immobilier: l'armée **liquide** son patrimoine (*sell off*); *[fig]* la France et l'Iran **liquident leur contentieux financier** (*settle their financial dispute*)

liquidités (*nfpl*): une crise mondiale des **liquidités**; le marché regorge encore de **liquidités** prêtes à s'investir (*liquid assets; available funds*)

lisibilité (*nf*): le manque évident de **lisibilité** de la politique du gouvernement (*clarity, coherence*)

liste (*nf*): la **liste** de la majorité présidentielle l'emporte dans l'Aveyron (*list of candidates [in list voting system]*); il reste encore un mois pour **s'inscrire sur les listes électorales** (*register on an electoral roll*); SEE ALSO **conduire, scrutin**

litige (*nm*): la soumission du **litige** à l'arbitrage des Nations Unies (*dispute*); la zone **en litige** recèle des richesses cachées (*disputed, in dispute*)

litigieux, -ieuse (*adj*): un service des contentieux s'occupe des questions **litigieuses** (*disputed, contentious*)

livraison (*nf*): l'embargo sur la **livraison d'armes** à la Bosnie (*supplying of arms*); dans la dernière **livraison** de la revue, parue en mars (*issue [of periodical]*); SEE ALSO **délai**

livre (*nm*): le **livre blanc** de la commission des Affaires sociales; un **livre blanc** remis au Premier ministre (*White Paper; official report*); un **livre vert** qui servira de document de réflexion (*Green Paper, policy proposals document*); l'imprimerie du *Parisien libéré*, occupée par les **ouvriers du livre** (*printworkers*); (*nf*): nouvelle baisse de la **livre sterling** (*[pound] sterling*)

livrer (*vt*): les malfaiteurs furent **livrés** à la police (*hand over, give up*); la Chine, accusée de **livrer** des matériaux nucléaires au Pakistan (*supply, deliver*); [se] (*vpr*): **se livrer** à des exactions contre la population civile (*carry out*)

livret (*nm*): le taux du **livret A [de caisse d'épargne]** a été baissé de 6 à 4,5% (*[French] National Savings "A" account*); titulaire d'un **livret d'Épargne-logement** (*Building Society pass book, savings book*); SEE ALSO **compte**

lobby (*nm*): le **lobby des armes** essuie une défaite aux États-Unis (*arms lobby*); sous la pression du **lobby des médecins** (*medical lobby*)

lobbying (*nm*): le **lobbying**, c'est l'influence d'un groupe de pression pour faire aboutir une revendication (*lobbying*); **mener un lobbying intense** en faveur de l'avion français (*lobby intensively*)

local, pl -aux (*nm*): des **locaux** entièrement rénovés (*premises*); dans un **local associatif** dans la cité ouvrière (*community room/hall*); les **locaux administratifs** du collège sont occupés depuis mardi (*administrative offices*); SEE ALSO **banalisé, occupation**

locataire (*nmf*): le précédent **locataire** n'a pas encore vidé les lieux (*tenant, occupier*); les avantages d'être **locataire** ou d'accéder à la propriété (*live in rented accomodation*); [*fig*] l'actuel **locataire de Matignon** (*French Prime Minister*)

locatif, -ive (*adj*): le montant du loyer et des **charges locatives** (*rental charges*); le **revenu locatif** des immeubles (*rental, proceeds from rents*); acheter de l'immobilier **à des fins locatives** (*for renting out*); SEE ALSO **logement**

location (*nf*): résilier un contrat de **location** (*renting, tenancy*); préférer la **location** à l'accession à la propriété (*renting [of accommodation]*)

lock-out (*nm*): après une grève de dix jours, la direction a décidé un **lock-out**; le patron réplique par une menace de **lock-out** [fermeture d'usine] pour briser la grève (*lock-out*)

locomotive (*nf*): le Japon refuse d'être la **locomotive** économique; le secteur privé doit être la **locomotive** de la croissance (*pacesetter, pacemaker*)

logement (*nm*): l'achat de leur **logement** par les locataires de HLM (*home; apartment*); un **logement social** réservé aux familles modestes (*local authority housing*); un salaire mensuel généreux et un **logement de fonction** (*company house/flat*); favoriser le **logement locatif** en milieu rural (*rented accommodation/housing*); SEE ALSO **conjoncture, crise, disette, épargne, indemnité, insalubre, parc, prêt, propriété**

loger (*vt/vi*): SEE **enseigne**

loi (*nf*): selon la **loi** en vigueur (*law*); faire campagne sur le thème de **la loi et l'ordre** (*law and order*); un projet de **loi-cadre** réformant le système actuel (*outline law*); voter une **loi-programme** militaire fastueuse (*act providing framework for government programme*); les grandes lignes de la **loi de finances** 1997 (*finance act/bill*); un mouvement **mis hors la loi** en 1985 (*outlawed*); depuis la **mise hors la loi** du PCF (*outlawing*); SEE ALSO **abrogation, anticasseur, enfreindre, initiative, prescription, projet, proposition, respecter, terme, texte**

loti, -e (*adj*): l'Europe est **la plus mal lotie** (*the least well off*); les étudiants en Lettres sont **mieux lotis** à cet égard (*better treated/provided for*); l'Allemagne est **mieux lotie** que la France (*better placed, in a better situation*)

lotir (*vt*): des **terrains à lotir** dans un quartier résidentiel de la ville (*[building] plots for sale; land for [housing] development*)

lotissement (*nm*): le **lotissement** ou a vente d'une propriété par lots (*division [of goods/land] into units*); d'immenses **lotissements** de maisons individuelles; des banlieues couvertes de **lotissements pavillonnaires** (*housing estate/development*)

loucher (*vi*): l'énorme marché américain vers lequel **louchent** tous les pays industrialisés (*look enviously at; have designs upon*)

louer (*vt*): **louer** un appartement en centre ville (*rent; rent out*); la solution qui consisterait à **louer du personnel** au fur et à mesure des besoins (*hire/engage staff*)

lourd, -e (*adj*): SEE **faute**

lourdeur (*nf*): les **lourdeurs** administratives de l'ANPE (*cumbersome procedures*)

loyer (*nm*): la libération totale des **loyers** (*rent, rental*); après le relèvement du **loyer de l'argent** aux États-Unis (*interest rates*); SEE ALSO **arrérages, encadrement, flambée, gratuité, habitation, impayé, libération, quittance, retard**

lucratif, -ive (*adj*): un trafic **lucratif** de papiers falsifiés (*profitable*); un établissement privé **à but lucratif** (*profit-making*); les associations d'entraide **à but non-lucratif** (*non-profit-making*)

lutte (*nf*): dans la **lutte** contre le terrorisme et l'ETA (*fight, struggle*); la proclamation de la **lutte armée** (*armed struggle*)

M

magasin (*nm*): de nouvelles mesures en faveur des **magasins de proximité** (*neighbourhood/local shops*); les **grands magasins**, victimes de la concurrence des hypermarchés (*department store*); les **magasins à succursales multiples** perdent du terrain face aux grandes surfaces (*chain store*); la popularité des **magasins à grande surface** (*hypermarket; supermarket*)

magasinage (*nm*): il faut y ajouter les frais de **magasinage** (*warehousing*)

magazine (*nm*): la bonne santé de la **presse magazine** (*magazine press*); SEE ALSO **mensuel**

Maghreb (*nm*): les pays francophones du **Maghreb** (*the Maghreb, North Africa*)

maghrébin, -e (*adj/nm,f*): parmi les immigrés, les **Maghrébins** sont les plus nombreux (*Maghrebi*)

magistrat (*nm*): un **magistrat** investi d'une autorité administrative ou politique (*officer, public servant*); les deux **magistrats instructeurs** chargés de l'enquête (*investigating judge*); le **premier magistrat** de Nice (*mayor*)

magistrature (*nf*): faire sa carrière dans la **magistrature** (*magistracy*); la **magistrature** est indépendante vis-à-vis de l'exécutif (*judiciary*); les magistrats du siège, inamovibles, ou **magistrature assise** (*the Bench/judges*); accéder à la **magistrature suprême** (*highest/supreme office [esp. presidency]*)

magouille (*nf*): l'Opposition parle de **"magouille"** à propos du redécoupage électoral (*election rigging*); certains crient à la **magouille politicienne** (*political skulduggery*)

main (*nf*): le gouvernement **met la dernière main** au projet d'ordonnances (*put the final touches to*); **tendre la main** aux partis du centre (*make overtures*); la **reprise en main** des médias par le gouvernement (*retaking control*)

main-d'œuvre (*nf*): avoir recours à la **main-d'œuvre** étrangère (*labour; workforce, manpower*); l'abondance d'une **main-d'œuvre bon marché** (*cheap labour*); les secteurs **à forte densité de main-d'œuvre** (*labour-intensive*)

mainmise (*nf*): freiner la **mainmise** du pouvoir sur la télévision (*control; hold*); la hantise de la **mainmise étrangère** (*foreign control/domination*)

maintenir [se] (*vpr*): se **maintenir** au second tour des élections (*stand again [for election]*); la droite pourra-t-elle se **maintenir au pouvoir**? (*stay in power, retain power*); SEE ALSO **investissement**

maintien (*nm*): un simple **maintien** du pouvoir d'achat du salaire horaire (*maintenance; preserving*); le préfet demeure chargé du **maintien de l'ordre** dans le département (*maintenance of law and order*); une opération de **maintien de la paix** à Chypre (*peace-keeping*)

maire (*nm*): dans le département de l'Allier, dix-sept femmes sont **maire**; le nouveau **maire**, Mireille Rousseau (*mayor; mayoress*); SEE ALSO **député, fauteuil, sénateur**

mairie (*nf*): les Communistes ont le tiers des **mairies** (*town hall; municipality; city council*); un Républicain **remporte la mairie** de New York (*become mayor*)

maison (*nf*): une **maison** établie depuis fort longtemps (*company, firm*); filiale à 50% de la **maison mère** (*parent company*); être écroué à la **maison d'arrêt** de Nîmes (*holding/short-stay prison*); SEE ALSO **employé, rapport**

maître, -esse (*adj/nm,f*): l'insertion et l'apprentissage ont été les **maîtres-mots** de la journée (*keyword; main theme*); la mairie de Sens est **maître-d'œuvre** du projet (*main contractor; project manager*); la commune, agissant en tant que **maître-d'ouvrage** (*contracting authority; developer*); SEE ALSO **pièce**

maîtrise (*nf*): la **maîtrise** de l'immigration (*control*); une **maîtrise** de philo, et un stage d'informatique (*Master's degree*); une lettre ouverte des ingénieurs et de la **maîtrise** au personnel; une vingtaine d'**agents de maîtrise** licenciés (*supervisory staff*); l'équipe lauréate **aura la maîtrise-d'œuvre complète** du projet (*will be the main contractor*); les travaux dont la **maîtrise-d'ouvrage** incombe au département du Bas-Rhin (*[role of] contracting authority*)

maîtriser (*vt*): on a à peu près **maîtrisé** l'inflation (*curb; bring under control*); une politique d'immigration **maîtrisée** (*controlled*); une immigration **mal maîtrisée** (*out-of-control*)

majeur, -e (*adj/nm,f*): le scrutin s'est déroulé sans incident **majeur** (*major, serious*); on est **majeur** à 18 ans (*person having attained his majority*)

major (*nm*): étudiant en médecine, et **major** de sa promotion (*top of the list/class*); les **majors** du bâtiment et des travaux publics (*leading name; [major] company*)

majoration (*nf*): une **majoration** pour retard de paiement (*surcharge*); il n'y aura pas de **majorations de prix** (*price increase*); SEE ALSO **prime**

majorer (*vt*): les constructeurs **majorent leurs prix** en janvier (*raise/mark up prices*); au **prix majoré**: plus 5% sur le prix initial (*increased price*)

majoritaire (*adj*): le PCF, **majoritaire** dans le canton (*having a majority, the majority party*); SEE ALSO **pondéré, uninominal**

majorité (*nf*): la **majorité** des électeurs se sont prononcés clairement (*majority*); il ne disposait plus que d'une **majorité simple** au Parlement (*relative majority*); cinq députés sur six de l'ancienne **majorité** (*party in power, governing party*); avant, la **majorité** était de 21 ans (*coming of age, majority*); **prendre la majorité** dans le capital de la société (*take a controlling stake*); SEE ALSO **verdict**

mal, *pl* **maux** (*nm*): le **mal de vivre** dans les grands ensembles (*depression [esp. caused by life in high-density housing]*); le chômage et le **mal des banlieues** (*social problems attendant on suburban life*)

maladie (*nf*): SEE **assurance, cotisation, indemnité**

malaise (*nm*): le **malaise** des banlieues (*unrest*); devant l'étendue du **malaise social** (*social unrest/discontent*)

mal-être (*nm*): un des symptômes du **mal-être** des jeunes (*malaise, discontent*); le **mal-être urbain** que nous connaissons (*urban malaise*)

malfaiteur (*nm*): un des **malfaiteurs** a tiré à cinq reprises sur lui; sévères condamnations pour les policiers devenus **malfaiteurs** (*law-breaker; criminal*); SEE ALSO **association**

mal-logés (*nmpl*): le nombre des sans-abris et des **mal-logés** dans la capitale (*persons living in substandard accommodation*)

maltraitance (*nf*): les moyens de lutte contre la **maltraitance à enfants** (*child abuse*)

maltraiter (*vt*): SEE **enfance**

malus (*nm*): les assurances frappent d'un **malus** spécial les automobilistes auteurs de graves infractions (*loaded [insurance] premium*)

malvenu, -e (*adj*): une rebuffade particulièrement **malvenue** (*untimely, inopportune*); l'armée française **malvenue** au Rwanda (*unwelcome*)

malversation (*nf*): inculpé après la découverte de **malversations financières** (*financial malpractice; embezzlement*)

mal-vivre (*nm*): la misère, le **mal-vivre** ne sont pas le lot exclusif des banlieues; ceux qui souffrent du **mal-vivre** des grands ensembles (*poor living conditions*)

manchette (*nf*): l'annonce **a fait la manchette** de la presse madrilène (*made the headlines*)

mandant, -e (*nm,f*): un député et ses **mandants** (*constituents*); les syndicats ouvriers et patronaux doivent rendre des comptes à leurs **mandants** (*members*)

mandat (*nm*): son **mandat** est de cinq ans (*term of office*); la reconduction du **mandat** de l'ONU (*mandate*); le procureur avait lancé un **mandat d'amener** contre les deux hommes (*arrest warrant*); sous le coup d'un **mandat d'arrêt international** (*international arrest warrant*); le **mandat de comparaître** lui a été communiqué à son domicile (*summons to appear; subpœna*); trois d'entre eux **ont été placés sous mandat de dépôt** (*have been served with a committal order*); SEE ALSO **cumul, électif, moitié, outrepasser, renouvellement**

mandataire (*nm*): confier ses intérêts à un **mandataire** (*proxy; authorized representative*)

mandater (*vt*): le député, **mandaté** pour représenter ses électeurs à Paris (*mandated*)

mandature (*nf*): l'ultime conseil général de sa deuxième **mandature**; les élus débutent leur **mandature** fin mars (*period of office*)

manifestant, -e (*nm,f*): des combats opposant **manifestants** et forces de l'ordre (*demonstrator*)

manifestation (*nf*): la présence de l'armée a directement inspiré la **manifestation** (*demonstration; unrest*)

manifester (*vt*): des dizaines de résidents **manifestaient leur colère** dans les rues (*demonstrate/show their anger*); (*vi*): une centaine de personnes **manifestent** devant l'ambassade (*demonstrate*)

manne (*nf*): la **manne financière** octroyée à l'Égypte (*financial windfall*); la **manne pétrolière** assurait 40% des exportations (*plentiful oil supplies*)

manœuvre (*nm*): la disparition progressive des postes de **manœuvres** et d'ouvriers spécialisés (*manual/unskilled worker*); (*nf*): le but de sa **manœuvre** a été atteint (*intrigue, scheme*); toutes les **manœuvres électorales** sont bonnes (*vote-catching manœuvre*)

manque (*nm*): l'État récupère ainsi le **manque à gagner** dû à la baisse des taxes; ceci entraîne un **manque à gagner** de 200F pour chaque homme (*loss of [expected] income*)

manqué, -e (*adj*): après le **coup d'État manqué** de juin 1992 (*failed coup*)

manquement (*nm*): on lui reprochait un **manquement** à la solidarité gouvernementale (*breach; violation*); par négligence ou **manquement aux règles de sécurité** (*breach of safety regulations*)

manufacture (*nf*): une **manufacture** de tabac, entreprise employant 2 000 personnes (*factory*)

manufacturier, -ière (*adj*): l'**activité manufacturière** ralentit sérieusement (*manufacturing activity*)

maquette (*nf*): la **maquette** a été rénovée, la pagination passe de 44 à 60 pages (*paste-up, layout [of newspaper]*)

marasme (*nm*): le **marasme** actuel du marché (*slump, stagnation*); en plus du **marasme économique** ambiant (*economic slump*)

marchand, -e (*adj/nm,f*): entre **marchands de canons**, la bataille sera féroce (*arms supplier/dealer*); SEE ALSO **valeur**

marchandage (*nm*): de bas calculs et de honteux **marchandages**; ces **marchandages** parlementaires nuisent à la crédibilité du parti (*bargaining; haggling*)

marche (*nf*): une **marche de protestation** aura lieu dimanche (*protest march*); un droit d'information et de consultation plus large sur la **marche de l'entreprise** (*running of the company*); le gouvernement vient d'**effectuer une marche arrière** assez spectaculaire (*back-pedal, backtrack*)

marché (*nm*): le **marché** qu'il a proposé à la Pologne (*deal*); l'entreprise espagnole, leader sur son **marché** (*market sector*); **passer d'importants marchés** auprès d'entreprises locales (*place large orders*); conquérir des **marchés à l'exportation** (*export markets*); le **marché parisien de l'habitat** continue de flamber (*the Paris housing market*); l'arrivée des jeunes **sur le marché du travail** (*in the job market*); partout dans l'ex-URSS les **marchés noirs** fleurissent (*black market*); préparer la France au **marché unique européen** (*single European market*); SEE ALSO **attribuer, attribution, effondrer, enlever, entente, leader, obtention, part, passation**

marge (*nf*): dans cette branche, les **marges** sont parfois abusives; les **marges bénéficiaires** des entreprises sont en hausse (*profit/trading margin*); disposer d'une certaine **marge de manœuvre** (*room for manœuvre*); vivre **en marge de la société** (*on the fringes of society*); SEE ALSO **laminer**

marginal, -e, *pl* **-aux** (*adj/nm*): certains sont des **marginaux**, qui refusent toute aide (*fringe elements of society; dropout*)

marginalité (*nf*): l'évolution technologique repousse les petits paysans vers la **marginalité sociale** (*fringes of society; second-class status*)

mariage (*nm*): un réseau de **mariages blancs** démantelé dans le Val-d'Oise (*contracting marriage [esp. to obtain residence permit]*); SEE ALSO **naître, reculer**

maroquin (*nm*): un autre **maroquin** éphémère, celui du secrétaire d'État chargé des travailleurs immigrés (*[minister's] portfolio; ministerial post*)

marquant, -e (*adj*): personnalité **marquante** du Parti socialiste (*prominent, influential*); un des événements **marquants** de cette fin de siècle (*significant; of outstanding importance*)

marque (*nf*): SEE **contrefaçon, image**

masse (*nf*): la nouvelle charge augmentera d'autant la **masse salariale** (*wage bill*); ce train de mesures ne manquera pas de **gonfler la masse monétaire** (*inflate the money supply*)

maternité (*nf*): la **maternité de substitution** doit être considérée comme licite (*surrogate motherhood*); le **congé maternité** passera à trente semaines pour toute naissance multiple (*maternity leave*)

matière (*nf*): **matières premières** en hausse à la Bourse de Tokyo (*raw materials*)

matrimonial, -e, *pl* **-aux** (*adj*): SEE **régime**

maussade (*adj*): une année **maussade** pour l'industrie automobile (*sluggish, lacklustre*)

mauvais, -e (*adj*): SEE **créance, payeur, traitement**

mécontent, -e (*adj*/*nm,f*): le chef d'État réunit 51% de **mécontents** (*malcontent; discontented voter*)

mécontentement (*nm*): canaliser le **mécontentement** populaire (*discontent, displeasure*); SEE ALSO **issu**

mécontenter (*vt*): les propositions de Moscou **mécontentent** les dirigeants baltes (*displease*)

média (*nm*): le conflit pour le contrôle des **médias**; la plupart des **médias** [quotidiens, radios et chaînes de télévision] (*[mass] media*)

médiateur, -trice (*adj*/*nm,f*): le **médiateur** défend les intérêts des citoyens face à l'administration (*mediator*); le **médiateur de la République** intervient quand il y a litige entre une personne physique et une administration de l'État (*Ombudsman*); **être le médiateur** entre le gouvernement, les élus et les acteurs socio-économiques (*mediate*)

médiation (*nf*): la tentative de **médiation** entreprise par le roi (*mediation*); après neuf mois de conflit, la **médiation** mise en place par le gouvernement a réussi (*mediation; arbitration*)

médiatique (*adj*): SEE **battage, exploitation, tapage**

médiatisation (*nf*): la **médiatisation** du procès risque de compliquer la recherche d'un compromis (*[extensive] media coverage*); devant la **médiatisation à outrance** de cette affaire (*media hype*)

médiatiser (*vt*): ces sommets exagérément **médiatisés**; jamais une maladie n'a été tant **médiatisée** (*give media coverage*)

mêler (*vt*): **être mêlé à** un trafic de devises (*be involved in*); [se] (*vpr*): les grandes puissances **s'en sont mêlées** (*get involved; intervene*)

membre (*nm*): devenir **membre à part entière** de l'édifice européen (*full member*); les **pays membres** de la Communauté (*member state*)

ménage (*nm*): plus d'allégements fiscaux pour les **ménages** (*household*); [*fig*] Juifs et Arabes ont souvent **fait bon ménage** (*get on well together*); SEE ALSO **consommation, dépense, épargne**

ménager (*vt*): pour **ménager** ses intérêts commerciaux avec l'Iran (*protect, look after*); Washington veut **ménager ses relations avec Pékin** (*take care not to upset Peking*)

ménager, -ère (*adj*/*nf*): SEE **eau, ordure, panier**

mendicité (*nf*): le nouveau code pénal ne considère plus la **mendicité** comme un délit (*begging*)

menées (*nfpl*): on les accuse de **menées** illégales (*intrigue; machinations*)

mener (*vt*): **mener** une enquête; **mener** une stratégie de diversification osée (*carry out*); **mener à bien** un vaste programme de réhabilitation (*carry out [successfully]; implement*); **mener à terme** les négociations avec les Palestiniens (*bring to a [successful] conclusion*)

meneur, -euse (*nm,f*): les **meneurs** responsables des massacres (*leader; agitator*)

mensonger, -ère (*adj*): SEE **publicité**

mensualisation (*nf*): la **mensualisation** des salaires s'est généralisée à partir de 1969 (*payment on a monthly basis*)

mensualité (*nf*): la **mensualité** pour un crédit de 1 000F sur un an passe de 912F à 926F; aider les ménages à payer leurs **mensualités de remboursement** (*monthly repayment/instalment*)

mensuel, -elle (*adj/nm*): salaire **mensuel**: 10 200F, plus une indemnité de la Ville de Paris (*monthly*); un **[magazine] mensuel** consacré aux questions financières (*monthly [magazine]*); SEE ALSO **tranche**

mention (*nf*): des jeunes brillants, qui ont récolté des **mentions** (*pass with distinction*); le DEUG Sciences compte désormais cinq **mentions** dont mathématiques et sciences de la vie (*specialism*)

menu, -e (*adj*): sans compter les **menus frais** (*incidental/minor expenses*); commettre des **menus larcins** (*petty theft*)

mercatique (*nf*): une carrière dans la **mercatique**; la **mercatique** et la promotion des ventes (*marketing*)

mère (*nf*): l'abolition de toute aide aux jeunes **mères célibataires** (*single/unmarried mother*); la question controversée des **mères porteuses** (*surrogate mother*); couper tout lien avec la **mère-patrie** (*mother country*); SEE ALSO **maison**

méridional, -e, *pl* **-aux** (*adj/nm,f*): dans les régions **méridionales** de la péninsule (*southern*)

mérite (*nm*): la promotion se fera **au mérite** (*by/on merit*); SEE ALSO **prime**

mesure (*nf*): décider une série de **mesures** concrètes (*measure*); prendre des **mesures d'urgence** (*emergency measures*); **prendre la mesure** des conséquences qui en résulteraient (*measure; calculate*); SEE ALSO **coercition, coup, draconien, kyrielle, paquet, rétorsion, saupoudrage, train**

mesurer (*vt*): on **mesure** ainsi l'ampleur du problème (*measure, assess*)

métier (*nm*): apprendre un **métier** (*trade, profession*); pour les candidats aux **métiers de l'enseignement** (*careers in teaching*); SEE ALSO **armée**

métropole (*nf*): dans les quatre lycées de la **métropole** lilloise (*metropolis; regional capital*); Nancy et Metz, réunies en une seule **métropole d'équilibre** (*regional growth centre*); les rapports tendus que les Corses entretiennent avec la **métropole** (*mainland France*)

métropolitain, -e (*adj/nm,f*): en Afrique du Nord et en France métropolitaine (*metropolitan/mainland France*)

meurtre (*nm*): lors d'un récent **procès pour meurtre** (*murder trial*); SEE ALSO **conclure, préméditation**

meurtrier, -ière (*adj/nm,f*): les auteurs de l'embuscade **meurtrière** (*lethal; murderous*); Tibet: tremblement de terre **meurtrier** (*causing great loss of life*); un suivi médical pour les **meurtriers d'enfants** (*child murderer*)

mévente (*nf*): avec la **mévente** actuelle de l'avion supersonique (*slump in sales; selling at a loss*)

mi- (*pref*): l'usine fermera **à la mi-juin** (*in mid-June*); **à mi-mandat** le président a besoin d'un second souffle (*half-way through his term of office*)

mieux (*nm*): un **mieux** se distingue au deuxième semestre (*improvement*)

mieux-être (*nm*): pour la résorption du chômage, pour le **mieux-être** de tous (*greater welfare; wellbeing*)

milieu, *pl* **-x** (*nm*): les **milieux d'affaires** allemands sont favorables à la monnaie unique (*business community*); les **milieux financiers** redoutent une reprise de l'inflation (*financial community*); dans les **milieux autorisés** français (*official circles*); SEE ALSO **rural**

militaire (*adj/nm*): les **militaires** avaient pris le pouvoir (*the military/army*); SEE ALSO **junte**

militant, -e (*adj/nm,f*): la presse quotidienne **militante** (*militant*); les **militants** d'autrefois, dévoués corps et âme au parti (*activist, active member*); SEE ALSO **pur**

militantisme (*nm*): la crise du **militantisme** et le déclin des idéologies (*militancy*); il a derrière lui 20 ans de **militantisme** syndical puis politique (*militant action; activism*)

militer (*vi*): **militer** pour l'arrêt du projet d'autoroute (*fight; campaign*); tout en continuant à **militer au parti** (*be an [active] party member*)

milliard (*nm*): le montant dépasse de loin le **milliard** de francs; l'octroi de 1,8 **milliard** de dollars (*billion; one thousand million*)

millier (*nm*): SEE **chiffrer**

mineur, -e (*adj/nm,f*): les parents de **mineurs** suspectés d'actes de délinquance (*minor, under-age person*); il existe une justice à part pour les **mineurs délinquants** (*young offender*); SEE ALSO **délit, détournement, viol**

minier, -ière (*adj*): SEE **bassin**

minimal, -e, *pl* **-aux** (*adj*): fixer des **prix minimaux** aux frontières européennes (*minimum prices*)

minimum (*adj/nm*): ne disposer même pas du **minimum vital** (*minimum living wage*); SEE ALSO **revenu, vieillesse**

ministère (*nm*): sous le **ministère** Juppé (*premiership*); la plupart des **ministères** devront faire des économies (*government department*); devant le **ministère de l'Éducation nationale**, rue de Grenelle (*Ministry of Education*); le **ministère public** a requis une peine de deux ans (*prosecution; the public/state prosecutor*)

ministériel, -ielle (*adj*): SEE **liquidation, remaniement**

ministrable (*adj/nmf*): après sa victoire, il prend rang parmi les **premiers ministrables** (*possible choice for Prime Minister*)

ministre (*nm*): nommé **ministre des Affaires étrangères** (*minister*); l'ancien **ministre délégué à la Santé** (*minister of state responsible for Health*); nommé ministre d'État **sans portefeuille** (*without portfolio*); il préférait consulter son **ministre de tutelle** (*minister with supervisory authority*); SEE ALSO **conseil**

minorer (*vt*): le montant des frais se trouve **minoré** d'autant (*cut, reduce*)

minoritaire (*adj*): un éventuel gouvernement **minoritaire** (*minority*)

minorité (*nf*): résoudre démocratiquement la question des **minorités** (*[ethnic] minority*); **mis en minorité** au sein du gouvernement (*in a minority; marginalized*); le gouvernement pourrait **être mis en minorité** lors du vote (*be defeated*); le gouvernement belge conserve une **minorité de blocage** de 25% dans Sabena (*minority blocking vote*)

mise (*nf*): la **mise initiale** est assez modique (*first payment*); la fermeté à l'égard de Bagdad est toujours **de mise** (*necessary*); un léger optimisme semble **de mise** (*justified*); SEE ALSO **application, avant, chantier, demeure, disposition, échec, écoper, épreuve, examen, fonds, garde, jour, œuvre, pied, place, point, route, sac, séquestre, valeur, veilleuse**

miser (*vt*): en **misant sur** une politique de qualité de leurs produits; le Niger **misait sur** l'agriculture (*bank/count on; place one's hopes on*)

misère (*nf*): la montée de la précarité et de la **misère** (*extreme poverty; squalor*); le **budget de misère** alloué au réseau routier (*grossly inadequate budget/funding*)

mission (*nf*): des **missions** clairement identifiées (*task, assignment*); partir **en mission** à l'étranger (*on assignment*); l'Inde a fermé sa **mission commerciale** à Johannesburg (*trade mission*); les emplois précaires, les **missions d'intérim** (*temporary work, "temping"*); SEE ALSO **chargé**

mi-temps (*nf*): une activité **à mi-temps** et sans perspective (*part-time*); (*nm*): on offre aux plus de 50 ans un **[emploi à] mi-temps** payé 65% (*part-time job*); SEE ALSO **préretraite**

mitigé, -e (*adj*): le bilan de l'action menée reste **mitigé** (*modest*); laisser une **impression mitigée** (*a mixed impression*); **satisfaction mitigée** dans les territoires occupés (*qualified satisfaction*)

mixité (*nf*): partisan de la **mixité à l'école** (*coeducational schooling*); la **mixité du travail** se généralise (*mixed male/female employment*)

mobilier, -ière (*adj/nm*): SEE **bien**

mobilisation (*nf*): faible **mobilisation** syndicale à Paris et en province (*participation, turn out [for industrial action, demonstration, etc.]*)

mobiliser (*vt*): l'appel CGT-FO a **mobilisé** moins de 30% de grévistes (*mobilize [esp. for strike action]*); [se] (*vpr*): emploi: les maires **se mobilisent** (*take action, mobilize*); à peine 10% des votants **s'étaient mobilisés pour le changement** (*vote for change*)

mobilité (*nf*): des aides à la **mobilité géographique** (*geographical mobility*); un chiffre qui met en valeur une assez faible **mobilité professionnelle** (*mobility of labour; job mobility*)

modalité (*nf*): les **modalités** de remboursement des frais sont les suivantes (*method, procedure*); les **modalités d'application** de la nouvelle loi (*mode of enforcement [of a law]*)

modérateur, -trice (*adj*): SEE **ticket**

modération (*nf*): la **modération** de sa politique d'inspiration socialiste (*moderation*)

modéré, -e (*adj/nm,f*): imposer un islam **modéré** (*moderate*); choisir un **modéré** pour diriger le ministère des Finances (*[political] moderate*); SEE ALSO **aile, reprise**

modicité (*nf*): la **modicité** des impôts indirects (*low level*); la **modicité des contraventions** prévues par la loi (*small [parking] fines*)

modique (*adj*): pour la **somme modique** de 10 000F (*modest sum*)

modulable (*adj*): SEE **horaire**

modulation (*nf*): la **modulation annuelle** de la durée de travail (*flexible working year*)

moduler (*vt*): une réforme de la fiscalité visant à **moduler à la hausse** la taxe professionnelle (*raise, increase*)

mœurs (*nmpl*): les **mœurs politiques** très particuliers de l'époque (*political behaviour*); SEE ALSO **outrage, police**

moindre (*adj*): on l'a vendu **à moindre prix** (*at a lower price*); travailler davantage **pour des rémunérations moindres** (*for less pay*); SEE ALSO **moitié**

moins-value (*nf*): provoquant une **moins-value** des appartements de 30% (*fall in value, depreciation*); en 1987 la Bundesbank a **subi une moins-value** d'environ sept milliards (*make a loss*)

mois (*nm*): SEE **creux, treizième**

moitié (*nf*): 800 000 barils par jour, soit **moitié moins que le normal** (*half the normal quantity/production*); un volume de transactions **moitié moindre** (*smaller by half; half as big/great*); **à la moitié de son mandat**, l'indice de popularité du président est en nette baisse (*half-way through his term of office*); l'Allemagne veut **réduire de moitié** le nombre de chômeurs en 5 ans (*halve, reduce by half*); la **réduction de moitié** de l'effectif actuel de 500 personnes (*halving*); SEE ALSO **amputer**

monde (*nm*): SEE **quart**

mondial, -e, *pl* **-aux** (*adj*): les stocks **mondiaux** ont diminué de moitié (*world; world-wide*)

mondialisation (*nf*): la **mondialisation**, ou le commerce à l'échelle planétaire; une réelle **mondialisation** de l'économie (*globalization*)

monétaire (*adj*): SEE **création**

monnaie (*nf*): le dinar, la **monnaie** nationale (*currency*); baisse de la **monnaie américaine** (*dollar*); en attendant la mise en place de la **monnaie unique** (*single currency*)

monnayer (*vt*): ces accords qu'il **monnayait** contre un monopole de représentativité syndicale (*trade; exchange*); un policier écroué pour avoir **monnayé** une enquête (*make money/financial gain from*)

mono- (*pref*): Eure-et-Loir: fin de la **mono-industrie** (*dependance on/ dominance of a single industry*)

monoparental, -e, *pl* **-aux** (*adj*): les **foyers monoparentaux** représentent 29% des allocataires du RMI (*one-parent household*); SEE ALSO **famille**

monopartisme (*nm*): le **monopartisme** est terminé au Zaïre (*one-party political system*)

monopole (*nm*): disposer d'un **monopole** en matière de radio et de télévision (*monopoly*); le **monopole d'embauche** syndical est illégal en France (*closed shop*); la société menace d'en saisir la **commission des monopoles et des fusions** (*French Monopolies and Mergers Commission*)

montage (*nm*): le **montage** d'une campagne de publicité (*organization, mounting*); un accord sur des **montages financiers** en faveur de la Hongrie et de la Bulgarie (*packet of financial measures*)

montant, -e (*adj/nm*): il dénonça la **criminalité montante** (*rising crime rate*); pour un **montant total** de 20 000F (*total [sum]*); la mise en place du système des **montants compensatoires** agricoles (*compensation payment*); SEE ALSO **global**

montée (*nf*): dans un contexte de **montée de chômage** (*rising unemployment*); la **montée en puissance** des classes moyennes (*rise; rise to power*)

monter (*vt/vi*): il avait **monté** sa propre société de carrosserie (*set up [business]*); [se] (*vpr*): la perte de salaire **se montait** à 2 000F par jour (*amount/come to*); SEE ALSO **créneau**, **épingle**, **flèche**

moral, -e, *pl* **-aux** (*adj*): SEE **personne**

moralisation (*nf*): la **moralisation** du financement de la vie politique (*cleaning up*)

moraliser (*vt*): ces deux textes vont **moraliser** le financement de la vie politique (*clean up*); tenter de **moraliser la vie publique** (*clean up public life*)

morceler (*vt*): une agglomération **morcelée** en une quarantaine de communes (*break up, divide, fragment*)

morcellement (*nm*): le **morcellement** de la fonction publique en des centaines de statuts particuliers (*division/splitting into small units*); le remembrement a résolu les problèmes causés par le **morcellement des terres** (*division of land into small units*)

morose (*adj*): après cinq années **moroses**, le marché a bondi cette année (*lacklustre*); dans un climat qualifié de **morose** (*gloomy; bearish [market]*)

morosité (*nf*): la **morosité** du secteur automobile persiste (*depressed mood; sluggishness [esp. of market]*); il déplorait la **morosité ambiante** (*the pervading atmospere of gloom*); SEE ALSO **heure**

mot (*nm*) **d'ordre**: manifester, mais sans **mot d'ordre** ni objectif déterminé (*slogan*); il a lancé un **mot d'ordre de grève** pour le 28 mars (*strike call*)

moteur, -trice (*adj/nm,f*): il jouait un **rôle moteur** dans la réforme des institutions (*leading role*); dans ce domaine, la France et l'Allemagne sont les **moteurs**; le principal **moteur** de la croissance en 1995 (*driving force*)

motif (*nm*): avoir un **motif valable** (*valid reason*); selon ses proches, elle aurait des **motifs de divorce** (*grounds for divorce*); SEE ALSO **exposé**

motion (*nf*): les communistes ont décidé de **voter la motion de censure** (*pass a vote of no confidence*)

motivé, -e (*adj*): un éventuel refus doit être **motivé** (*well founded; justifiable*)

motiver (*vt*): on lui demanda de **motiver** sa décision (*justify, explain*)

mouiller (*vi*): la flotte **mouille** en rade de Toulon (*be at anchor*); **[se]** (*vpr*): le maire radical **s'est mouillé** dans une affaire de pots-de-vin (*be implicated/involved*)

mouture (*nf*): la première **mouture** de ces propositions (*draft, version*); la **mouture finale** de l'accord (*final draft/version*)

mouvance (*nf*): le dialogue entre le pouvoir et la **mouvance islamique** (*Islamic circles*); les hommes de la **mouvance présidentielle** (*presidential party/circles*)

mouvement (*nm*): les différents **mouvements** de l'opposition ne sont pas d'accord sur la question (*movement, group*); ce **mouvement ministériel** était attendu (*ministerial reshuffle*); des **mouvements de grève** ont paralysé hier les transports parisiens (*strike*); le gouvernement mis à l'épreuve par l'extension des **mouvements sociaux** (*industrial action in pursuit of workers' demands*); SEE ALSO **autonomiste, euphorie, guérilla, haussier, revendicatif, séparatiste**

mouvementé, -e (*adj*): dans un contexte social et politique **mouvementé** (*eventful; turbulent*)

moyen, -enne (*adj/nm,f*): les étudiants réclament **plus de moyens** pour les universités (*more resources/funding*); le rôle des nouveaux **moyens de communication de masse** (*mass media*); chiffre plus bas que la **moyenne nationale** (*national average*); SEE ALSO **ancienneté, importance**

moyennant (*prep*): **moyennant** une cotisation annuelle de 100F (*at a charge of, in consideration of*); **moyennant** des contreparties territoriales (*in exchange for*)

muet, -ette (*adj*): malaise au sein de la **grande muette** (*the [French] army*)

multipartisan, -e (*adj*): une commission **multipartisane** sur la refonte du service national (*multi-party, cross-party*)

multipartisme (*nm*): enfin le **multipartisme** va devenir une réalité; la transition d'un régime de parti unique au **multipartisme** (*multi-party system/politics*)

multipartite (*adj*): des pourparlers **multipartites** sur le projet d'élections en Irlande du Nord (*multi-party; multipartite*)

multiplication (*nf*): la **multiplication** des contacts entre les deux parties (*increasing number*)

multiplier (*vt*): Londres **multiplie les avertissements** au régime des ayatollahs (*give numerous warnings*); [se] (*vpr*): les mesures en faveur des femmes **se multiplient** (*increase in number*)

multipropriété (*nf*): la **multipropriété**, la méthode moderne de gérer ses vacances (*time-sharing system*); les méthodes de vente des **sociétés de vacances en multipropriété** (*time-share company*)

multirécidiviste (*adj/nmf*): des centres destinés aux jeunes **multirécidivistes** (*habitual offender*)

municipal, -e, *pl* **-aux** (*adj/nfpl*): en vue des [élections] **municipales** de l'an prochain (*municipal elections*); SEE ALSO **arrêté, conseil municipal, receveur, régie**

municipalité (*nf*): les deux **municipalités** vont se retrouver pour discuter de cette question; espérer une aide de la **municipalité** (*town/city council*)

munir (*vt*): des jeunes **munis d'un CAP** [certificat d'aptitude professionnelle] (*equipped with a vocational training qualification*); [se] (*vpr*): il est conseillé de **se munir** d'une assurance médicale privée (*obtain*)

musclé, -e (*adj*): [*fig*] des interpellations **musclées**; il a prononcé un réquisitoire **musclé** contre le libéralisme (*vigorous, no-nonsense*)

mutation (*nf*): dans la période de **mutation** profonde que traverse actuellement l'économie (*change, transformation*); refuser une **mutation** pour raisons d'ordre familial (*job transfer/move*)

muter (*vt*): en poste dans le Nord, il **se trouve muté** en Alsace (*be transferred/moved*)

mutualisme (*nm*): écrire l'histoire du **mutualisme** français (*mutual benefit insurance system*)

mutualiste (*nm*): un Français sur deux est **mutualiste** (*member of a mutual insurance company*)

mutualité (*nf*): la **mutualité**, l'assurance maladie complémentaire à celle de la Sécurité sociale; les représentants de patronat, des syndicats et de la **mutualité** (*French mutual benefit insurance system*)

mutuel, -elle (*adj/nf*): adhérer à une **mutuelle**; les **mutuelles** complètent les remboursements de la Sécurité sociale (*French complementary insurance scheme; mutual benefit society*); SEE ALSO **consentement, reconnaissance, respect**

mutuellement (*adv*): les deux pays s'accusent **mutuellement** (*each other, one another*)

N

naissance (*nf*): SEE **bulletin, extrait, taux**

naître (*vi*): un enfant sur deux **naît hors mariage** pour les mères de moins de 25 ans (*be born out of wedlock*)

nanti, -e (*adj*): le fossé qui sépare les pays **nantis** et les pays pauvres (*rich, prosperous*); une commune particulièrement **bien nantie** (*well equipped*); (*nmpl*) par rapport aux autres salariés, ils sont des **nantis** (*prosperous, well-off; privileged*)

napoléon (*nm*): la prime du **napoléon** a subi d'importantes variations (*gold coin worth 20 old francs*)

natalité (*nf*): l'accroissement de la **natalité** française; le **taux de natalité** est partout en baisse (*birth rate*)

nation (*nf*): au siège des **Nations Unies [ONU]** (*United Nations*); SEE ALSO **commerçant**

national, -e, *pl* -aux (*adj/nm,f*): prendre la **nationale** 10 en direction de Chartres (*trunk road, A road [UK]*); réservé aux **nationaux** de ces deux pays (*national*); SEE ALSO **préférence, service**

nationaliser (*vt*): chasser les anciens colons blancs et **nationaliser** leurs biens (*nationalize*)

nationalité (*nf*): acquérir la **nationalité française** (*French citizenship*); SEE ALSO **accès**

naturaliser (*vt*): les étrangers voulant se faire **naturaliser français** (*acquire French nationality/citizenship*)

nature (*nf*): SEE **avantage, payer**

navette (*nf*): malgré les multiples **navettes** qu'il effectue (*shuttle*); le projet de loi a **fait la navette** pendant trois mois entre l'Assemblée et le Sénat (*be sent backwards and forwards*)

nécessiteux, -euse (*adj/nm,f*): les familles **nécessiteuses**, vivant dans le dénuement le plus complet (*in need*); venir en aide aux **nécessiteux** (*needy*)

néfaste (*adj*): les conséquences **néfastes** d'un dollar surévalué; une montée des taux d'intérêt serait **néfaste** pour l'économie (*harmful, pernicious; dangerous*)

négoce (*nm*): **faire du négoce** avec des pays asiatiques (*trade, do business*); le **négoce des céréales** continue entre les deux pays (*trade in grain/cereals*)

négociant, -e (*nm,f*): un célèbre **négociant en vins** du Bordelais (*wine merchant*); un **négociant en gros** du Havre (*wholesaler*)

négociation (*nf*): les **négociations commerciales** ont repris avec le Japon (*trade talks*); la cause de l'échec des **négociations salariales** (*pay talks*); SEE ALSO **séance, serré, table**

négocier [se] (*vpr*): à 232F, le titre se **négocie** peu au-dessus de son cours le plus bas de l'année (*change hands, sell*)

nervosité (*nf*): la **nervosité** du pouvoir lorsqu'il doit faire face à la contestation (*irritability; touchiness*); **nervosité** à la Bourse de Paris hier (*nervous trading*)

nettoyage (*nm*): le **nettoyage ethnique** mené en Yougoslavie (*ethnic cleansing*)

nier (*vt*): il est difficile de **nier l'évidence** (*deny the obvious*); ils avaient **nié les faits** (*deny the allegation/charge*)

niveau, pl -x (*nm*): une élévation sensible du **niveau de vie** (*living standards*); discussions bilatérales **au plus haut niveau** (*top-level; at the highest level*); SEE ALSO **faible, remise**

niveler (*vt*): les indemnités de chômage ont été **nivelées par le bas** (*level down*)

nivellement (*nm*): le **nivellement** des rémunérations sera long à obtenir (*evening-out; equalizing*); il y aura inévitablement un **nivellement par le bas** (*levelling-down*)

nocturne (*adj/nf*): **nocturne** hebdomadaire, vendredi jusqu'à 22h (*late opening; late-night shopping*); SEE ALSO **tapage**

noir, -e (*adj*): Lagos, la métropole la plus peuplée d'**Afrique noire** (*Black Africa*); SEE ALSO **caisse, marché, or, travail**

nombreux, -euse (*adj*): SEE **famille**

nommément (*adv*): le rapport les met **nommément** en cause; sans les citer **nommément** (*by name*)

nommer (*vt*): sans le **nommer** ouvertement (*name, mention by name*); des enseignants titulaires nouvellement **nommés** (*appoint [to a post]*)

non-accord (*nm*): un **non-accord sur la question** n'empêchera pas la tenue d'un sommet (*failure to agree on the matter*)

non-aligné, -e (*adj/nm*): lors de la conférence au sommet des **[pays] non-alignés** (*nonaligned countries*)

non-assistance (*nf*): inculpé de coups et blessures et de **non-assistance à personne en danger** (*failing to come to the aid of a person in danger*)

non autorisé, -e (*adj*): sa participation à une manifestation **non autorisée** (*unauthorized; illegal*)

non conforme (*adj*): l'installation **non conforme** de stations de pompage (*not conforming to regulations/standards*); un texte déclaré **non conforme à la constitution** (*unconstitutional*)

non-droit (*nm*): dans ce pays **de non-droit** (*where the rule of law does not apply*)

non-ingérence (*nf*): au nom de la **non-ingérence** dans les affaires d'un autre pays (*non-interference*)

non-inscrit, -e (*adj*): la majorité des maires, RPR-UDF et **non-inscrits** (*independent*); le **député non-inscrit** des Bouches-du-Rhône (*deputy without party affiliation*)

non-lieu, pl -x (*nm*): l'inculpation s'est terminée par un **non-lieu** (*dismissal [of a case]*); le juge d'instruction a **rendu une ordonnance de non-lieu** (*dismiss a case [for lack of evidence]; decide there is no case to answer*)

non marié, -e (*adj*): SEE **couple**

non-observation (*nf*): la **non-observation du règlement** peut exposer à des poursuites (*failure to comply with regulations*)

non-paiement (*nm*): un mouvement de protestation contre le **non-paiement** de leurs salaires (*non-payment*)

non-port (*nm*): le **non-port de la ceinture de sécurité** ou du casque (*failure to wear a seat-belt*)

non publié, -e (*adj*): d'après ce rapport encore **non publié** (*as yet unpublished*)

non qualifié, -e (*adj*): un personnel féminin **non qualifié** (*unqualified, without qualifications*)

non-recevoir (*nm*): **opposer une fin de non-recevoir** à tout projet d'augmentation d'impôts (*flatly refuse*)

non rentable (*adj*): une fermeture systématique des **puits non rentables** (*unprofitable mines*)

non résolu, -e (*adj*): le nombre d'affaires criminelles **non résolues** (*unsolved*)

non-respect (*nm*): dans les cas de **non-respect de la loi** (*infringement of the law*); le principal reproche des usagers, c'est le **non-respect des horaires** (*poor punctuality; failure to run on time*)

non-satisfaction (*nf*): **en cas de non-satisfaction des revendications**, une nouvelle grève sera lancée (*if their demands are not met*)

normal, -e, *pl* **-aux** (*adj/nf*): permettre un retour à la **normale** (*normality*)

normalien, -ienne (*adj/nm,f*): diplômé de l'ÉNA et **normalien** (*graduate of the* École normale supérieure)

normalisation (*nf*): l'accord de **normalisation des relations** entre la Grèce et la Macédoine (*normalizing of relations*); vers une **normalisation** des législations nationales (*standardization*)

normaliser (*vt*): il faudra **normaliser** l'écartement des voies de chemin de fer en Europe (*standardize*); le Maroc **normalise ses relations** avec Israël (*normalize relations*); [se] (*vpr*): depuis, l'approvisionnement **s'est normalisé** (*return to normal*)

norme (*nf*): compte tenu des **normes** nationales et internationales (*norms, standards*); **mettre aux normes** le patrimoine existant (*bring up to standard*)

notable (*adj/nm*): être désigné par un collège de **notables** (*notable; important personality*)

notaire (*nm*): passer par un **notaire** (*notary, lawyer*); tout acquéreur devrait **faire appel à un notaire en droit** (*call on the services of a solicitor*); SEE ALSO **charge**

notation (*nf*): la **notation** des professeurs par leurs étudiants; la promotion dépend de ces **notations** (*grading; assessment*)

note (*nf*): cette pratique, précisée en juin 1996 par une **note interne** (*memorandum, memo*); présenter sa **note de frais** (*claim for expenses*); **note d'admission**: 6/20 (*pass mark*)

noter (*vt*): les militaires sont **notés** par leur supérieur hiérarchique (*assess; grade*)

notifier (*vt*): **se faire notifier** sa mise en examen par le juge (*be advised/notified*); SEE ALSO **congé**

notoire (*adj*): SEE **concubinage**

notoriété (*nf*): l'exceptionnelle **notoriété** de cette société; outre-Rhin, la **notoriété** de ces vins reste très faible (*reputation, fame*)

noyau, *pl* **-x** (*nm*): le **noyau dur** des chômeurs de longue durée (*hard core*); les **noyaux durs** des actionnaires, constitués par le gouvernement dans les sociétés qu'il privatisait (*hard-core shareholders*)

noyautage (*nm*): le **noyautage du pouvoir** par les communistes (*infiltration of government*); le **noyautage opéré par les gauchistes** paralyse le syndicat (*left-wing infiltration*)

noyauter (*vt*): le parti au pouvoir du gouvernement qui veut **noyauter** la radio et la télévision (*infiltrate*)

nuancé, -e (*adj*): adopter une position plus **nuancée** (*balanced; finely shaded*)

nue-propriété (*nf*): la **nue-propriété**: le droit de posséder un bien sans avoir le droit de l'utiliser (*ownership without usufruct; freehold*)

nuire (*vt*): un fanatisme qui **nuit fortement** à l'image de l'islam (*do great harm/be detrimental to*)

nuisance (*nf*): une **nuisance** d'odeurs ou de bruits provoquée par un commerce (*pollution*); le problème des **nuisances sonores** que subissent les riverains d'aéroports; en cas de **nuisance par le bruit** (*noise pollution*); les produits **sans nuisance pour l'environnement** (*environmentally harmless*)

nuisible (*adj*): sans avoir des conséquences **nuisibles** sur l'économie (*harmful*)

nuit (*nf*): SEE **travail**

nul, nulle (*adj*): ses chances de gagner sont pratiquement **nulles** (*nil; non-existent*); s'abstenir ou **voter nul** (*spoil a voting paper*); déclarer **nulle et non avenue** la consultation populaire proposée (*null and void*); SEE ALSO **bulletin**

nullité (*nf*): les conditions de son arrestation **entachent de nullité** l'ensemble de la procédure; le non-respect des règles **entraîne la nullité** de l'acte (*render [null and] void*)

numéraire (*adj/nm*): exiger d'être payé **en numéraire** (*in cash*)

numérique (*adj*): le progrès de la cartographie **numérique** (*digital*)

numériser (*vt*): **numériser** le cadastre national (*digitize*)

numéro (*nm*): le quotidien *Libération*, dans son **numéro** du 28 mars (*issue, edition*); des cas d'abus sexuels signalés au **numéro vert** spécialisé (*freephone number*); SEE ALSO **un**

O

obédience (*nf*): dans les régimes **d'obédience communiste** (*of communist allegiance; communist*); parmi les **musulmans de stricte obédience** (*devout Muslims*)

objectif (*nm*): son **objectif**: 1,3 millions d'abonnés en 1995 (*aim, target*); l'aviation a bombardé plusieurs **objectifs industriels** (*industrial target*); il **se fixe comme objectif** de réduire d'un million le nombre des chômeurs (*set oneself a target*)

objet (*nm*): les mutins **feront l'objet de sanctions** (*will be punished*)

obligation (*nf*): convertir la dette en **obligations** négociables sur le marché international (*bond; debenture; fixed-interest stock*); la loi **fait obligation** aux associations de tenir des comptes (*oblige*); les jeunes Français toujours **soumis aux obligations militaires** (*liable for military service*)

obligatoire (*adj*): le système de santé américain n'est ni **obligatoire** ni national (*obligatory, compulsory*)

obtempérer (*vi*): devant leur **refus d'obtempérer**, le policier fit usage de son arme (*refusal to obey [instruction/order]*)

obtention (*nf*): la procédure pour l'**obtention** de pièces d'identité (*obtaining*); l'**obtention d'un important marché d'armement** en Chine (*winning of a large arms contract*)

occidental, -e, *pl* **-aux** (*adj/nm,f*): le premier chef d'État **occidental** à s'y rendre (*Western*); face aux Serbes, les **Occidentaux** opposent hésitations et incohérences (*Western powers*); SEE ALSO **ouvrir**

occulte (*adj*): des commissions **occultes** dégagées sur des marchés publics (*undisclosed; under-the-counter*); SEE ALSO **financement**

occulter (*vt*): le régime tenta d'**occulter** ces années de quasi-guerre civile (*gloss over; conceal*)

occupation (*nf*): des grèves avec **occupation de locaux** ont associé étudiants et professeurs (*sit-in*); le **taux d'occupation** des hôtels de luxe (*occupancy rate*); la modification du **POS [plan d'occupation des sols]** de la commune (*land-use plan*); SEE ALSO **coefficient**

occuper (*vt*): une centaine de grévistes **occupent les lieux** (*occupy the premises*)

octroi (*nm*): décider l'**octroi** d'un jour de congé (*granting*)

octroyer (*vt*): une prime spéciale est **octroyée** au personnel (*grant, give, award*); **[s']** (*vpr*): la France pense pouvoir **s'octroyer** 10% de ce marché (*obtain; win for oneself*)

œuvre (*nf*): la décentralisation fut l'**œuvre** de l'ancien ministre de l'Intérieur (*work, achievement*); cette réforme était difficile à **mettre en œuvre** (*implement*); les observateurs de l'ONU surveillent sur place la **mise en œuvre** du cessez-le-feu (*implementation*)

œuvrer (*vi*): **œuvrer** ensemble à la recherche de solutions (*work*); les superpuissances **œuvrent pour** une limitation des armes (*work for; strive to bring about*)

office (*nm*): les employés de l'**Office** des HLM (*bureau, office*); le nouveau Premier ministre **fera office** aussi de ministre de la Justice (*hold office; serve as*); **être nommé d'office** à la commission (*be appointed by virtue of one's position*); SEE ALSO **cartel**

officialiser (*vt*): un décret qui **officialise** le droit au multipartisme (*make official; formalize*)

officiel, -ielle (*adj/nm*): SEE **journal**

officieux, -ieuse (*adj*): établir des contacts **officieux** entre les belligérants (*unofficial*); faire un voyage **à titre officieux** à Bonn (*in an unofficial capacity; unofficially*)

officine (*nf*): les 22 000 **officines de pharmacie** en France (*dispensary, pharmacy*)

offrant (*nm*): l'**offrant** ne peut revenir sur son offre (*bidder, offeror*); vendre **au plus offrant** (*to the highest bidder*)

offre (*nf*): l'**offre** crée sa propre demande (*supply*); son **offre** reste insuffisante dans beaucoup de secteurs (*supply, availability*); le nombre des **offres d'emploi** est en forte progression (*job vacancy*); en lançant une **OPA [offre publique d'achat]** sur le grand quotidien (*launch a take-over bid*); une **OPA inamicale** lancée sur la firme de Rennes (*unwelcome take-over bid*); SEE ALSO **appel**

omnipraticien, -ienne (*nm,f*): 6 000 généralistes, soit 11% de l'ensemble des **omnipraticiens** (*general [medical] practitioner*)

onéreux, -euse (*adj*): les traites à payer sembleront à long terme très **onéreuses** (*expensive, costly*)

onusien, -ienne (*adj*): Jérusalem rejette les conclusions des **experts onusiens** (*United Nations experts*); la force multinationale, **placée sous le pavillon onusien** (*flying the United Nations flag*)

OPA (*nf*): SEE **offre**

opérer (*vt*): **opérer** une transition en douceur (*effect*); les conditions dans lesquelles les vols ont été **opérés** (*carry out*); [s'] (*vpr*): un transfert des compétences **s'est opéré** du préfet vers le président du conseil général (*take place; come about*); SEE ALSO **perquisition**

opinion (*nf*): une bonne partie de l'**opinion** prend position en faveur du ministre (*public opinion*); en prison pour **délit d'opinion** (*holding/ expressing subversive views*); SEE ALSO **décalé, enquête, liberté, presse, prisonnier, sensibiliser, sondage**

opportunité (*nf*): mettre en question l'**opportunité** de cette mesure (*opportuneness, timeliness; appropriateness*); **saisir les opportunités** qu'offre le marché unique de 1993 (*seize the opportunity/chance*)

opposant, -e (*adj/nm,f*): les **opposants** au régime militaro-islamiste; dix **opposants** iraniens expulsés de France (*opponent; member of the opposition*)

opposer (*vt*): des heurts ont **opposé** étudiants et policiers (*bring into conflict*); [s'] (*vpr*): l'Arabie Saoudite et l'Iran **s'opposent** sur les quotas de production de pétrole (*clash, disagree*); ils **s'étaient opposés avec succès** au projet de l'Algérie (*foil, block*); SEE ALSO **non-recevoir**, **véto**

opposition (*nf*): les **chefs de l'opposition** demandent la démission du président (*opposition leaders*); la faculté de **faire opposition à un chèque** (*stop a cheque*); SEE ALSO **formation, siéger**

opprimé, -e (*adj/nm,f*): un pays refuge pour les **opprimés** (*oppressed person*)

optimal, -e, *pl* **-aux** (*adj*): pour une gestion **optimale** des ressources (*optimum, optimal*)

optimiser (*vt*): essayer d'**optimiser les bénéfices** (*maximize profits*)

optique (*nf*): dans **l'optique américaine**, l'affaire est plus compliquée (*from the American perspective*)

or (*nm*): **l'or noir** rapporte beaucoup moins de devises; les financiers surveillent anxieusement les caprices de **l'or noir** (*oil, black gold*)

ordination (*nf*): le Parlement approuve l'**ordination** des femmes anglicanes (*ordination*)

ordonnance (*nf*): recourir aux **ordonnances** pour accélérer les choses (*[government] decree/edict*); la chambre d'accusation avait infirmé l'**ordonnance de mise en détention** (*detention order*); SEE ALSO **injonction, non-lieu**

ordonner (*vt*): un juge de la cour d'appel avait **ordonné** sa libération (*order*)

ordre (*nm*): l'**ordre** et la répression, une obsession de la droite (*[law and] order*); les 150 000 membres de l'**ordre des avocats** (*lawyers' association*); l'**ordre du jour** comportera, notamment, la question de l'emploi (*agenda; business of the meeting*); [*fig*] la réduction du temps de travail **revient à l'ordre du jour** (*be back on the agenda*); SEE ALSO **force, loi, maintien, trouble, troubler**

ordure (*nf*): la collecte des **ordures ménagères** (*household refuse*)

organe (*nm*): le Conseil des ministres, l'**organe décisionnel** de l'Union européenne (*decision-making body*); l'**organe suprême** de l'État algérien (*supreme/highest body*)

organisation (*nf*): SEE **humanitaire**

organisme (*nm*): une initiative subventionnée par les **organismes** régionaux et départementaux (*body, organism*)

oriental, -e, *pl* **-aux** (*adj/nm,f*): les pays d'Europe centrale et **orientale** (*Eastern*)

orientation (*nf*): une permanence d'accueil, d'information et d'**orientation** pour les 16-25 ans (*careers guidance*); définir les grandes **orientations** de sa politique étrangère (*[policy] direction*)

orienter (*vt*): **orienter** un élève vers la vie active (*direct, steer [esp. in careers advice]*); depuis mars, le marché est **orienté à la hausse** (*on the upturn, on the rise*); [s'] (*vpr*): la politique d'immigration **s'oriente vers le laxisme** (*become more permissive*)

outrage (*nm*): inculpé d'**outrages à agent** (*[verbal] assault of police officer; insulting behaviour*); condamné pour **outrage à magistrat** pour avoir tu ce qu'il savait du complot (*contempt of court*); coupable d'**outrage aux bonnes mœurs** (*affront to public decency; publication of obscene material*); le juge d'instruction l'a inculpé d'**outrage public à la pudeur** (*indecent exposure*)

outrance (*nf*): la majorité se mobilise contre les **outrances de son discours** (*his/her extreme views*); la militarisation **à outrance** du Nicaragua (*large-scale; excessive*); SEE ALSO **médiatisation**

outre (*prep*): ceci a été abondamment commenté **outre-Manche** (*in Britain; across the Channel*); **outre-Atlantique**, on est en période d'élections (*in America; across the Atlantic*); à l'encontre des **sociétés d'outre-Rhin** (*German companies*); SEE ALSO **passer**

outremer (*adv/nm*): un nouveau ministre de l'**Outremer** (*overseas territories*)

outrepasser (*vt*): le Premier ministre avait **outrepassé** son pouvoir (*exceed, go beyond, overstep*); le négociateur a-t-il **outrepassé son mandat**? (*go beyond one's mandate/remit*)

ouverture (*nf*): demander l'**ouverture** d'une enquête (*opening*); prévoyant l'**ouverture totale** du ciel européen à la concurrence (*opening up [to competition]*); un gouvernement d'**ouverture vers le centre** (*alliance with the centre*); le débat sur l'**ouverture dominicale** rebondit (*Sunday trading*); les **ouvertures** faites en direction de Washington (*overtures*)

ouvrable (*adj*): on appelle **jours ouvrables** tous les jours de la semaine sauf celui consacré au repos hebdomadaire et les jours fériés; 25 jours ouvrés, ou 30 **jours ouvrables** (*working day*)

ouvrage (*nm*): Eurotunnel: comment faire face au surcoût de l'**ouvrage** (*construction; project*); les **ouvrages d'art** [ponts, viaducs] seront réalisés en premier lieu (*structure [bridge, tunnel, etc.]*)

ouvré, -e (*adj*): on appelle **jours ouvrés** les jours du lundi au vendredi inclus (*working day*)

ouvrier, -ière (*adj/nm,f*): l'écart entre l'**ouvrier** le plus mal payé et le cadre supérieur (*worker; workman*); 20 000 emplois d'**ouvrier qualifié [OQ]** ne trouvent pas preneurs (*skilled worker*); un maçon qui est devenu **OS [ouvrier spécialisé]** dans l'automobile (*unskilled/semi-skilled worker*) ; SEE ALSO **banlieue, livre, polyvalent, syndicat**

ouvrir [s'] (*vpr*): le congrès qui doit **s'ouvrir** dimanche (*start, open, begin*); l'Irak prêt à **s'ouvrir aux occidentaux** (*open up to the West/to Western firms*)

P

pacifique (*adj*): SEE **résolution**

pactole (*nm*): le marché de l'environnement n'offre pas le **pactole** espéré par les industriels (*windfall*); **un vrai pactole** pour la société de Courbevoie (*a veritable gold-mine; worth a small fortune*)

page (*nf*): SEE **placard**

pagination (*nf*): une réduction de la **pagination** du quotidien *Libération* (*number of pages*)

paie (*nf*): on ne verse plus de **paie** au personnel réduit à l'inactivité; il touchait une bonne **paie** d'ouvrier (*wage, pay*); SEE ALSO **feuille, fiche**

paiement (*nm*): le **paiement** des indemnités auxquelles il a droit (*payment*); le **paiement** de la dette (*repayment, paying [off]*); SEE ALSO **cessation, défaut, échelonner**

paix (*nf*): **ramener la paix** en Irlande du Nord (*restore peace*); SEE ALSO **aboutir, accord, gardien, juge, justice, maintien, plan, pourparlers, processus**

palais (*nm*): les **sages du Palais-Royal** se sont réunis pour donner leur avis (*[in France] the* Conseil d'État); au **palais de justice** de Nanterre (*law courts*)

palliatif (*nm*): les nouvelles mesures ne sont que des **palliatifs** (*stop-gap measure*)

pallier (*vt*): pour **pallier** cette honteuse carence (*make up/compensate for*)

palmarès (*nm*): la société bretonne s'est hissée à la première place du **palmarès** de l'agro-alimentaire (*order of merit; honours list*)

panachage (*nm*): l'électeur ne peut exprimer ni vote préférentiel ni **panachage** (*alteration by voter of names on the voting list by subtraction or replacement*)

panacher (*vt*): cette fois-ci, ils vont sans doute **panacher** (*alter names on voting list; vote for candidates from different parties/voting lists*)

panier (*nm*): un **panier** de monnaies (*basket*); le **panier de la ménagère**, mesure de l'évolution des prix à la consommation (*housewife's shopping basket; housekeeping bill*)

pantouflage (*nm*): le **pantouflage**, ou le passage du secteur public au secteur privé (*[in France] leaving a civil service post to work in the private sector*)

pantoufler (*vi*): les hauts fonctionnaires, **pantouflant dans le privé** (*leave a civil service post [in France] to work in the private sector*)

paquet (*nm*): un **paquet de mesures** de relance (*package of measures*)

parachever (*vt*): leur ambition: **parachever** la construction de l'Europe (*complete*)

parachutage (*nm*): la pratique du **parachutage**, mal acceptée par les instances locales du parti (*imposing an outside electoral candidate*)

parachuter (*vt*): **parachuté** dans l'Orne, il fut battu sans appel dans les élections (*brought in from outside [esp. of an electoral candidate]*)

paradis (*nm*): les enquêteurs se heurtent au système des **paradis fiscaux** (*tax haven*)

parallèle (*adj*): SEE **économie**

parapher (*vt*): le Premier ministre refusa de **parapher** cette ordonnance (*initial; sign, put a signature to*); seule la CGT refuse de **parapher** l'accord (*sign the agreement*)

parc (*nm*): avec le **parc d'automobiles** le plus important d'Europe (*total number of cars*); le **parc français du logement** a doublé en trente ans (*French housing market*); un **parc d'activités** de 66 hectares (*business park; enterprise zone*)

parcelle (*nf*): s'acheter une **parcelle de terre** (*plot of land*); un lotissement de douze **parcelles privatives** (*individual plot*)

parent, -e (*nm,f*): les contentieux entre parents par le sang et **parents adoptifs** (*adoptive/foster parents*); **parent isolé** avec un enfant à charge (*lone parent*); SEE ALSO **charge**

parental, -e, *pl* **-aux** (*adj*): avoir droit à un **congé parental [d'éducation]** (*parents' right to time off work without pay after birth of child*); SEE ALSO **autorité**

pari (*nm*): un **pari** économique, mais aussi un défi politique (*gamble; challenge*); l'ex-RFA **a fait le pari de** l'ancrage à l'Ouest (*gamble on; stake all on*)

paritaire (*adj*): une **gestion paritaire** patronat-syndicats (*joint management*); une **commission mixte paritaire**, les parties étant représentées à parts égales (*joint committee with equal representation*)

parité (*nf*): **parité** entre le statut des magistrats du siège et du parquet (*parity*); leur exigence principale, la **parité des salaires** (*equal pay*); SEE ALSO **siéger**

parjurer [se] (*vpr*): **se parjurer** pour faire condamner des innocents (*commit perjury*)

parlement (*nm*): devant le **parlement** réuni; renforcer le rôle des **parlements** nationaux (*parliament; parliamentary chamber*); SEE ALSO **croupion**, **dissoudre**, **unicaméral**

parlementaire (*adj/nmf*): respectueux de la procédure **parlementaire** (*parliamentary*); le **parlementaire** continue à percevoir ses indemnités (*member of parliament*)

parole (*nf*): il va **prendre la parole** au nom de ses collègues (*speak*)

parquet (*nm*): la section antiterroriste du **parquet** de Paris; le **parquet** a ordonné l'ouverture d'une enquête (*office of the public prosecutor*); **sur le parquet**, les titres s'échangeaient à un rythme soutenu (*on the trading floor [of the Paris Stock Exchange]*); SEE ALSO **déférer**

parrain (*nm*): les États-Unis, **parrain** du processus de paix (*sponsor*)

parrainage (*nm*): le **parrainage** d'une équipe cycliste professionnelle (*sponsorship*); le **parrainage publicitaire** envahit les écrans de télévision (*advertising sponsorship*); il a recueilli 75 000 signatures de **parrainage** (*[political] backing/support*)

parrainer (*vt*): une liste de 500 élus **parrainant** la candidature de l'écologiste (*back, sponsor*); interdiction de **parrainer** des manifestations sportives (*sponsor*)

part (*nf*): la **part** des hydrocarbures dans les exportations est tombée à 50% (*share, proportion*); six terroristes ont **pris part** à cette action (*take part; participate*); de nouveaux pays producteurs pourront **prendre de grosses parts de marché** au détriment de la France (*take a large market share*); SEE ALSO **membre, tailler**

partage (*nm*): le vote sur le **partage** de la Palestine (*division, partition*); un **partage du pouvoir** avec les communistes (*power-sharing*); l'accord sur le **partage du travail** évitera 128 licenciements (*work-sharing*)

partagé, -e (*adj*): les spécialistes restent très **partagés** (*divided; in disagreement*)

partenaire (*nm*): plusieurs **partenaires** qui détiennent globalement 27% du capital (*partner; associate*); le ministre discuta de l'affaire avec tous les **partenaires sociaux** (*management and labour/unions*)

partenariat (*nm*): un **partenariat** industriel franco-espagnol (*partnership; association*)

parti (*nm*): le **Parti** conservateur triomphe à nouveau (*party*); les candidats du **parti au pouvoir** (*party in power*); le **régime du parti unique** est un facteur de cohésion (*one-party regime*); hésiter à **prendre parti** dans la dispute (*take sides*); SEE ALSO **permanent, vert**

participation (*nf*): les deux complices nient leur **participation** dans l'affaire (*involvement*); une **participation** modique de quelques francs est demandée (*contribution*); certains actionnaires ont déjà accru leurs **participations** (*share/stock holding, stake*); l'ordonnance sur la **participation des salariés aux bénéfices des entreprises** (*profit-sharing scheme*); la faible **participation électorale** impose un second tour (*electoral/voter turnout*)

particularisme (*nm*): une preuve du **particularisme** régional bavarois (*distinctive identity*); en tenant compte des **particularismes locaux** (*specific local conditions*)

particulier, -ière (*adj/nm*): la production de voitures **particulières** (*private; privately owned*); le nombre de **particuliers** à détenir directement des actions; les mesures concernent les **particuliers** et les entreprises (*person; private individual*); SEE ALSO **hôtel, préjudice**

partie (*nf*): faire venir les **parties belligérantes** autour d'une table (*warring faction; both sides*); les avocats de la **partie adverse** (*opposing party*); l'avocat de la **partie civile** (*plaintiff in civil action*); les États **parties** à cette convention (*signatory/party to*); la Chine **est partie prenante** à tout règlement cambodgien (*be directly involved/concerned in*); notre armement nucléaire est une **partie intégrante** de la sécurité européenne (*integral part*); SEE ALSO **constituer**

partiel, -ielle (*adj*): des [élections] **partielles** auront lieu dans le Doubs (*by-election*); SEE ALSO **chômage, temps**

partisan, -e (*adj/nm,f*): quelle que soit leur préférence **partisane** (*party-political*); beaucoup de ses **partisans** sont passés à l'opposition (*supporter*); **être partisan** d'un renforcement de l'autorité du chef de l'État (*be in favour of*); les plus chauds **partisans de la peine de mort** (*advocate of capital punishment*); SEE ALSO **affiliation, farouche**

partition (*nf*): depuis les accords de Genève et la **partition** du Vietnam (*partition*)

pas (*nm*): la production industrielle semble **marquer le pas** (*remain stationary, make no progress*); un débat où l'idéologie préconçue **prend le pas sur** les faits (*override, take precedence over*)

passage (*nm*): lors de leur **passage à la douane** (*passing through customs*); le **passage** à la monnaie unique (*change, transition*); SEE ALSO **privé, servitude, tabac**

passation (*nf*): dans la **passation de marchés** pour la réhabilitation d'habitats anciens (*signing of contract*); au moment de la **passation des pouvoirs** à l'hôtel Matignon (*handing-over of an office; transfer of power*)

passer (*vi*): l'allocation **passe** à 770F (*rise/be increased to*); il faut utiliser différents moyens pour **faire passer son message** (*get/put across one's message*); Taiwan, **passant outre** au véto de Pékin (*defy; disregard*); SEE ALSO **acte, aveu, marché, revue, rouge, tabac**

passerelle (*nf*): créer des **passerelles** avec d'autres emplois; une **passerelle** entre deux cursus universitaires (*bridge, link*)

passible (*adj*): un crime **passible** de la peine de mort (*punishable by*); tout contrevenant sera **passible d'une amende** (*liable to a fine*); les contrevenants **sont passibles des tribunaux** (*are liable to prosecution*)

passif, -ive (*adj/nm*): le **passif** atteint 3 MF pour un chiffre d'affaires de 29 millions en 1988 (*deficit; liabilities, debt*); il a un **passif** très lourd de truand et de malfaiteur (*long criminal record*); SEE ALSO **apurer**

patente (*nf*): le remplacement de la **patente** par la taxe professionnelle en 1975 (*business/trading tax*)

pâtir (*vi*): les relations entre les deux pays risquent d'**en pâtir** (*suffer [as a result]*); le tourisme **pâtit de** la désaffection des étrangers (*suffer from; be a victim of*)

patrie (*nf*): SEE **mère**

patrimoine (*nm*): la fiscalité qui frappe le **patrimoine** (*inheritance, estate; property*); la publication du **patrimoine des hommes politiques** (*details of a politician's financial situation*); des associations de défense du **patrimoine** (*heritage [architectural/environmental]*); SEE ALSO **transparence**

patron, -onne (*nm,f*): un petit **patron** avec quatre employés (*employer*); le **patron d'usine** accueillit les invités (*factory owner*)

patronal, -e, *pl* **-aux** (*adj*): deux propositions faites par l'**organisation patronale** (*employers' organization*); SEE ALSO **contribution, cotisation, grève**

patronner (*vt*): les firmes qui **patronnent** des spectacles et des manifestations sportives (*sponsor*)

paupérisation (*nf*): avec pour conséquence la **paupérisation** de la commune (*impoverishment*); résultat: **la paupérisation de l'éducation nationale** (*the education system is starved of resources*)

paupériser (*vt*): la lente progression des salaires **paupérise** les classes moyennes (*impoverish*); [se] (*vpr*): une population qui **se paupérise** (*become impoverished*)

pauvreté (*nf*): une nouvelle **pauvreté urbaine** a fait son apparition (*urban poverty*); la lutte contre la **grande pauvreté** (*extreme poverty*); la **pauvreté** du budget général de la justice (*poverty; inadequacy*); SEE ALSO **seuil**

pavillon (*nm*): habiter un **pavillon** de banlieue (*[detached] house*); les armateurs placent souvent leurs navires sous **pavillon de complaisance** (*flag of convenience*); un navire **battant pavillon russe** (*flying the Russian flag*); SEE ALSO **onusien**

pavillonnaire (*adj*): le centre ancien, et les **zones pavillonnaires** (*area of low-rise housing; housing estate*); SEE ALSO **lotissement**

payant, -e (*adj*): la stratégie s'est révélée **payante** (*profitable, worthwhile*); SEE ALSO **tiers**

paye (*f*): SEE **paie**

payer (*vt*): Taiwan **paye comptant** ses achats d'armements (*pay in cash/cash down*); des versements officieux **payés en liquide** (*paid in cash*); préférer **se faire payer en nature** (*receive payment in kind*)

payeur, -euse (*adj/nm,f*): des sanctions automatiques contre les **mauvais payeurs** (*bad debtor*)

paysage (*nm*): [*fig*] dans un **paysage socio-économique** profondément remanié (*socio-economic environment*); le **paysage politique** d'**Afrique** s'en est trouvé profondément remanié (*the political map of Africa*); un **paysage audiovisuel** moins réglementé et mieux régulé (*broadcasting environment/system*)

paysan, -anne (*adj/nm,f*): propositions agricoles au GATT: les **paysans** sont-ils sacrifiés? (*small farmers; peasantry*)

paysannerie (*nf*): le niveau de vie de la **paysannerie** suisse (*small farmers*)

peaufiner (*vt*): la nouvelle chaîne **peaufine** sa grille de programmes (*put the finishing touches to*); son image, **peaufinée** par son entourage (*polish, refine*)

peine (*nf*): purger sa **peine [de prison]** à la centrale de Melun (*prison sentence*); Pédophilie: vers des **peines aggravées** (*stiffer penalties/ sentences*); la disparition de la **peine-plancher** (*minimum sentence*); les partisans d'une **peine de substitution** à la peine de mort (*alternative punishment/sentence*); SEE ALSO **confusion, encourir, incompressible, partisan, prononcé, remise, renforcer**

peloton (*nm*): [*fig*] figurer **dans le peloton de tête** des pays exportateurs (*in the leading group*)

pénal, -e, *pl* **-aux** (*adj*): la législation civile et **pénale** (*criminal*); les honoraires des avocats **en matière pénale** (*in criminal cases*); la **population pénale** est en hausse de 1% (*prison population*); SEE ALSO **chambre, code, droit, sanction**

pénaliser (*vt*): un des seuls pays d'Europe à **pénaliser** l'usage de drogues (*punish by law*)

pénalité (*nf*): SEE **renforcement**

pencher [se] (*vpr*): **se pencher** longtemps sur la question (*examine, look into*); la Grèce et la Turquie **se penchent sur Chypre** à Paris (*discuss the Cyprus question*)

pénitentiaire (*adj*): l'**administration pénitentiaire** voit ses crédits augmentés d'un tiers (*prison authorities*)

pension (*nf*): toucher la **pension de base** de la Sécurité sociale (*basic [retirement] pension*); recevoir une **pension de retraite à taux plein** (*full [retirement] pension*); avoir droit à une **pension d'invalidité** (*disability pension*); la **pension alimentaire** qu'il doit à son ancienne épouse (*alimony, maintenance*); SEE ALSO **bloquer**

pénurie (*nf*): certains biens, sujets à de fréquentes **pénuries** (*shortage, scarcity, dearth*); la **pénurie alimentaire** est la plus grave de l'histoire du pays (*food shortage; famine*)

percée (*nf*): il a qualifié cet accord de "**percée historique**" (*historic breakthrough*); **réaliser une percée** de taille sur le marché américain (*make a breakthrough*)

percepteur (*nm*): protester contre la suppression du poste de **percepteur** (*tax inspector; tax collector*)

perception (*nf*): le ministre veut moderniser la **perception** de la redevance (*collection; levying [of tax/charge]*); aller à la **perception** payer ses contributions (*tax collector's office, tax office*); SEE ALSO **recette**

percer (*vt*): pour **percer** le marché intérieur américain (*penetrate, break into*)

percevoir (*vt*): soupçonné d'avoir **perçu** des dessous-de-table (*receive [esp. payment]*); une baisse des **revenus perçus** par l'État (*state revenue*); la façon dont ceci **est perçu** par les différents partenaires sociaux (*be perceived/seen*)

perchoir (*nm*): l'ancien Premier ministre a été investi pour le **perchoir** (*seat/office of President of the French National Assembly*)

pérenniser (*vt*): la nécessité de **pérenniser** un régime qui a fait ses preuves (*make permanent; ensure the continuance of*); [se] (*vpr*): à en croire le ministre, le plan Vigipirate est appelé à **se pérenniser** (*become permanent; be continued indefinitely*)

pérennité (*nf*): des incidents qui prouvent la **pérennité** du sentiment raciste (*permanence; lasting quality*); cette prise de contrôle devra **assurer la pérennité** de la firme (*ensure the survival*)

péréquation (*nf*): un **fonds de péréquation** au profit des communes les plus pauvres (*adjustment fund*)

performant, -e (*adj*): les entreprises les plus grosses ou les plus **performantes** (*high-performance; outstanding*)

péricliter (*vi*): faute de dynamisme, l'entreprise **périclite** (*be in a bad way; be going downhill*)

péril (*nm*): les désordres monétaires **mettent en péril** les revenus des agriculteurs (*threaten; endanger*)

période (*nf*): pendant la **période électorale** (*election time*); embauché après une **période d'essai** (*trial period*)

périodicité (*nf*): la **périodicité** peut être semestrielle ou trimestrielle (*periodicity; interval, frequency*)

permanence (*nf*): devant la **permanence** et l'ampleur des troubles en Cisjordanie (*persistence, continuation*); dans les **permanences** des partis de l'opposition (*[political] party headquarters*); le député **tient une permanence** le samedi dans sa circonscription (*hold a surgery*)

permanent, -e (*adj/nm*): élu **permanent** fédéral CFDT pour la branche Tourisme (*[union] official*); devenu **permanent du parti** (*party worker*); SEE ALSO **formation**

permis (*nm*): un **permis** de construire a été accordé (*permit, licence*); se procurer un **permis de travail** (*work permit*)

perpétrer (*vt*): deux attentats à la bombe **perpétrés** simultanément; le sabotage fut **perpétré** par des agents français (*carry out, commit*)

perpétuité (*nf*): condamné à la **prison à perpétuité**; une **perpétuité** réelle pour assassinat de mineur précédé de viol (*life sentence; prison for life*)

perquisition (*nf*): la police a **opéré une perquisition** chez l'accusé (*carry out a search of premises*)

perquisitionner (*vi*): la police **perquisitionna** à son domicile (*carry out a [police] search*)

persister (*vi*): le chancelier **persiste et signe** (*continue with the same policy; stick to his guns*)

personnage (*nm*): SEE **clé**

personnalisé, -e (*adj*): un suivi pédagogique **personnalisé** (*personalized; individual*)

personne (*nf*): l'abattement est plafonné à 30 000F pour une **personne morale** (*legal entity; corporate body*); cette allocation est soumise à un plafond de 70 000F pour une **personne physique** (*individual; natural person*); SEE ALSO **atteinte, circulation, dépendant, droit, troisième âge, valide**

personnel, -elle (*adj/nm*): l'ensemble du **personnel** est prêt à faire grève (*staff, personnel*); l'usine a un **personnel** de 220 (*staff, payroll*); SEE ALSO **actionnariat, apport, campagne, compression, équipe, louer, prévoyance, réduction, rotation, vacataire**

perspective (*nf*): une **perspective** peu séduisante pour Paris (*prospect*); **dans la perspective des** législatives de 1998 (*bearing in mind; with a view to*); l'absence complète de **perspectives d'emploi** (*employment prospects*)

perte (*nf*): les **pertes** se sont élevées à 70 millions de francs (*financial loss*); l'entreprise avait enregistré 200 millions de **pertes d'exploitation** (*operating/trading loss*); **fortes pertes** pour la filiale allemande (*heavy losses*); une **perte sèche** de 2,36 milliards de francs (*total loss*); SEE ALSO **alourdissement**

perturbation (*nf*): de nouvelles **perturbations** dans le trafic aérien; des **perturbations** prévisibles dans les transports (*disruption, disturbance*)

perturber (*vt*): les services des Finances **perturbés** par des arrêts de travail (*disrupt; disorganize*)

pervers, -e (*adj*): les réformes ont engendré des **effets pervers** (*undesirable consequences*)

pesanteur (*nf*): les **pesanteurs** de l'administration parisienne (*sluggishness, slowness*)

peser (*vt*): le groupe **pèse** un demi-milliard de francs de chiffre d'affaires (*be worth/valued at*); (*vi*): les charges sociales excessives qui **pèsent** sur les salaires (*be a heavy burden*); l'augmentation de la **fiscalité pesant sur l'épargne** (*tax on savings*)

petit, -e (*adj*): 400 000 **petits porteurs** sont devenus actionnaires de la chaîne privatisée (*small shareholder*); SEE ALSO **actionnaire, souscripteur**

pétition (*nf*): apposer sa signature sur une **pétition** (*petition*)

pétitionner (*vi*): **pétitionner** contre l'implantation d'une aire de nomades (*petition; organise a petition*)

phase (*nf*): SEE **engager**

pic (*nm*): le **pic** ayant été atteint en 1985, avec 36,6% (*peak; high point*)

pièce (*nf*): se munir d'une **pièce d'identité** (*identity papers; means of identification*); sur présentation de **pièces justificatives** (*supporting evidence; documentary proof*); Washington a fait de Riyad la **pièce maîtresse** de son dispositif au Proche-Orient (*cornerstone, key element*); des produits **vendus à la pièce** (*sold individually*); un nouveau ministère **créé de toutes pièces** (*newly created/set up*); SEE ALSO **annexe**

pied (*nm*): la société de Rennes a **mis à pied** plus de 400 employés (*lay off*); la direction décida la **mise à pied** immédiate des grévistes (*suspension*); la **mise sur pied** d'une commission parlementaire (*setting up, forming*); cette décision tranche en faveur des **pieds-noirs** et d'autres rapatriés d'Afrique (*Algerian of European stock; French settler in Algeria*); SEE ALSO **écoper**

pierre (*nf*): [*fig*] la Constitution reste la **pierre angulaire** de l'édifice politique américain (*cornerstone*); la **pierre d'achoppement** qui empêche de faire avancer les négociations (*stumbling block, obstacle*); octroyer des **aides à la pierre** (*construction/building grant*); SEE ALSO **jet**

piétinement (*nm*): pour masquer le **piétinement de l'enquête** (*slow progress of the investigation*)

piétiner (*vt*): [*fig*] les droits de l'homme sont quotidiennement **piétinés** (*trample under foot*); (*vi*): alors que le dialogue inter-cambodgien **piétine** (*make no progress/make no headway*); le manque de crédits **fait piétiner** le mouvement (*slow down, hamper*)

pignon (*nm*): [*fig*] si on est une société **ayant pignon sur rue** (*successful; well-established*)

pilotage (*nm*): le **comité de pilotage** définit le programme de travail (*steering group*)

pilote (*adj*): le tourisme, **secteur pilote** de l'économie (*leading/principal sector*); Reims et Angers, **villes-pilotes** en matière de transports en commun (*innovating towns/cities*); SEE ALSO **expérience**

piquet (*nm*): installer un **piquet de grève** devant l'entrée de l'établissement (*strike picket, picket line*)

piratage (*nm*): le **piratage informatique** entraîne une peine de trois ans de prison (*computer crime*)

pirate (*nm*): les **pirates de l'air** impliqués dans le détournement de l'avion (*hijacker*)

piraterie (*nf*): la **piraterie** en matière de droits d'auteur (*pirating; illegal copying*)

placard (*nm*): insérer un **placard pleine page** dans cinq quotidiens (*full-page advertisement*); l'affaire des fausses factures: **un nouveau dossier est mis au placard** (*another "affair" is put on ice/shelved*)

placarder (*vt*): ils **placardent** sur les murs des milliers d'affiches (*stick up, post*)

place (*nf*): chercher une **place** d'employé de maison (*position, situation*); la **place** française a moins baissé que les autres (*stock exchange/ market*); les forces russes ont bombardé la **place forte** tchétchène (*stronghold*); **mettre en place** un plan de réformes économiques (*set up*); la **mise en place** de ces mesures sera très coûteuse (*putting into effect, implementation*); SEE ALSO **postuler, pouvoir**

placement (*nm*): le juge d'enfants décide un **placement** dans une famille d'accueil (*placement*); ces actions constituent un **placement très sûr** (*a very secure investment*); 500 offres d'emploi par semaine arrivent au **bureau de placement** (*employment agency*)

placer (*vt*): **placer** un enfant en danger (*find a placement for, place [esp. with foster family]*); **placer un enfant à la DDASS** à 650F par jour (*place child in local-authority care*); SEE ALSO **assistance**

plafond (*nm*): le **plafond** mensuel de la Sécurité sociale; le dépassement du **plafond** des dépenses électorales (*ceiling, upper limit*); des prestations familiales versées sans **plafond de ressources** (*upper limit on income*); SEE ALSO **cours**

plafonnement (*nm*): en refusant le **plafonnement** des dépenses de santé (*setting of upper limit/ceiling*); on assiste à un **plafonnement** des recettes publicitaires (*levelling-off*)

plafonner (*vt*): une retraite qui **serait plafonnée** à trois fois le SMIC (*be subject to a maximum/ceiling/upper limit*); (*vi*): le salaire minimum qui **plafonne** depuis 5 ans à 21F l'heure (*reach a ceiling; level off*)

plage (*nf*): la nouvelle **plage horaire** s'étend de 9h à 17h (*broadcasting slot*); les émissions sont interrompues par des **plages publicitaires** (*commercial break*)

plaider (*vt/vi*): un Algérien expulsé avant que son avocat ait pu **plaider** (*plead [case]; go to court*); la défense **plaide l'acquittement** (*plead not guilty*); pris en flagrant délit, il **plaide coupable** (*plead guilty*); l'affaire **sera plaidée** devant le TGI de Marseille (*be heard in court*); [*fig*] **plaider** pour une coopération étroite entre leurs deux pays (*appeal/ make a plea*); SEE ALSO **foi, légitime, relaxe**

plaideur, -euse (*nm,f*): le **plaideur** peut se défendre sans l'assistance d'un avocat (*litigant*)

plaidoirie (*nf*): après les **plaidoiries** des avocats de l'accusation et de la défense (*speech/plea [for the defence]*)

plaidoyer (*nm*): [*fig*] se livrer à un vibrant **plaidoyer** en faveur du désarmement (*plea*)

plaignant, -e (*adj/nm,f*): le **plaignant** fut débouté de sa plainte (*plaintiff, complainant*); la **partie plaignante** a eu gain de cause (*litigant*); SEE ALSO **débouter, raison**

plainte (*nf*): ces agressions ont suscité plus de cinquante **plaintes [en justice]** (*complaint*); **porter plainte** pour incitation à la haine raciale; il pourra décider de **porter plainte en justice** (*lodge an official complaint, press charges*)

plan (*nm*): le **plan de paix** qui entérine la partition de la Bosnie (*peace plan*); le **plan social** offre à tout licencié 200 000F de dédommagement (*planned redundancy scheme*); la diminution des **plans de charge** dans les chantiers navals (*order book*); le Caire cherche à assurer son **rôle de premier plan** dans la région (*key/leading role*); SEE ALSO **cadastral, contrat, épargne, occupation, prévoyance, restructuration, rigueur, sauvetage**

planche (*nf*): financer le progrès social par la **planche à billets** (*printing of money*)

plancher (*nm*): SEE **cours, peine**

plancher (*vi*): [*fam*] patrons et syndicats **planchent** sur l'insertion (*work on, study*); un groupe de spécialistes vont **plancher sur le rapport** (*work on the report*)

planification (*nf*): la **planification à la française** est de conception assez souple (*French economic planning*); l'encouragement à la **planification familiale** (*family planning*)

planifier (*vt*): l'explosion d'hier avait dû être **planifiée** depuis longtemps (*plan*)

planning (*nm*): établir un **planning** (*programme, schedule*); le libre accès des femmes au **planning familial** (*family planning*)

plaque (*nf*): la vente et la pose de **plaques [d'immatriculation]** (*vehicle number-plate*); [*fig*] véritable **plaque tournante** du commerce international (*hub, centre; nerve centre*)

plaquette (*nf*): éditer une nouvelle **plaquette** d'information (*booklet*)

plastiquage (*nm*): après le **plastiquage** d'un poste de police près de Bastia (*bomb attack [on], bombing*)

plastiquer (*vt*): des usines détruites, des immeubles d'habitation **plastiqués** (*bombed, blown up*)

plat, -e (*adj*): le ministre propose de **mettre à plat** ce problème insoluble (*have a close look at*); attribution des logements sociaux: **une mise à plat** s'impose (*the whole question needs a thorough examination*); plaider en faveur d'une **remise à plat** du dossier (*thorough re-examination*)

plate-forme (*nf*): appliquer la **plate-forme [électorale]** RPR-UDF (*electoral platform/programme*)

plébisciter (*vt*): les militants socialistes l'avaient **plébiscité** par référendum (*elect by an overwhelming majority*)

plein, -e (*adj*): obtenir une croissance soutenue qui mènera l'économie au **plein emploi** (*full employment*); tous ne désirent pas **travailler à temps plein** (*work full-time*)

plénier, -ière (*adj*): SEE **séance**

pléthorique (*adj*): les surplus **pléthoriques** se résorbent peu à peu (*excessive, over-abundant*); le problème des **effectifs pléthoriques** (*over-staffing; excessive numbers*)

plier [se] (*vpr*): **se plier** à la loi sur la transparence (*obey, respect*); **se plier à des méthodes nouvelles** n'est pas chose aisée (*adapt to new methods*)

pluralisme (*nm*): réaffirmer le **pluralisme** linguistique (*pluralism*); s'engager sur la voie du **pluralisme politique** (*multi-party political system*); le **pluralisme des candidatures** étant la règle (*multiple candidates; multi-candidate system*)

pluraliste (*adj*): les premières **élections pluralistes** que le pays a connues (*multi-party elections*); la **liberté d'information pluraliste** est-elle respectée dans ce pays? (*access to both official and unofficial sources of information*)

pluralité (*nf*): **en cas de pluralité d'infractions**, les peines s'additionnent (*if more than one offence has been committed*); un régime démocratique fondé sur la **pluralité des partis** (*multi-party system*)

pluripartisme (*nm*): les pays de l'Est s'ouvrent au **pluripartisme** (*multi-party political system*)

plus-value (*nf*): l'État réalisera ainsi une **plus-value** substantielle (*profit*); la **plus-value** sera alors totalement exonérée (*capital gain*); SEE ALSO **fiscalité, juteux**

poids (*nm*): réduire le **poids** des cotisations sociales (*burden*)

point (*nm*): **faire le point** de la situation (*take stock; sum up*); le plan social **mis au point** par Bata France (*devised; finalized*); le quai d'Orsay **diffusa une mise au point** pour dissiper les malentendus (*issue a statement to set the record straight/clarify a point*); au cours d'un **point de presse** tenu à l'issue de la réunion (*press briefing; meeting with the press*); SEE ALSO **achoppement**

pointage (*nm*): **au dernier pointage**, un train sur cinq circulait en région parisienne (*at the last/most recent check*)

pointe (*nf*): après une **pointe**, le titre a fait marche arrière (*high spot; peak*); le Japon, **à la pointe** de l'innovation (*at the forefront*); leader dans les **technologies de pointe** (*leading-edge/state-of-the-art technology*)

pointer (*vi*): aller **pointer** au bureau de chômage (*check in, sign on*); son mandat de député non-renouvelé, il a dû **pointer au chômage** (*register at the unemployment office*)

pointu, -e (*adj*): des formations spécifiques, très **pointues**; acquérir une spécialisation plus **pointue** (*specialized*)

pôle (*nm*): la création de **pôles de croissance** soigneusement situés (*growth centre*); toute la région a été déclarée **pôle de conversion** (*special relocation/redevelopment area*); la ville de Nîmes constitue un véritable **pôle régional** (*regional centre*)

polémique (*adj/nf*): essais nucléaires: la **polémique** continue (*argument, debate*); ses déclarations **suscitent de vives polémiques** en Grande-Bretagne (*spark off heated debate*)

polémiquer (*vi*): éviter de **polémiquer** avec la direction du parti (*enter into a debate*)

police (*nf*): en l'absence d'une **police** internationale (*policing authority*); la **police judiciaire [PJ]** parisienne, quai des Orfèvres (*criminal investigation department*); la **police des mœurs** enquête sur les affaires crapuleuses (*vice squad*); plastiquage d'un **poste de police** en Corse (*police station*); souscrire une **police d'assurance tous risques** (*comprehensive insurance policy*); SEE ALSO **préfecture, préfet, quadriller, tribunal**

policier, -ière (*adj/nm*): quatre **policiers** dont un commissaire (*police officer*); la présence obligatoire d'une **femme policier** (*policewoman*); SEE ALSO **enquête**

politicien, -ienne (*adj*): SEE **magouille, politique**

politique (*adj/nmf*): la **politique intérieure** préoccupe le gouvernement (*domestic policy/politics*); il dédaigne souverainement la **politique politicienne** (*politicking; politics for its own sake*); on ne peut plus pratiquer **la politique de l'autruche** (*burying one's head in the sand*); SEE ALSO **actualité, asile, classe, clivage, imprévoyance, inflexion, institution, paysage, pluralisme, récupération, réfugié, salarial, volonté**

polyvalence (*nf*): un poste exigeant **polyvalence** et motivation (*adaptability, versatility*); la **polyvalence** fait craindre une perte d'identité professionnelle (*[need for] flexibility in the workplace*)

polyvalent, -e (*adj*): il s'agissait d'une brigade d'intervention **polyvalente** (*all-purpose*); on hébergea les sinistrés dans la **salle polyvalente** (*multi-purpose hall*); la création d'un emploi d'**ouvrier polyvalent** à temps complet (*worker with flexible duties*)

ponction (*nf*): une inflation maîtrisée, et des **ponctions fiscales en baisse** (*lower taxes*)

ponctionner (*vt*): l'impôt sur le revenu en France **ponctionne** moins de 6% de la richesse nationale (*take out, tap*)

ponctuel, -elle (*adj*): des opérations **ponctuelles** de baisse des prix (*one-off, isolated*); des **cas ponctuels** ont été signalés (*isolated cases*); des **mesures ponctuelles** pour lutter contre le chômage (*individual/selective measures*)

ponctuellement (*adv*): convaincre ses adversaires de se rallier **ponctuellement** à tel ou tel projet (*selectively; in individual/specific cases*)

pondéré, -e (*adj*): le **vote majoritaire pondéré** est le plus fréquent au conseil des ministres (*majority weighted voting*)

pondérer (*vt*): on a retenu sept critères, en les **pondérant** (*weight; give weighting to*)

pont (*nm*): avant le **pont** du 11 novembre; des repos supplémentaires pour les **ponts** non chômés (*extra holidays/days off [between public holiday and weekend]*); frais émoulu des **Ponts et Chaussées** (*French national school of civil engineering*); SEE ALSO **tête**

populaire (*adj*): SEE **légitimité, secours**

population (*nf*): le chômage a atteint 10% de la **population active** (*population of working age; working population*); SEE ALSO **pénal, vieillissement**

port (*nm*): interdire le **port** des signes religieux à l'école (*wearing; carrying*); SEE ALSO **défaut, non-port, voile**

porte-à-faux (*adv*): le Président est **en porte-à-faux** après Irangate; ceci place le PCF **en porte-à-faux** (*in an awkward/a delicate position*)

portée (*nf*): la **portée** de ses remarques n'a pas échappé à ses interlocuteurs (*significance*); sa visite risque d'avoir une **portée considérable** (*far-reaching consequences*)

portefeuille (*nm*): le chef de l'État lui a confié le difficile **portefeuille** de l'Intérieur (*ministerial portfolio*); la gestion d'un **portefeuille** d'un montant de 2 MF (*share portfolio*); SEE ALSO **gérer, ministre**

porte-parole (*nm*): selon le **porte-parole** de la commission d'enquête (*spokesperson*)

porter (*vt*): le coup d'État qui **porta au pouvoir** le régime militariste (*bring to/put in power*); tous les matins, votre journal **porté à domicile** (*delivered to one's home*); le montant de l'allocation est **porté à 63F** par jour (*raise/increase to*); des conversations **portant sur** les problèmes de l'Afrique australe (*concerning*); SEE ALSO **acquéreur, garant, plainte, préjudice**

porteur, -euse (*adj/nm,f*): l'industrie manufacturière, dopée par une conjoncture très **porteuse** (*buoyant*); les **porteurs** Eurocard (*holder*); SEE ALSO **créneau, mère, petit**

position (*nf*): il **prend position** contre la dénucléarisation de l'Europe (*take a stance; declare oneself*); sa **prise de position** en faveur des minorités opprimées (*stand; position*); SEE ALSO **durcir**

positionner [se] (*vpr*): la société essaie de **se positionner** sur ce nouveau créneau (*occupy a [market] slot*); chercher à **se positionner** en vue des prochaines élections (*establish a position*)

possédant, -e (*adj/nm,f*): l'explosion de la Bourse a fait la joie des **possédants** (*owning class*); SEE ALSO **classe**

posséder (*vt*): **posséder** sa résidence principale demeure un bon investissement (*own, possess*)

postal, -e, *pl* **-aux** (*adj*): SEE **franchise**

poste (*nm*): les dépenses, réparties en différents **postes [budgétaires]** (*[budget] heading; item*); en 1995, six millions de **postes [de travail]** utiliseront l'informatique (*post; position, job*); décrocher un **poste définitif**; ne pas chercher un stage, mais un **poste fixe** (*permanent position*); deux fonctionnaires de l'OTAN **en poste** à Bruxelles (*in post*); (*nf*): une employée des **Postes** (*Post Office*); on va vers la **privatisation des postes** (*privatizing postal services*); SEE ALSO **clé, création, débloquer, exclure, honorifique, police, pourvoir, responsabilité**

posté, -e (*adj*): des salariés **postés** (*on shift work*); ceux qui **travaillent en posté** (*do shift work, work shifts*); SEE ALSO **travail**

postulant, -e (*adj/nm,f*): pour 4 000 **postulants**, on propose 400 places (*applicant, candidate*)

postuler (*vt*): **postuler une place** de représentant (*apply for a job/position*)

pot-de-vin (*nm*): les poursuites pour versement de **pots-de-vin** (*bribe, sweetener; backhander*); **toucher des pots-de-vin** pour l'obtention de marchés (*accept bribes*)

pouce (*nm*): **donner un coup de pouce** au tourisme rural (*boost, help*); un **coup de pouce fiscal** de 5 000F décidé par le ministre (*tax incentive*)

poumon (*nm*): [*fig*] l'Asie, nouveau **poumon** de l'économie mondiale (*economic dynamo/force*); le puits fut longtemps **le poumon économique de la région** (*the economic lifeline of the region*)

pourcentage (*nm*): rémunération: fixe plus **pourcentage** sur le chiffre d'affaires réalisé (*percentage, commission*)

pourparlers (*nmpl*): des **pourparlers** indirects entre Kaboul et Islamabad (*talks; negotiations*); les **pourparlers de paix** doivent s'ouvrir le 10 juin (*peace talks*)

pourrir (*vi*): au risque de **laisser pourrir la situation** (*allow the situation to deteriorate*)

pourrissement (*nm*): ces affrontements illustrent le **pourrissement de la situation** (*the worsening situation*); le gouvernement a choisi la **stratégie du pourrissement** (*allowing a situation to deteriorate*)

poursuite (*nf*): le plan prévoit la **poursuite** de l'aide humanitaire (*continuation*); la société a fait l'objet de **poursuites en justice** (*legal action/proceedings*); **engager des poursuites judiciaires** pour factures non réglées (*bring a legal action, prosecute*)

poursuivre (*vt*): les dirigeants de la secte **sont poursuivis** pour escroquerie (*be prosecuted*); [se] (*vpr*): cette tendance devrait **se poursuivre** cette année encore (*continue, carry on*)

pourvoi (*nm*): le **pourvoi** a été rejeté (*appeal*); le défenseur a **déposé un pourvoi en cassation** contre le verdict de la cour (*take a case to the supreme court of appeal*)

pourvoir (*vt*): 600 emplois sont créés pour **pourvoir aux** besoins immédiats (*cater for; satisfy*); douze sièges sont encore à **pourvoir** (*fill, allot*); il y a 4 000 postes d'infirmière **non pourvus** (*unfilled*); **pourvoir un poste**, sans petites annonces (*fill a post/position*); [se] (*vpr*): il **s'est pourvu devant la cour d'appel**, qui a confirmé la première décision (*appeal [against conviction]*); condamné en appel, il **se pourvoit en cassation** (*take a case to the supreme court of appeal*)

pourvoyeur, -euse (*nm,f*): principal **pourvoyeur en armes** de l'armée ira-kienne (*arms supplier*)

pourvu, -e (*adj*): la région est **bien pourvue** sur le plan médical (*well provided for*)

poussée (*nf*): la **poussée** des inégalités sociales (*increase*); la nouvelle **poussée** du parti d'extrême droite (*upsurge*)

pousser (*vt*): les Serbes **poussent à** un arrêt des combats (*push/press for*)

pouvoir (*nm*): le **pouvoir** s'est ressaisi face à l'agitation universitaire (*government*); **les pouvoirs publics** ont décrété le couvre-feu (*the authorities*); il dénonçait **les pouvoirs en place** (*the powers that be; the government in office*); facilitant ainsi la **prise de pouvoir** des communistes (*seizure of power; [political] takeover*); des gains de **pouvoir d'achat** consécutifs à une progression des salaires (*purchasing power*); SEE ALSO **accaparer, coulisse, décision, écarter, élargi, étendu, éviction, fondé, inféoder, maintenir, noyautage, parti, passation, porter, usure, venue**

praticien, -ienne (*nm,f*): le sollicitor anglais est un **praticien** général du droit (*practitioner*); consulter son **praticien** (*GP, general practitioner*)

pratique (*nf*): la **pratique [religieuse]** dominicale est en baisse en France (*church attendance*); SEE ALSO **discriminatoire**

pratiquer (*vt*): inférieurs aux **taux pratiqués** la semaine dernière (*last week's rates*); [se] (*vpr*): les **prix qui se pratiquent à Paris** sont très chers (*Paris prices*)

préalable (*adj/nm*): exiger le retrait **préalable** des troupes soviétiques (*prior*); négocier **sans préalable** (*without preconditions*); (*adv*): faire arrêter **au préalable** un certain nombre de gens (*first of all; as a preliminary*)

préalablement (*adv*): donner **préalablement** son accord (*first, beforehand*)

préavis (*nm*): le licenciement sans **préavis** de 19 ouvriers (*warning, notice*); partir sans **effectuer son préavis** (*work one's notice*); le syndicat des cheminots dépose un **préavis de grève** pour le 15 septembre (*notice of strike*)

précaire (*adj*): entassés dans des logements **précaires** et insalubres (*unsafe; dangerous*); une société où **l'emploi est si précaire** (*the job situation is so uncertain/insecure*); les intérimaires, et autres **travailleurs précaires** (*person without job security*)

précarité (*nf*): le travail féminin reste synonyme de **précarité** et de petits salaires (*job insecurity*); la **précarité de l'emploi** s'est accentuée (*lack of job security*); la traditionnelle **précarité des relations** entre Hanoï et Pékin (*strained/difficult relationship*)

préciser (*vt*): à une date qui reste à **préciser** (*fix, decide*); le ministre **précise** son calendrier de réforme de l'université (*clarify, spell out*); il a **précisé** qu'il briguera un nouveau mandat (*make clear, reveal*); [se] (*vpr*): si l'offre **se précise** d'ici à la fin du mois (*be confirmed*)

précision (*nf*): le communiqué **n'a fourni aucune précision** (*gave no [further] details*)

préconiser (*vt*): l'Algérie **préconise** une augmentation des quotas de production (*advocate, advise*)

prédateur, -trice (*nm,f*): toutes les valeurs susceptibles d'intéresser les grands **prédateurs**; à condition que le **prédateur** y mette le bon prix (*predator, corporate raider*)

préemption (*nf*): la municipalité fait usage de son **droit de préemption** pour acquérir ce terrain (*pre-emptive right to acquire*)

préfectoral, -e, *pl* **-aux** (*adj*): aspirer à une **carrière préfectorale** (*post as* préfet); des **arrêtés préfectoraux** appellent aux économies d'eau (*edict from the* préfet)

préfecture (*nf*): interdit par un arrêté pris par la **préfecture** (*office of the* préfet); Créteil, la **préfecture** du Val-de-Marne (*prefecture; main administrative town in* département); à Marseille, devant la **préfecture** (*residence of the* préfet); la **préfecture de police** a autorisé le défilé (*[office of] the* préfet de police)

préférence (*nf*): il propose un référendum sur la **préférence nationale** (*[policy of] putting France/the French first*)

préfet (*nm*): les maires ne craignent plus la tutelle du **préfet** (préfet; *administrative head of* département); le **préfet de police** dépend hiérarchiquement du ministre de l'Intérieur (*prefect of police; police chief*); SEE ALSO **valse**

préjudice (*nm*): obtenir réparation d'un **préjudice** subi (*damage; loss*); les vols commis **au préjudice des particuliers** (*against the individual*); l'attraction de Paris **porte préjudice** au développement des autres grands centres (*be detrimental*)

prélèvement (*nm*): un **prélèvement** de 0,5% sur tous les revenus (*deduction, levy*); les **prélèvements obligatoires** [impôts et cotisations sociales] vont augmenter (*tax and social security deductions*); le **prélèvement à la source** de l'impôt direct (*deduction at source*); régler une facture par **prélèvement automatique sur compte bancaire** (*direct debit*)

prélever (*vt*): les versements peuvent être **prélevés** automatiquement sur un compte-chèques ou un livret (*deduct*); l'État **prélève** une part importante du PNB (*take in the form of taxes*)

préméditation (*nf*): le tribunal n'a pas retenu la **préméditation** (*premeditation; intent [to commit a crime]*); inculpé de **meurtre avec préméditation** (*premeditated/first-degree murder*)

premier, -ière (*adj/nm.f*): SEE **matière, ministrable**

prépondérance (*nf*): ceci leur y a garanti une **prépondérance économique** (*dominant [economic] position*)

prépondérant, -e (*adj*): **jouer un rôle prépondérant** dans la recherche d'une solution pacifique (*play a prominent/major part*); SEE ALSO **voix**

préposé, -e (*nm.f*): sous le regard dubitatif du **préposé des douanes** (*customs official*); le **préposé des postes** doit absolument vérifier votre identité (*post office clerk/employee*)

préretraite (*nf*): des **préretraites** massives et de plus en plus précoces (*early retirement*); de nouvelles règles pour les **préretraites à mi-temps** (*pre-retirement scheme*); SEE ALSO **départ**

préretraité, -e (*nm.f*): la CE compte 2 millions de **préretraités** (*person having taken early retirement*)

prérogative (*nf*): il abuse des **prérogatives** présidentielles (*privilege, prerogative*)

près (*prep*): procureur général **près** la cour des comptes (*appointed, attached to*)

prescription (*nf*): selon les **prescriptions de la loi** (*terms of the law*); la promotion du produit incite à des **prescriptions [médicales]** abusives (*medical prescription*)

prescrire (*vt*): la liberté de **prescrire** des médecins sera encadrée (*prescribe medicine/treatment*)

présenter [se] (*vpr*): le maire décida de ne pas **se présenter** au scrutin du 25 septembre (*stand [for election]*)

présidence (*nf*): date à laquelle débute la **présidence** française de la CE; une femme a été nommée à la **présidence** (*presidency, chairmanship*); la **présidence tournante** exercée à tour de rôle par chacun des États (*revolving chairmanship*); lors des élections à la **présidence de la République** (*presidency of the Republic*); SEE ALSO **prétendant**

président, -e (*nm.f*): **président du conseil de direction** (*chairman*); c'est le **P-DG [président-directeur général]** lui-même qui annonça la nomination (*chairman and managing director*); SEE ALSO **relever**

191

présidentiable (*adj/nmf*): il est, de l'avis de tous, le meilleur **présidentiable** (*potential presidential candidate*)

présidentialisme (*nm*): le **présidentialisme** à la française (*presidential regime*)

présidentiel, -ielle (*adj*): les [élections] **présidentielles** de 1988 furent un triomphe pour la gauche (*presidential elections*); SEE ALSO **mouvance**

présomption (*nf*): bénéficier de la **présomption d'innocence** (*presumption of innocence*); les accusations s'appuyaient sur un faible **faisceau de présomptions** (*body of evidence*)

presse (*nf*): ce sera une année décisive pour la **presse écrite** (*press, newspaper industry*); les ventes de la **presse hebdomadaire d'information** en baisse (*news weeklies*); déclin de la **presse d'opinion** en Israël (*newspapers specializing in political analysis*); la **presse à sensation** s'est emparée de l'affaire (*popular press; gutter press*); SEE ALSO **délit, liberté, magazine, point, tirage**

pressenti, -e (*adj*): la liste des **pressentis** s'allonge (*person sounded out [for post/office]*); **Premier ministre pressenti**, mais sans majorité au parlement (*prospective Prime Minister*); de tous les **candidats pressentis à sa succession** (*favourites for the succession*)

pressentir (*vt*): le président des centristes a été **pressenti** dans la Somme (*sound out [to stand for election/office]*)

presser (*vt*): Bruxelles **presse** les Quinze de débloquer le financement des grands travaux (*press, urge*)

pression (*nf*): les **pressions** politiques dont ils sont l'objet (*pressure*); une **pression à la baisse** des salaires (*downward pressure*); une aggravation de la **pression fiscale** (*tax burden*); SEE ALSO **groupe**

prestataire (*nm*): le nombre de **prestataires** a augmenté de 25% en deux ans (*recipient of a state benefit*); les **prestataires de services** indépendants s'estiment lésés par cette loi (*supplier of a service*)

prestation (*nf*): les factures correspondaient à des **prestations** réelles (*service*); la directive européenne sur la libre **prestation de services** (*supplying of a service*); des **prestations sociales** qui tiennent lieu de revenu (*social security benefits*); le gel des **prestations familiales** (*family benefits*); Zaïre: **prestation de serment** du gouvernement (*taking/swearing of oath*)

présumé, -e (*adj*): auteur **présumé** du meurtre d'un quinquagénaire (*alleged, supposed; presumed*); l'**assassin présumé** a été écroué (*murder suspect*)

prêt (*nm*): obtenir un nouveau **prêt** (*loan*); les **prêts au logement** comptent pour la moitié du bilan du Crédit Agricole; l'attribution de logements HLM et de **prêts immobiliers** (*housing loan*); l'octroi d'un **prêt hypothécaire** (*mortgage loan*); SEE ALSO **annuité**

prétendant, -e (*nm,f*): l'assassinat du **prétendant à la présidence** (*presidential candidate*)

prétendu, -e (*adj*): les **prétendus** excès de la politique commerciale de la CE (*alleged, claimed*)

prétendument (*adv*): lors d'une opération **prétendument** anti-terroriste (*allegedly*)

prétention (*nf*): la Libye a abandonné ses **prétentions** sur ce territoire (*claim*); l'Italie n'a aucune **prétention territoriale** sur la Dalmatie (*territorial claim*); (*pl*): envoyer une lettre de candidature manuscrite, avec **prétentions [salariales]** (*expected salary*)

prêter (*vt*): le gouvernement a **prêté serment** devant le Président (*swear/ take an oath*); la cour **fait prêter serment à douze jurés** (*swear in a jury of twelve*); les propos **prêtés au ministre** (*attributed to the minister*); 200 bénévoles **prêteront leur concours** (*give their help, lend support*)

prétoire (*nm*): la bataille va donc se poursuivre **dans les prétoires** (*in court, in the courtroom*)

preuve (*nf*): après audition des témoins et examen des **preuves** (*evidence*); **faire preuve** d'une grande prudence (*show, display*)

prévaloir (*vi*): le souci de ne pas isoler la Russie **prévaut** à Washington (*prevail; be the prime consideration*); il n'a pas **fait prévaloir ses idées** sur la question (*impose one's ideas*); [se] (*vpr*): Tokyo a pu **se prévaloir d'une très forte croissance** (*boast/point to a high growth rate*)

prévenir (*vt*): afin de **prévenir** toute augmentation du prix du brut (*anticipate*); dans la perspective de **prévenir** d'éventuels conflits (*avert, prevent*); afin de **prévenir** les dangers d'un nationalisme anti-russe (*guard against; stave off*)

préventif, -ive (*adj/nf*): un raid **préventif** serait-il justifié? (*pre-emptive*); cinq ans de prison, dont un ferme, couvert par la **préventive** (*custody while awaiting trial*)

prévention (*nf*): le projet de loi relatif à la **prévention** du licenciement économique (*prevention*); adjoint au maire chargé de la sécurité et de la **prévention** (*crime prevention*); comment lever les **préventions bruxelloises?** (*opposition from Brussels*)

prévenu, -e (*adj/nm,f*): le **prévenu**, confronté aux témoins, a reconnu les faits (*accused; defendant*); les simples **prévenus en attente de jugement** (*prisoner awaiting trial*); il est **prévenu de** détournement (*accused of/charged with*); SEE ALSO **banc**

prévisible (*adj*): il s'agit d'anticiper l'augmentation **prévisible** de la population (*likely, predictable*); l'évolution de la situation est **difficilement prévisible** (*not easy to predict*)

prévision (*nf*): la **prévision** d'une croissance de 6% en 1996 paraît optimiste (*forecast, prediction*); **en prévision** de l'ouverture des frontières du grand marché européen (*in anticipation*)

prévisionnel, -elle (*adj*): un chiffre d'affaires **prévisionnel** pour 1995 de 200 millions de dollars (*projected/estimated*)

prévisionniste (*nm*): les **prévisionnistes** parient sur une nouvelle explosion du chômage (*[economic] forecaster*)

prévoir (*vt*): les accords **prévoient** deux réunions par an (*provide for, envisage*); le groupe **prévoit** un chiffre d'affaires de 4,5 milliards pour 1996 (*anticipate; expect*); l'article 226 du code pénal **prévoit** des peines de prison (*stipulate*); la récession est **plus forte que prévu** (*worse than expected*)

prévoyance (*nf*): l'assurance suppose chez l'intéressé un esprit de **prévoyance** (*forethought; foresight*); Jonquille: votre **plan personnel de prévoyance** (*personal savings/insurance scheme*)

primaire (*adj/nf*): désigner, dans des [**élections**] **primaires**, le candidat unique; l'éventualité de **primaires** à gauche n'est pas exclue (*primary; preliminary election; eliminating contest*)

primauté (*nf*): la **primauté** du droit français sur le droit européen (*primacy; pre-eminence*); l'écrasante **primauté** de Paris ne s'est pas démentie (*pre-eminence, dominance*)

prime (*nf*): le syndicat réclame le versement d'une **prime d'ancienneté** (*seniority bonus*); toucher une **prime d'intéressement** égale à 20% de son salaire annuel (*profit-sharing bonus*); les **primes au mérite** sont distribuées en fin d'année (*merit bonus*); toucher des **primes de rendement** (*efficiency bonus*); recevoir une **prime de départ** de 150 000F (*golden handshake*); recevoir une **prime de licenciement** (*severance pay*); on peut résilier un contrat d'assurance quand il y a **majoration de prime** (*rise in the insurance premium*)

principal, -e, *pl* **-aux** (*adj/nm*): les **principaux de collège** et les proviseurs de lycée (*college principal*)

principauté (*nf*): la **principauté** d'Andorre quitte la tutelle de la France et de l'Espagne (*principality*)

prise (*nf*): la **prise** de la ville par les rebelles (*seizure, capture*); la France **est aux prises avec** l'âpre concurrence de ses voisins (*is faced by/fighting against*); SEE ALSO **bénéfice, charge, commande, conscience, contrôle, position, pouvoir**

prison (*nf*): SEE **encombrement, peine, perpétuité, purger, surpopulation**

prisonnier, -ière (*adj/nm,f*): une centaine de ces détenus sont des **prisonniers d'opinion**; la libération de nombreux **prisonniers de conscience** (*political prisoner*) SEE **constituer**

privatif, -ive (*adj*): SEE **parcelle**

privation (*nf*): avec **privation du droit de vote** et inéligibilité pour cinq ans (*loss/forfeiture of the right to vote*); condamné à cinq années de **privation de ses droits civiques** (*forfeiture of civil rights*)

privatisation (*nf*): relancer la **privatisation des terres** (*[return to] private ownership of land*)

privatiser (*vt*): l'idée de **privatiser** les établissements pénitentiaires ne semble plus choquer personne (*privatize*)

privé, -e (*adj/nm*): le retour au **[secteur] privé** de Rhône-Poulenc (*private sector*); les syndicats de l'entreprise ont accepté le **passage au privé** (*privatization*); SEE ALSO **cession, école, intimité, vente**

priver (*vt*): la récente loi les **prive** de certains droits essentiels (*deprive*); **[se]** (*vpr*): l'Opposition **ne s'est pas privée de** dénoncer la lâcheté du gouvernement (*have no hesitation in*)

privilégié, -e (*adj/nm,f*): un allié **privilégié** dans la région du Golfe (*special; privileged*); l'octroi de prêts sans garantie et **à des taux privilégiés** (*at very favourable rates of interest*)

privilégier (*vt*): faut-il **privilégier** la solidarité sociale aux dépens d'une relance de l'économie? (*favour, give priority to*); **privilégier** la lutte contre la drogue (*give more importance to*)

prix (*nm*): les fabricants diffusent des **prix conseillés** pour leurs produits (*manufacturer's recommended price, MRP*); les **prix de détail** n'ont progressé que de 0,1% (*retail prices*); se procurer des marchandises **au prix de gros** (*at wholesale prices*); après la fixation du **prix de vente** (*selling price*); le **prix de revient** est donc de 35F pièce (*cost price; production cost*); des articles vendus **à prix coûtant** (*at cost price*); SEE ALSO **avantageux, blocage, casser, casseur, concurrence, dissuasif, écraser, fourchette, guerre, indexer, libération, majoration, majorer, minimal, pratiquer, réglementation, serré, soutenir, vérité**

probant, -e (*adj*): la démonstration paraît **peu probante** (*unconvincing; not very convincing*)

probatoire (*adj*): pendant une période **probatoire** (*trial; probationary*); il s'était soustrait aux obligations du **contrôle probatoire** (*probation*)

problème (*nm*): la chasse à courre est devenue un **problème de société** (*social problem*)

procédé (*nm*): nous nous sommes refusés à de tels **procédés** (*methods, practices*); le **procédé [de fabrication]** est protégé par un brevet exclusif (*manufacturing process*)

procéder (*vt*): les Américains pourraient **procéder** à un essai nucléaire; on a décidé de **faire procéder** à de nouvelles élections (*carry out; conduct*); SEE ALSO **constatation**

procédure (*nf*): réformer le Code pénal et aussi amender la **procédure** (*legal procedure*); on a intérêt à éviter la **procédure judiciaire** (*legal proceedings*); engager une **procédure au civil** en dommages et intérêts (*civil action*); SEE ALSO **frais, vice**

procès (*nm*): le **procès** s'est déroulé à huis clos (*trial*); un des plus grands **procès criminels** de l'époque (*criminal trial*); lors du **procès d'appel** (*appeal hearing*); elle a **perdu son procès** contre le tabloïde (*lose her case*); le maire envisage de **faire un procès** à la Caisse des dépôts et consignations (*bring a court action against, sue*); [*fig*] dans un véritable réquisitoire, il a **fait le procès du** gouvernement (*put in the dock; criticize*); SEE ALSO **diffamation, intenter, intention, meurtre**

processus (*nm*): faire avancer le **processus de paix** au Proche-Orient (*peace process*)

procès-verbal (*nm*): extrait du **procès-verbal** des délibérations du conseil municipal (*minutes; written record*); la contractuelle de service lui a **dressé un procès-verbal pour stationnement interdit** (*issue a parking ticket*)

prochain, -e (*adj/nm*): la **prochaine** suppression de 22 000 lits d'hôpitaux; la **prochaine** reprise des essais nucléaires français (*impending; imminent*)

proche (*adj/nm*): les **proches** du Premier ministre le nient formellement (*person/source close to*); **proche du Président** depuis une trentaine d'années (*a close aide to the President*)

procuration (*nf*): **avoir une procuration** sur le compte en banque de sa femme (*have authorization [esp. to operate a bank account]*); il est possible aux Français d'outre-mer de **voter par procuration** (*vote by proxy*)

procureur (*nm*): le magistrat du parquet, qu'il soit **procureur** ou substitut; le **procureur [de la République]** a requis trois ans de prison ferme (*public prosecutor*)

producteur, -trice (*adj/nm*): onzième **producteur** mondial de brut en 1994 (*producer*); face à la concurrence de nouveaux **pays producteurs de café** (*coffee-producing country*)

production (*nf*): SEE **capacité, serrer**

productivité (*nf*): la **productivité** ou la valeur produite par heure de travail (*productivity*); la quête d'une **productivité accrue** (*improved productivity*); l'ambition du nouveau directeur financier: **renouer avec la productivité** (*a return to greater productivity*); SEE ALSO **gain**

produit (*nm*): le **produit** des taxes sur les cartes grises (*proceeds, yield; [tax] revenue*); la Belgique exporte 70% de son **produit intérieur brut [PIB]** (*gross domestic product*); la progression du **produit national brut [PNB]** a été de 1,7% (*gross national product*); SEE ALSO **blanc**

professionnel, -elle (*adj/nm,f*): SEE **armée, formation, taxe**

profit (*nm*): améliorer le **profit** des entreprises (*profit, profitability*); le **retour au profit** est pour cette année (*return to profitability*); rééquilibrer les transports **au profit du rail** (*in favour of the railway system*); les pays ayant **tiré profit** de l'embargo contre l'Irak (*take advantage of*); SEE ALSO **répartition**

profondeur (*nf*): procéder à une réforme **en profondeur** du financement de la protection sociale (*in-depth*)

progresser (*vi*): les prix à la consommation ont **progressé** de 0,9% (*increase, rise*)

progression (*nf*): la forte **progression** dans les ventes de magnétoscopes (*increase, rise*); les dépenses d'éducation, **en progression** de 14,5% (*up, higher*)

progressiste (*adj*): lors de la constitution de la nouvelle **alliance progressiste** (*alliance for progress*)

projet (*nm*): un **projet libéral** susceptible d'attirer des électeurs (*liberal programme*); le **projet d'extension** de l'aéroport de Roissy (*planned extension*); un **projet de loi** sera déposé en automne (*[government] bill*); SEE ALSO **fusion**

projeter (*vt*): la firme **projette** de fermer son usine de Gien (*plan*); la junte militaire **projette** un retour par étapes à la démocratie (*plan, prepare*)

prolongation (*nf*): obtenir une **prolongation** de la trêve (*extension, prolongation*)

prolongement (*nm*): l'UEO constitue le **prolongement** militaire de l'Union européenne (*extension*)

prolonger (*vt*): l'état d'urgence a été **prolongé** de six mois (*extend, prolong*)

promotion (*nf*): sortir major de sa **promotion** à HEC (*year, intake*); le poste sera pourvu **par promotion interne** (*by an internal appointment*); la **promotion sociale** des enfants issus de l'immigration (*upward mobility; social advancement*); les consommateurs n'achètent plus qu'en solde ou lors des **promotions** (*special offer/promotion*)

promouvoir (*vt*): abaisser les barrières commerciales et ainsi **promouvoir** le commerce mondial (*promote, foster*); il a été **promu** au grade d'adjudant-chef (*promote, raise*)

promulguer (*vt*): le décret devra être **promulgué** avant juin 1996; de nouvelles législations ont été **promulguées** (*enact [legislation]*)

prôner (*vt*): **prôner** le retour de son pays au sein de l'OTAN; la politique **prônée** par le gouvernement en matière d'immigration (*advocate; make a plea for*)

prononcé (*nm*): au moment du **prononcé du verdict** (*verdict*); il a fait appel dès le **prononcé de sa peine** (*announcement of the sentence*)

prononcer (*vt*): les peines **prononcées** à l'encontre des putschistes (*pass/ pronounce [sentence]*); [se] (*vpr*): la Cour suprême **se prononcera** sur leur sort (*decide, reach a verdict*); les Polonais **se prononcent** les 4 et 18 juin (*vote, go to the polls*); 38% des sondés **ne se prononcent pas** (*are undecided; express no opinion*)

pronostic (*nm*): son **pronostic de croissance** a été révisé à la baisse (*growth forecast*); le **pronostic de vie** d'un malade frappé du sida (*life expectancy*)

pronostiquer (*vt*): tous deux **pronostiquent** une aggravation de la tension dans le pays (*forecast; foresee*)

proportionnel, -elle (*adj/nf*): le scrutin majoritaire avec une dose de [**représentation**] **proportionnelle** (*proportional representation, PR*); les sièges sont désignés **à la proportionnelle** (*by proportional representation*); SEE ALSO **rétablir**

propos (*nm*): il se dit "étonné" des réactions suscitées par ses **propos** (*remark, comment*)

proposer (*vt*): **proposer** une nouvelle législation (*bring forward [legislation]*); **proposer** un candidat (*nominate; put forward*)

proposition (*nf*): un certain nombre de **propositions** ont déjà été faites (*proposal, suggestion*); la **proposition de loi** émane d'un groupe de socialistes (*private member's bill*)

propriétaire (*nmf*): nouvelle loi sur le logement: les **propriétaires** mécontents (*landlord; owner*); 70% d'entre eux sont **propriétaires** (*homeowner, householder*); dans le nouveau Congrès, les **propriétaires fonciers** dominent (*landowners*)

propriété (*nf*): libérer la **propriété de la terre** (*ownership of land*); le gouvernement a démocratisé la **propriété du logement** (*home ownership*); SEE ALSO **accédant, accéder, accession, titre**

prorogation (*nf*): l'ONU appelle à la **prorogation** de la trêve en Bosnie (*continuation; extension*); la **prorogation** d'un an des baux à loyer (*renewal*)

proroger (*vt*): le gouvernement a annoncé qu'il **proroge** de 30 jours supplémentaires la trêve (*extend, continue*)

protection (*nf*): gagner un poste **grâce à des protections** (*through influence/friends in high places*); une réforme du financement de la **protection sociale** [Sécurité sociale, retraite, chômage] (*state-provided social welfare*)

protestataire (*adj/nmf*): SEE **vote**

protestation (*nf*): arrêter le travail **en signe de protestation** (*as a protest*); SEE ALSO **marche, réunion**

protocole (*nm*): cet accord va plus loin que le **protocole** signé en 1987 (*formal agreement*); un **protocole d'accord** a été signé (*outline/draft agreement*)

provenance (*nf*): nous avons pu nous assurer de sa **provenance** (*[place of] origin*); d'importantes liquidités **en provenance de l'étranger** (*originating from abroad*)

provenir (*vi*): le tiers du PNB allemand **provient de** l'exportation; 45% de ses recettes **proviennent de** l'assurance-maladie (*come from, arise out of*)

province (*nf*): une série d'attentats dans la capitale et **en province** (*in the provinces*); SEE ALSO **délocaliser**

proviseur (*nm*): principaux et **proviseurs** veulent une répression accrue de la violence à l'école (*grammar-school headteacher*)

provision (*nf*): le non-paiement d'un chèque en raison d'une **insuffisance de provision** (*insufficient funds*); SEE ALSO **chèque**

provisionnel, -elle (*adj*): SEE **tiers**

provisoire (*adj*): SEE **détention, liberté**

provocateur, -trice (*adj/nm,f*): rejeter la responsabilité sur d'éventuels **provocateurs** (*agitator, troublemaker*)

provocation (*nf*): le désir d'ignorer ces nouvelles **provocations** de l'extrême droite (*provocation, provocative behaviour*); la nouvelle infraction de **provocation à la haine ou à la violence raciale** (*inciting racial hatred or violence*)

provoquer (*vt*): accident qui a **provoqué** la mort de 37 personnes (*cause*); SEE ALSO **tollé**

proxénète (*nmf*): **proxénète**, il obligeait sa propre femme à se livrer à la prostitution (*procurer, pimp*)

proxénétisme (*nm*): inculpé de **proxénétisme** (*living off immoral earnings, pimping*)

proximité (*nf*): la **proximité** des élections européennes (*imminence*); SEE ALSO **magasin**

prudence (*nf*): **prudence** aussi du côté travailliste (*circumspection; caution*); appel à la **prudence salariale** (*moderation in pay claims/pay awards*)

prudent, -e (*adj*): se montrer très **prudent**; Gatt: la France reste **prudente** (*cautious; careful*)

prud'homal, -e, *pl* **-aux** (*adj*): le **juge prud'homal**, le juge des litiges liés au contrat de travail (*judge on industrial tribunal*); aux **élections prud'homales**, 54% des ouvriers se sont abstenus (*election to an industrial disputes tribunal*)

prud'homme (*nm*): la CGT respecte la décision des **prud'hommes**: la direction fait appel; condamné par le **tribunal des prud'hommes** pour le licenciement d'un employé (*industrial disputes tribunal*); obtenir gain de cause **en prud'homme** (*before an industrial tribunal/labour court*)

public, -que (*adj/nm*): le ministère de la Défense a **rendu public** un livre blanc sur la défense (*publish*); par contre, **dans le [secteur] public** les augmentations ont été rares; hausse des salaires **dans les entreprises publiques** (*in the public/state sector*); le géant européen de l'électronique **grand public** (*consumer electronics*); SEE ALSO **argent, dépense, école, fonds, ministère, puissance, rumeur, utilité**

publication (*nf*): SEE **interdire**

publicitaire (*adj*): SEE **encart, parrainage, plage, spot**

publicité (*nf*): poursuivi pour **publicité mensongère**; il s'estime victime d'une **publicité trompeuse** (*misleading advertising*)

pudeur (*nf*): SEE **attentat, outrage**

puissance (*nf*): une reconnaissance de leur statut de **grande puissance** (*major power*); **la puissance publique** dispose de la faculté de s'y opposer (*the authorities; the state*); SEE ALSO **montée**

pur, -e (*adj/nm,f*): quelques **militants purs et durs** du PC (*hard-liner*); coordination des infirmières: la grève **pure et dure** (*hard-line, uncompromising*)

purge (*nf*): procéder à une **purge** d'éléments politiquement indésirables (*purge*)

purger (*vt*): cette mesure vise les détenus **purgeant** une première condamnation (*serve [sentence]*); **purger une peine de prison** pour séjour irrégulier (*serve a prison sentence*)

putsch (*nm*): l'armée a réussi un **putsch** samedi, sans effusion de sang (*military coup, putsch*); au moment du **putsch raté** d'août 1991 (*failed coup*); SEE ALSO **tentative**

pyramide (*nf*): la **pyramide des âges** est éloquente (*age pyramid, diagram showing structure of population by age group*)

pyromane (*adj/nmf*): un **pyromane** serait à l'origine des incendies dans le Midi (*arsonist, pyromaniac*)

Q

quadrangulaire (*nf*): une **quadrangulaire** l'opposant à la droite, aux Verts, et au Front national (*four-way [electoral] contest*)

quadrillage (*nm*): les forces de sécurité ont accentué leurs opérations de **quadrillage**; le **quadrillage policier** de la ville (*tight police control*)

quadriller (*vt*): le secteur est **quadrillé par la police** (*under tight police control*)

qualification (*nf*): la **qualification** n'est pas le seul critère de recrutement (*qualifications*); une main-d'œuvre **sans qualification** donc à très bon marché (*unqualified*)

qualifié, -e (*adj*): un monde de travail qui rejette les **moins qualifiés** (*those with least qualifications*); SEE ALSO **ouvrier**

qualifier (*vt*): des idées que certains **qualifient** de subversives; Londres a **qualifié** de prématurée la décision palestinienne (*label, term*)

qualité (*nf*): on lui avait refusé la **qualité** de réfugié (*status*); **en sa qualité de** secrétaire de l'ambassadeur (*in one's capacity as*); **avoir qualité** pour signer les traités (*be competent*); l'amélioration de la **qualité de la vie** (*quality of life*)

quart (*nm*): un **quart** des Français vivent en HLM (*quarter*); toutes les catégories sociales, des oubliés du **quart monde** aux nantis (*the least developed countries; the most deprived sector of the population*)

quartier (*nm*): dans le **quartier des affaires** (*business district*); des demandes de subventions venues des associations **de quartier** (*local; neighbourhood*); un collège situé dans un **quartier difficile** (*deprived area*)

quasi- (*adv*): jouir d'un **quasi-monopole** (*virtual monopoly*); la poursuite de la grève a été votée **à la quasi-unanimité** (*almost unanimously*)

quasiment (*adv*): l'adoption, **quasiment** sans débats, du projet de résolution du congrès (*virtually, almost*)

quémander (*vt*): les associations **quémandent** des subventions (*beg [for], fish/angle for*)

querelle (*nf*): le réveil de la **querelle** algéro-marocaine (*dispute*); faire étalage de leurs **querelles de chapelle**; des **querelles intestines** déchiraient le parti (*internal wrangling/squabbles*)

question (*nf*): la **question** n'est pas à l'ordre du jour (*item [on agenda]*); la séance de **questions orales** (*oral questions [in Parliament]*); le gouvernement est acculé à **poser la question de confiance** (*ask for a vote of confidence*); on ne saurait **mettre en question** son autorité (*challenge, call into question*); une **remise en question** de la sécurité nucléaire (*reappraisal; reassessment*); SEE ALSO **fond, non-accord, sécuritaire**

quête (*nf*): une presse de gauche, **en quête de** financement (*in need/search of*)

quêter (*vi*): **quêter** dans la rue pour soutenir les grévistes (*collect money*)

queue (*nf*): la France est **en queue** des nations industrielles (*in last position, at the tail-end*)

quinquennal, -e, *pl* **-aux** (*adj*): la nouvelle loi **quinquennale** sur l'emploi (*quinquennial, five-year*); l'élection européenne est **quinquennale** (*five-yearly*)

quinquennat (*nm*): il préconise le **quinquennat** pour tous les mandats électifs (*five-year term of office*)

quittance (*nf*): une **quittance** d'électricité à laquelle on ne peut faire face (*bill*); pour pouvoir être inscrit, on demande une **quittance de loyer** (*rent receipt*)

qui-vive (*nm*): les forces en présence **restent sur le qui-vive** (*remain on the alert*)

quolibet (*nm*): partir sous les **quolibets** de ses adversaires (*gibe, jeer, taunt*)

quorum (*nm*): absence de **quorum** de 50% des actionnaires (*quorum*)

quota (*nm*): protéger un marché par des **quotas d'importation** (*import quotas*); des produits agricoles **soumis à quotas** (*subject to quotas*); SEE ALSO **instauration**

quote-part (*nf*): [*fig*] la **quote-part** des États-Unis était de 40% en 1945 (*share*)

quotidien, -ienne (*adj/nm*): responsable de la **gestion quotidienne** (*day-to-day management*); des **quotidiens** diversement touchés par la grève (*daily [newspaper]*); la presse écrite, **quotidiens régionaux** exceptés (*regional daily*)

quotient (*nm*): la suppression du **quotient familial** dans le calcul de l'impôt sur le revenu (*dependents' allowance set against tax*)

R

rabais (*nm*): bénéficier d'un **rabais** de 80F par rapport au tarif (*rebate, reduction*); accorder un **rabais** pour paiement au comptant (*discount*); SEE ALSO **consentir**

raccordement (*nm*): la taxe de **raccordement** au tout-à-l'égout (*connection, linking [up]*); SEE ALSO **bretelle**

raccorder (*vt*): demander un devis pour faire **raccorder** deux canalisations (*connect together/up*); [se] (*vpr*): la nouvelle ligne pourra par la suite **se raccorder** au réseau du TGV (*be connected*)

rachat (*nm*): le **rachat** en bourse de 5% des actions (*purchase, acquisition*); un autre candidat potentiel au **rachat** (*buy-out*)

racheter (*vt*): une société du Mans **rachetée** par une firme allemande (*take over [a company]*)

racial,-e, *pl* **-aux** (*adj*): SEE **injure, provocation**

racisme (*nm*): le **racisme** devenait un délit puni par la loi (*racism, racial prejudice*)

raciste (*adj*): des écrits à caractère **raciste** et antisémite (*racist*)

racket (*nm*): dans des collèges où sévissent la drogue, l'intimidation et le **racket** (*racketeering; extortion through blackmail*)

racolage (*nm*): arrêtée pour **racolage sur la voie publique** (*soliciting for purposes of prostitution*)

racoler (*vt*): **racoler** des clients (*tout [for custom]; solicit [esp. for prostitution]*)

radiation (*nf*): pratiquer des **radiations** des listes de l'ANPE; l'ordre des médecins réduit sa **radiation** à deux ans (*striking off/from a register*)

radical,-e, *pl* **-aux** (*adj/nm*): pour isoler les plus **radicaux** des intégristes (*extreme, radical*); les quelques **radicaux** de gauche seront un appoint précieux pour les Socialistes (*Radical*); SEE ALSO **aile**

radicalisation (*nf*): une soudaine **radicalisation du conflit** (*hardening of a conflict*)

radicaliser [se] (*vpr*): les positions **se radicalisent** dans ce conflit (*become more extreme; harden*)

radicalisme (*nm*): face à la montée du **radicalisme** intégriste (*extremism*)

radier (*vt*): **radier** les jeunes chômeurs qui refusent un emploi (*remove [from register of unemployed]*); il vient d'être **radié** de la fonction publique (*be struck off*)

raffermir [se] (*vpr*): la confiance des patrons **se raffermit** (*grow firmer/stronger*); la monnaie américaine **s'est raffermie** hier (*strengthen*)

raffermissement (*nm*): cette bonne nouvelle a contribué au **raffermissement** de Wall Street (*strengthening; steadying*)

rafle (*nf*): le juge ordonna une **rafle** de tous les établissements du quartier; la police a lancé une vaste **rafle** dans des quartiers protestants (*[police] raid/roundup*)

rafler (*vt*): la liste arrivant en tête **rafle** tous les sièges (*win; make a clean sweep of*)

raid (*nm*): le groupe a fait l'objet d'un **raid boursier** (*surprise bid on the Stock Exchange*); on assiste à une fièvre d'acquisitions et de **raids** dans le monde des assurances (*raid; take-over bid*)

raider (*nm*): [*fig*] la firme est constamment à l'affût des **raiders**; le groupe agro-alimentaire américain semble intéresser les **raiders** (*corporate raider*)

raidir (*vt*): Washington **raidit sa position** (*take a tougher line*); [se] (*vpr*): si Tokyo **se raidit** sur la question de l'aide (*take a tougher line*)

raidissement (*nm*): comment s'expliquer le brusque **raidissement** de l'Iran?; face à chaque crise, le premier réflexe des dirigeants est le **raidissement** (*hardening of attitude; taking a tough line*)

raison (*nf*): le tribunal a **donné raison au plaignant** (*find for/in favour of the plaintiff*); les **raisons sociales** successives du groupe (*corporate/trading name*)

ralenti (*nm*): [*fig*] l'économie espagnole toujours **au ralenti** (*idling, ticking-over*); les chantiers navals **tournent au ralenti** (*idle; run under capacity*)

ralentir (*vt/vi*): les dépenses des hôpitaux ont **ralenti** (*slow down; decrease*)

ralentissement (*nm*): se traduire par un **ralentissement** de la croissance (*slowing-down; slackening*)

ralliement (*nm*): Congo: **ralliement** du principal parti d'opposition; son récent **ralliement** à la motion socialiste (*conversion/coming over to*)

rallier (*vt*): des propositions susceptibles de **rallier** la Grande-Bretagne (*bring over; gain the support of*); une bonne partie des autres a **rallié les rangs de l'UDF** (*join/rejoin the UDF*); [se] (*vpr*): la Grèce **s'est ralliée** au compromis adopté la semaine dernière; combattre un mouvement pour finalement **s'y rallier** (*join, come over*)

rallonge (*nf*): revendiquer une **rallonge** à l'accord salarial (*extension*); obtenir une **rallonge** de 100 MF (*additional sum/grant*)

rallonger (*vt*): inciter les entreprises à **rallonger** leurs horaires de travail (*lengthen, extend*)

ramener (*vt*): **ramener** les effectifs à 21 000; **ramener** le déficit de la Sécurité sociale à 4 milliards de francs (*reduce, bring down*); SEE ALSO **paix**

rang (*nm*): un diplomate **de haut rang** (*senior, high-ranking*); la France doit pouvoir **tenir son rang** dans le monde (*maintain one's rank/position*); Usinor Sacilor **est sur les rangs** pour racheter le sidérurgiste espagnol (*be in the running; be a candidate*); SEE ALSO **rallier**

ranger [se] (*vpr*): finalement il **s'est rangé** à l'argument de ses collègues (*come round to; fall in with*); d'autres **se sont rangés au point de vue français** (*agreed with the French position*)

rapatrié, -e (*adj/nm,f*): les mesures prises en faveur des **rapatriés** (*repatriated person*)

rapatriement (*nm*): une aide au **rapatriement** des étrangers (*repatriation*)

rapatrier (*vt*): les bénéfices seront **rapatriés** en France (*bring home/back capital investment*)

rappel (*nm*): Paris annonce le **rappel** de son ambassadeur (*recall*); à la suite d'une augmentation, il touche un **rappel [de salaire]** de 2 000F (*back pay; retroactive pay rise*); Washington **bat le rappel** des réservistes (*call up; call to arms*)

rappeler (*vt*): la Chine **rappelle** son ambassadeur aux États-Unis (*recall, call back*)

rapport (*nm*): le **rapport** établira la vérité sur l'affaire (*report*); il a quelques **maisons de rapport** (*investment property*); le **rapport cours-bénéfice** de ce titre est de 12,6 en avril (*price/earnings ratio*); SEE ALSO **décloisonner, envenimer, expertise**

rapporter (*vt*): une nouvelle **rapportée** par l'agence France-Presse (*report*); l'impôt sur le capital **rapporte** 100 milliards par an (*yield; earn*); la proportion de ceux qui travaillent **rapportée à la population totale** (*in relation to the total population*); (*vi*): ce type de fraude **rapporte gros** (*is very lucrative*)

rapporteur (*nm*): nommé **rapporteur** de la Commission des finances (*chairman of a committee*); le **rapporteur** d'un projet de loi (*rapporteur, reporter [esp. of a parliamentary bill]*)

rapprochement (*nm*): le **rapprochement** franco-turc intervenu récemment (*reconciliation; bringing together*); le **rapprochement** des taux de TVA en Europe (*bringing closer together*); l'accord vise à favoriser des **rapprochements d'entreprises** (*collaboration/link-up between companies*)

rapprocher (*vt*): il faudra **rapprocher** les taux de TVA (*bring closer together*); [se] (*vpr*): les positions des négociateurs se **sont rapprochées** (*come closer together; converge*); deux géants de l'édition vont se **rapprocher**, en échangeant des participations (*collaborate; come together*)

rapt (*nm*): une condamnation pour **rapt** et détournement de mineur (*abduction; kidnapping*)

raréfier [se] (*vpr*): les acheteurs solvables se **raréfient** (*become scarce*); dès lors que l'**emploi se raréfie** (*job opportunities become scarcer*)

ras-le-bol (*nm*): comment canaliser le **ras-le-bol** des étudiants? (*dissatisfaction; feeling of frustration*)

rassemblement (*nm*): la CGT organise des **rassemblements** pour rappeler ses revendications (*[political] rally/meeting*); un large **rassemblement** de tous ceux qui sont sincèrement européens (*union; grouping; party*); le gaullisme de **rassemblement national** (*national unity*); SEE ALSO **signe, unitaire**

rassembler (*vt*): le seul à pouvoir **rassembler** toute la gauche (*unite, bring together*)

ratissage (*nm*): lors d'une opération de **ratissage** de l'armée israélienne (*thorough search/combing of an area*)

ratisser (*vt*): les gendarmes avaient **ratissé le secteur** (*comb/search the area thoroughly*)

ratonnade (*nf*): des **ratonnades**, des expéditions punitives; des **ratonnades** dirigées contre les Pakistanais (*racially motivated beating; attack on immigrants*)

rattrapage (*nm*): le **rattrapage** du pouvoir d'achat (*catching up*); pour obtenir un **rattrapage** de 10% (*wage increase to keep up with costs*); suivre des **cours de rattrapage** (*remedial class*)

rattraper (*vt*): les prix dans les magasins **rattrapent** le pouvoir d'achat (*catch up [with]*); SEE ALSO **demande**

ravir (*vt*): pour **ravir** la municipalité clermontoise aux socialistes (*take, win*)

ravisseur, -euse (*nm,f*): d'éventuelles tractations entre Paris et les **ravisseurs** (*kidnapper; abductor*)

ravitaillement (*nm*): pour assurer le **ravitaillement en essence** (*provision of fuel supplies*)

ravitailler (*vt*): comment **ravitailler** en eau ces populations? (*supply*); [se] (*vpr*): la France se **ravitaille** difficilement en sources énergétiques (*obtain supplies; be supplied*)

raz-de-marée (*nm*): le **raz-de-marée** socialiste n'épargne pas le Midi (*landslide [electoral]*)

réactualisation (*nf*): effectuer une **réactualisation** des données de l'INSEE (*updating*)

réactualiser (*vt*): on **réactualise** tous les chiffres au 31 décembre (*bring up to date; update*)

réalisation (*nf*): c'est la **réalisation** d'un rêve vieux de 20 ans (*fulfilment, realization*); la **réalisation** de travaux de voirie (*carrying out; completion*); le ministre souligna les **réalisations** de son gouvernement (*achievement*)

réaliser (*vt*): le premier essai nucléaire **réalisé** par la Chine (*carry out*); il tente en vain de **réaliser** l'unité arabe (*achieve, bring about*); la Grande-Bretagne **réalise la moitié de son commerce** avec l'Europe (*conduct half her trade*); [se] (*vpr*): comment va **se réaliser** l'union monétaire? (*come about; be achieved*); SEE ALSO **bénéfice**

réaménagement (*nm*): un **réaménagement** de la fiscalité des carburants (*restructuring*); des mesures de **réaménagement** des quartiers les plus défavorisés (*renovation; redevelopment*); un cas réussi de **réaménagement urbain** (*urban redevelopment*)

rébellion (*nf*): la **rébellion** refuse la proposition de Kaboul d'un cessez-le-feu unilatéral (*rebel movement, rebels*); placé en garde à vue pour **rébellion** et outrage à agent (*rebellion; resisting arrest*)

rebond (*nm*): baisse du chômage, **rebond** de la production industrielle (*improvement; increase*)

rebondir (*vi*): le candidat pourrait **rebondir** dans les mois qui viennent (*bounce back*); l'affaire, qu'on croyait enterrée, vient de **rebondir** (*have a new/fresh development*)

rebondissement (*nm*): il y a eu un **rebondissement** hier dans l'affaire Greenpeace; sauf **rebondissement** de dernière minute (*[fresh/new] development*)

recaser (*vt*): le tiers seulement des ouvriers licenciés ont pu être **recasés** (*re-employ; find new employment for*)

recel (*nm*): le **recel**, une infraction de droit commun; impliqué dans de nombreuses affaires de **recel** (*receiving/being in possession of stolen goods*)

receleur (*nm*): soupçonnés d'être d'importants **receleurs** d'objets volés (*receiver of stolen goods*)

recensement (*nm*): procéder à un **recensement** des habitants (*census; count*)

recenser (*vt*): **recenser** les jeunes pour le service national (*register*); plus de 200 offres d'emploi ont été **recensées** (*compile a register of*); aucune victime n'a été **recensée** (*report; count*)

recentrage (*nm*): le **recentrage** de la gauche opéré par le Président (*occupation of the centre ground*); le **recentrage** du groupe sur l'agro-alimentaire (*concentration [on core activities]*)

recentrer (*vt*): **recentrer** la politique sociale sur les plus défavorisés (*concentrate, focus*); [se] (*vpr*): la firme entend **se recentrer** sur ses activités les plus rémunératrices (*concentrate production*)

récession (*nf*): frappé de plein fouet par la **récession** de ses marchés en Europe; sur fond de **récession** nationale et mondiale (*recession*); l'Europe **connaît la pire récession** depuis un demi-siècle (*experience its worst recession*); SEE ALSO **sortie**

recette (*nf*): les **recettes** pétrolières du Mexique (*income, revenue*); les hydrocarbures représentent 95% des **recettes d'exportation** de l'Algérie (*export revenue*); les **recettes fiscales** rentrent toujours aussi mal (*tax revenue*); à la **recette des impôts** (*tax collector's office*); les services de la **recette-perception** (*tax/revenue office*)

recevabilité (*nf*): la décision du Trésor sur la **recevabilité** de cette OPA sera un test important (*admissibility*)

recevable (*adj*): le vote de la motion de censure, pour être **recevable**, doit être signé par 58 députés (*admissible, allowable*)

receveur, -euse (*nm,f*): au bureau du **receveur municipal** (*rate/tax collector*); payable au **receveur des Postes** (*postmaster*)

rechange (*nf*): disposer d'une politique économique **de rechange** (*alternative*); SEE ALSO **solution**

réchauffement (*nm*): le **réchauffement des relations** entre Londres et Moscou (*improvement in relations*)

réchauffer (*vt*): le Qatar cherche à **réchauffer ses relations** avec l'Arabie Saoudite (*improve relations*); [se] (*vpr*): les **relations se réchauffent** entre Moscou et Pékin (*improved relations*)

rechute (*nf*): la **rechute** des prix de l'immobilier (*fall back, fall*)

récidive (*nf*): le fort taux de **récidive** parmi les jeunes délinquants (*committing of a further offence*)

récidiver (*vi*): 97% des jeunes qui vont en prison **récidivent** (*commit a further offence, reoffend*)

récidiviste (*nmf*): Yvelines: le violeur **récidiviste** inculpé (*repeat offender, habitual criminal*)

réclamation (*nf*): inutile de faire **une réclamation** (*complain, lodge a complaint*)

réclamer (*vt*): les nationalistes **réclament** le statut de république (*call for, demand*); [se] (*vpr*): sur l'essentiel, le Front national **se réclame des** mêmes valeurs que la majorité (*claim allegiance/fidelity to*)

reclassement (*nm*): la CGT exige un **reclassement** des partants dans les PME locales (*transfer, redeployment*); faciliter la formation et le **reclassement** des salariés (*finding of new employment for*)

reclasser (*vt*): une expérience pour **reclasser** 1 000 intérimaires en fin de mission; on compte **reclasser** les deux tiers des sureffectifs dans d'autres emplois (*redeploy [esp. worker into a new job]*); les salariés de 45 à 55 ans **se reclassent difficilement** (*are difficult to place in a job*)

réclusion (*nf*): requérir une peine de 15 ans de **réclusion criminelle** (*imprisonment*)

recommander [se] (*vpr*): dans les pays **qui se recommandent de l'Islam** (*claiming allegiance to Islam*)

recomposition (*nf*): la **recomposition** du parti est en route (*restructuring*); un accord avec le groupe CGE entérinant la **recomposition du capital** de Framatome (*capital restructuring*)

reconductible (*adj*): une grève de 24 heures, **reconductible** tous les jours (*renewable*)

reconduction (*nf*): le P-DG a obtenu la **reconduction** de son mandat d'administrateur (*renewal, extension*); avec, pour 1996, une **reconduction** exacte des déductions appliquées en 1995 (*renewal, continuation*)

reconduire (*vt*): le cessez-le-feu a été **reconduit** indéfiniment (*extend; renew*); les électeurs belges **reconduisent** la coalition gouvernementale (*re-elect*); le ministre **a été reconduit dans ses fonctions** à la tête des Socialistes du Vaucluse (*re-elect; reappoint*)

reconduite (*nf*): ressortissants étrangers: 44 affaires de **reconduite à la frontière** (*expulsion [of illegal immigrant]*); SEE ALSO **frapper**

reconnaissance (*nf*): manifester pour obtenir la **reconnaissance** de ses diplômes (*recognition*); appeler à une **reconnaissance mutuelle** entre la Serbie et la Bosnie (*mutual recognition*)

reconnaître (*vt*): l'Irak a **reconnu** l'indépendance du Koweït (*recognize*); il a **reconnu les faits** au cours de sa garde à vue (*admit to the deed; confess*); les inculpés, **reconnus coupables** de conspiration (*found guilty*)

reconversion (*nf*): un programme d'aide à la **reconversion** des bassins miniers (*redevelopment*); les suppressions d'emplois se feront par départs en préretraite et **reconversions** (*redeployment [of staff]*)

reconvertir (*vt*): les Charbonnages ont **reconverti** près de 10 000 salariés (*redeploy [staff]*); [se] (*vpr*): **se reconvertir** dans l'immobilier (*switch [to new type of employment/new sector]*)

recourir (*vt*): ils **recourent** à la violence en désespoir de cause (*have recourse to; take refuge in*)

recours (*nm*): quels sont les **recours** en cas de litige? (*appeal; recourse*); l'ultime **recours en appel** s'est soldé par une fin de non-recevoir (*appeal against a judgment*); le **recours en grâce** fut rejeté (*petition for reprieve*); **déposer un recours** devant le Conseil constitutionnel (*register an appeal*); **avoir recours** à des moyens illégaux (*resort to*); SEE ALSO **voie**

recouvrement (*nm*): la lutte pour le **recouvrement** des droits palestiniens inaliénables (*recovering*); le **recouvrement** ou la perception de sommes dues (*levying, collecting [money, taxes]*); pour simplifier les procédures de **recouvrement des créances** (*debt-collecting*)

recouvrer (*vt*): une amnistie leur a permis de **recouvrer** leurs droits civiques (*recover, regain*); **recouvrer** les impôts (*collect [tax]*)

recrudescence (*nf*): on assiste à une **recrudescence** de la fraude électorale (*renewed outbreak*); on peut s'attendre à une **recrudescence de la guérilla** (*renewed outbreak of guerrilla activity*)

recrue (*nf*): 24% des jeunes **recrues** n'ont pas été incorporées; une armée mixte mêlant à parité cadres de métier et **recrues du contingent** (*national service recruit*); mobiliser des engagés, ou des **recrues volontaires** (*volunteer*)

recrutement (*nm*): le **recrutement** se fait sur concours (*recruitment*); SEE ALSO **apprenti**

recruter (*vt*): la majorité a été **recruté sur concours** (*recruit by competitive examination*)

recteur (*nm*): on changea la moitié des **recteurs** et 40 inspecteurs d'Académie; la compétence d'un **recteur d'Académie** (*[in France] chief regional education officer*)

rectificatif, -ive (*adj/nm*): *Le Monde* publia un **rectificatif** dans son numéro de mardi (*correction, amendment*)

rectoral,-e, *pl* **-aux** (*adj*): l'épiscopat attaque deux **décisions rectorales** supprimant le congé du mercredi (*decision by* recteur/*French chief regional education officer*)

rectorat (*nm*): une concertation entre l'Assemblée régionale, les **rectorats** et les enseignants; les **rectorats** ont dû engager des maîtres-auxiliaires (*French regional education authority*)

reçu, -e (*adj/nm,f*): la proportion de **reçus** parmi les candidats (*successful candidate*); obtenir un **reçu** du vendeur (*receipt*)

recueillement (*nm*): une journée de deuil et de **recueillement** (*meditation; reverence*)

recueillir (*vt*): les Libéraux **recueillent** en général quelque 12% des voix (*obtain*); propos **recueillis** par un reporter sur place (*report; record*); SEE ALSO **adhésion**

recul (*nm*): le **recul** du pouvoir d'achat est supérieur à 10%; on table sur un léger **recul** de la demande (*reduction; downturn, decline*); les Libéraux **sont en recul** (*are on the decline/in retreat*)

reculade (*nf*): Bruxelles: nouvelle **reculade** de la Grande-Bretagne (*climbdown; back-tracking*)

reculer (*vi*): le commerce mondial du pétrole a fortement **reculé** depuis 1973 (*decline, regress*); certes, **le mariage a reculé** depuis 20 ans (*people marry less*); (*vt*): on parle de **reculer** le scrutin au 13 janvier (*put off, postpone*)

récupération (*nf*): la **récupération** des thèmes régionalistes par les Socialistes (*takeover; appropriating*); on peut déplorer la **récupération** d'un meurtre à des fins racistes (*exploiting*); faire de la **récupération** **politique** (*exploiting for political ends*); la **récupération** des déchets d'emballage (*recycling for reuse*)

récupérer (*vt*): **récupérer** une somme prêtée (*recoup, get back*); Zagreb a toujours affiché sa volonté de **récupérer** son territoire (*regain, win back*); **récupérer** de la ferraille (*salvage; reprocess*); leur intention est de **récupérer** le mouvement (*hijack, take over [esp. for political ends]*)

récuser (*vt*): il **récuse** totalement la démarche de son président (*reject*); l'accusé **récuse** les compétences de la cour (*challenge*)

recyclable (*adj*): SEE **déchet**

recyclage (*nm*): le **recyclage** des matériaux d'emballage (*[industrial] recycling*); le **recyclage** de l'argent de la drogue (*recycling, laundering*); le développement technique impose un **recyclage** périodique (*retraining*)

recycler [se] (*vpr*): **se recycler dans** le marketing (*retrain for*); une partie du grand banditisme **s'est recyclée dans l'automobile** (*turn to crime involving [stolen] cars*)

rédacteur, -trice (*nm,f*): l'un des **rédacteurs** du code de procédure civile (*author; drafter; editor*)

rédaction (*nf*): la préparation et la **rédaction** du contrat d'assurance (*drawing up, drafting*); la **rédaction** est composée d'une centaine de journalistes (*editorial staff*)

reddition (*nf*): tenter d'obtenir la **reddition** des rebelles (*surrender*)

redécoupage (*nm*): le **redécoupage du calendrier scolaire** a été bien accueilli (*reorganization of the school year*); le projet de **redécoupage électoral** (*redrawing of electoral boundaries*)

redémarrage (*nm*): un **redémarrage** de l'activité industrielle (*take-off; resurgence*)

redémarrer (*vi*): la production **redémarre**, les commandes affluent (*take off/get going again*)

redéploiement (*nm*): devant la chute des commandes, la société envisageait un **redéploiement** industriel (*diversification; conversion*)

redéployer [se] (*vpr*): contraint de **se redéployer** pour sortir de la crise (*diversify*)

redevable (*adj*): les **redevables** de l'impôt de solidarité sur la fortune [ISF] (*person liable [for tax]*)

redevance (*nf*): la société payera une **redevance** à IBM pour l'utilisation de ses brevets (*licence fee; royalties*); la **redevance audiovisuelle** augmentera de 4,5% en 1997 (*radio/TV licence fee*)

rédiger (*vt*): un rapport confidentiel **rédigé** par son supérieur hiérarchique (*draft; write*)

redressement (*nm*): démographie: le **redressement** se confirme (*recovery*); un **plan de redressement** comportant une réduction des effectifs (*recovery plan*); la société **a été placée en redressement judiciaire** (*be put into receivership*); le fisc lui a imposé un **redressement fiscal** pour les deux exercices écoulés (*notification of arrears of tax*); une maison de correction ou un **centre de redressement** (*reformatory, approved school*)

redresser (*vt*): réussir à **redresser** l'économie nationale (*redress, put right*); un nouveau P-DG saura vite **redresser l'affaire** (*turn a company round*); [se] (*vpr*): **l'action s'est redressée** à l'annonce d'un exercice bénéficiaire (*the share price recovered*)

réduction (*nf*): obtenir une **réduction** des heures de travail (*cut, reduction*); des **réductions de personnel** sont annoncées (*staff cutbacks*); la **réduction des coûts** a également fait son apparition (*cost-cutting measures*); une **réduction d'impôt** pour garde d'enfant (*tax allowance*); SEE ALSO **moitié**

réduire (*vt*): la France compte **réduire** son aide à l'Algérie (*reduce, cut*); SEE ALSO **moitié**

rééchelonnement (*nm*): la Pologne obtient un **rééchelonnement** de sa dette (*rescheduling*)

rééquilibrage (*nm*): un certain **rééquilibrage** des pouvoirs institutionnels entre les communautés (*redistribution*); à la suite du **rééquilibrage** de la diplomatie égyptienne en faveur de la Syrie (*realignment*)

réévaluer (*vt*): si le mark est **réévalué**, le franc le sera dans les mêmes proportions (*revalue*); les barèmes n'ont pas été **réévalués** (*re-evaluate, reassess*)

réévaluation (*nf*): une **réévaluation [à la hausse]** des salaires des infirmières (*revaluation; upgrading*)

réfection (*nf*): procéder à la **réfection** des toitures (*repairing, rebuilding*)

référé (*nm*): une procédure simplifiée, le **référé**, permet d'obtenir d'une juridiction une décision provisoire (*summary court hearing*); ils ont saisi le **tribunal des référés** de Créteil (*court of summary jurisdiction*)

référence (*nf*): fournir une **référence bancaire** satisfaisante (*bank reference*)

référendaire (*adj*): au fur et à mesure de la **campagne référendaire** (*referendum campaign*)

référendum (*nm*): soumettre une question à **référendum** (*referendum*); la réforme a été réalisée **par voie de référendum** (*by referendum*)

réfléchir (*vt*): la commission chargée de **réfléchir à** une réforme de la procédure pénale (*consider; study*)

réflexion (*nf*): une **réflexion** en profondeur sur l'efficacité de l'ensemble de l'éducation (*debate; reflection*); les travaux de la **commission de réflexion** sur le système éducatif (*think tank; working group*); SEE ALSO **cellule, délai**

reflux (*nm*): nouveau **reflux** du dollar (*retreat; fall [in value]*); l'échec de la grève va précipiter un **reflux** syndical (*decline*)

refondre (*vt*): il faudrait **refondre** l'ensemble du système (*remodel, overhaul*)

refonte (*nf*): un projet de **refonte** du code de la nationalité (*revision*); l'opposition demande une **refonte complète** du texte (*complete revision/recasting*)

réformateur, -trice (*adj/nm,f*): le candidat **réformateur** a été battu (*reforming; for reform [esp. of French Communist party]*)

réforme (*nf*): un rapport propose une **réforme** de l'impôt (*reform*); SEE ALSO **abandon, enterrement, enterrer, geler**

réformer (*vt*): engagé volontaire pour trois ans, puis **réformé** et rendu à la vie civile (*declare unfit [for military service]*)

réformiste (*adj*): un parti profondément divisé entre ses ailes **réformiste** et orthodoxe (*reforming*)

refoulement (*nm*): le **refoulement** d'étrangers se rendant en France (*turning-back/expulsion [esp. of immigrant]*)

refouler (*vt*): il risque d'**être refoulé** à la frontière (*be sent/turned back*)

réfractaire (*adj/nmf*): l'Espagne et la Grande-Bretagne **réfractaires** à un accord sur la minorité de blocage (*hostile/opposed to*)

réfugié, -e (*nm,f*): déposer une demande de statut de **réfugié politique** (*political refugee*)

refus (*nm*): SEE **obtempérer**

refuser (*vt*): thèse que le gouvernement **refuse en bloc** (*reject absolutely*); [se] (*vpr*): le porte-parole du gouvernement **se refuse à tout commentaire** (*decline/refuse to comment*)

réfuter (*vt*): avant de **réfuter** les accusations portées contre lui (*refute*)

regain (*nm*): le **regain** du catholicisme aux États-Unis est dû aux hispaniques (*revival*); les négociations suscitent un **regain d'espoir** chez les Blancs (*renewed hope*); l'Ulster connaît un brusque **regain de tension** (*renewed tension*)

régie (*nf*): la **régie des bus municipaux** a fait faillite (*municipal bus company*); les P et T, une **régie [d'État]** avec monopole (*partly state-owned company; guaranteed state group*)

régime (*nm*): le **régime** en place est soutenu par l'étranger (*regime; government*); peut-on modifier un **régime matrimonial** après le mariage? (*marriage settlement*); l'équilibre financier des **régimes de retraite** (*retirement pension scheme*); SEE ALSO **dérogatoire**

région (*nf*): la **région**, une collectivité territoriale à part entière; dans la **région** Provence-Alpes-Côte d'Azur (*region*)

régional, -e, *pl* **-aux** (*adj*): SEE **conseil régional, quotidien, schéma**

régir (*vt*): les nouvelles règles qui **régissent** son fonctionnement (*govern, control*)

règle (*nf*): la **règle de droit** s'applique à toutes les personnes vivant en France (*rule of law*); on a intérêt à **être en règle avec l'administration** (*be in order with the authorities*); SEE ALSO **avertissement, contrevenir, déroger, réquisitoire**

règlement (*nm*): les **règlements** internationaux s'en trouvent facilités (*settlement, payment*); parvenir à un **règlement négocié** du problème (*negotiated settlement*); un **règlement** est plus contraignant qu'une directive (*regulation [esp. Community]*); le proviseur a fondé sa décision sur le **règlement intérieur** de l'établissement (*rules [school]; policies and procedures [company]*); des **règlements de compte** entre truands (*settling of scores*); la société est **en règlement judiciaire**, ne pouvant pas faire face à ses dettes (*in compulsory liquidation*); SEE ALSO **amiable, comptant, entorse, non-observation**

réglementation (*nf*): la libération des prix exige une **réglementation** de la concurrence (*control, regulation*); la **réglementation** ici a tendance à être un peu protectionniste (*regulations, laws*); aucun de ces pays n'a recouru à la **réglementation des prix** (*price controls*); SEE ALSO **répressif**

réglementer (*vt*): décider de **réglementer** par voie législative; une proposition de loi visant à **réglementer** la publicité subliminale (*regulate, control*)

régler (*vt*): pour **régler** le problème des sureffectifs (*solve, settle*); en lui **réglant** les indemnités prévues à son contrat (*pay [out]*)

régresser (*vi*): les infractions à la législation sur les stupéfiants ont nettement **régressé** [–11,6%] (*decline, fall [in numbers]*)

régression (*nf*): nette **régression** des valeurs minières à la Bourse (*decline, fall back*); le pouvoir d'achat du consommateur **en régression** (*declining*)

regroupement (*nm*): travailler pour un **regroupement** de communes (*association; merging, fusion*); autorisés à séjourner en France **au titre du regroupement familial** (*under a scheme for family entry and settlement*)

regrouper (*vt*): les Progressistes **regroupent** tous les mécontents du pays ; la francophonie **regroupe** un ensemble de communautés et de peuples (*bring together*); l'agglomération **regroupe** entre 40 000 et 50 000 habitants (*comprise, contain*)

régularisation (*nf*): afin d'**obtenir une régularisation de sa situation** (*regularize one's situation; put one's papers in order*)

régulariser (*vt*): l'Espagne va **régulariser** 50 000 clandestins (*legalize*); permettre ainsi à 130 000 étrangers de **régulariser leur situation** (*regularize their situation*)

régularité (*nf*): contrôler la **régularité** du séjour des étrangers en France (*legality*); veiller à la **régularité du scrutin** (*fairness of an election*)

régulation (*nf*): la nouvelle **instance de régulation** de l'audiovisuel (*regulatory body*)

réguler (*vt*): afin de **réguler** le marché du travail (*regulate*)

régulier, -ière (*adj*): ces premières élections ont-elles été **régulières?** (*legal; properly conducted*); apporter la preuve de cinq années de **résidence régulière** en France (*lawful residence*)

régulièrement (*adv*): arrivé **régulièrement** en France en 1988 (*legally, lawfully*)

réhabilitation (*nf*): une opération de **réhabilitation** de l'habitat ancien (*regeneration; restoration*); se lancer dans une politique de **réhabilitation urbaine** (*urban renewal*)

réhabiliter (*vt*): les moyens de **réhabiliter** les habitations dégradées (*rehabilitate; restore*)

rehausser (*vt*): ceci n'a fait que **rehausser** son prestige dans le pays (*enhance, increase*)

réinsérer (*vt*): les chômeurs les plus difficiles à **réinsérer** (*find new employment for*); [se] (*vpr*): aider les drogués à **se réinsérer dans la société** (*become rehabilitated into society*)

réinsertion (*nf*): la **réinsertion** des anciens détenus dans la société (*reintegration; rehabilitation*); un **centre de réinsertion** pour jeunes cas sociaux (*rehabilitation centre*); les difficultés de la **réinsertion des chômeurs de longue durée** (*putting back to work the long-term unemployed*)

réintégration (*nf*): la **réintégration** du Caire au sein de la Ligue arabe (*readmission; re-entry*); entraînant la **réintégration** automatique du salarié licencié (*reinstatement*)

réintégrer (*vt*): la France ne doit pas **réintégrer** l'OTAN (*rejoin*); la femme refusa de **réintégrer le domicile conjugal** (*return to the marital home*); **réintégrer** les employés renvoyés par l'ancienne direction (*reinstate, re-engage*)

réinvestir (*vt*): si les bénéfices sont **réinvestis** (*plough back; reinvest*)

rejet (*nm*): l'électorat manifeste son **rejet** de la classe politique; renforçant le sentiment de **rejet** (*rejection*); le Nil, pollué par les **rejets urbains** (*urban waste*)

rejoindre (*vt*): le niveau de vie des plus de 60 ans a **rejoint** celui des actifs (*catch up with*); la livre sterling va-t-elle **rejoindre** le SME? (*join, become a member of*); [se] (*vpr*): malgré leurs différences, les deux candidats **se rejoignent sur l'essentiel** (*agree on essentials*)

relâche (*nf*): poursuivre **sans relâche** les auteurs des assassinats (*without let-up, unceasingly*)

relâchement (*nm*): il critique un **relâchement** dans la lutte contre l'inflation (*slackening; laxity*)

relâcher (*vt*): interpellé, interrogé, puis **relâché** (*set free, release*)

relais (*nm*): les Chinois vont **prendre le relais** des Japonais; les services y ont **pris le relais** de l'agriculture (*take over from; replace*)

relance (*nf*): la **relance** de l'économie se fait toujours attendre (*reflation; boost*); la **relance** du processus de paix (*revival, relaunching*)

relancer (*vt*): pour **relancer** à l'Est le rôle politique de la France (*revive, boost*); l'Allemagne refuse de **relancer**, mais accepte une réévaluation de sa monnaie (*stimulate the economy; expand*)

relation (*nf*): les **relations** de la Colombie avec les États-Unis (*relations*); SEE ALSO **inamical, ménager, normaliser, réchauffement, réchauffer**

relativiser (*vt*): le score du Front national doit être **relativisé** par l'abstention massive des électeurs (*put into proper perspective*); la chute de Wall Street est importante, mais il faut **relativiser les choses** (*put matters into perspective*)

relaxe (*nf*): demander la **relaxe** pour les trois prévenus (*acquittal, discharge*); les avocats de la défense **plaident la relaxe** (*ask for the acquittal of a defendant*)

relaxer (*vt*): le cinquième prévenu a été **relaxé**; les auteurs de la tuerie **relaxés** par le tribunal de Nouméa (*acquit, discharge*)

relevé (*nm*): un **relevé** des opérations passées à votre compte en banque (*summary, statement*); les versements et retraits figurent sur le **relevé de compte** (*bank statement*)

relève (*nf*): une élite indigène qui pourra **prendre la relève** au moment de l'indépendance (*take over; take charge*)

relèvement (*nm*): un **relèvement** de la cotisation vieillesse (*raising, increase*)

relever (*vt*): le constructeur vient de **relever ses tarifs** (*raise prices*); **relever le défi** des nouvelles technologies (*take up the challenge*); une force de paix de 50 000 hommes va **relever** les Casques bleus (*relieve, take over from*); le Président l'a **relevé de ses fonctions** (*dismiss, sack*); (*vi*): la mise en route de la dissuasion nucléaire **relève du Président seul** (*is a matter for the President alone*); SEE ALSO **compétence**

remaniement (*nm*): toute la défense de l'OTAN **est en cours de remaniement** (*is being reorganized*); un **remaniement ministériel** est intervenu à Bonn (*cabinet reshuffle*)

remanier (*vt*): Phnom Penh **remanie** profondément son gouvernement (*reshape, reshuffle*); la législation a été **remaniée** à plusieurs reprises (*revise, amend; redraft*)

remboursement (*nm*): le **remboursement** d'une dette (*reimbursement, repayment*); la part des revenus des particuliers consacrée au **remboursement de crédit** (*loan repayment*); SEE ALSO **mensualité**

rembourser (*vt*): les frais d'hospitalisation sont **remboursés** à 80% (*reimburse*)

remédier (*vt*): pour **remédier au** surpeuplement dans les prisons (*find a remedy for; cure*)

remembrement (*nm*): favoriser le **remembrement** des terres cultivables; grâce au **remembrement**, les exploitations seront d'une taille rentable (*reallotment; restructuring [of land]*)

remercier (*vt*): le gouvernement envisage de **remercier** le P-DG d'Elf-Aquitaine (*sack, dismiss*)

remettre (*vt*): le document qu'il vient de **remettre** au ministre (*submit, hand in*); son adjoint aux finances **remet sa démission** (*tender one's resignation*); la société **remet à plus tard** son introduction en Bourse (*postpone*); SEE ALSO **cause, huitaine**

remise (*nf*): consentir des **remises** importantes (*discount, reduction*); la **remise en état** des infrastructures (*repair*); des formations de **remise à niveau des connaissances** (*refresher course*); solliciter une **remise de peine** ou une libération conditionnelle (*reduction of sentence; remission*); SEE ALSO **cause, question**

remontée (*nf*): la **remontée** du chômage (*rise, increase*); rechute du dollar, **remontée** du yen (*rise; recovery*)

remonter (*vt*): la nouvelle direction a bien **remonté** la société (*put back on its feet*); (*vi*): le chômage **remonte**, on assiste à une baisse des reprises d'emploi (*go up, rise*); la dernière augmentation **remonte au** 1er juillet (*date from, go back to*)

remous (*nm*): l'affaire a **provoqué des remous** au sein du gouvernement (*cause a stir/discontent*)

remplaçant, -e (*adj/nm,f*): l'affectation de **remplaçants** supplémentaires (*replacement [esp. supply teacher]*)

remplacement (*nm*): des enseignants chargés d'effectuer des **remplacements** (*supply teaching*)

remporter (*vt*): l'opposition a **remporté** la majorité absolue; d'autres gros contrats ont été **remportés** par des Français en 1989 (*gain, win*)

rémunérateur, -trice (*adj*): on a préféré les cultures les plus hautement **rémunératrices** (*profitable; lucrative*)

rémunération (*nf*): avoir droit à une **rémunération** décente de son travail (*pay, earnings*); une **hausse des rémunérations** est survenue dans le secteur du bâtiment (*pay rise*); SEE ALSO **évolutif, fourchette, moindre**

rémunérer (*vt*): la banque **rémunère** les compte-chèques de 6 à 7% (*pay interest on*); un stage de formation **rémunéré** (*paid*); un allégement des cotisations sociales pour les emplois **faiblement rémunérés** (*poorly paid*); SEE ALSO **compte**

renchérir (*vi*): on a vu le brut **renchérir** constamment (*get dearer, increase in price*); **renchérir sur** toute OPA lancée sur le fabricant de whisky (*bid higher than*); et le ministre de **renchérir**, en disant: . . . (*add; go further*)

renchérissement (*nm*): le **renchérissement** très sensible du coût de l'habitat (*rise in price/cost*); le Japon, ébranlé par le **renchérissement de l'énergie** (*rise in energy costs*)

rendement (*nm*): son **rendement** est passé de 20 milliards en 1975 à 50 en 1988 (*yield, output*); les obligations sont des placements **à rendement fixe** (*fixed-return, with a fixed return*); l'usine travaillait **à plein rendement** (*at full capacity*); SEE ALSO **course, prime**

rendre (*vt*): SEE **décision, sentence**

renflouement (*nm*): le **renflouement** de la Sécurité sociale ne sera pas chose aisée (*refloating; bailing out*)

renflouer (*vt*): des sommes destinées à **renflouer** des filiales déficitaires (*bail out; refloat*); en offrant ses services aux entreprises, la société **renfloue ses caisses** (*return to a sound financial situation*)

renforcement (*nm*): le **renforcement** des troupes cubaines en Afrique australe (*strengthening, reinforcement*); un **renforcement** des droits de douane (*increase; raising*); malgré le **renforcement des pénalités** pour crimes de violence (*heavier penalties*)

renforcer (*vt*): les États-Unis **renforcent** l'embargo sur Haïti (*reinforce, strengthen*); **renforcer les peines** prévues pour la fabrication et l'usage de faux documents (*fix/set stiffer penalties*); [se] (*vpr*): le cimentier entend **se renforcer** en Espagne (*strengthen its trading position; expand*); SEE ALSO **lien**

renfort (*nm*): des **renforts** occidentaux, dont un millier de soldats français (*reinforcements*); des gendarmes mobiles envoyés **en renfort** (*as reinforcements; in support*)

reniement (*nm*): les **reniements** du maire sortant, et sa gestion incohérente (*broken promises*); la paix, mais pas au prix du **reniement** (*going back on all one has stood for*)

renier (*vt*): **renier** les idées de son prédécesseur (*disown, repudiate*)

renouer (*vt*): l'Irak veut **renouer le dialogue** avec l'ONU sans perdre la face (*resume discussions, reopen talks*); la France voudrait **renouer avec** Canberra (*get back on good terms with*); les entreprises françaises **renouent avec le profit** (*return to profitability*)

renouveau, *pl* **-x** (*nm*): accusé d'être le saboteur du **renouveau** économique (*revival, recovery*); **renouveau de tension** indo-pakistanais (*renewed tension*)

renouveler (*vt*): les élections permettront de **renouveler** le personnel (*renew, replace, change*); onze sièges **sont à renouveler** (*are up for re-election*)

renouvellement (*nm*): le **renouvellement** partiel du comité central (*renewal, replacement*); lors d'un **renouvellement de bail** le propriétaire demande souvent une hausse de loyer (*renewing of a lease*); ne pas souhaiter le **renouvellement de son mandat** (*re-election*)

rénovateur, -trice (*adj/nm,f*): les élus PC se sont constitués en groupe des élus **rénovateurs** (*reformist; modernizing*); les **rénovateurs** refusent de voter pour la liste communiste (*reformer, modernizer [esp. Communist]*)

rénovation (*nf*): une politique de **rénovation** de l'habitat ancien (*renovation, restoration*); la constitution d'une liste du centre et de **rénovation**; le vent de la **rénovation** souffle aussi au Sénat (*modernization; reform*)

rénover (*vt*): le conseil général décide de **rénover** le collège d'Étampes (*renovate, refurbish*); les institutions ont été **rénovées** et l'économie modernisée (*reform; overhaul*)

renseignement (*nm*): la France accroît fortement ses moyens de **renseignement** (*intelligence, information gathering*); la police judiciaire, en liaison avec les **Renseignements généraux [RG]** (*French general intelligence service*)

rentabiliser (*vt*): un éditeur **rentabilise** un ouvrage lorsqu'il en vend 2 000 exemplaires; **rentabiliser** au mieux son investissement (*make profitable; make pay*)

rentabilité (*nf*): par souci de **rentabilité** et d'économie (*profitability; financial viability*); la **rentabilité de l'investissement** demeure faible (*return on investment*); SEE ALSO **seuil**

rentable (*adj*): un investissement qui sera **rentable** à long terme (*profitable; cost-effective*)

rente (*nf*): une épargne versée sous forme de capital ou de **rente** (*income, annuity*); percevoir une **rente viagère** (*life annuity*); avec l'amenuisement de la **rente pétrolière** (*oil revenue*); vivre largement de ses **rentes** (*unearned income*)

rentier, -ière (*nm,f*): la fin de la société des **rentiers** (*person of independent/ private means*)

rentrée (*nf*): les dépenses étaient supérieures aux **rentrées** (*income; revenue*); se procurer de précieuses **rentrées de devises** (*foreign currency revenue*); grâce à de bonnes **rentrées fiscales** (*tax revenue*); la **rentrée sociale** promet d'être chaude (*return to work [after summer vacation]*); SEE ALSO **irrégularité**

rentrer (*vi*): en deux ans d'activité, il est **rentré dans ses fonds** (*recoup one's costs/investment*)

renversement (*nm*): l'opposition appelle au **renversement** militaire du régime (*overthrow*); un **renversement de tendance** s'est produit dès l'ouverture de Wall Street (*reversal of trend*)

renverser (*vt*): les auteurs du putsch qui a **renversé** le régime nigérien (*overthrow, topple*)

renvoi (*nm*): le **renvoi** devant une cour d'assises des six membres de la bande (*committal [for trial]*); demander le **renvoi** de la discussion au lendemain (*postponement*); 40% des sondés souhaitent le **renvoi** des travailleurs étrangers (*sending back; expulsion*); des sanctions allant jusqu'au **renvoi définitif** de l'élève (*expulsion*)

renvoyer (*vt*): pas question de **renvoyer** jusqu'après 1995 cette question cruciale (*put off; postpone*); les inculpés sont **renvoyés** devant la cour d'assises (*send, refer*); SEE ALSO **barreau**

répartir (*vt*): elle a 280 filiales **réparties** dans 31 pays (*distribute, spread*)

répartition (*nf*): une **répartition** plus équilibrée du logement social (*division; sharing-out*); la mise en place d'un **plan de répartition des profits** (*profit-sharing scheme*)

répercussion (*nf*): les **répercussions** des mouvements du dollar sur les prix (*repercussion, knock-on effect*)

répercuter (*vt*): **répercuter** une charge sur le client; les entrepreneurs **répercutent** souvent ces augmentations dans leurs prix (*pass on [the cost]*); [se] (*vpr*): ces incidents **se répercutent sur** la vie de chaque Français (*have an effect on; have repercussions on*)

répertorier (*vt*): Amnesty International a **répertorié** la disparition de 272 personnes (*list; itemize*)

replâtrage (*nm*): on imagine mal un **replâtrage** de leur alliance (*repairing; patching-up*)

replâtrer (*vt*): afin de **replâtrer** les fissures de la majorité (*paper over; patch up*)

repli (*nm*): un **repli nationaliste** serait regrettable (*retreat into nationalism*); la consommation des biens manufacturés a connu un **repli** sensible en mars (*reduction; decline*); sensible **repli des cours du cuivre** sur le marché de Londres (*fall in copper prices*); SEE ALSO **solution**

replier [se] (*vpr*): **se replier** provisoirement (*withdraw, retreat*); la bourse d'Amsterdam **s'est repliée** mardi, dans un marché terne (*fall [back]; drop*)

répondre (*vi*): SEE **accusation**

report (*nm*): demander le **report** de la conférence (*postponement*); un **report d'incorporation** pour cause d'études supérieures (*deferment of national service*); le candidat a bénéficié de très bons **reports de voix** des électorats communiste et radical (*transfer of vote*)

reporter (*vt*): **reporter** la scolarité obligatoire jusqu'à l'âge de 18 ans (*put back*); l'élection présidentielle au Liban a été **reportée** (*postpone, put off*); une partie des électeurs ont **reporté** leurs suffrages sur le candidat d'union (*transfer*)

repos (*nm*): les commerces sont condamnés au **repos dominical** (*ban on Sunday trading; Sunday closing*)

repousser (*vt*): **repousser** à lundi sa décision (*put back*); la justice irlandaise a **repoussé** la démarche visant à interdire cette publicité (*reject, throw out*); la motion de censure a été **repoussée** par 130 voix à 105 (*defeat*)

reprendre (*vt*): les autorités de Zagreb **reprennent** la Krajina aux Serbes (*retake, recapture*); ils voulaient **reprendre** l'entreprise en perdition (*take over; acquire*); les fonctionnaires **reprennent le travail** (*restart/go back to work*); (*vi*): le travail **reprend** dans l'usine de Belfort (*restart, resume*); SEE ALSO **dessus**

repreneur (*nm*): le **repreneur** désigné devra injecter 15 MF avant le 3 août (*company rescuer*); le nouveau **repreneur** n'est pas totalement étranger à cette activité (*new owner; buyer*)

représailles (*nfpl*): la menace de **représailles** aériennes (*reprisals*); la décision a été prise **en représailles** (*in retaliation*); SEE ALSO **éventuel**

représentation (*nf*): le Parlement, en France, assure la **représentation** du peuple (*representation*); les industriels français ont rouvert des **représentations** dans la capitale irakienne (*office; agency, branch*); SEE ALSO **proportionnel**

représenter [se] (*vpr*): le président **se représentera** aux prochaines élections (*stand again [for election]*)

répressif, -ive (*adj*): une politique très **répressive** (*repressive*); Pékin renforce sa **réglementation répressive** (*repressive measures*)

répression (*nf*): à la **répression** on préférait la négociation (*repressive measures*); les dépenses pour la **répression de la criminalité** (*dealing with crime*); un tournant dans la **répression de la Mafia** en France (*crackdown on the Mafia*)

réprimer (*vt*): l'armée **réprime** brutalement des manifestations de rue (*quell; put down*); une loi destinée à **réprimer** la violence dans les stades (*curb, crack down upon*); ce délit **est réprimé par l'article 425** du Code (*comes under article 425*); en Belgique, seul l'usage collectif des stupéfiants **est réprimé** (*is an indictable offence*)

repris de justice (*nm*): l'homme, **repris de justice** notoire, est activement recherché par la police (*habitual offender*)

reprise (*nf*): l'ONU craint une **reprise** de la guerre civile (*restart, resumption*); les salariés votent la **reprise du travail** (*return to work*); une **reprise modérée** de la consommation (*modest recovery, upturn*); après l'échec du projet de **reprise** de la firme allemande (*taking control; acquisition*); SEE ALSO **appel**, **main**

reprocher (*vt*): les **faits reprochés** à l'ancien ministre; tous nient en bloc les **faits qui leur sont reprochés** (*allegations, charges*)

requérant, -e (*adj/nm,f*): le tribunal débouta les **requérants** (*plaintiff; claimant*); tous les **requérants d'asile** déboutés en première instance (*asylum seeker*)

requérir (*vt*): l'avocat général a **requis** une peine de prison de dix ans (*call for, demand [sentence]*); **requérir** la force publique pour expulser les occupants (*request [the intervention of]*)

requête (*nf*): le Conseil constitutionnel rejeta la **requête**; examiner les **requêtes** des plaignants (*appeal*)

réquisition (*nf*): la **réquisition** du parquet est accablante pour lui; contrairement aux **réquisitions** du procureur de la République (*closing speech [for prosecution]*)

réquisitoire (*nm*): dans son **réquisitoire**, l'avocat général a insisté sur l'horreur du crime (*charge*); [*fig*] prononcer un **réquisitoire en règle** contre la politique du gouvernement (*denunciation/indictment*)

réseau, *pl* **-x** (*nm*): un vaste **réseau** commercial dans les cinq continents (*network*); grève SNCF: **réseau** perturbé hier (*network; [transport] system*); un **réseau d'espionnage** opérant au profit de la Roumanie (*spy ring*)

réserve (*nf*): la Banque de France doit reconstituer ses **réserves de change** (*foreign currency reserves*); SEE ALSO **devoir**

résidence (*nf*): le placement en **résidence surveillée** du chef du parti de l'opposition (*house arrest*); SEE ALSO **assignation, assigner, régulier**

résiliation (*nf*): la **résiliation** d'un contrat de location (*termination, cancellation*)

résilier (*vt*): il y a un temps de préavis à respecter pour **résilier** un contrat (*terminate/cancel [esp. insurance policy]*)

résolution (*nf*): chercher une **résolution pacifique** du conflit (*peaceful resolution*); selon la **résolution 232 de l'ONU** (*UN resolution 232*)

résorber (*vt*): le déficit prévu sera **résorbé** grâce à l'augmentation des cotisations; **résorber** la violence urbaine (*reduce, bring down*); [se] (*vpr*): la crise de recrutement d'enseignants a tendance à **se résorber** (*resolve itself*)

résorption (*nf*): la **résorption du chômage** tarde à se réaliser (*bringing down of/fall in unemployment*)

résoudre (*vt*): un plan d'action visant à **résoudre** la crise pacifiquement (*resolve; settle*)

respect (*nm*): des relations de **respect mutuel** et de bon voisinage (*mutual respect*); une force de paix chargée de surveiller le **respect du cessez-le-feu** (*observance of the cease-fire*)

respecter (*vt*): être là pour **faire respecter la loi** (*enforce the law*)

responsabilité (*nf*): accéder à un **poste à responsabilité** (*post/position of responsibility*); en cas de blocage, il peut **engager la responsabilité du gouvernement** en vertu de l'article 49/3 de la Constitution (*[in France] stake government survival on the acceptance of a bill without a vote*); SEE ALSO **Sàrl**

responsable (*adj/nmf*): un **responsable** américain a démenti cette affirmation (*official; representative*); plusieurs **hauts responsables** démis de leurs fonctions (*high-ranking official*); il est à la fois délégué du personnel et **responsable syndical** (*trade-union official*)

ressentiment (*nm*): il n'y a pas de **ressentiment** ici contre les Américains (*antagonism, resentment*)

ressentir (*vt*): des restrictions budgétaires **mal ressenties** dans la marine (*unpopular*); une décision qui devait **être très mal ressentie** en Belgique (*be very unpopular*)

resserrement (*nm*): le **resserrement** de la politique monétaire vise à mettre fin à la faiblesse du mark (*tightening; squeeze*)

resserrer (*vt*): aux États-Unis, la Réserve fédérale a préféré **resserrer** sa politique du crédit (*tighten*); SEE ALSO **employer**

ressort (*nm*): utiliser tous les **ressorts** de la procédure parlementaire pour retarder l'adoption du texte (*resource; possibility*); la défense **est du ressort du** chef de l'État (*be the responsibility of; fall within the competence of*); [*fig*] c'est lui qui décide, **en dernier ressort** (*in the final analysis; finally*)

ressortir (*vi*): c'est ce qui **ressort** du rapport établi par les enquêteurs (*emerge*); les traitements nets **font ressortir** une baisse du pouvoir d'achat (*indicate, reveal*)

ressortissant, -e (*nm,f*): un **ressortissant espagnol** recherché par la justice de son pays (*Spanish national*)

ressource (*nf*): la principale **ressource** du Koweït est le pétrole (*resource*); les **ressources** prises en compte ne comprennent pas les allocations familiales (*means, resources*); père de trois enfants, **sans ressources** (*with no means of support*); l'importance d'une bonne gestion des **ressources humaines** (*human resources, staffing*); SEE ALSO **condition, plafond**

restituer (*vt*): le voleur a promis de **restituer** les objets volés; **restituer** la péninsule du Sinaï à l'Égypte (*return, give back*)

restitution (*nf*): la **restitution** du chef du gouvernement déchu (*reinstatement*); la **restitution** de Hongkong à la Chine (*return, giving back*)

restreindre (*vt*): c'est le budget global qui **restreint** les dépenses hospitalières (*curb, limit, keep down*); abroger les articles **restreignant** les libertés démocratiques (*restrict, limit*)

restreint, -e (*adj*): SEE **comité**

restructuration (*nf*): 8% de la population active ont été touchés par les **restructurations**; la crise devrait accélérer les **restructurations industrielles** (*restructuring; shake-up*); approuver le **plan de restructuration** (*restructuring plan*)

restructurer [se] (*vpr*): le groupe **se restructure**: bilan, 400 personnes sans emploi (*restructure; reorganize*)

résultat (*nm*): baisse des **résultats** des constructeurs automobiles (*profit*); la firme enregistra un **résultat d'exploitation** de 5,2 millions de francs (*operating profit*); SEE ALSO **intéressement**

rétablir (*vt*): **rétablir** des conditions de vie normales (*re-establish*); avoir l'intention de **rétablir le scrutin proportionnel** (*bring back proportional representation*)

rétablissement (*nm*): il faut attendre 1995 pour que la firme achève son **rétablissement** (*recovery*); le **rétablissement de la peine de mort** (*restoration of the death penalty*)

retard (*nm*): le **retard** pris par la mise en œuvre de l'accord se prolonge (*delay*); expulsé à cause de ses **retards de loyer** (*arrears of rent*)

retenir (*vt*): la zone où sont **retenus** les otages (*detain, hold*); les régions **retenues** pour l'aide au développement (*choose, select*); l'impôt sur le revenu sera **retenu à la source** (*deducted at source*); cette journée de grève **leur sera retenue sur le salaire** (*will be deducted from their pay*)

rétention (*nf*): la **rétention** du permis de conduire et le retrait de six points du capital du permis à points (*withholding*); les conditions de **rétention des clandestins** en voie de reconduite à la frontière (*holding of illegal immigrants*)

retenue (*nf*): la **retenue** dont avaient fait preuve les autorités (*restraint*); les **retenues** pour la Sécurité sociale étaient de 6,5% (*deduction, stoppage*); une **retenue à la source** par l'employeur sur tous les salaires (*deduction of tax at source*)

réticence (*nf*): le ministre s'est heurté aux **réticences** des députés socialistes (*reservations; resistance*); malgré les **réticences syndicales** (*trade-union opposition*)

réticent, -e (*adj*): les partenaires de la France restent **réticents** (*reluctant; hostile*); ce peuple, conservateur et **réticent au changement** (*opposed to change*)

retirer (*vt*): **retirer** de l'argent (*withdraw*); **retirer** une plainte (*withdraw, take back*); les dossiers sont à **retirer** et déposer avant le 31 mai (*pick up, collect*); [se] (*vpr*): **se retirer** avant le second tour des élections (*withdraw, stand down*)

retombée (*nf*): des **retombées** du boom pétrolier (*spin-off; beneficial effects*); cette mesure pourrait avoir des **retombées politiques** négatives (*political consequences*)

rétorsion (*nf*): mettre en place des **mesures de rétorsion** économique (*retaliatory measures*)

retour (*nm*): son **retour** à la politique (*comeback*); la gauche, pour assurer à tout prix son **retour aux affaires** (*return to power*); SEE ALSO **profit**

retournement (*nm*): des entreprises en voie de **retournement** (*turn-round; recovery*); ce **retournement d'alliance** évoque une comédie de boulevard (*change of alliance; changing sides*); les constructeurs craignent un **retournement de conjoncture** (*change of economic conditions*)

retourner [se] (*vpr*): **se retourner contre** le fabricant pour obtenir réparation d'un préjudice (*take legal action against*)

rétracter [se] (*vpr*): le principal témoin à charge **s'était rétracté** (*retract, withdraw one's statement*); **se rétracter** après avoir signé un prêt (*withdraw*)

retrait (*nm*): le **retrait** du corps expéditionnaire libyen (*withdrawal*); un **retrait de fonds** de votre compte peut s'effectuer à n'importe quel guichet (*withdrawal of funds*); la date limite de **retrait des dossiers** (*collecting an application form*); SEE ALSO **espèce**

retraite (*nf*): pour obtenir une **retraite à taux plein** (*full pension*); des militaires **à la retraite** (*retired, in retirement*); prendre une **retraite anticipée** (*early retirement*); SEE ALSO **départ, pension, régime**

retraité, -e (*nm,f*): la France comptera davantage de **retraités** que d'actifs (*retired person; [old age] pensioner*)

retravailler (*vi*): les femmes désirant **retravailler** (*go back to work*)

rétribuer (*vt*): faire un **travail rétribué** (*paid work*); il leur est interdit d'**occuper un emploi rétribué** (*be in paid employment*)

rétrocéder (*vt*): **rétrocéder** ses parts dans l'entreprise (*sell back*); Hongkong sera **rétrocédé** à la Chine en 1997 (*retrocede, give back*)

rétrocession (*nf*): à trois ans de la **rétrocession** de la colonie à la Chine (*handing-back*)

rétrograder (*vt*): douze commissaires de la République sont **rétrogradés** (*downgrade; demote*)

retrouver [se] (*vpr*): Occidentaux et Russes **se retrouvent** aujourd'hui à Genève (*meet [again]*)

réunion (*nf*): les ministres PR ont tenu une **réunion** (*meeting*); au cours d'une **réunion de protestation** (*protest meeting*); l'interdiction de toute **réunion** de plus de cinq personnes (*gathering, assembly*); SEE ALSO **compte, liberté, viol**

réunir (*vt*): des réunions **réunissant** plus de 40 000 personnes (*bring together*); [se] (*vpr*): une table ronde nationale devrait **se réunir** à la mi-juin (*meet, get together*)

revalorisation (*nf*): la **revalorisation** de l'enseignement du chinois en France (*promotion; giving greater importance [to]*); demander une **revalorisation de leur statut** (*regrading*); l'urgence de **revalorisations salariales** massives (*wage rise, pay increase*)

revaloriser (*vt*): il faut **revaloriser** le rôle du Parlement (*give greater importance to*); l'ensemble des rémunérations sera **revalorisé** de 1 500F au moins (*raise, increase*)

revendicateur, -trice (*adj/nm,f*): envoyer une **lettre revendicatrice** à la direction (*letter stating demands*)

revendicatif, -ive (*adj*): la CFDT est prête à s'associer à d'éventuels **mouvements revendicatifs** (*protest movement; action in support of claims*)

revendication (*nf*): la **revendication** des syndicats pour une retraite à 60 ans (*demand*); se limiter à des **revendications catégorielles** (*sectional claims/demands*); face aux **revendications identitaires corses** (*demand for recognition of their Corsican identity*); SEE ALSO **salarial, solidaire**

revendiquer (*vt*): l'attentat a été **revendiqué** par un groupe loyaliste (*claim responsibility for*); le mouvement **revendique 20 000 adhérents** (*claim a membership of 20,000*); territoire **revendiqué** à la fois par le Tchad et la Libye (*claim*); les ouvriers **revendiquent** de nouvelles hausses de salaire (*demand, put in a claim for*)

revenir (*vi*): le coût a chuté de 2 milliards de francs, **revenant** à 1,2 milliards en 1986 (*come down to*); la décision **revient au** Président, et à lui seul (*be the prerogative of; fall to*); le gouvernement n'entend pas **revenir sur** la liberté totale des prix (*reconsider, go back upon [decision, promise]*); l'assassin présumé **revient sur ses aveux** (*retract his confession*)

revenu (*nm*): seul le **revenu du travail** est imposable (*earned income*); pour ceux qui touchent le **revenu minimum d'insertion [RMI]** (*[in France] minimum welfare payment made to person with no other source of income*); SEE ALSO **déclarer, disponible, imposable, impôt, percevoir**

revers (*nm*): un **revers** personnel pour le nouveau leader; un nouveau **revers** pour l'intégration européenne (*setback; defeat*); SEE ALSO **enregistrer, essuyer**

revirement (*nm*): le **revirement** de la politique sociale (*reversal; turn-around*); ceci apparaît un **revirement total** (*complete turn-around; U-turn*)

réviser (*vt*): la Cour de cassation peut **réviser** ou non le procès (*review; rehear [trial]*); l'INSEE **révise à la baisse** ses estimations (*revise downward*)

révocation (*nf*): le ministre de la Justice a prononcé au moins 118 **révocations**; sous peine de sanctions allant jusqu'à la **révocation** (*dismissal [of civil servant]; removal from office*)

revoir (*vt*): il faut **revoir** un projet qui s'annonce trop coûteux (*re-examine, review*); l'OCDE **revoit en hausse** ses prévisions (*revise upwards*)

révoquer (*vt*): le premier président d'industrie nationalisée à être **révoqué** (*be sacked/dismissed*); la Cour d'appel peut **révoquer la décision** (*cancel/quash the decision*)

revue (*nf*): une **revue** de la presse (*review*); ils ont **passé en revue** l'état des négociations en cours (*review, survey*)

rigidité (*nf*): la Finlande déçue par la **rigidité** de Paris (*inflexibility; strictness*)

rigueur (*nf*): une **rigueur** accrue contre les sectes (*strong measures; severity*); manifestations contre la **rigueur**; les effets du **plan de rigueur** se font déjà sentir (*austerity measures*); l'incident est clos: la Turquie semble ne pas **tenir rigueur** à la Grèce (*blame, feel resentment towards*)

ristourne (*nf*): un dossier-clef: la **ristourne** accordée à la Grande-Bretagne (*rebate*); proposer une **ristourne** de 20% sur le prix affiché (*discount*)

riverain, -e (*adj/nm,f*): les dirigeants des États **riverains** de la Méditerranée (*countries on the Mediterranean*); accès interdit sauf aux **riverains** (*local resident*); permettre aux **riverains d'aéroports** d'insonoriser leurs habitations (*people living in the vicinity of an airport*)

rocade (*nf*): l'ouverture de la **rocade** Nord-Est diminuera le flux des camions (*bypass*); une seconde **rocade de contournement** de l'agglomération rennaise (*ring road*)

rogatoire (*adj*): SEE **commission**

rompre (*vt*): le PS demande au RPR de **rompre** ses accords régionaux avec le Front national (*break off, cancel*)

rose (*adj*): l'**Assemblée rose** arrivée au Palais-Bourbon en 1981 (*Socialist-dominated assembly*); proposer de la législation pour mettre fin au scandale des **messageries roses** (*sex chatlines [esp. on Minitel]*)

rotation (*nf*): la **rotation du personnel** donne à penser que les cadences y sont trop élevées (*turnover/rotation of staff*)

rouage (*nm*): connaître les **rouages** de l'administration (*ins and outs, workings*)

rouge (*adj/nm*): conséquence: France Télécom **passe dans le rouge** (*go into the red*)

roulement (*nm*): travailler avec un **roulement** de trois équipes (*rota system; system of shift-working*); SEE ALSO **fonds**

route (*nf*): la **mise en route** de nouveaux chantiers (*starting-up; establishment*); SEE ALSO **compagnon**

routier, -ière (*adj*): SEE **désenclavement**

rubrique (*nf*): il tenait longtemps la **rubrique financière** dans *Le Monde* (*financial column/section*); SEE ALSO **fait divers**

rude (*adj*): la concurrence est **rude** dans ce secteur (*tough, fierce*); les prochains mois s'**annoncent rudes** (*promise to be difficult/hard*)

rue (*nf*): Roumanie: **la rue** à l'assaut du pouvoir (*the people; the mob*); une décision qui mécontente **la rue**; le Premier ministre tente d'ouvrir le dialogue avec **la rue** (*the people; the man in the street*); SEE ALSO **pignon**

ruine (*nf*): sa gestion désastreuse va **conduire son pays à la ruine** (*bankrupt his country*)

ruiner (*vt*): des investissements qui l'avaient **ruiné**, l'acculant à la faillite (*ruin*); s'installer sans **se ruiner** (*go bankrupt*)

rumeur (*nf*): la **rumeur publique** l'accuse, malgré le démenti de ses amis (*hearsay; rumour*)

rupture (*nf*): une **rupture** de la coalition gouvernementale ne saurait tarder (*collapse, breakdown*); une **rupture diplomatique** entre Londres et Damas (*breaking-off of diplomatic relations*); une **rupture** totale avec la politique suivie jusqu'alors (*break; change*); des jeunes **en rupture de milieu familial** (*who have left the parental home*); le magasin est **en rupture de stock** (*out of stock*)

rural, -e, *pl* **-aux** (*adj/nm,f*): s'installer **en milieu rural** (*in a rural area*); la fermeture de services publics **en zone rurale** (*in rural areas*); SEE ALSO **espace**

ruralité (*nf*): paysans et **ruralité**; l'agriculture et la **ruralité** sont omniprésentes (*country/rural life*)

rythme (*nm*): l'ampleur et surtout le **rythme** des réformes sont décon-certants (*tempo; frequency, rate*); la réforme des **rythmes scolaires** (*pattern of school day/week*); SEE ALSO **sage**

rythmer (*vt*): une semaine boursière **rythmée par** les évolutions du titre Compagnie du Midi (*marked by*); une année **rythmée par** grèves et arrêts de travail (*punctuated by*)

S

sabbatique (*adj*): une année **sabbatique** (*sabbatical*); prendre un **congé sabbatique** d'une durée de six mois (*sabbatical leave*)

sabotage (*nm*): le **sabotage** du *Rainbow Warrior*, le 10 juillet 1985 (*sabotage*)

saboter (*vt*): routes et voies ferrées **sabotées**; veulent-ils **saboter** le processus de paix? (*sabotage*)

sac (*nm*): une incitation à la **mise à sac** du siège du Parti socialiste (*ran-sacking*); l'ambassade du Pakistan **mise à sac** par des manifestants (*ransack*)

saccage (*nm*): l'armée tente de mettre fin au **saccage** de la capitale (*[wanton] destruction; vandalizing*)

saccager (*vt*): mairie **saccagée**, bâtiments publics pillés (*vandalize, wreck*)

sage (*adj/nm*): les prix de gros progressent à **un rythme plus sage** (*less rapidly, more slowly*); **les neuf sages** vont plancher sur le projet de loi gouvernemental (*[the members of] the French Constitutional Council*); SEE ALSO **palais**

sagesse (*nf*): une compression de la demande, et la **sagesse** de la consommation outre-Rhin (*moderation; modest level*)

saisie (*nf*): ordonner la **saisie** de l'hebdomadaire (*seizure; confiscation*); il y aura encore des **saisies** et des expulsions (*seizure of property; repossession*); assurer la **saisie informatique** des résultats d'examen (*data capture, keyboarding, information input*)

saisine (*nf*): la **saisine** du Conseil constitutionnel par le simple citoyen; demander la **saisine** de la Chambre criminelle de la Cour de cassation (*seisin; submission of a case before a court*)

saisir (*vt*): ses créanciers ont **saisi** tous ses biens (*seize; take possession of*); **saisir la justice** et demander des dommages et intérêts (*go to law*); **saisir** la Commission européenne des Droits de l'homme (*refer a matter to a court; complain to*); les familles des victimes pourraient **saisir les tribunaux** (*go to court*); [se] (*vpr*): le Sénat à son tour va **se saisir du dossier** (*examine the case*); SEE ALSO **opportunité**

saisonnier, -ière (*adj/nm,f*): exercer un emploi **saisonnier** (*seasonal*); en été on emploie surtout des **saisonniers** (*seasonal worker; migrant labour*); SEE ALSO **donnée**

salaire (*nm*): un **salaire d'embauche** de 30 000F (*starting salary*); le nombre de **familles à salaire unique** (*single-wage family*); SEE ALSO **baisse, bas, blocage, bordereau, brut, égalité, éventail, gel, grille, hiérarchie, parité, SMIC**

salarial, -e, *pl* **-aux** (*adj*): la **politique salariale** a été extrêmement sévère (*wage/pay policy*); il s'agit, comme toujours, de **revendications salariales** (*wage claims/demands*); SEE ALSO **augmentation, barème, charge, coût, masse, négociation, prétention, revalorisation**

salariat (*nm*): le **salariat** est aujourd'hui un privilège (*being a salaried employee; being in employment*)

salarié, -e (*adj/nm,f*): dix mois d'**activité salariée** (*paid employment*); un **salarié** sur cinq n'a pas un emploi stable (*wage-earner, salaried employee*)

sanction (*nf*): la **sanction** des infractions aux règles de la navigation (*penalty*); s'exposer à des **sanctions pénales** (*legal action*); ils craignent la **sanction** de l'opinion publique (*verdict, judgment*); un DEUG, **sanction de deux années d'études** (*awarded after two years of study*); SEE ALSO **objet, vote**

sanctionner (*vt*): des fautes qui devraient être **sanctionnées** (*punish; penalize*); le vote de confiance a **sanctionné** sa déclaration de politique générale (*ratify; express approval of*)

sang (*nm*): en Allemagne, la nationalité s'obtient par le **droit du sang** (jus sanguinis, *right to citizenship by virtue of kinship*); SEE ALSO **effusion**

sanglant, -e (*adj*): les **sanglantes** émeutes d'octobre (*bloody*); une colonie éprouvée par **une sanglante guerre civile** (*a bloody civil war*)

sanitaire (*adj*): l'**état sanitaire** du pays est déplorable (*health/sanitary conditions*); une détérioration des **services sanitaires** dans ce pays (*health service*); SEE ALSO **schéma**

sans-abri (*nmf*): Soudan: plus d'un million de **sans-abri** à Khartoum (*homeless person*)

sans-emploi (*nmf*): au total, 16 millions de **sans-emploi** dans les pays de la CE (*unemployed person*)

sans-papiers (*nmf*): des **sans-papiers** africains occupent la mairie du 18e arrondissement (*illegal immigrant*)

santé (*nf*): le **système de santé gratuit** est également menacé (*free health service*)

Sàrl (*nf*): l'Assemblée générale de la **Sàrl** *Le Monde*; il n'y a ni conseil d'administration ni P-DG dans une **société à responsabilité limitée [Sàrl]** (*private limited company*)

satisfaction (*nf*): le décret du 27 juin vient de leur **donner satisfaction** (*satisfy*); SEE ALSO **mitigé, non-satisfaction**

satisfaire (*vt*): les candidats doivent **satisfaire** à certaines conditions (*fulfil, satisfy*)

satisfecit (*nm*): [*fig*] OCDE: **satisfecit** à l'économie française (*glowing report; commendation*); Washington **décerne des satisfecit** à l'OLP (*commend, congratulate*)

saupoudrage (*nm*): le problème ne pourra être résolu par un **saupoudrage de mesures** (*series of small measures*)

sauvage (*adj*): l'immigration **sauvage** ou clandestine (*uncontrolled; unrestricted*); SEE ALSO **grève, concurrence**

sauvegarde (*nf*): garantissant ainsi la **sauvegarde** de 85 emplois (*protection, saving*); **veiller à la sauvegarde** des intérêts vitaux européens (*safeguard, protect*)

sauvetage (*nm*): mettre au point un **plan de sauvetage** (*rescue plan*)

savoir (*nm*): recentrer les programmes scolaires sur les **savoirs** essentiels (*knowledge, learning*); un musée du **savoir-faire** artisanal (*skill*); les usines du tiers-monde offrent des débouchés aux exportateurs d'équipements et de **savoir-faire** (*know-how, expertise*)

scander (*vt*): les manifestants **scandaient des slogans** (*shout/chant [political] slogans*)

scénario (*nm*): le même **scénario** est en train de se reproduire (*scenario, pattern of events*); trois **scénarios** peuvent être envisagés (*possibility, eventuality*)

schéma (*nm*): les Pays de la Loire adoptent un **schéma régional** d'aménagement des transports (*outline regional plan*); Bretagne: le **schéma sanitaire régional** inquiète élus et professionnels (*regional health plan*)

scinder [se] (*vpr*): le PC lituanien **s'est scindé** en deux factions (*split*)

scission (*nf*): cette décision entraîna une **scission** au sein du parti (*split*); les socialistes refusent l'union de la gauche et **font scission** (*split, secede*)

scolaire (*adj/nmf*): SEE **cursus, échec, effectif, établissement, rythme**

scolariser (*vt*): une famille avec cinq **enfants scolarisés** (*children at school/receiving an education*); les jeunes **scolarisés dans les filières techniques** (*receiving a technical education*)

scolarité (*nf*): terminer sa **scolarité** sans diplôme (*schooling, education*); payer les **frais de scolarité** de ses enfants (*school fees*)

scrutin (*nm*): le nouveau **scrutin** impose un regroupement des partis (*vote, ballot*); les prochaines élections se feront selon le **mode de scrutin** actuel (*electoral voting system*); le **scrutin de liste** dans le cadre de la représentation proportionnelle (*list system [for elections]*); SEE ALSO **dépouiller, régularité, rétablir, tour, uninominal**

séance (*nf*): au terme de cinq **séances de négociations** (*negotiating session*); six mois de travaux marqués par 37 **séances de travail** (*working session*); lors des **séances plénières** suivantes (*plenary session*)

sécession (*nf*): l'indépendance ne signifie pas la **sécession** (*secession*); Yougoslavie: le PC slovène **fait sécession** (*secede*)

sécheresse (*nf*): intervenir en faveur des victimes de la **sécheresse** (*drought*)

secouer (*vt*): les militants ont été fortement **secoués**; la crise politique qui **secoue** la Russie (*shake*)

secourir (*vt*): on chiffre à 2 500 les personnes officiellement **secourues** (*aid, help*)

secours (*nm*): le **Secours populaire [français]** cherche des bénévoles (*French charity organization giving help to the poor*)

sectaire (*adj/nmf*): un Islam de plus en plus **sectaire** (*intolerant, fanatical*); un féminisme **sectaire** et dépassé (*narrow-minded*); c'était un **sectaire**, mais qui savait se montrer conciliant (*doctrinaire*)

sectarisme (*nm*): le danger que ce **sectarisme** fait courir à l'unité du pays; un puissant lobby qui se distingue par son **sectarisme** (*sectarianism; intolerance*)

secteur (*nm*): les **secteurs** les plus touchés: la poste, l'enseignement (*area, sector*); SEE ALSO **privé, public, ratisser, valoriser**

section (*nf*): dans les **sections** et les fédérations du Parti socialiste (*local grouping*); patronat et **section syndicale [d'entreprise]** sont accusés de complicité dans la mauvaise gestion de l'entreprise (*trade-union representation within the workplace*)

sectoriel, -ielle (*adj*): les crises **sectorielles** sont de plus en plus aiguës (*sector-based*)

séculaire (*adj*): c'est une tradition **séculaire** dans ce pays (*ancient; time-honoured*); les **haines séculaires** entre Allemands et Polonais renaissent (*centuries-old hatred*)

sécuriser (*vt*): la loi aura pour conséquence de **sécuriser** les immigrés (*give a sense of security to*)

sécuritaire (*adj*): la droite exploite l'argument **sécuritaire** (*law and order*); la **question sécuritaire** figure en bonne place dans les manifestes des partis (*law and order issues*)

sécurité (*nf*): la **sécurité** de la détention des grands criminels (*security*); un projet de loi sur la **sécurité**; la maîtrise de la **sécurité publique** (*public safety; public order*); la **sécurité de l'emploi** sera un des principaux enjeux de l'élection (*job security*); SEE ALSO **dispositif, jouir**

séduire (*vt*): cette idée **séduit** les conservateurs (*attract; win over*); un atout important pour **séduire la clientèle** (*attract customers/custom*)

séduisant, -e (*adj*): une perspective **séduisante** pour les petits investisseurs (*attractive*)

seing (*nm*): l'acte de vente peut être établi **sous seing privé** (*as a private agreement/simple contract*); inculpé de **blanc seing** et de faux en écritures privées (*putting one's signature to a blank document*)

séjour (*nm*): les conditions d'entrée et de **séjour** des étrangers en France (*residence*); des personnes âgées accueillies dans des **unités de long séjour** (*long-stay unit*); SEE ALSO **autorisation, délivrer, interdire, taxe, titre**

séjourner (*vi*): perdre le droit de **séjourner** en France (*stay*)

sélection (*nf*): en France, la **sélection** s'effectue sur dossier scolaire (*selection; selective entry*)

sellette (*nf*): [*fig*] déjà **sur la sellette** à propos d'histoires de pots-de-vin (*coming under attack; in the hot seat*); la révision des listes électorales **sur la sellette** (*undergoing reappraisal*)

semaine (*nf*): EDF et GDF proposent la **semaine** de 32 heures à leurs agents (*[working] week*); pratiquer la **semaine anglaise** (*five-day [working] week*)

semestre (*nm*): la société a enregistré de très bons résultats pour le premier **semestre** (*half-year, six-month period*)

semestriel, -ielle (*adj*): SEE **bénéfice**

semonce (*nf*): [*fig*] adresser une **verte semonce** à ceux qui perdaient l'espoir (*strong reprimand*); ces abstentions constituent un **coup de semonce** pour le gouvernement (*warning shot, shot across the bows*)

sénat (*nm*): le **Sénat**, la Chambre haute du parlement français (*Senate*)

sénateur (*nm*): ancien Premier ministre, **sénateur maire** de Lille (*senator and mayor*)

sénatorial, -e, *pl* **-aux** (*adj*): membre de plusieurs **commissions sénatoriales** (*senate committee*); (*nfpl*): les **sénatoriales** ont lieu tous les trois ans (*elections to the Senate*)

sens (*nm*): envoyer une lettre **en ce sens** (*to this effect*); les autres pays ont fait savoir qu'ils **iraient dans le même sens** (*do likewise; follow*); tout cela **va dans le sens de l'apaisement** (*is a move in the direction of reconciliation*); SEE ALSO **abonder, argumenter**

sensation (*nf*): SEE **presse**

sensibilisation (*nf*): un problème de **sensibilisation des jeunes** (*increasing awareness among the young*)

sensibiliser (*vt*): il faut **sensibiliser l'opinion publique** à l'intérêt de la question (*heighten public awareness*)

sensibilité (*nf*): des parlementaires **de toutes sensibilités** (*of all parties, of all shades of opinion*); les **sensibilités de gauche** ou d'extrême gauche (*left-wing opinion*)

sensible (*adj*): la question étant électoralement **sensible** (*delicate, sensitive*); un autre **dossier sensible** (*sensitive subject*); une réduction **sensible** des effectifs (*marked, appreciable*)

sensiblement (*adv*): la retraite à 60 ans n'a pas **sensiblement** abaissé l'âge réel de cessation d'activité (*significantly, markedly, appreciably*)

sentence (*nf*): le choix entre les différentes **sentences** possibles (*sentence*); la **sentence a été rendue**: la mort (*pronounce/pass sentence*); SEE ALSO **exécution**

séparation (*nf*): les parents étaient **en instance de séparation** (*in the middle of separation proceedings*); les époux mariés sous le régime de la **séparation de biens** (*matrimonial division of property*); la **séparation de corps** dispense les époux du devoir de cohabitation sans rompre les liens du mariage (*legal separation*)

séparatiste (*adj/nmf*): le principal **mouvement séparatiste** corse (*separatist movement*); régionalistes, mais se défendant d'être **séparatistes** (*separatist*)

séparé, -e (*adj*): chez les SDF, il y a beaucoup de divorcés et de **séparés** (*[person] separated from partner/spouse*)

séparer [se] (*vpr*): lorsque les parents divorcent ou **se séparent** (*split up, separate*); le conseil **s'est séparé** sans être arrivé à voter aucun des projets (*split up; break up*); Thomson **se sépare de ses activités financières** (*sell off its financial interests*)

septennat (*nm*): la fin du **septennat** s'approche (*seven-year period of office*)

septentrional, -e, *pl* **-aux** (*adj*): SEE **frontière**

séquestre (*nm*): demander la **mise sous séquestre** de ces actions vendues illégalement (*confiscation, impounding*)

séquestrer (*vt*): en son absence, tous ses biens furent **séquestrés** (*sequester; impound*)

serein, -e (*adj*): les autres pays ont des raisons de rester **sereins** (*calm; confident, optimistic*)

sérénité (*nf*): appeler à la **sérénité** dans le débat sur le port du foulard islamique (*calm, reason; moderation*); le débat doit être mené **dans la sérénité** (*calmly, dispassionately*)

série (*nf*): la **construction en série** n'est pas prévue avant janvier (*mass production*); **limogeages en série**: 20 responsables mis à l'écart (*a large number of dismissals*); SEE ALSO **fabriquer**

serment (*nm*): prononcer un **serment d'allégeance** à la couronne (*oath of allegiance*); SEE ALSO **prestation, prêter**

serré, -e (*adj*): au terme d'un scrutin **serré** (*tight, close-fought*); une **négociation serrée** se joue dans les coulisses (*hard bargaining*); une concurrence acharnée et des **prix serrés** (*keen prices*)

serrer (*vt*): **serrer** étroitement les dépenses (*cut, reduce*); une stratégie pour **serrer les coûts de production** (*cut/squeeze production costs*)

service (*nm*): tout dépend du **service** dans lequel on travaille (*department; section*); les **activités de service** ne cessent de s'étendre (*service industries; tertiary sector*); effectuer son **service national** dès l'âge de seize ans (*national/military service*); (*pl*) les **services** en ont été les principaux bénéficiaires (*services, service industries*); SEE ALSO **exempt, prestataire, prestation, sanitaire**

servitude (*nf*): le **droit de servitude**, c'est-à-dire l'obligation de laisser le passage sur son terrain; compte tenu des **servitudes de passage** de la RATP (*easement; right of way*)

session (*nf*): le projet de loi sera présenté au Parlement **à la session de printemps** (*in the spring session*)

seuil (*nm*): le **seuil de tolérance** a été largement dépassé (*threshold of tolerance*); des personnes dont les ressources sont inférieures au **seuil de pauvreté** (*poverty threshold*); le **seuil d'imposition** est très bas: 250 000F par personne (*tax threshold*); décider le **seuil de rentabilité** (*break-even point*)

sévices (*nmpl*): les **sévices** subis par les femmes (*violence, ill-treatment*); soupçonnés d'avoir **exercé des sévices** sur leurs enfants (*ill-treat*); on ignore si la fillette a **subi des sévices sexuels** (*be subjected to sexual abuse*)

sévir (*vi*): l'ampleur de la crise qui **sévit** dans l'ex-Union soviétique (*be rife; hold sway*); motos sur le trottoir: la police va **sévir**; le gouvernement va devoir **sévir durement** (*crack down; come down heavily*)

sexe (*nm*): SEE **discrimination**

sexuel, -elle (*adj*): SEE **abus, agression, harcèlement, sévices, vagabondage, violence**

siège (*nm*): perdre son **siège** de conseiller général aux élections cantonales (*seat*); au **siège** du quartier-général des forces armées (*headquarters*); les Éts Duforge ont désormais leur **siège social** à Lyon (*head office; registered office*); SEE ALSO **emporter**

siéger (*vi*): le Parlement européen **siège** à Strasbourg (*sit, meet*); il **siège dans l'opposition** (*sit on the Opposition benches*); les représentants des syndicats et de l'administration y **siègent à parité** (*are represented in equal numbers*)

signalement (*nm*): les photos et **signalements** des deux malfaiteurs (*description*)

signature (*nf*): la **signature** officielle du cessez-le-feu (*signing*); 25 000 **signatures** ont été recueillies (*signature*)

signe (*nm*): l'université d'été du RPR **est placée sous le signe du rassemblement** (*has unity as its theme*)

signer (*vt*): SEE **persister**

significatif, -ive (*adj*): on a constaté une amélioration **significative** (*significant*)

simple (*adj/nm*): selon le quartier, **le prix peut varier du simple au double** (*the price can be twice as high*); SEE ALSO **majorité**

sinistre (*nm*): on ne peut pas déclarer plus d'un **sinistre** par an (*accident; damage*); le **sinistre** a été rapidement maîtrisé (*fire*); SEE ALSO **déclaration**

sinistré, -e (*adj/nm,f*): les **régions sinistrées** par la sécheresse (*disaster-stricken areas*); la reconversion des sites sidérurgiques **sinistrés** (*stricken; depressed*); plusieurs communes du Doubs sont déclarées **zone sinistrée** (*disaster area*); l'aide aux **sinistrés** (*disaster victim; homeless [after flood/earthquake]*)

sinistrose (*nf*): après l'unification allemande, **sinistrose** à l'Est (*doom and gloom; pessimism*)

site (*nm*): Bull ferme son **site** de Franche-Comté; l'entreprise, qui comprend deux **sites**, à Lille et à Douai (*factory, operation*) SEE also **fermeture**

situation (*nf*): SEE **irrégulier, pourrir**

situer [se] (*vpr*): la véritable alternative **se situe** ailleurs (*be found, reside*); **où l'Europe se situe-t-elle** dans ce conflit? (*where does Europe stand?*)

SMIC (*nm*): le **SMIC** [salaire minimum interprofessionnel de croissance] est indexé sur l'évolution des prix (*[in France] national minimum wage*)

smicard, -e (*nm,f*): [fam] les **smicards** ont leur salaire indexé sur l'évolution des prix (*[in France] minimum wage earner*)

social, -e, *pl* **-aux** (*adj*): à l'issue d'une semaine sociale agitée (*a week in which social issues loomed large*); cette **Europe** sociale qu'appelle de ses vœux le Président (*a Europe of social justice*); SEE ALSO **accompagnement, action, agitation, aide, animation, capital, cas, charge, cohésion, conflit, couverture, fracture, inadaptation, inégalité, justice, logement, mouvement, plan, prestation, promotion, protection, travailleur, volet**

sociétaire (*nmf*): la mutuelle regroupe 1 260 000 **sociétaires** (*member [of club/association]*)

société (*nf*): les rapports complexes entre les enseignants et la **société civile** (*society [as a whole]*); une entreprise d'État transformée en **société anonyme** (*public company*); SEE ALSO **capital, consommation, impôt, joint venture, problème, réinsérer**

soin (*nm*): le Portugal veut privatiser son **système de soins** (*health care/ medical treatment system*); SEE ALSO **gratuité**

sol (*nm*): un étranger expulsé du **sol français** peut faire appel (*French soil/territory*); le **droit du sol**: tout enfant né sur le territoire français est citoyen français (jus soli; *right of nationality by birth within that country*); SEE ALSO **occupation**

solde (*nm*): le **solde** doit être réglé un an plus tard (*balance; remainder; sum outstanding*); le **solde déficitaire** ce mois-ci dans l'industrie; 20 000 postes supprimés et 7 000 créés, soit un **solde négatif** de 13 000 (*negative balance; deficit*); (*nf*): une **solde** correcte et des conditions de vie décentes (*pay [military]*); des meneurs professionnels **à la solde de l'OLP** (*in the pay of the PLO*); SEE ALSO **congé**

solder (*vt*): des sommes utilisées pour **solder** les dettes de la campagne électorale (*discharge, settle, pay off*); il leur faudra bien un jour **solder ce contentieux** (*settle the dispute*); [se] (*vpr*): [*fig*] l'affrontement **s'était soldé par** la mort de trois soldats; le scrutin **se solda par** un succès inattendu de la gauche (*result in*)

solidaire (*adj*): les médecins d'hôpital **sont solidaires des revendications des infirmières** (*support the nurses' demands*)

solidariser [se] (*vpr*): ils **se solidarisent** tous avec leurs collègues moins fortunés (*make common cause; sympathize with*)

solidarité (*nf*): ministre des Affaires sociales et de la **solidarité** (*national solidarity*); renoncer à certains avantages, **au nom de la solidarité** (*to show solidarity [with others]*)

sollicitation (*nf*): faire parvenir votre **lettre de sollicitation** le plus rapidement possible (*letter of application*)

solliciter (*vt*): il **sollicitera** aux élections de mars un troisième mandat (*seek; ask for*); la Grande-Bretagne, **sollicitée d'y participer**, réserve sa réponse (*asked to join/participate*); éviter les filières **les plus sollicitées** (*the most popular/in demand*)

solution (*nf*): il n'y a pas de **solution de rechange** à la coopération franco-allemande (*alernative, alternative solution*); avoir une **solution de repli** en cas d'échec (*fall-back solution*); SEE ALSO **adapté**

solutionner (*vt*): une question **qui n'est pas près d'être solutionnée** (*which is not close to being solved*)

solvabilité (*nf*): les problèmes de **solvabilité** des familles les plus démunies (*solvency, creditworthiness*)

solvable (*adj*): les banques prêtent de préférence à des débiteurs **solvables** (*solvent, creditworthy*)

sommation (*nf*): recevoir une **sommation** de quitter les lieux (*demand; injunction*); le policier aurait tiré **sans sommation** (*without giving a warning*)

somme (*nf*): SEE **forfaitaire, modique**

sommer (*vt*): un ultimatum **sommant** les étrangers de quitter le pays (*order, instruct*); **être sommé** de se présenter (*be ordered/instructed*)

sommet (*nm*): après le **sommet** franco-allemand de Dijon (*summit [meeting]*); une série de **sommets restreints** entre pays arabes (*mini-summit*)

sondage (*nm*): les **sondages d'opinion** lui donnent un avantage de 9 points (*opinion poll, survey*)

sondé, -e (*adj/nm,f*): 31% des **sondés** se déclarent prêts à abandonner leur droit de grève (*person questioned in opinion poll; responder*)

sonder (*vt*): on a **sondé** toutes les catégories de personnel (*canvass, poll the opinion of*)

sortant, -e (*adj/nm*): l'équipe municipale **sortante** se représentera (*retiring, outgoing*); élections en Martinique: le PS reconduit ses **sortants** (*sitting member, incumbent*)

sortie (*nf*): pas de **sortie de récession** sans une croissance rapide de la consommation (*end of the recession*); avant même sa **sortie en librairie** (*publication [of book]*); SEE ALSO **visa**

sortir (*vi*): SEE **attribution, compétence, indemne**

souche (*nf*): nos compatriotes de **souche** nord-africaine (*origin, stock*); la moitié des pieds-noirs n'étaient pas **de souche française** (*of French extraction; French born and bred*)

souci (*nm*): le **souci** du parti de se présenter comme le défenseur du peuple (*concern, desire, intention*)

soucier [se] (*vpr*): sans avertir ses alliés ni **se soucier** des réactions du Congrès (*care/be concerned*)

soucieux, -ieuse (*adj*): les États-Unis, **soucieux de** promouvoir la stabilité des taux de change (*concerned/anxious to*); on est **soucieux de** ses possibles effets négatifs sur la démocratie (*concerned about*)

souffrance (*nf*): beaucoup de problèmes restent **en souffrance** (*pending*); conséquence de la grève des postes: activité ralentie, **créances en souffrance** (*payments backlog*)

soulèvement (*nm*): la tentative de **soulèvement** avortée de mercredi dernier (*uprising*)

soulever (*vt*): en dépit de l'émotion que **soulève** cette affaire (*arouse; excite*); **soulever** le problème du monopole (*raise, bring up*); [se] (*vpr*): le peuple est prêt à **se soulever** contre le dictateur (*rise up*)

soumettre (*vt*): on **soumet** le peuple à des pressions intolérables (*subject*); **être soumis aux** restrictions du pays où on vit (*be subject to/bound by*); le plan **sera soumis au Parlement** au printemps (*be put before Parliament*); [se] (*vpr*): le préfet est tenu de **se soumettre à l'avis de la commission** (*obey the committee's ruling*)

soumis, -e (*adj*): le régime, **soumis** à des pressions venues de l'extérieur (*subject/subjected to*); tous les contribuables **soumis à l'impôt sur la fortune** (*liable for wealth tax*); SEE ALSO **quota**

souple (*adj*): avec des conditions très **souples** de durée et de taux (*flexible*); il a invité les deux pays à **se montrer plus souples** dans la négociation (*be more flexible*)

souplesse (*nf*): le patronat n'entend pas renoncer à cette **souplesse** (*flexibility*)

source (*nf*): **selon de bonnes sources**, Washington y serait favorable (*according to reliable sources*); l'ISF impose la fortune **à la source** (*at source*); SEE ALSO **prélèvement, retenir, retenue**

souscripteur, -trice (*nm,f*): la liste des **souscripteurs** s'allonge (*contributor, subscriber*); 70 millions de titres achetés par 270 000 **petits souscripteurs** (*small investor*); une bonne nouvelle pour les **souscripteurs d'une assurance-vie** (*life-insurance policyholder*)

souscrire (*vt*): être disposé à **souscrire** un contrat de vente (*sign [esp. contract]*); dans l'état actuel du plan, nous ne pouvons y **souscrire** (*subscribe/give one's approval to*)

sous-préfecture (*nf*): Thionville, chef-lieu d'arrondissement et **sous-préfecture** (*sub-prefecture, administrative subdivision of French département*)

sous-préfet (*nm*): nommé **sous-préfet** dans la Sarthe; le **sous-préfet**, représentant de l'État dans l'arrondissement (*sub-prefect; ministerial representative in French arrondissement*)

sous-traitance (*nf*): développer des activités de **sous-traitance** (*subcontracting*)

sous-traiter (*vt*): la firme **sous-traitait** plus de 70% des travaux à une firme anglaise (*subcontract, contract [work] out*)

soutenir (*vt*): Tripoli aurait promis de ne pas **soutenir** les islamistes algériens (*give support to, help*); les dépenses consacrées à **soutenir les prix agricoles** dans la CE (*support agricultural prices*); **soutenir** le contraire (*argue, maintain*)

soutenu, -e (*adj*): la demande reste **soutenue** (*buoyant; sustained*)

soutien (*nm*): l'Occident, qui est le **soutien** d'Israël (*support, mainstay*); les dépenses communautaires affectées au **soutien du lait** (*price support for dairy products*); une réduction de 30% des **soutiens agricoles** (*agricultural support payments*); SEE ALSO **acquérir**

souverain, -e (*adj/nm,f*): la principauté de Monaco est un État **souverain** (*sovereign*)

souveraineté (*nf*): permettre au peuple le plein exercice de sa **souveraineté** (*sovereignty*); SEE ALSO **abandon, délégation**

sponsor (*nm*): la liste des **sponsors** du Parti républicain (*sponsor*)

sponsorat (*nm*): de plus en plus d'entreprises se convertissent au **sponsorat** (*sponsorship*)

sponsoriser (*vt*): parrainer, ou **sponsoriser,** des épreuves sportives (*sponsor*); **se faire sponsoriser** par un grand brasseur australien (*obtain [commercial] sponsorship*)

spot (*nm*): les **spots publicitaires** sont le dernier cri en matière de publicité médiatique (*advertising slot*)

stage (*nm*): accomplir un **stage professionnel** de six mois (*vocational training course*); prévoir un **stage en entreprise** (*work experience/placement*); le développement des **stages d'insertion à la vie professionnelle** (*work-placement scheme*); SEE ALSO **formation**

stagiaire (*nmf*): un poste de **stagiaire** (*in-house trainee; probationer*)

statuer (*vi*): en dernier ressort, ce sera le tribunal qui **statuera** sur ce litige (*try [a case]; rule, give a ruling*); les juges **statuent cas par cas** (*give an individual ruling in each case*)

statut (*nm*): la nouvelle loi sur le **statut** du personnel des collectivités locales (*status*); le **statut juridique** des syndicats est bien établi (*legal status*); les syndicats doivent déposer leurs **statuts** et les noms de leurs administrateurs (*articles of association*); SEE ALSO **revalorisation**

structure (*nf*): il n'existe aucune **structure** permanente pour accueillir les exclus (*facility; organization*); le ministre a visité une **structure d'accueil** pour personnes âgées (*shelter, refuge*); ouverture d'une nouvelle **structure d'accueil des jeunes enfants** (*nursery; facility for young children*)

structurel, -elle (*adj*): ne pas confondre le conjoncturel et le **structurel** (*structural; underlying*)

stupéfiant (*nm*): la législation draconienne sur les **stupéfiants** (*drug, narcotic*); l'affaire a été confiée à la **brigade des stupéfiants** (*drugs squad*)

subalterne (*adj*): un soulèvement d'officiers **subalternes**; passer quelques années dans des emplois **subalternes** (*junior, low-ranking*)

subir (*vt*): **subir** un contrôle d'identité (*undergo, be subjected to*); **subir** un préjudice (*suffer*); la ville a **subi quelques dégâts** (*suffer/sustain damage*); **subir une concurrence féroce** d'une société hongroise (*face fierce competition*); SEE ALSO **déroute, moins-value, sévices**

subornation (*nf*): la tentative de **subornation de témoin** dont il a fait l'objet (*bribing a witness*)

suborner (*vt*): essayer de **suborner** le témoin principal (*bribe*)

subside (*nm*): les travailleurs sans emploi ne bénéficient d'aucun **subside** (*grant, allowance*); recevoir aides et **subsides** de Paris (*grants; subsidies*)

subsidiarité (*nf*): appliquer le principe de la **subsidiarité** (*subsidiarity*)

substitut (*nm*): le **substitut**, spécialement détaché à la section anti-terroriste (*deputy public prosecutor*)

substitution (*nf*): SEE **maternité, peine**

subvenir (*vt*): incapables de **subvenir** à leurs besoins alimentaires (*satisfy, provide for*); des pays incapables de **subvenir à leurs propres besoins** (*be self-sufficient*)

subvention (*nf*): on débattra à Bruxelles des **subventions à l'agriculture** (*agricultural subsidies*)

subventionner (*vt*): l'État **subventionne** le gros œuvre, la municipalité se charge du reste (*subsidize*); l'agriculture est très largement **subventionnée** (*subsidized*)

succéder (*vt*): le ministre des Affaires étrangères **succède au** président à la tête du parti (*succeed, take over [from]*); [se] (*vpr*): il compte bien **se succéder à lui-même** (*be re-elected; be returned to office*)

succession (*nf*): une **succession** de crises politiques (*succession, series*); un impôt progressif sur les **successions** (*inheritance*); 80% des héritiers ne paient aucun **droit de succession** (*inheritance tax; death duty*); SEE ALSO **candidat, pressenti**

succursale (*nf*): les banques vont-elles fermer leurs **succursales** dans les petites communes? (*branch; agency*); SEE ALSO **magasin**

suffrage (*nm*): s'il veut rallier les **suffrages** des centristes (*vote*); le chef de l'État est élu au **suffrage universel** (*universal suffrage*); SEE ALSO **dépouillement**

suite (*nf*): décider la **suite à donner** à ces propositions; le parquet décidera des **suites à donner** à l'affaire (*action to be taken*); l'acheteur ou le propriétaire peut ne pas **donner suite** (*continue, proceed, take a matter further*); SEE ALSO **classer**

suivi, -e (*adj/nm*): mouvement de grève **peu suivi** (*poorly supported*); la mise en chantier et le **suivi** des travaux (*monitoring*); la mise en place d'un véritable **suivi médical** des sportifs (*medical monitoring*); des frais supplémentaires pour le **suivi du courrier** (*forwarding of mail*)

suivre (*vt*): les enfants **sont suivis sur le plan médical** (*receive health care*)

sujet, -ette (*adj/nm*): les nouvelles en provenance de Pékin sont **sujettes à caution** (*unreliable; unconfirmed*); un **sujet** qui en 1994 était d'une brûlante actualité (*issue, question*); SEE ALSO **conflictuel**

supercherie (*nf*): les documents étaient des **supercheries** (*fake*); sept personnes sont inculpées pour avoir participé à la **supercherie** (*deception, deceit*)

suppléance (*nf*): un enseignant qui préfère **faire des suppléances** (*do supply teaching*); il avait refusé la **suppléance de député** qui lui était offerte (*position of running mate in elections to parliament*)

suppléant, -e (*adj/nm,f*): le **suppléant** à l'Assemblée du secrétaire d'État à la Jeunesse et aux Sports (*replacement, stand-in*); être remplacé par un **juge suppléant** non professionnel (*replacement/stand-in judge*)

suppléer (*vt*): **suppléer** un professeur absent pour cause de maladie (*replace, stand in/supply for*)

supplétif, -ive (*adj/nm*): l'armée populaire, un **corps de supplétifs** de l'armée régulière (*reservist corps*)

suppression (*nf*): la **suppression** des subventions gouvernementales (*abolition*); on redoute des **suppressions massives d'emplois** (*massive job losses*)

supprimer (*vt*): plus de 350 **emplois supprimés** chez Michelin (*job cuts*)

surcapacité (*nf*): il faut réduire une **surcapacité** de 20% et des prix trop élevés de 25% (*excess productive capacity*); la sidérurgie est **en surcapacité** de 30 millions de tonnes (*in a situation of overcapacity*)

surchauffe (*nf*): une reprise de l'inflation, due à une **surchauffe de l'économie** (*overheating of the economy*)

surcoût (*nm*): le **surcoût** sera très important pour les petites entreprises; le **surcoût** résultant de l'abaissement de l'âge de la retraite (*additional cost*)

surcroît (*nm*): le **surcroît de travail** que cela occasionnerait (*additional workload*); bénéficier d'un **surcroît de crédits** (*extra/additional funds*)

sureffectif (*nm*): la chasse aux **sureffectifs** (*overmanning; surplus staff/labour*); des entreprises déjà **en sureffectifs** (*overstaffed, overmanned*)

surenchère (*nf*): préparer une **surenchère** à l'offre de l'industriel australien (*higher bid*); la CGT, vite dépassée par la **surenchère de la base** (*increasing demands from the rank and file*); les syndicats **font de la surenchère** (*make exaggerated demands*)

surenchérir (*vi*): obligé de **surenchérir**, ou de renoncer à son OPA (*raise the bid/offer; raise the stakes*)

surendetté, -e (*adj*): 10% des ménages **surendettés** disposent de revenus inférieurs au SMIC (*heavily in debt*)

surendettement (*nm*): le **surendettement**, un phénomène qui touche plus de 100 000 ménages (*overborrowing; debt burden*)

surendetter [se] (*vpr*): pouvoir rembourser sans se **surendetter** (*get heavily into debt*)

sûreté (*nf*): vers un accord sur la **sûreté** des centrales nucléaires (*safety*); des atteintes à la **sûreté de l'État** (*state security*); les policiers de la **Sûreté** urbaine de Strasbourg (*French criminal investigation department*); le créancier demande des **sûretés**, des garanties supplémentaires de paiement (*guarantee; security*); condamné à quinze ans de réclusion **avec une période de sûreté de dix ans** (*with no release before ten years of sentence have been served*)

surévaluation (*nf*): la raison de cette dégradation: la **surévaluation** du dollar (*overvaluation*)

surévaluer (*vt*): la livre sterling est **surévaluée** par rapport au mark (*overvalue*)

surface (*nf*): les **grandes surfaces** alimentaires dominent le marché (*large store; hypermarket*)

surimposer (*vt*): le fisc l'a **surimposé** deux années de suite; la nécessité de ne pas **surimposer** les artisans et les commerçants (*overtax*)

surimposition (*nf*): ayant payé une **surimposition**, il aura droit à un abattement sur la prochaine imposition (*excess tax*)

surnombre (*nm*): le problème du **surnombre** auquel fait face l'administration pénitentiaire; le problème des 1 500 salariés **en surnombre** (*excess, surplus*)

surpeuplé, -e (*adj*): les prisons toujours **surpeuplées**; allant de squats miteux à studios **surpeuplés** (*overcrowded*)

surpeuplement (*nm*): les gardiens sont les premières victimes du **surpeuplement carcéral** (*prison overcrowding*)

surpopulation (*nf*): le combat contre la **surpopulation des prisons** (*prison overcrowding*)

surprime (*nf*): pas de **surprime** pour les conducteurs novices; un aménagement de cette clause vous coûtera une **surprime** (*extra/excess insurance premium*)

sursaut (*nm*): un brusque **sursaut** de la livre sterling (*sharp rise*)

surseoir (*vi*): le maire a accepté de **surseoir à sa décision** (*defer/suspend his decision*); c'est au Président de recommander que l'on **surseoie à l'exécution** des deux condamnés à mort (*grant a stay of execution*)

sursis (*nm*): aboutissant en général à des **peines de prison avec sursis** (*suspended prison sentence*); les jeunes Français peuvent bénéficier d'un **sursis d'incorporation** (*deferment of military call-up*); **sursis à exécution** de l'arrêté d'expulsion (*temporary reprieve; stay of execution*)

sursitaire (*adj/nm*): en tant que **sursitaire**, il fera son service militaire plus tard (*deferred conscript*)

surveillance (*nf*): sous la **surveillance étroite** du ministère de la Santé (*close supervision/monitoring*); attaché à la **Direction de la surveillance du territoire [DST]** (*French counter-intelligence agency*); se transformer en société à **conseil de surveillance** et directoire (*supervisory board*)

surveillé, -e (*adj*): SEE **liberté, résidence**

survie (*nf*): se battre pour la **survie** de la langue; la **survie** du gouvernement, de plus en plus problématique (*survival*)

sus (*adv*): **sus** aux illettrés (*away with!; an end to!*)

susciter (*vt*): un discours qui a **suscité bien des controverses** (*cause/give rise to much controversy*); SEE ALSO **émoi**

sympathisant, -e (*nm,f*): affrontements entre manifestants de l'opposition et **sympathisants** du gouvernement; comment transformer les **sympathisants** en adhérents? (*sympathizer, supporter*)

syndic (*nm*): pour la reprise de la société, les **syndics** se sont prononcés pour le groupe belge (*official government receiver*); la mission du **syndic** est d'assurer la gestion de l'immeuble (*tenants' managing agent*)

syndical, -e, pl -aux (*adj*): la délégation **syndicale** CGT-CFDT (*[trade] union*); SEE ALSO **central, confédération, délégué, responsable, réticence, section**

syndicalisation (*nf*): avec le taux de **syndicalisation** le plus faible d'Europe (*union membership; unionization*)

syndicat (*nm*): les co-propriétaires groupés en un **syndicat** (*association*); de moins en moins de Français appartiennent à un **syndicat ouvrier** (*trade union*)

syndiqué, -e (*adj/nm,f*): en 1979, les **syndiqués** y étaient encore au nombre de 12 millions (*member of a trade union*)

syndiquer [se] (*vpr*): les femmes de 30 à 40 ans **se syndiquent** plus fréquemment que leurs aînées (*join a union*)

synergie (*nf*): [*fig*] une véritable **synergie** entre le commerce, les affaires et les loisirs; on voit s'esquisser des **synergies** entre les deux villes (*synergy; complementarity*)

système (*nm*): SEE **santé, soin**

T

tabac (*nm*): le **passage à tabac** de jeunes immigrés et autres bavures (*beating [up]; handling roughly [esp. by police]*); deux policiers, accusés d'avoir **passé à tabac** trois suspects (*treat roughly, beat up*); SEE ALSO **bureau**

tabagisme (*nm*): la lutte contre le **tabagisme** engagée par le gouvernement (*addiction to tobacco*)

table (*nf*): retourner à la **table de négociation** (*negotiating table*); une **table ronde** entre pouvoirs publics, syndicats et élus (*round-table talks*); on ne saurait **faire table rase** de la législation sociale du gouvernement sortant (*sweep away*); SEE ALSO **tour**

tableau, *pl* -**x** (*nm*): des cartes et des **tableaux** comparatifs (*table, chart*)

tabler (*vi*): les experts **tablent sur** une baisse des prix des céréales de l'ordre de 15% (*assume, expect; count upon*)

taille (*nf*): la seule société française **de taille** européenne (*of European size/stature*); SEE ALSO **enjeu**

tailler (*vi*): il faudrait **tailler dans les aides** à l'emploi (*make big cuts in the social programmes*); [se] (*vpr*): **se tailler** une réputation d'incorruptible (*secure/gain for oneself*); lors des élections le RPR **s'est taillé la part du lion** (*gain the lion's share of seats/votes*)

tampon (*nm*): SEE **zone**

tapage (*nm*): une politique menée **sans tapage** et loin des objectifs des caméras de télévision (*without fuss; unostentatiously*); à l'écart du **tapage médiatique** (*media hype*); le **tapage nocturne** et autres troubles de voisinage (*disturbance of the peace [at night]*)

tarder (*vi*): si le gouvernement **tarde** à négocier avec les mineurs (*be slow to; delay*); aller de l'avant **sans tarder** (*without delay*)

tardif, -**ive** (*adj*): la mobilisation des lycéens a été **tardive** (*slow; slow in coming*)

tardivement (*adv*): la crise a touché **tardivement** la France (*late*)

tarif (*nm*): les compagnies baissent leurs **tarifs** (*scale of charges; fare*); la guerre des **tarifs aériens** se rallume (*air fare*); les **tarifs douaniers** vont baisser de 40% environ (*customs/tariff duties*); SEE ALSO **hausse, relever**

tarifaire (*adj*): une plus grande souplesse dans le domaine **tarifaire** (*pertaining to prices/charges*)

tarifer (*vt*): le ministre a autorisé les banquiers à **tarifer** les chèques (*make a charge for; fix a price for*)

tarification (*nf*): les banques renoncent à la **tarification** des chèques (*charging for; putting a charge on*); les **tarifications réduites** proposées par la SNCF (*fare reductions*)

tas (*nm*): SEE **former, grève**

tassement (*nm*): hausse des exportations, **tassement** des importations (*drop; fall-off*); un **tassement** de l'activité économique (*downturn, slowdown*)

tasser (*vt*): on a beau **tasser les prix** (*squeeze prices*); [se] (*vpr*): les ventes vers les États-Unis **se sont tassées** en 1990 (*stagnate; slow down*)

taux (*nm*): un secteur à fort **taux d'immigrés** (*with a high immigrant population*); la chute du **taux des naissances** (*birth rate*); une baisse des **taux d'intérêt** (*interest rates*); les banques relèvent leur **taux de base [bancaire]** (*base lending rate; prime rate*); les variations des **taux de change** (*exchange rate*); la Banque du Japon avait abaissé son **taux d'escompte**, taux auquel elle prête aux établissements (*bank rate*); SEE ALSO **abaisser, attractif, dégressif, détente, pratiquer, privilégié, zéro**

taxation (*nf*): un alignement de la **taxation** du gasoil sur celle de l'essence (*taxation, taxing*)

taxe (*nf*): l'augmentation des **taxes sur les carburants** (*fuel tax*); la **taxe d'habitation** payée par tous les occupants d'immeubles (*tax on house occupancy; residence tax*); dans certaines communes, on doit payer une **taxe de séjour** (*tourist tax*); la ville reçoit 1,5 MF de **taxe professionnelle** par an (*local tax levied on business*); SEE ALSO **foncier**

taxer (*vt*): les plus-values sont **taxées** à 15% (*tax*); **se voir taxé** de protectionnisme par les États-Unis (*be accused of*)

tchador (*nm*): le **tchador**, la grande cape noire qui couvre la femme musulmane de la tête aux pieds (*chador*)

témoignage (*nm*): de nouveaux **témoignages** sur les circonstances de la mort des otages (*account, testimony*); recevoir des **témoignages** de soutien et de solidarité (*mark, expression*); ouvrir une information pour **faux témoignage** (*perjury, false witness*)

témoigner (*vi*): et s'il refusait de **témoigner en justice**? (*testify/give evidence in court*); ceci **témoigne de** l'importance que la France attache à ses rapports avec le Maroc (*testify to, reflect*)

témoin (*nm*): l'absence de ce **témoin** crucial pour la défense (*witness*); il y avait deux **témoins à charge** (*prosecution witness*); être requis comme **témoin à décharge** (*defence witness*); SEE ALSO **audition, auditionner, barre, citer, subornation**

temps (*nm*): la réduction programmée du **temps de travail** à 35 heures (*working week*); remplacer des emplois stables par des emplois à **temps partiel** (*part-time*); SEE ALSO **aménager, antenne**

tenant (*nm*): les **tenants** de la ligne dure voulaient proclamer la loi martiale; les **tenants** de l'enseignement confessionnel (*advocate, supporter*)

tendance (*nf*): la **tendance** était à une augmentation annuelle du nombre de chômeurs (*trend*); l'homme de la **tendance dure du parti** (*hardline tendency within the party*); SEE ALSO **renversement**

tendre [se] (*vpr*): les relations entre Washington et Pékin **se sont tendues** (*become strained*)

tendu, -e (*adj*): c'est dans un climat très **tendu** que les discussions ont commencé (*tense*)

tenir [se] (*vpr*): les élections **se tiennent** en juin (*take place*); le gouvernement **s'en tient** à la politique menée en Corée depuis 1988 (*keep to; continue*)

ténor (*nm*): [*fig*] les principaux **ténors** du PS ont pris la parole (*leading personality*)

tension (*nf*): **tension** entre la Chine et les Philippines (*tension*); **la tension s'accroît** entre l'Équateur et le Pérou (*increased tension*); SEE ALSO **foyer, regain**

tentative (*nf*): la mutinerie militaire s'est transformée en **tentative de putsch** (*attempted putsch*); une **tentative de coup d'État** échoua (*attempted coup d'état*)

tenue (*nf*): la **tenue** d'un nouveau scrutin (*holding*); la relative **bonne tenue** du franc suisse (*healthy state; firmness*); policiers **en tenue** et policiers en civil (*uniformed*)

tergiversation (*nf*): de longues **tergiversations** ont précédé l'adoption du projet (*prevarication; shilly-shallying*)

tergiverser (*vi*): Téhéran, après avoir **tergiversé** pour ne pas répondre à l'appel lancé par le Conseil de sécurité (*shilly-shally; play for time*)

terme (*nm*): **mettre un terme** à 40 ans de socialisme (*bring to an end*); son mandat, qui va **venir à terme** en juin (*expire; come to an end*); c'est à **terme** un mariage sur trois qui se terminera par un divorce (*sooner or later; eventually*); **aux termes de la loi,** l'employeur n'est pas obligé de le faire (*according to [the terms of] the law; legally*)

terrain (*nm*): la pénurie de **terrains à bâtir** (*building plot; building land*); la montée en flèche du prix du **terrain agricole** (*agricultural land*); des **terrains vagues** en bordure de la ville (*waste land*); [*fig*] trouver un **terrain d'entente** (*common ground; basis for agreement*); SEE ALSO **étude, expérience, lotir**

terre (*nf*): le Gabon constitue une **terre d'asile** pour les régions limitrophes (*refuge; sanctuary*); la France, première **terre d'accueil** d'Europe (*haven; country of immigration*); SEE ALSO **gel, geler, morcellement, parcelle, privatisation, propriété**

tertiaire (*adj/nm*): l'industrie décline au profit du **[secteur] tertiaire** (*service industries; tertiary sector*)

testament (*nm*): SEE **léguer**

tête (*nf*): **tête de liste** pour les élections municipales (*principal candidate on an electoral list*); [*fig*] les industriels étrangers trouvent ainsi une **tête de pont** en France (*bridgehead; foothold*); SEE ALSO **peloton, turc**

texte (*nm*): voter un **texte** visant à réduire les pouvoirs du Président (*piece of legislation; bill*); amender un **texte de loi** (*law*)

thèse (*nf*): favorable aux **thèses** des séparatistes (*argument, idea*); cette **thèse** ne convainc pas tout le monde (*theory, hypothesis*)

ticket (*nm*): ce **ticket modérateur** peut être partiellement remboursé par les mutuelles (*patient's contribution to cost of medical treatment*)

tiers, tierce (*adj/nm,f*): le troisième **tiers** de l'impôt sur le revenu (*third*); nos revenus publicitaires ont diminué **d'un tiers** (*by a third*); la pratique du **tiers payant** favorise une surconsommation médicale (*part of fee for medical treatment paid directly to doctor/hospital by patient's insurers*); le **tiers provisionnel**, un acompte sur l'impôt sur le revenu (*interim tax payment [equal to one-third of annual tax]*)

tiers-monde (*nm*): les pays du **tiers-monde** ont réagi de façon positive (*Third World*); SEE ALSO **endettement**

tiers-mondisme (*nm*): le **tiers-mondisme** cher à certains intellectuels (*interest in/action in favour of the Third World*)

tiers-mondiste (*adj/nmf*): 1981–91: dix ans d'utopies **tiers-mondistes** (*Third World*)

tirage (*nm*): aucun journal français n'avait un **tirage** supérieur à 50 000 exemplaires (*circulation [figures]*); les sujets préférés de la **presse à grand tirage** (*high-circulation press*)

tirer (*vt*): les exportations **tirent la croissance** dans la plupart des secteurs de l'industrie (*stimulate [economic] growth*); un quotidien qui **tire** à 400 000 exemplaires par jour (*have a circulation of*); SEE ALSO **profit**

titre (*nm*): titulaires d'un **titre de séjour** en cours de validité (*residency permit*); un justificatif de domicile [un bail ou un **titre de propriété**] (*title deed*); 70 000 **titres** changèrent de main à la Bourse de Londres (*stock; share*); des jeunes, employés **au titre de la coopération** (*under a scheme for working abroad on an aid project*); SEE ALSO **bénévole, délivrer, expérimental, flamber, officieux, regroupement**

titrer (*vi*): *Le Monde* **titrait**: "Une victoire pour les eurosceptiques" (*run a headline*)

titulaire (*adj/nmf*): tous les postes ont été pourvus de nouveaux **titulaires** (*incumbent*); les **titulaires** de la double nationalité (*person holding/in possession of*)

titularisation (*nf*): le statut des enseignants qui n'optent pas pour la **titularisation** (*tenure; granting of tenure*)

titulariser (*vt*): **titularisé** à l'issue d'une période de stage de deux ans; en 1967, il fut **titularisé dans ses fonctions** (*confirm in a post; establish*)

toilettage (*nm*): procéder à un **toilettage** du code civil français; le **toilettage** d'une loi vieille de 150 ans (*updating, superficial reform [of law]*)

tollé (*nm*): ce fut un **tollé** de la part des syndicats (*outcry, protest*); une décision qui a **provoqué un tollé général** dans les milieux laïques (*provoke an outcry*); SEE ALSO **déclencher**

tort (*nm*): redresser un **tort** (*wrong*); une loi qui va **faire du tort** aux producteurs (*harm, hurt*); la Cour européenne **donne tort** à la France (*blame; find against*)

total, -e, *pl* -aux (*adj/nm*): SEE **montant**

totalité (*nf*): en cas de retard, la **totalité des droits** peut être exigée immédiatement (*the whole [registration] fee*)

toucher (*vt*): le chômage **touche** 17% des actifs (*affect*); un pétrolier **touché** par un missile en Méditerranée (*hit, strike*); il aurait **touché** d'importantes sommes d'argent (*receive*); SEE ALSO **fouet, pot-de-vin**

tour (*nm*): lors du premier **tour [du scrutin]** (*electoral ballot/round*); Groupama **entre dans le tour de table** pour 2,5 milliards de francs (*become a major shareholder*); (*nf*): la démolition des **tours** du quartier des Minguettes à Vénissieux (*tower/high-rise housing block*)

tournant, -e (*adj/nm*): ce **tournant** historique s'est fait dans le calme (*turning point*); l'opposition fait des gorges chaudes de ce **tournant** du PC (*change of direction*); SEE ALSO **grève, plaque, présidence**

tournée (*nf*): le Premier ministre entame une importante **tournée** diplomatique (*round of visits; tour*)

tourner (*vt*): les firmes d'armement **tournent** l'embargo vers le golfe Persique (*get round; find a loophole in*); (*vi*): les entreprises sont loin de **tourner** à pleine capacité (*run; operate*); SEE ALSO **court, dos, ralenti**

tract (*nm*): des **tracts** manuscrits et anonymes appelant à une grève générale; éditer et diffuser des **tracts** et affiches électoraux (*tract, pamphlet, leaflet*)

tractation (*nf*): les **tractations** sur les échanges de prisonniers; après six mois de **tractations**, les deux partis sont arrivés à un accord (*negotiation, bargaining*)

traduire (*vt*): 13 personnes ont été **traduites en justice** (*bring before the courts*)

trafic (*nm*): l'Office central de répression du **trafic illicite** des stupéfiants (*[illegal] trade, dealings in*); inculpé de corruption et de **trafic d'influence** (*trading of favours; bribery and corruption*); le **trafic passager** avec la Corse et l'Afrique du Nord (*passenger traffic*)

trahison (*nf*): la **trahison**, le crime le plus grave commis contre l'État (*treason*); les Serbes se réjouissent, les musulmans **crient à la trahison** (*denounce it as a betrayal*)

train (*nm*): l'entrée en vigueur d'un **train de mesures** d'austérité économique (*batch/package of measures*); la réduction du **train de vie** américain apparaît comme la seule issue (*lifestyle; standard of living*)

traite (*nf*): des accédants à la propriété étranglés par leurs **traites**; les **traites** de la villa qu'il venait de se faire construire (*[mortgage] repayment*)

traité (*nm*): un **traité**, une convention écrite entre deux ou plusieurs États (*treaty*); aux termes du **traité de Rome** (*Treaty of Rome*); SEE ALSO **conclusion**

traitement (*nm*): les **traitements** dans le secteur du bâtiment restent stables (*wages*); un ancien des RG, suspendu **avec plein traitement** (*on full pay*); la collecte et le **traitement** des ordures ménagères (*treatment, processing*); mettre l'accent sur le **traitement économique du chômage** (*legislation designed to mitigate effects of unemployment*); les cas notifiés de **mauvais traitements à enfants** (*cruelty to children, child cruelty*); SEE ALSO **convenir, insuffisance**

traiter (*vt*): on n'a pas pu **traiter** toutes les questions à l'ordre du jour (*discuss, deal with*); il **traita** l'auteur du livre d'affabulateur et de menteur (*call; denounce*)

tranche (*nf*): la première **tranche** du projet (*phase, stage*); l'augmentation du chômage a touché toutes les **tranches d'âge** (*age bracket*); le prêt sera versé **par tranches mensuelles** (*in monthly instalments*); toutes les **tranches d'imposition** sont relevées (*tax band*)

trancher (*vt*): **trancher** des litiges (*settle, resolve*); (*vi*): le tribunal s'est donné jusqu'au 28 mai pour **trancher** (*take a decision*); le gouvernement pourra **trancher dans** les effectifs et les équipements (*make cuts*); le ministre soviétique **tranche avec** son successeur (*contrast sharply with; be very different from*)

transalpin, -e (*adj/nm,f*): les services secrets **transalpins** y furent pour quelque chose (*transalpine; Italian*)

transférer (*vt*): **transférer** la production dans une autre usine (*transfer, relocate*)

transfert (*nm*): le **transfert des voix** entre les deux partis est de 1,7% au profit du Labour (*electoral swing*)

transfuge (*nmf*): **transfuge** du RPR, qu'il avait quitté en 1989 (*defector; deserter*)

transiger (*vi*): refuser de **transiger** avec les principes (*compromise*)

transition (*nf*): les membres du **gouvernement de transition** (*transitional government*)

transitoire (*adj*): la mise en place de mesures **transitoires** (*transitional, provisional*); ils auront un mandat de cinq ans **à titre transitoire** (*as a transitional measure*)

transmettre (*vt*): **transmettre** seulement la nue-propriété et se réserver l'usufruit (*hand down, pass on*)

transmission (*nf*): organiser la **transmission** de son patrimoine (*transfer*)

transparence (*nf*): sa volonté d'assurer la **transparence** de sa gestion (*openness [esp. of government/administration]*); le débat sur la **transparence du patrimoine** des élus (*full divulging of one's financial situation*)

transparent, -e (*adj*): rendre plus **transparentes** les compétences des collectivités territoriales (*make clearer, define more clearly*)

travail, *pl* **-aux** (*nm*): le **travail** féminin (*employment*); le **travail posté**, avec trois équipes successives (*shift-working*); le **travail de nuit** des femmes dans l'industrie (*night-working*); la lutte contre le **travail au noir** et l'immigration clandestine (*moonlighting*); embaucher des sans-emploi pour des **petits travaux** (*small jobs*); les **grands travaux** ont l'avantage de créer des milliers d'emplois (*major building programme*); 400 000 personnes en stages, dont 190 000 en **TUC [travaux d'utilité collective]** (*paid community work for young unemployed*); le parquet a requis 60 heures de **travail d'intérêt général [TIG]** contre les jeunes casseurs (*community service*); SEE ALSO **aménager, atelier, biais, bleu, bourse, cessation, chaîne, droit, groupe, inapte, incapacité, insertion, législation, marché, partage, reprendre, reprise, rétribuer, séance, volontariat**

travailler (*vi*): SEE **plein, posté**

travailleur, -euse (*nm,f*): les **travailleurs sociaux** dans les quartiers réputés difficiles (*social worker*); SEE ALSO **clandestin, précaire**

travailliste (*adj/nmf*): les **travaillistes** ont remporté deux élections partielles (*Labour Party*)

treizième (*adj*): supprimer le **treizième mois** et les primes d'ancienneté (*bonus equal to a month's salary*)

tremper (*vi*): accusés de **tremper dans** le trafic de drogues (*be involved in/mixed up in*)

trésor (*nm*): c'est le **Trésor public** qui finance ces activités (*French government department in charge of public finance*)

trésorerie (*nf*): une baisse de sa **trésorerie** (*funds, cash reserves*); surmonter ses **problèmes de trésorerie** (*cash problems*); une **gestion de trésorerie** personnalisée et sans risque (*money management*)

trésorier, -ière (*nm,f*): le **trésorier** d'une association (*treasurer*); verser une somme à l'ordre du **trésorier [général]** (*paymaster; head of* Trésor public *in each French region*)

trêve (*nf*): une fragile **trêve** s'est instaurée entre Palestiniens et miliciens chiites; la **trêve** annonce-t-elle une paix définitive? (*truce*); le mouvement Hamas propose une **trêve sous conditions** (*conditional truce*); SEE ALSO **décréter**

triangulaire (*adj/nf*): dans une [élection] **triangulaire** au deuxième tour (*three-way election contest*)

tribunal, *pl* **-aux** (*nm*): renvoyer une affaire devant un autre **tribunal** (*court*); le gouvernement décida de **porter l'affaire devant les tribunaux** (*bring the matter before the courts*); il sera jugé par un **tribunal pour enfants** (*juvenile court*); le **tribunal de police** juge les contraventions (*police court*); les **tribunaux d'instance** ont remplacé les justices de paix (*magistrate's court*); le **tribunal de grande instance [TGI]** siège au chef-lieu du département (*county court*); SEE ALSO **citer, correctionnel, passible, référé, saisir**

tribune (*nf*): on a organisé une **tribune** sur les questions sociales (*discussion, forum*)

tributaire (*adj*): la progression des transports maritimes **est tributaire de** l'évolution de la conjoncture (*depend/be dependent on*)

tricolore (*adj/nm*): la plupart des grandes marques **tricolores** étaient représentées (*French*); SEE ALSO **écharpe**

trimestre (*nm*): dès le premier **trimestre** de 1996 (*term; quarter, three-month period*)

trimestriel, -elle (*adj*): le paiement d'un loyer **trimestriel** (*quarterly*); un bulletin **trimestriel** (*end-of-term, termly*)

trinquer (*vi*): [*fam*] les femmes, les ouvriers, les beurs **trinquent** pour les nantis (*take the rap; pay the price*)

tripotage (*nm*): une sombre histoire de **tripotage électoral** (*electoral skulduggery*)

troc (*nm*): dans le cadre d'un accord de **troc** conclu récemment (*barter; exchange*)

trois (*adj*): faire les **trois-huit** pour optimiser la production (*operate three eight-hour shifts*)

troisième âge (*nm*): les promesses du candidat aux **personnes du troisième âge** (*elderly person; senior citizen*)

tronc (*nm*): les matières scolaires constituant le **tronc commun** (*common-core syllabus*)

trou (*nm*): [*fig*] le **trou** du régime général de la Sécurité sociale dépasse quatre milliards pour l'année; le bilan cache un **trou** de 100 millions de francs (*deficit*)

trouble (*adj/nm*): [*fig*] les innombrables dossiers **troubles** qui ont émaillé sa carrière (*shady, dubious*); **troubles** sanglants à la suite d'une manifestation anti-nucléaire à Rome (*disturbance, unrest*); on ne peut pas leur reprocher directement un **trouble de l'ordre public** (*disturbance of the peace*); un des symptômes d'un **trouble de la personnalité** (*personality disorder*); les **troubles de comportement** chez les enfants (*behavioural problems*)

troubler (*vt*): ces gestes étaient de nature à **troubler l'ordre public** (*cause a breach of public order; disturb the peace*)

truchement (*nm*): à travers l'ONU et non pas **par le truchement de l'OTAN** (*through NATO*); l'État exerçait sa tutelle **par le truchement du préfet** (*through the intervention of the* préfet)

trust (*nm*): la mise en place de **législations anti-trust** (*anti-trust laws*)

truster (*vt*): les énarques **trustent** toutes les premières places; ses supporters ont **trusté** les places au Congrès (*make a clean sweep of; monopolize*)

turc, turque (*adj/nm,f*): [*fig*] un des **jeunes turcs** de la nouvelle opposition (*young radicals*); on en veut aux centristes, **têtes de turc** traditionnelles (*whipping boy, scapegoat*)

turpitude (*nf*): une enquête qui montrerait les **turpitudes** du pouvoir; la **turpitude** de certains élus (*corruptness; corruption*)

tutelle (*nf*): enfin libéré de la **tutelle** soviétique; les départements sont soumis à la **tutelle** de Paris (*administrative supervision*); SEE ALSO **ministre**

tuteur, -trice (*nm,f*): le parent survivant devient **tuteur** légal des enfants (*guardian*)

U

ulcéré, -e (*adj*): il se déclara **ulcéré** par le retrait du projet de loi (*appalled, sickened*)

ultérieur, -e (*adj*): les versements **ultérieurs** sont de 3 600F (*subsequent; later*)

ultime (*adj*): mais l'**ultime** séance de négociations n'avait rien donné (*last, final*); SEE ALSO **cour**

ultra (*adj/nm*): la surveillance des **milieux ultra de droite** (*extreme right-wing groups*); les **ultras** de la mouvance islamiste (*[extreme] reactionary; extremist*)

un, une (*nmf*): le **numéro un** mondial de l'informatique (*leader, number one*); le quotidien lui consacrait la **une** de son supplément dominical (*front page*); la visite **faisait la une des journaux** (*make the front page*)

unanimité (*nf*): on regrette que l'**unanimité ne se soit pas faite** à ce sujet (*there was not unanimous agreement*); être réélu à l'**unanimité** (*unanimously*); une réforme qui **fait l'unanimité contre elle** (*be unanimously unpopular*); SEE ALSO **quasi-**

unicaméral, -e, *pl* **-aux** (*adj*): la Chambre du peuple [**parlement unicaméral**, 400 sièges] (*a single-chamber parliament*)

uninominal, -e, *pl* **-aux** (*adj*): on adoptera pour les législatives le **scrutin uninominal majoritaire** (*single candidate majority voting; first-past-the-post voting system*)

union (*nf*): il appelle la majorité à privilégier l'**union** (*unity*); les couples qui **vivent en union libre** (*cohabit*); le secrétaire de l'**union locale** CGT (*local interprofessional trade-union grouping*)

unique (*adj*): SEE **monnaie, parti, salaire**

unitaire (*adj*): un État **unitaire**, mais décentralisé (*unified, united*); une manifestation **unitaire** CGT-CFDT (*combined*); appeler à un large **rassemblement unitaire** (*alliance for union*)

unité (*nf*): la construction d'une nouvelle **unité** de 30 salariés (*production unit; factory*); une **unité de CRS** fait face aux émeutiers (*unit of French riot police*); SEE ALSO **séjour**

universel, -elle (*adj*): SEE **suffrage**

université (*nf*): cette deuxième journée de l'**université d'été** du RPR (*summer school/conference*)

urbain, -e (*adj*): les **urbains**, coupés du monde rural (*urban population*); Tours est peu de chose à côté des grands **centres urbains** (*urban centre*); SEE ALSO **aménagement, croissance, district, émeute, réaménagement, réhabilitation, rejet**

urbaniser (*vt*): SEE **ZUP**

urbanisme (*nm*): un plan d'**urbanisme** et de résorption des bidonvilles (*town planning/development*); la **commission d'urbanisme** a émis un avis défavorable (*planning committee*); SEE ALSO **adjoint**

urbaniste (*adj/nmf*): ancien **urbaniste** en chef de la ville de Lyon (*town planner*)

urgence (*nf*): demander une aide communautaire **d'urgence** (*emergency*); l'**urgence** de rétablir un équilibre conventionnel en Europe (*urgent need*); l'**état d'urgence** a été décrété (*state of emergency*); des **centres d'urgence** pour accueillir les sans-abri (*hostel offering emergency accommodation*); SEE ALSO **cellule, mesure**

urne (*nf*): dimanche prochain les Français **se rendent aux urnes** (*go to the polling booth; vote*); le parlement **sorti des urnes** en mars 1986 (*voted in, elected*); SEE ALSO **verdict**

us (*nmpl*): ceux qui ne sont pas familiers avec les **us et coutumes** du pays (*ways and customs*)

usage (*nm*): une résolution autorisant l'**usage de la force** pour faire respecter l'embargo (*use of force*); les policiers ont **fait usage** de leurs armes (*use, employ*); **contraire aux usages** et au droit actuel de la mer (*contrary to custom*); avec toutes les garanties **d'usage** (*usual, customary*); SEE ALSO **constatation, faux**

usager (*nm*): grèves: les **usagers** mis à rude épreuve (*customer; user of public service/facility*)

user (*vt*): il a prévenu qu'il **userait de** son droit de véto (*use, exercise*)

usine (*nf*): SEE **patron**

usufruit (*nm*): l'**usufruit**, ou le droit d'utiliser un bien sans pouvoir en disposer librement; il a l'**usufruit** du terrain, qui passera à son fils après sa mort (*use; usufruct*)

usufruitier, -ière (*adj/nm.f*): l'**usufruitier** d'un bien a le droit d'user de la chose et d'en percevoir les revenus sa vie durant (*usufructuary, beneficial owner*)

usure (*nf*): le Parti socialiste, victime de la corruption et de l'**usure du pouvoir** (*wearing effect of the exercise of power*); SEE ALSO **guerre**

utile (*adj*): **voter utile** en donnant sa voix au candidat socialiste (*vote tactically*)

utilité (*nf*): une association **déclarée d'utilité publique** (*state-approved*); SEE ALSO **travail**

V

vacance (*nf*): la **vacance** du poste de président (*vacancy; period when no one is officially in power*); assurer l'intérim pendant la **vacance du pouvoir** (*power vacuum*)

vacant, -e (*adj*): un poste, **vacant** depuis janvier (*vacant, unfilled*)

vacataire (*adj/nmf*): le **personnel vacataire** ne bénéficie pas de couverture sociale; on préférait employer des **vacataires**, payés à l'heure (*temporary employee*)

vacation (*nf*): son traitement d'instituteur et ses **vacations d'élu** (*parliamentary allowance*)

vagabond, -e (*adj/nm.f*): un lieu d'accueil pour sans-abri et **vagabonds** (*vagrant, vagabond*)

vagabondage (*nm*): le délit de **vagabondage** ayant été supprimé dans le nouveau code pénal (*vagrancy*); les gens qui ont contracté le virus par **vagabondage sexuel** (*sexual promiscuity*)

valable (*adj*): un ticket de métro **valable** (*valid*); SEE ALSO **interlocuteur, motif**

valeur (*nf*): pour la défense des **valeurs** traditionnelles (*values, attitudes*); se présenter comme le garant des **valeurs familiales** (*family values*); une hausse record des **valeurs** françaises (*securities; stocks and shares*); les **valeurs vedettes** étaient les plus demandées hier en bourse (*blue-chip shares*); le secteur public représente 30% de la **valeur ajoutée** industrielle (*added value*); la drogue, dont la **valeur marchande au détail** est estimée à 3 millions de dollars (*retail street value*); la région nantaise essaie de **mettre en valeur** sa production (*promote; exploit*); un comité pour l'étude et la **mise en valeur** du patrimoine industriel (*promotion; exploiting*)

valide (*adj*): les écoutes téléphoniques sont **valides** dans ces cas-là (*valid; justifiable*); des logements pour **personnes encore valides** (*the able-bodied/fit*); plusieurs centaines de **personnes non valides** (*invalid, disabled person*)

valider (*vt*): l'Assemblée **valide** la loi sur la bioéthique (*ratify [law]*); travail temporaire: **accord validé** (*an agreement has been ratified*)

validité (*nf*): avec un visa touristique **en cours de validité** (*valid*); la carte de résident **a une durée de validité de trois ans** (*is valid for three years*)

valoir (*vt*): une opération manquée **qui lui a valu une peine de prison de quatre ans** (*which earned him a four-year prison sentence*); (*vi*): les adversaires du projet **font valoir** qu'il sera très coûteux (*argue, point out*); **faire valoir ses droits** auprès de l'administration (*assert one's rights*)

valorisant, -e (*adj*): une **fonction valorisante** et bien rémunérée (*post which brings personal satisfaction*)

valorisation (*nf*): assurer la promotion et la **valorisation** de l'image de la marque (*promotion*); la **valorisation** des cités-ghettos et des quartiers dégradés (*renovation, redevelopment*); une **valorisation** de 90% des emballages, dont 60% par recyclage (*treatment; reuse*)

valoriser (*vt*): **valoriser** le patrimoine communal (*exploit, develop*); **valoriser** les déchets d'emballage (*recycle, reuse*); en **valorisant** voiture et logement de fonction, on arrive à 20 000F nets mensuels (*put a value on*); l'agroalimentaire, **un secteur qui se valorise** (*a growth sector/industry*)

valse (*nf*): après les élections, ce fut la **valse des préfets** (*wholesale replacement of préfets*); la mesure a provoqué immédiatement une **valse des étiquettes** (*spiralling prices*)

valser (*vi*): hôteliers et restaurateurs **font valser les étiquettes** (*raise prices constantly*)

vaquer (*vi*): pour la fête de l'Assomption, les bureaux **vaquent** (*be on vacation; be closed*)

variation (*nf*): SEE **donnée**

vedette (*nf*): sa mort a **ravi la vedette** dans la presse outre-Rhin (*steal the headlines*); SEE ALSO **valeur**

véhicule (*nm*): SEE **effraction**

véhiculer (*vt*): il **véhicule** ouvertement les obsessions racistes de l'extrême droite (*promote; express*)

veiller (*vt*): la force qui sera chargée de **veiller** à l'application de l'accord de paix (*oversee; supervise*); SEE ALSO **sauvegarde**

veilleuse (*nf*): la **mise en veilleuse** du droit de vote des étrangers (*shelving; putting on the back burner*)

velléitaire (*adj*): le gouvernement est très **velléitaire** sur ce chapitre (*indecisive, lacking in resolution*)

velléité (*nf*): pour contrer les **velléités** néo-impériales russes (*ambition, design*); il y a eu en 1981 des **velléités** de révolution culturelle (*hint, sign of*); une opinion britannique réticente devant **toute velléité supranationale** (*any idea of setting up a supranational body*)

vendre (*vt*): SEE **pièce**

venir (*vi*): **venir en aide** aux plus démunis (*help, bring help*); une proposition qui a peu de chances de **venir à bout de la grogne des syndicats** (*overcome union hostility*) SEE also **terme**

vente (*nf*): la **mise en vente** de 55% de son capital (*offering/putting up for sale*); la **vente au privé** de Saint-Gobain (*privatization*); SEE ALSO **adjudication, compromis, prix**

ventilation (*nf*): une **ventilation** géographique du déficit commercial américain (*analysis, breakdown*)

ventiler (*vt*): les enquêteurs ont **ventilé** les divers contrats de ces sociétés (*analyse, break down*)

venue (*nf*): encourager la **venue** d'activités nouvelles (*arrival; setting-up*); depuis sa **venue au pouvoir** il y a cinq ans (*coming to power*)

verbaliser (*vt*): l'agent **verbalisait pour stationnement non-autorisé** (*report a motorist for a parking offence*)

verdict (*nm*): rendre un **verdict à la majorité** (*majority verdict*); il faut respecter **le verdict des urnes** (*the electorate's verdict*); SEE ALSO **contester, énoncé, prononcé**

véreux, -euse (*adj*): des opportunistes et des hommes d'affaires **véreux** (*crooked*); encore une affaire de **policiers véreux** (*police corruption*)

vergogne (*nf*): exploiter le thème raciste **sans vergogne** (*shamelessly*)

vérification (*nf*): Désarmement: le problème de la **vérification** (*inspection, checking*); dans le cadre d'une simple **vérification d'identité** (*identity check*)

vérifier (*vt*): **vérifier** le texte d'un projet de loi (*scrutinize, check*); la commission de l'ONU chargée de **vérifier** le désarmement de l'Irak (*check; monitor*); [se] (*vpr*): si les prévisions de fréquentation **se vérifient** (*turn out to be true/accurate; be confirmed*)

vérité (*nf*): Bruxelles exige la **vérité des prix**; le mot d'ordre sera: **vérité des prix** (*fair/realistic prices*); SEE ALSO **épreuve**

verrou (*nm*): un citoyen belge **mis sous les verrous** en France (*put behind bars; imprison*)

verrouiller (*vt*): la police a **verrouillé** le quartier (*cordon off, seal*); la France **verrouille ses frontières** (*close borders to immigrants*); les Socialistes **verrouillent les postes clefs** en région parisienne (*hold the key posts*); **verrouiller** le marché informatique (*gain a dominant [market] position*)

versement (*nm*): après le **versement** d'une caution (*payment*); payable en 12 **versements** annuels (*payment, instalment*); SEE ALSO **commission, dessous**

verser (*vt*): des sommes **versées** sur un compte en banque (*pay [in], deposit*); (*vi*): **verser dans** la délinquance (*lapse/fall into*)

vert, -e (*adj*): le problème récurrent des **politiques vertes** (*agricultural policy*); l'**Europe verte** sera à l'ordre du jour du sommet (*farming within the EC*); un vendredi noir pour le **billet vert** (*dollar, greenback*); le **Parti vert** a recueilli 14% des suffrages (*Ecology/Green Party*); le **tourisme vert**, une panacée pour revitaliser la campagne (*rural tourism*); un POS, distinguant zones d'aménagement, **espaces verts**, etc. (*parks, green areas, open spaces*); (*nmpl*): la gauche – **les Verts** compris – a fait bloc derrière le maire (*the French Green party*); SEE ALSO **ceinture, livre, numéro, semonce**

vertigineux, -euse (*adj*): la hausse **vertigineuse** du dollar (*dizzy; very great*)

véto (*nm*): l'OLP a **mis son véto** à un tel projet; le Président va pouvoir **opposer son véto** à la loi sur le commerce (*veto*); la France n'hésitera pas à user de son **droit de véto** (*right of veto*)

vétuste (*adj*): des locaux **vétustes**, délabrés (*dilapidated, decrepit*); la nécessité de renouveler les installations **vétustes** (*old, worn out*)

vétusté (*nf*): en raison de la **vétusté** de nombreux établissements (*dilapidated state [of buildings/premises]*)

veuf, veuve (*adj/nm,f*): la veuve ou le **veuf** d'un conjoint assuré au régime général (*widower*); toucher une pension en tant que **veuve de guerre** (*war widow*)

veuvage (*nm*): l'**allocation-veuvage**, une allocation de la Sécurité sociale destinée au conjoint survivant (*widow's allowance/pension*)

viabilisation (*nf*): le coût de la **viabilisation** de la zone [voirie, alimentation en eau potable] (*equipping with mains services*)

viabiliser (*vt*): 75 000 m^2 de terrains, **viabilisés tous réseaux**; on met à la disposition des SDF un lieu d'accueil et un terrain **viabilisé** (*equipped with all mains services*)

viabilité (*nf*): ainsi la **viabilité** de l'entreprise serait compromise (*viability*)

viable (*adj*): des entreprises pourtant économiquement **viables** (*viable, healthy*)

viager, -ère (*adj/nm*): il **vendit** la ferme **en viager** moyennant une rente qu'il toucherait jusqu'à sa mort (*dispose of [a property] in return for a life annuity*); SEE ALSO **rente**

vice (*nm*): le consommateur a droit à la garantie légale des défauts et **vices cachés** (*hidden defect/fault*); la demande fut rejetée pour **vice de forme** (*legal flaw, irregularity*); le jugement fut cassé **pour vice de procédure** (*on a procedural irregularity*)

vide (*nm*): un **vide** politique dangereux (*vacuum*); en profitant d'un **vide juridique** (*gap in the law*)

vie (*nf*): être en âge d'**entrer dans la vie active** (*enter employment*); la lutte des travailleurs contre la **vie chère** (*high prices/cost of living*); SEE ALSO **associatif, cadre, couple, durée, espérance, pronostic, train**

vieillesse (*nf*): des régimes d'assistance tels que le **minimum vieillesse** garanti à toute personne âgée (*minimum old-age pension*)

vieillir (*vi*): mieux vaut **vieillir** chez soi que dans une institution (*grow old*)

vieillissement (*nm*): en raison du **vieillissement de la population** (*ageing population*)

vif, vive (*adj*): faire l'objet de **vifs débats** (*lively debate/discussion*)

vigile (*nm*): des affrontements entre les jeunes du quartier, les **vigiles** et la police (*security guard; vigilante*)

vignette (*nf*): les impôts indirects tels que la **vignette automobile** (*road-fund licence, tax disc*)

vigueur (*nf*): les taux de cotisation **en vigueur** au 1er novembre 1996 (*in force/operation*); l'**entrée en vigueur** du cessez-le-feu (*coming into effect/force, implementation*); la nouvelle Constitution **entre en vigueur** le 4 décembre (*come into force*)

viol (*nm*): pour **viol** des règlements nationaux et internationaux (*violation*); mis en examen pour **viol aggravé** (*aggravated rape*); dix années de réclusion pour **viol sur mineures** (*sexual offences against under-aged girls*); trois adolescents mis en question pour **viol en réunion** (*gang rape*)

violation (*nf*): en **violation** des résolutions votées par le Conseil de sécurité (*violation, breach*); porter plainte pour **violation de domicile** (*forcible entry [into person's home]*)

violence (*nf*): une recrudescence des actes de **violence** contre les forces de l'ordre (*violence*); interrogé sur l'origine de la **violence au foyer** (*domestic violence*); les **violences racistes** sont restées stables en France en 1994 (*racial violence*); le meurtre d'une femme après **violences sexuelles** (*sexual violence; rape*); SEE ALSO **provocation**

violenter (*vt*): une jeune mère de famille **violentée** par deux hommes masqués (*sexually assault; rape*); chez les jeunes qui ont été **violentés** (*[sexually] abuse*)

violer (*vt*): une jeune Ivoirienne tue son employeur qui la **violait** (*rape*); Bonn accuse Moscou de **violer** les droits de l'homme (*violate*); il perd le bénéfice de l'amnistie s'il **viole ses engagements** (*break a promise*)

virage (*nm*): un **virage** dans la politique hongroise (*change of direction*); le **virage** de 1983 explique la défaite de 1986 (*shift [of policy]*)

virement (*nm*): le transfert de fonds s'est effectué par **virement bancaire** (*bank transfer*); [*fig*] les pressions se multiplient pour un complet **virement de bord** (*change of direction/policy*)

virer (*vt*): la somme a été **virée** sur un compte de dépôt (*transfer*); le chef d'état-major brésilien **viré** pour avoir trop parlé (*fire, sack*); (*vi*): la province canadienne de l'Ontario **vire à droite** (*swing to the right*)

visa (*nm*): un **visa** validant le document (*visa*); obtenir un **visa de sortie** (*exit visa*); la suppression des **visas d'entrée** en France (*entry visa*)

visée (*nf*): les **visées gouvernementales** n'échappent à personne (*government intentions*); il déplora les **visées expansionnistes** d'Israël (*expansionist policy*)

viser (*vt*): notre démarche **vise** la catégorie des 18 ans (*target/be directed at*); le texte **vise à garantir** les droits des petits épargnants (*seek to protect*); il faut **faire viser le formulaire** à la mairie du domicile (*have a form stamped/visaed*)

vivre (*vi*): l'année 1996 **a été vécue** comme une année noire (*experience*); le service national dans sa formule actuelle **aura vécu** (*be a thing of the past*); en être réduit à **vivre d'expédients** (*live on one's wits; resort to short-term measures*); SEE ALSO **mal**, **union**

vocation (*nf*): une région **à vocation agricole** (*agricultural, farming*); le revenu minimum d'insertion **avait une double vocation** (*had a dual purpose*)

vœu, *pl* -**x** (*nm*): la presse reçoit les **vœux** du Premier ministre (*good wishes*); le changement de régime qu'un grand nombre de Russes **appelaient de leurs vœux** (*were ardently hoping for*)

voie (*nf*): en empruntant la **voie rapide** (*expressway*); interdire la mendicité **sur la voie publique** (*on the public highway*); d'où ils sont expédiés **par voie terrestre** (*overland; by land*); les **voies d'eau** pourraient être mieux utilisées (*waterways*); dans le cas des **pays en voie de développement** (*developing countries*); une procédure judiciaire pour outrage et **voies de fait** (*violence against the person*); pour toute décision de justice, il existe une **voie de recours** (*appeal procedure*); SEE ALSO **hiérarchique**, **liaison**, **racolage**, **référendum**

voile (*nm*): opposés au **port du voile** dans les écoles d'État (*wearing of the [Islamic] veil*)

voirie (*nf*): les routes ont été dégagées par la **voirie** municipale (*roads maintenance department*); mettre un article au rebut, ou l'envoyer à la **voirie** (*refuse dump*); SEE ALSO **entretien**

voix (*nf*): le candidat centriste a reçu 12 000 **voix** (*vote*); la **voix prépondérante** du président (*casting vote*); le projet sera **mis aux voix** le 11 juillet (*vote on; put to the vote*); SEE ALSO **comptage**, **déplacement**, **report**, **transfert**

vol (*nm*): la délinquance urbaine: **vols simples**, violences (*common theft*); son inculpation pour **vol à l'étalage** (*shoplifting*); deux cambrioleurs inculpés de **vol avec effraction** (*burglary; theft with breaking and entering*); les **vols à la roulotte** ont particulièrement progressé cette année (*theft of objects from cars*); le **vol de voiture** a augmenté de 20% en un an (*car theft*)

volet (*nm*): les deux **volets**, politique et économique, du dossier (*section, constituent part*); après le compromis américano-européen sur le **volet agricole** (*agricultural clause/chapter*); le **volet social** du traité de Maastricht (*social chapter*)

volontaire (*adj/nmf*): inculpé de coups et blessures **volontaires** sur un enfant âgé de moins de 15 ans (*deliberate, intentional*); une politique d'immigration très **volontaire** (*firm, determined*); un réseau national de 3 500 **volontaires** (*volunteer*); SEE ALSO **départ, engagé, homicide**

volontairement (*adv*): le Japon limite **volontairement** ses ventes aux États-Unis (*voluntarily, freely*); cette convention se résume en 21 articles **volontairement vagues** (*intentionally vague*)

volontariat (*nm*): une journée de **travail en volontariat** (*unpaid work*); les départs se sont faits **sur la base du volontariat** (*on a voluntary basis*)

volontarisme (*nm*): le Premier ministre prône **un volontarisme industriel** (*a vigorous industrial policy*)

volontariste (*adj*): pour une politique **volontariste** de l'environnement (*energetic, vigorous*); **mener une politique volontariste** pour reconstituer le tissu rural (*implement a vigorous policy*)

volonté (*nf*): il a affirmé sa **volonté** de voir la Turquie entrer dans la CE (*will, determination*); l'absence de **volonté de démocratisation** du pays (*wish/desire for democratic institutions*); c'est un problème de **volonté politique** (*political will*)

volontiers (*adv*): il se reconnaissait **volontiers** une parenté avec le FN (*willingly, readily*); une Turquie mieux armée et **volontiers offensive** (*given to aggressive gestures*)

volte-face (*nf*): cette **volte-face** se traduit par une grave crise de confiance pour le gouvernement conservateur (*volte-face; U-turn*)

votant, -e (*nm,f*): l'élément déterminant du choix des **votants** (*voter*)

vote (*nm*): avant même le décompte des **votes**, il était donné gagnant (*vote*); le **vote** du budget interviendra la semaine prochaine (*voting; vote on*); grâce à la procédure du **vote bloqué**, le gouvernement s'assura la victoire (*package vote; single vote on whole bill*); l'on s'attendait à un **vote sanction** lors des élections cantonales; c'est là une des raisons des **votes protestataires** (*protest vote*); SEE ALSO **consigne, défiance, intention, pondéré, privation**

voter (*vt*): le Sénat **votera** le projet de loi en première lecture (*vote on*); le groupe centriste n'a pas **voté** la motion de censure (*vote; vote in favour of*); faire **voter** l'abolition de la peine de mort (*vote, pass [measure/law]*); SEE ALSO **blanc, confiance, nul, procuration, utile**

voyager (*vi*): **voyager** pour une entreprise de textile (*travel, work as a commercial traveller/sales representative*)

voyageur, -euse (*nm,f*): le **voyageur [de commerce]** est payé uniquement à la commission (*commercial traveller; sales representative*)

voyant, -e (*adj/nm*): tous les **voyants** sont au rouge (*indicator; warning light*)

vu (*prep*): **vu** l'article 126 du code pénal (*in view of*); le conseil municipal, **au vu de** la lettre circulaire, demande la reconduction de la subvention (*taking note of*)

vue (*nf*): l'application **à courte vue** des lois du marché (*short-sighted*); SEE ALSO **garde**

X

X (*nm*): l'ouverture d'une information judiciaire contre **X**; déposer plainte contre **X** (*a person/persons unknown*); on a confié la direction commerciale à un **X** (*graduate of the* École polytechnique)

xénophobe (*adj/nmf*): une vague de violences **xénophobes** (*xenophobic*)

xénophobie (*nf*): manifester contre la **xénophobie** et le racisme (*xenophobia*)

Z

ZAC (*nf*): les **ZAC [zones d'aménagement concerté]** et les opérations de rénovation se succèdent; la **ZAC** prévoyait la réalisation de 250 logements sociaux neufs (*integrated development zone*)

ZAD (*nf*): les **zones d'aménagement différé [ZAD]** permettent à la collectivité de s'assurer des réserves de terrains pour logements ou équipements collectifs (*designated development area*)

zélateur, -trice (*nm,f*): les **zélateurs** de cette solution étaient nombreux (*advocate, supporter*)

zèle (*nm*): appliquer **avec zèle** la législation sur la maîtrise de l'immigration (*zealously, enthusiastically*) SEE **grève**

zénith (*nm*): [*fig*] il est **au zénith de sa popularité** (*at the height of his popularity*)

zéro (*nm*): des prêts **à taux zéro** (*at zero per cent*)

zizanie (*nf*): un diviseur qui **crée la zizanie** au sein du PS marseillais; cette affaire **sème la zizanie** au conseil municipal (*cause discord/ill-feeling*)

zonage (*nm*): élaborer un POS, c'est-à-dire un **zonage** de son territoire (*zoning*)

zone (*nf*): un enfant d'immigrés, né dans la **zone** (*slum belt*); des entreprises nouvelles installées sur les **zones d'activités** du district (*business park*); on réclame l'instauration d'une **zone de conversion** (*redevelopment area*); la **zone d'exclusion** autour de la capitale bosniaque (*exclusion zone*); une sorte de **zone tampon** entre l'Est et l'Ouest (*buffer zone*); SEE ALSO **abattement, libre-échange, rural, sinistré**

ZUP (*nf*): les **zones à urbaniser en priorité [ZUP]** sont une forme aujourd'hui périmée d'urbanisme concerté (*priority development area*); dans un immeuble au cœur de la **ZUP** de Poitiers (*new suburb comprising mainly low-cost housing*)

ACRONYMS AND ABBREVIATIONS

Besides the most commonly met acronyms and abbreviations, the following list contains addresses of ministries, headquarters of political parties, trade unions, etc. These are widely used as convenient shorthand for the bodies, offices and organizations to which they refer.

Certain acronyms referring to new taxes, social security or housing benefits, or recently formed political parties (e.g. APL, PAP, RDS) may prove ephemeral and disappear rapidly from common use, but they are included here for reasons of completeness.

ACP	Afrique, Caraïbes, Pacifique
AELE	Association européenne de libre échange [UK: EFTA]
AFNOR	Association française de normalisation
AFP	Agence France-Presse
AFR	Allocation formation-reclassement
AGIRC	Association générale des institutions de retraite des cadres
ALPE	Association laïque des parents d'élèves
ANPE	Agence nationale pour l'emploi
APE	Allocation parentale d'éducation
APEL	Association des parents d'élèves de l'école libre
APL	Aide personnalisée au logement
Ardt	Arrondissement
ARRCO	Association des régimes de retraite complémentaire
ASSEDIC	Association pour l'emploi dans l'industrie et le commerce
Beauvau	[place] Ministère de l'Intérieur
BEP	Brevet d'études professionnelles
BEPC	Brevet d'études du premier cycle
Bercy	[rue de] Ministère de l'économie et des Finances
BIT	Bureau international du travail
BNP	Banque Nationale de Paris
BO	Bulletin officiel
Bourbon	[palais] Assemblée nationale
BPF	Bon pour francs
Branly	[quai] Conseil supérieur de la Magistrature
Brienne	[Hôtel de] Ministère de la Défense
Brongniart	[palais] Bourse de Paris
BSP	Brigade des stupéfiants et du proxénétisme
BT	Brevet de technicien
BTP	bâtiments et travaux publics
BTS	Brevet de technicien supérieur

CA	Conseil d'administration
CAC	Compagnie des agents de change
CAC 40	Paris Stock Exchange 40 Share Index
CAF	Coût, assurance, fret;
	Caisse d'allocations familiales
Cambon	[rue] Cour des comptes
CAP	Certificat d'aptitude professionnelle
CAPES	Certificat d'aptitude au professorat de l'enseigne- ment du second degré
CC	Corps consulaire
CCI	Chambre de commerce et d'industrie
CCP	Compte chèque postal; centre de chèques postaux
CD	Corps diplomatique
CDD	Contrat à durée déterminée
CDS	Centre des démocrates sociaux
CE	Comité d'entreprise
CEDEX	Courrier d'entreprise à distribution exceptionnelle
CEE	Communauté économique européenne
CEG	Collège d'enseignement général
CEI	Communauté des États indépendants
CERC	Centre d'études des revenus et des coûts
CERES	Centre d'études, de recherches et d'éducation socialiste
CERN	Conseil européen pour la recherche nucléaire
CES	Conseil économique et social;
	Collège d'enseignement secondaire
CET	Collège d'enseignement technique
CF	Communauté française
CFA	Communauté financière africaine;
	Centre de formation d'apprentis
CFAO	conception et fabrication assistées par ordinateur
CFDT	Confédération française démocratique du travail
CGE-CGC	Confédération générale de l'encadrement – Confération générale des cadres
CFI	crédit (de) formation individualisé
CFTC	Confédération française des travailleurs chrétiens
CGC	Confédération générale des cadres
CGT	Confédération générale du travail
CGT-FO	Confédération générale du travail – Force ouvrière
CHU	Centre hospitalier universitaire
Cie	Compagnie
CIF	congé individuel de formation
CNAL	Comité national d'action laïque
CNCL	Commission nationale de la communication et des libertés
CNI	Centre national des indépendants
CNPF	Conseil national du patronat français
CNRS	Centre national de la recherche scientifique
COB	Commission des opérations de Bourse
CODER	Commission de développement économique régional

CODEVI	Compte pour le développement industriel
Conti	[quai] Académie française
CPA	Classe préparatoire à l'apprentissage
CPAM	Caisse primaire d'assurance maladie
CREDOC	Centre de recherches, d'études et de documentation sur la consommation
CRIF	Conseil représentatif des institutions juives de France
CRS	Compagnie républicaine de sécurité
CSA	Conseil supérieur de l'audiovisuel
CSG	Contribution sociale généralisée
CSM	Conseil supérieur de la magistrature
CU	Communauté urbaine
DAB	distributeur automatique de billets
DATAR	Délégation à l'aménagement du territoire et à l'action régionale
DDASS	Direction départementale à l'action sanitaire et sociale
DES	Diplôme d'études supérieures
DEUG	Diplôme d'études universitaires générales
DGE	Dotation globale d'équipement
DGF	Dotation globale de fonctionnement
DGSE	Direction générale de la sécurité extérieure
DPU	Droit de préemption urbain
DOM	Département d'outre-mer
DSQ	Développement social des quartiers
DST	Direction de la surveillance du territoire
DTS	Droits de tirage spéciaux
DUEL	Diplôme universitaire d'études littéraires
DUES	Diplôme universitaire d'études scientifiques
DUP	Déclaration d'utilité publique
DUT	Diplôme universitaire de technologie
EDF	Électricité de France
Élysée	[palais de l'] résidence du Président de la République
ENA	École Nationale d'Administration
ENS	École Normale supérieure
ESC	École Supérieure de Commerce
ESSEC	École Supérieure des Sciences économiques et sociales
ETAM	Employé, technicien, agent de maîtrise
E-U	États-Unis
Fabien	[place du colonel] siège de la CGT
FCP	fonds commun de placement
FD	Force démocrate
FDES	Fonds de développement économique et social
FED	Fonds européen de développement
FEN	Fédération de l'éducation nationale
FFA	Forces françaises en Allemagne
FIS	Front islamique du salut
FIV	fécondation in vitro
FMI	Fonds monétaire international [UK: IMF]

FN	Front national
FNS	Fonds national de solidarité
FO	Force ouvrière
GDF	Gaz de France
GE	Génération écologie
GIE	Groupement d'intérêt économique
GIGN	Groupe d'intervention de la Gendarmerie nationale
Grenelle	[rue de] Ministère des Affaires Sociales; Ministère de l'Industrie; Ministère du Travail
HEC	[école des] Hautes études commerciales
HLM	Habitation à loyer modéré
Iéna	[palais d'] Conseil économique et social
IFOP	Institut français d'opinion publique
IGAME	Inspecteur général de l'administration en mission extraordinaire
IGF	Impôt sur les grandes fortunes
IGR	Impôt général sur le revenu
INSEE	Institut national de la statistique et des études économiques
INSERM	Institut national de la santé et de la recherche médicale
IRPP	Impôt sur le revenu des personnes physiques
IS	Impôt sur les sociétés
ISF	Impôt de solidarité sur la fortune [ex-IGF]
IUT	Institut universitaire de technologie
IVD	Indemnité viagère de départ
IVG	Interruption volontaire de grossesse
JCR	Jeunesse communiste révolutionnaire
JEC	Jeunesse étudiante chrétienne
JO	Jeunesse ouvrière; Journal officiel; Jeux Olympiques
Lassay	[Hôtel de] résidence du Président de l'Assemblée nationale
LEP	Livret d'épargne populaire; Lycée d'enseignement professionnel
Lille	[rue de] siège du RPR
LO	Lutte ouvrière
Luxembourg	[palais du] Sénat
MATIF	Marché à terme international de France; Marché à terme d'instruments financiers
Matignon	[hôtel] résidence du Premier ministre
MJC	Maison des jeunes et de la culture
MOCI	Moniteur officiel du commerce et de l'industrie
MRAP	Mouvement contre le racisme, l'antisémitisme et pour la paix
MRG	Mouvement des radicaux de gauche
MST	maladie sexuellement transmissible
NDLR	Note de la Rédaction [UK: Editor's note]
NF	norme française

OAS	Organisation de l'armée secrète
OCDE	Organisation de coopération et de développement économique [UK: OECD]
OFPRA	Office français de protection des réfugiés et apatrides
OLP	Organisation de libération de la Palestine [UK: PLO]
OMS	Organisation mondiale de la santé [UK: WHO]
ONG	organisation non gouvernementale
ONU	Organisation des Nations Unies [UK: UNO]
OP	Ouvrier professionnel
OPA	offre publique d'achat
OPE	offre publique d'échange
OPEP	Organisation des pays exportateurs de pétrole [UK: OPEC]
OQ	Ouvrier qualifié
Orfèvres	[quai des] Police judiciaire de Paris
Orsay	[quai d'] Ministère des Affaires étrangères
ORSEC	[plan] plan d'organisation des secours
OS	Ouvrier spécialisé
OTAN	Organisation du Traité de l'Atlantique Nord [UK: NATO]
PAC	Politique agricole commune [UK: CAP]
PAF	Paysage audiovisuel français; Police de l'air et des frontières
Palais-Royal	[rue du] Conseil d'État [place du] Conseil constitutionnel
PAO	publication assistée par ordinateur
PAP	Prêts aidés pour l'accession à la propriété
PC	Prêt conventionnel; Parti communiste; poste de commandement
PCC	pour copie conforme
PCF	Parti communiste français
P-DG	Président-Directeur Général
P et C	Ponts et Chaussées
PEEP	Fédération des parents d'élèves de l'enseignement public
PEL	Plan d'épargne-logement
PER	Plan d'épargne-retraite
PIB	Produit intérieur brut [UK: GDP]
PIL	Programme d'insertion locale
PJ	Police judiciaire
PLA	Prêt locatif aidé
PLM	Paris-Lyon-Marseille
PME	Petite[s] et moyenne[s] entreprise[s]
PMI	Petite[s] et moyenne[s] industrie[s]
PMU	Pari mutuel urbain
PNB	Produit national brut [UK: GNP]
POS	Plan d'occupation des sols
PR	Parti républicain
PS	Parti socialiste
PSU	Parti socialiste unifié

PTT	Postes, Télécommunications et Télédiffusion
PV	procès-verbal
QG	Quartier général
RAID	Recherche, Assistance, Intervention, Dissuasion
RATP	Régie autonome des transports parisiens
RC[S]	Registre du commerce [et des sociétés]
RDS	remboursement de la dette sociale
R et D	Recherche et développement
RER	Réseau express régional
RES	Rachat d'entreprise par les salariés [UK: MBO]
RF	République française
RG	Renseignements généraux
Rivoli	[rue de] Ministère de l'économie et des Finances [29 rue de] Hôtel de Ville de Paris
RMI	Revenu minimum d'insertion
RN	Route nationale
RPR	Rassemblement pour la République
SA	Société anonyme
SAFER	Société d'aménagement foncier et d'établissement rural
Sàrl	Société à responsabilité limitée
SDAU	Schéma directeur d'aménagement et d'urbanisme
SDECE	Service de documentation extérieure et de contre-espionnage
SDF	[personne] sans domicile fixe
Ségur	[avenue de] Ministère de la Santé
SEITA	Société nationale d'exploitation industrielle des tabacs et allumettes
SEM	Société d'économie mixte
SERNAM	Service national des messageries
SFIO	Section française de l'Internationale ouvrière
SGDG	Sans garantie du gouvernement
SICAV	Société d'investissement à capital variable
SICOB	Salon des industries du commerce et de l'organisation du bureau
SIDA	Syndrome immunodéficitaire acquis [UK: AIDS]
SIVOM	Syndicat intercommunal à vocation multiple
SIVOS	Syndicat intercommunal à vocation spécialisée
SIVP	Stage d'initiation à la vie professionnelle
SIVU	Syndicat intercommunal à vocation unique
SME	Système monétaire européen [UK: EMS]
SMIC	Salaire minimum interprofessionnel de croissance
SNC	Société en nom collectif
SNCF	Société nationale des chemins de fer français
SOFRES	Société française d'enquêtes par sondage
Solférino	[rue de] siège du Parti socialiste
SR	Service des renseignements
SS	Sécurité sociale
TGI	Tribunal de grande instance
TGV	Train à grande vitesse

TIG	Travail d'intérêt général
TOM	Territoire d'outre-mer
TTC	Toutes taxes comprises
TUC	Travaux d'utilité collective
TVA	Taxe sur la valeur ajoutée [UK: VAT]
UDC	Union du centre
UDF	Union pour la démocratie française
UE	Union européenne
UEO	Union de l'Europe occidentale
UER	Unité d'enseignement et de recherche
UFR	Unité de formation et de recherche
Ulm	[rue d'] École Normale supérieure
UNAPEL	Union nationale des associations de parents d'élèves de l'école libre
UNEDIC	Union nationale pour l'emploi dans l'industrie et le commerce
Université	[126, rue de l'] Assemblée nationale
URSSAF	Union pour le recouvrement des cotisations de Sécurité sociale et d'allocations familiales
UV	Unité de valeur
Valois	[place de] Parti radical-socialiste
	[rue de] Ministère de la Culture et des Arts
Varenne	[rue de] Hôtel Matignon; Ministère de l'Agriculture
Vaugirard	[15 rue de] Sénat
Vendôme	[place] Ministère de la Justice
Vivienne	[rue] Bourse de Paris
VRP	Voyageur représentant placier
VVF	village vacances famille
ZAC	Zone d'aménagement concerté
ZAD	Zone d'aménagement différé
ZAE	Zone d'activité économique
ZEP	Zone d'environnement protégé; Zone d'éducation prioritaire
ZI	Zone industrielle
ZIF	Zone d'intervention foncière
ZUP	Zone à urbaniser en priorité